**Marketing Planning**
**2005–2006**

 The Chartered Institute of Marketing

# Marketing Planning 2005–2006

Karen Beamish and Ruth Ashford

ELSEVIER
BUTTERWORTH
HEINEMANN

AMSTERDAM  BOSTON  HEIDELBERG  LONDON  NEW YORK  OXFORD
PARIS  SAN DIEGO  SAN FRANCISCO  SINGAPORE  SYDNEY  TOKYO

Elsevier Butterworth-Heinemann
Linacre House, Jordan Hill, Oxford OX2 8DP
30 Corporate Drive, Burlington, MA 01803

First published 2005

Copyright © 2005, Karen Beamish and Ruth Ashford. All rights reserved

The rights of Karen Beamish and Ruth Ashford to be identified
as the authors of this work has been asserted in accordance with the
Copyright, Designs and Patents Act 1988

No part of this publication may be reproduced in any material form (including
photocopying or storing in any medium by electronic means and whether
or not transiently or incidentally to some other use of this publication) without
the written permission of the copyright holder except in accordance with the
provisions of the Copyright, Designs and Patents Act 1988 or under the terms of
a licence issued by the Copyright Licensing Agency Ltd, 90 Tottenham Court Road,
London, England W1T 4LP. Applications for the copyright holder's written
permission to reproduce any part of this publication should be addressed
to the publisher

Permissions may be sought directly from Elsevier's Science and Technology Rights
Department in Oxford, UK: phone: (+44) (0) 1865 843830; fax: (+44) (0) 1865 853333;
e-mail: permissions@elsevier.com. You may also complete your request
on-line via the Elsevier homepage (http://www.elsevier.com), by selecting
'Customer Support' and then 'Obtaining Permissions'

**British Library Cataloguing in Publication Data**
A catalogue record for this book is available from the British Library

**Library of Congress Cataloguing in Publication Data**
A catalogue record for this book is available from the Library of Congress

ISBN 0 7506 6647 1

For information on all Elsevier Butterworth-Heinemann publications
visit our website at http://books.elsevier.com

Typeset by Integra Software Services Pvt. Ltd, Pondicherry, India
www.integra-india.com
Printed and bound in Italy

Working together to grow
libraries in developing countries

www.elsevier.com | www.bookaid.org | www.sabre.org

ELSEVIER    BOOK AID International    Sabre Foundation

# Contents

| Preface | Welcome to the CIM coursebooks | ix |
|---|---|---|
| **Unit 1** | **Introduction to marketing planning** | **1** |
| | Introduction | 1 |
| | The marketing planning process | 2 |
| | Marketing Planning in context | 2 |
| | Understanding the aims and objectives of Marketing Planning and achieving your learning outcomes | 4 |
| | The importance of reading | 5 |
| | Approaching the Marketing Planning examination | 6 |
| | An overview of the strategy and planning hierarchy | 7 |
| | Corporate planning – what is it? | 8 |
| | Marketing strategy – what is it? | 10 |
| | Planning – what is it? | 12 |
| | Relationship marketing with the wider public and society | 15 |
| | Marketing and social responsibility | 16 |
| | Legislation | 18 |
| | The rise in consumerism | 19 |
| | Social response to consumerist pressure | 19 |
| | Ethical issues for consumers and marketers | 20 |
| | Ethical implications for the marketing mix | 21 |
| **Unit 2** | **The marketing audit** | **25** |
| | Introduction | 25 |
| | Conducting a marketing audit | 26 |
| | Stage 1 – Analysis of the macro environment | 30 |
| | Stage 2 – Analysis of the micro environment | 35 |
| | Identifying key opportunities | 46 |
| | Developing a marketing information system | 49 |
| **Unit 3** | **Marketing planning, implementation and control** | **53** |
| | Introduction | 53 |
| | How to take the marketing audit to the planning process | 54 |
| | Stage 3 – The setting of objectives | 55 |
| | The balanced scorecard | 57 |
| | Gap analysis | 61 |
| | Formulation of the marketing strategy | 63 |
| | Market segmentation and competitive positioning | 71 |
| | The role of a marketer in positioning | 81 |
| | The marketing plan | 82 |
| | Implementation of the marketing plan | 83 |
| | A supportive and effective marketing structure | 87 |
| | The control process | 94 |
| **Unit 4** | **Promotional operations** | **101** |
| | The marketing mix in the context of marketing planning | 101 |
| | Profiling marketing segments for promotional activities | 103 |

|  |  |  |
|---|---|---|
|  | Push and pull strategy | 103 |
|  | Promotional operations and the planning framework | 104 |
|  | Aims and objectives of the promotional communications process | 105 |
|  | Branding | 106 |
|  | Brand values | 107 |
|  | The promotional mix | 112 |
|  | Advertising | 114 |
|  | Advertising and the marketing mix | 116 |
|  | Sales promotions | 117 |
|  | Sales promotion techniques | 118 |
|  | Retailer to consumer sales promotions | 120 |
|  | Manufacturer to consumer sales promotions | 120 |
|  | Public relations | 123 |
|  | Public relations and attitude change? | 124 |
|  | Public relations techniques | 125 |
|  | Direct and interactive marketing | 126 |
|  | Objectives of direct marketing | 127 |
|  | Database marketing | 128 |
|  | Direct marketing techniques | 129 |
|  | Telemarketing | 130 |
|  | Sponsorship | 132 |
|  | Personal selling | 135 |
| Unit 5 | **Product operations** | **139** |
|  | Product operations | 139 |
|  | Product management | 143 |
|  | The product life cycle | 144 |
|  | Managing the product life cycle | 146 |
|  | Product portfolio planning tools | 148 |
|  | New product development | 153 |
|  | The new product development process | 154 |
|  | The product adoption process | 157 |
|  | Targeting decision-makers | 161 |
| Unit 6 | **Price operations** | **164** |
|  | Introduction | 164 |
|  | Price perception and the customer | 165 |
|  | Perspective of price and the organization | 165 |
|  | Pricing in relation to demand | 166 |
|  | Influences on price | 166 |
|  | Correlating price with value | 168 |
|  | Strategic pricing determinants | 169 |
|  | Price sensitive markets as a determinant | 170 |
|  | Pricing objectives and strategies | 174 |
|  | Strategic pricing | 175 |
|  | Tactical pricing strategies | 176 |
|  | Eight stages to establishing a price | 178 |
|  | The route to setting higher prices | 178 |
| Unit 7 | **Place operations** | **181** |
|  | Introduction | 181 |
|  | Influences on distribution | 182 |
|  | Marketing issues for distribution | 183 |
|  | Distribution channels | 183 |
|  | Channel members | 184 |
|  | Why use intermediaries? | 185 |
|  | The distribution channel and the customer | 187 |

|   |   |   |
|---|---|---|
|   | Selecting the channels of distribution | 188 |
|   | Intermediary selection criteria | 188 |
|   | The balance of power within the distribution channel | 189 |
|   | Vertical channel integration | 191 |
|   | Horizontal channel integration | 192 |
|   | Physical distribution management | 192 |
|   | Push and pull strategies | 194 |
|   | The impact of the Internet on channel decisions | 195 |
|   | Evaluating channel effectiveness | 200 |
| **Unit 8** | **Managing marketing relationships** | **203** |
|   | Introduction | 203 |
|   | Relationship marketing | 204 |
|   | From transactional to relationship marketing | 204 |
|   | The scope of marketing relationships | 206 |
|   | Planning for relationship management | 207 |
|   | Customer retention management | 210 |
|   | The marketing mix for customer retention management | 213 |
|   | Managing internal marketing relationships | 214 |
|   | The relationship marketing plan | 217 |
| **Unit 9** | **International marketing** | **219** |
|   | Introduction | 219 |
|   | Why go international? | 220 |
|   | Levels of international marketing | 220 |
|   | The international marketing environment | 222 |
|   | Know your markets | 225 |
|   | Understanding the external marketplace | 226 |
|   | Understanding consumer and business buying behaviour | 227 |
|   | International research | 227 |
|   | Developing an international marketing information system | 227 |
|   | Acquiring primary research | 230 |
|   | Potential barriers to entry | 232 |
|   | The implications on marketing plans | 233 |
|   | Globalization | 235 |
| **Unit 10** | **Industrial/business-to-business, FMCGs and services marketing (including the services mix)** | **240** |
|   | Business-to-business marketing | 241 |
|   | Developing a marketing strategy for FMCGs | 251 |
|   | Marketing of services | 255 |
| **Unit 11** | **Not-for-profit, SMEs and virtual marketing** | **269** |
|   | Charities – not-for-profit marketing | 269 |
|   | What is a non-profit-making organization? | 273 |
|   | Marketing for SMEs | 279 |
|   | The virtual marketing environment | 282 |

**Appendices**

| | | |
|---|---|---|
| 1 | Guidance on examination preparation | 290 |
| 2 | Assignment-based assessment | 302 |
| 3 | Answers and debriefings | 319 |
| 4 | Sample exam questions and answers | 336 |
| 5 | Past examination papers and examiners' reports | 364 |
| 6 | Curriculum information and reading list | 397 |

**Index**     **408**

# Preface: welcome to the CIM coursebooks

## An introduction from the academic development advisor

In the last 2 years we have seen some significant changes to CIM Marketing qualifications. The changes have been introduced on a year-on-year basis, with Certificate changes implemented in 2002, and the Professional Diploma in Marketing being launched in 2003. The Professional Postgraduate Diploma in Marketing was launched in 2004. The new qualifications are based on the CIM Professional Marketing Standards developed through research with employers.

Study note © CIM 2005

As a result the authoring team, Elsevier Butterworth-Heinemann and I have all aimed to rigorously revise and update the coursebook series to make sure that every title is the best possible study aid and accurately reflects the latest CIM syllabus. This has been further enhanced through independent reviews carried out by CIM.

We have aimed to develop the assessment support to include some additional support for the assignment route as well as the examinations, so we hope you will find this help.

There are a number of new authors and indeed Senior Examiners in the series, who have been commissioned for their CIM course teaching and examining experience, as well as their research into specific curriculum-related areas and their wide general knowledge of the latest thinking in marketing.

*Preface*

We are certain that you will find these coursebooks highly beneficial in terms of the content and assessment opportunities and a study tool that will prepare you for both CIM examinations and continuous/integrative assessment opportunities. They will guide you in a logical and structured way through the detail of the syllabus, providing you with the required underpinning knowledge, understanding and application of theory.

The editorial team and authors wish you every success as you embark upon your studies.

*Karen Beamish*
*Academic Development Advisor*

## How to use these coursebooks

Everyone who has contributed to this series has been careful to structure the books with the exams in mind. Each unit, therefore, covers an essential part of the syllabus. You need to work through the complete coursebook systematically to ensure that you have covered everything you need to know.

This coursebook is divided into units, each containing a selection of the following standard elements:

- *Learning objectives* – tell you what you will be expected to know, having read the unit.
- *Syllabus references* – outline what part of the syllabus is covered in the module.
- *Study guides* – tell you how long the unit is and how long its activities take to do.
- *Questions* – are designed to give you practice – they will be similar to those you get in the exam.
- *Answers* – (at the end of the book) give you a suggested format for answering exam questions. *Remember* there is no such thing as a model answer – you should use these examples only as guidelines.
- *Activities* – give you a chance to put what you have learned into practice.
- *Debriefings* – (at the end of the book) shed light on the methodologies involved in the activities.
- *Hints and tips* – are tips from the senior examiner, examiner or author and are designed to help you avoid common mistakes made by previous candidates and give you guidance on improving your knowledge base.
- *Insights* – encourage you to contextualize your academic knowledge by reference to real-life experience.
- *Key definitions* – highlight and explain the key points relevant to that module.
- *Definitions* – may be used for words you must know to pass the exam.
- *Summaries* – cover what you should have picked up from reading the unit.
- *Further study* – provides details of recommended reading in addition to the coursebook.

While you will find that each section of the syllabus has been covered within this text, you might find that the order of some of the topics has been changed. This is because it sometimes makes more sense to put certain topics together when you are studying, even though they might appear in different sections of the syllabus itself. If you are following the reading and other activities, your coverage of the syllabus will be just fine, but don't forget to follow up with trade press reading!

## About MarketingOnline

Elsevier Butterworth-Heinemann offers purchasers of the coursebooks free access to MarketingOnline (www.marketingonline.co.uk), our premier online support engine for the CIM marketing courses. On this site you can benefit from:

- Fully customizable electronic versions of the coursebooks enabling you to annotate, cut and paste sections of text to create your own tailored learning notes.
- The capacity to search the coursebook online for instant access to definitions and key concepts.
- Useful links to e-marketing articles, provided by Dave Chaffey, Director of Marketing Insights Ltd and a leading UK e-marketing consultant, trainer and author.
- A glossary providing a comprehensive dictionary of marketing terms.
- A Frequently Asked Questions (FAQs) section providing guidance and advice on common problems or queries.

## Using MarketingOnline

### Logging on

Before you can access MarketingOnline you will first need to get a password. Please go to www.marketingonline.co.uk and click on the registration button where you will then find registration instructions for coursebook purchasers. Once you have got your password, you will need to log on using the onscreen instructions. This will give you access to the various functions of the site.

MarketingOnline provides a range of functions, as outlined in the previous section, that can easily be accessed from the site after you have logged on to the system. Please note the following guidelines detailing how to access the main features:

1. *The coursebooks* – buttons corresponding to the three levels of the CIM marketing qualification are situated on the home page. Select your level and you will be presented with the coursebook title for each module of that level. Click on the desired coursebook to access the full online text (divided up by chapter). On each page of text you have the option to add an electronic bookmark or annotation by following the onscreen instructions. You can also freely cut and paste text into a blank Word document to create your own learning notes.
2. *e-Marketing articles* – to access the links to relevant e-marketing articles simply click on the link under the text 'E-marketing Essentials: useful links from Marketing Insights'.
3. *Glossary* – a link to the glossary is provided in the top right hand corner of each page enabling access to this resource at any time.

If you have specific queries about using MarketingOnline then you should consult our fully searchable FAQs section, accessible through the appropriate link in the top right hand corner of any page of the site. Please also note that a *full user guide* can be downloaded by clicking on the link on the opening page of the website.

# unit 1
# introduction to marketing planning

## Learning objectives

Marketing Planning is the mainstay module of the Professional Diploma, formerly known as the Advanced Certificate in Marketing. It is the backbone of marketing, and builds clearly upon the Fundamentals of Marketing at Certificate level and firmly underpins Planning and Control and Integrated Marketing Communications at Postgraduate Diploma level.

This unit will:

- Help you to understand the basis and focus of the Marketing Planning Course Book
- Help you to understand the nature of the CIM Learning Outcomes, and what you should achieve through your studies
- Encourage you to read more broadly around the Marketing Planning area
- Focus on the nature of the examination
- Explain the synergistic planning process – analysis, planning, implementation and control
- List the components of the marketing plan
- Assess the potential impact of wider macro-environmental forces relating to the role of culture, ethical approach, social responsibility, legal frameworks and sustainability.

Syllabus reference: 1.1, 1.2, 1.3, 1.4, 1.5

## Introduction

The Marketing Planning module within the Professional Diploma, formerly known as the Advanced Certificate has a very clear focus and is based upon four key elements overall:

1. The marketing plan and its organizational and wider marketing context (15 per cent)
2. Marketing planning and budgeting (20 per cent)
3. The extended marketing mix and related tools (50 per cent)
4. Marketing in different contexts (15 per cent).

A brief insight into each of these components appears below. You might find it useful at this stage to look closely at the CIM syllabus, which can be found either the CIM website in the Student Zone at www.cim.co.uk, as this will put your study into context.

## The marketing planning process

This element of the text focuses on the process of effectively 'doing' marketing. It looks at the concepts and applications of 'the marketing planning process', from the marketing audit through to developing objectives and marketing strategies. One of the key success factors (KSF) of marketing is the successful utilization and integration of the marketing mix. The marketing mix is a set of tools for the trade; if they are not carefully managed, in a co-ordinated and defined way, then the strategy may crumble and the process may fall apart.

Organizations will often be found analysing their capabilities, assessing their true position and overall potential in the marketplace, both home and abroad. This analysis provides the foundations of the planning process, which are critical to the direction of the organization in the future.

Malcolm McDonald, Cranfield University School of Management, defines the overall purpose of planning at this stage as follows:

> *The overall purpose of marketing planning and its principal focus is the identification and creation of sustainable competitive advantage.* (Quoted in Dibb, Simkin, Pride and Ferrell, 2001, p. 689)

Implementing the marketing plan is probably one of the most challenging and often fraught areas of business strategy. Each division and department will be involved in fighting for their share of the budget and appropriate resource allocations, in order to achieve the objectives that are the fundamental basis of the future success of the organization. Ultimately this can often result in one of the most dramatic changes of all, i.e. change in the organizational structure. It is necessary to consider carefully the nature, structure and culture of any organization, in order that it can clearly meet the challenges to achieve a sustainable competitive advantage and remain at the heart of the marketplace.

## Marketing Planning in context

This syllabus has been designed and structured in a logical way to provide marketers with an understanding of the different concepts applicable to operational marketing management. Marketers are required to develop a range of transferable skills that aid creativity, innovation and the potential to exploit and develop new marketing opportunities.

In order that you can successfully achieve some elements of this, the CIM syllabus, and this text in association with it, has presented you with an opportunity to look at marketing in a range of different contexts. Therefore the latter part of your studies will see you starting to apply the 'process' and 'relationship' elements of Marketing Planning, into a range of contextual situations, such as:

- Industrial/business-to-business marketing
- Services marketing
- SMEs
- Charity and not-for-profit marketing
- International marketing.

Unit 1 Introduction to marketing planning

Being able to apply marketing in different contexts is vital to your own individual success and continuing professional development. You will be in a much stronger position to add value to your own position within the organization as well as to the organization as a whole.

At this early stage of your studies, it is useful to highlight how these concepts can actually work in practice.

## Case history

### The Easy Group

One of the greatest success stories of recent years is Stelios Haji-Ioannou and the 'Easy Group'. According to *Marketing Week*, the 'Easy Group is flag-waver for branding' and is described by *EuroBusiness* as Europe's most successful brand since Richard Branson's Virgin. Haji-Ioannou has clearly taken a planned approach to ensuring this high level of success for his organization, and has achieved a strong positioning for easyJet, 'the Web's favourite airline'.

Haji-Ioannou is famous for single-handedly revolutionizing low-cost air travel in Europe and has made a significant fortune in the process.

Haji-Ioannou's vision was to provide what the consumer wants, wherever they want it. Clearly he played a game as good as the one he talks. His brand translated into reality immediately, with some 3 per cent of Britons initially having heard of the airline, and 90 per cent of Europeans recognizing the brand and some 18 million passengers flying with easyJet annually within 5 years.

Whilst 2001 proved to be a devastating year for the airline industry, easyJet continued to thrive and grow, producing results completely contrary to the rest of the global airline business.

As a result, early in 2002 easyJet announced the acquisition of Go Airlines, who have subsequently been absorbed into easyJet and have expanded passenger numbers considerably. Since 2002 easyJet have continued to expand and in February 2004 easyJet announced their will to expand further into the EU – here is an extract from that announcement.

> Ten new countries joined the EU on the 1st May 2004 and easyJet has been seen to take advantage of enlarging and extending its services to Hungary and Slovenia from that date. EasyJet is also expanding further to Switzerland, with a new service linking London to Geneva Airport.

In essence the complete 'travel solutions package' for 'Easy' customers has been achieved and continues to be developed. EasyJet extends across all consumer and business sectors, meeting a variety of customer needs, from corporate business through to the individual consumer, with an increasingly innovative product/services portfolio that can see the brand being continually stretched. This is a prime example of the success of a sound planning basis, taking into consideration all of the components of the marketing plan and developing customer relationships in the context of the 'travel' services industry.

In recent times easyJet has also extended its provision of B2B business – go the the website www.easyjet.com to find out more.

Unit 1 Introduction to marketing planning

Like people, organizations are far from perfect, and the Easy Group will be no exception. Within many businesses it is clear to see that while the concept is good, the reality has scope for improvement. The purpose of your studies is to prepare you to add value to your organization, with a combination of knowledge, understanding and application abilities and skills that could really make the difference, make your organization stand out from the crowd and achieve 'sustainable competitive advantage'.

## Understanding the aims and objectives of Marketing Planning and achieving your learning outcomes

Having read the CIM syllabus overview for Marketing Planning, it is clear that the syllabus is broken down into three tiers:

1. Aims and objectives
2. Learning outcomes
3. Indicative content and weighting.

Understanding the role of each of these areas is quite important, as together they culminate in the acquisition of the knowledge and understanding that underpins the examination process.

### Aims and objectives

The aims and objectives clearly explain the basis of your learning and what that learning is designed to achieve. It is this basis that this text seeks to promote:

- To build on your knowledge and understanding of marketing fundamentals.
- To enable you to apply modern marketing theory to the understanding and solution of practical marketing problems and situations.
- To provide a sound understanding of the process of marketing planning, analysis, strategy and implementation.
- To provide a sound understanding of the marketing mix tools that contribute towards the effective implementation of marketing strategy.
- To enable you to evaluate the relative effectiveness and costs of elements of the promotional mix, providing underpinning operational knowledge for progression on to the Postgraduate Diploma in Marketing.
- To explore the multiple relationships which need to be formed and maintained to enable successful and ongoing exchange in the marketplace.
- To examine the need to adapt Marketing Planning to a variety of different contexts.

Table 1.1 provides a list of key learning outcomes, linked to the units of study, so that it is clear to see how the coursebook provides you with the underpinning knowledge and understanding to support a successful outcome to your studies, and of course the all-important examination. This should provide you with a useful reference for structuring your learning.

## Learning outcomes

Table 1.1 Learning outcomes/unit guide

| Learning outcomes | Study units/ syllabus reference |
|---|---|
| Explain the role of the marketing plan within the context of the organization's strategy and culture and broader marketing environment (ethics, social responsibility, legal frameworks and sustainability) | Unit 1 |
| Conduct a marketing audit considering appropriate internal and external factors | Unit 2 |
| Develop marketing objectives and plans at an operational level | Unit 3 |
| Develop the role of branding and positioning within the marketing plan | Unit 4 |
| Integrate marketing mix tools to achieve effective implementation of plans | Units 4–7 |
| Select an appropriate co-ordinated marketing mix incorporating appropriate stakeholder relationships for a particular marketing context | Units 8–11 |
| Set and justify budgets for marketing plans and mix decisions | Unit 3 |
| Define and use appropriate measurements to evaluate the effectiveness of marketing plans and activities | Unit 3 |
| Make recommendations for changes and innovations to marketing processes based on an understanding of the organizational context and evaluation of past marketing activities | Unit 3 |

All learning outcomes are designed in order that you can apply marketing in practice in a range of different contexts.

## Indicative content

The third and final tier of the syllabus is the indicative content and weighting. This explains in detail the different elements of the syllabus that you will cover to achieve the learning outcomes. These have been referenced in Table 1.1 for your information.

You should endeavour to familiarize yourself with these key syllabus points as they form the basis of the examination process. The examination questions are formulated by the CIM Senior Examiners and are written with a clear focus upon the indicative content. There is more on examinations later in this book.

# The importance of reading

While you might be taking the Marketing Planning module with the sole objective of achieving the Professional Diploma, hopefully you will broaden your horizons considerably along the way.

In order to do this, you should not only use this particular course text, but also read around the subject. CIM have clearly specified a range of recommended reading texts, which are listed in your Study Manual and also in *Curriculum information* in Appendix 6 of this text. Many of the texts within the reading list have been used to develop this book and you are encouraged to read and follow up on these and the other references interspersed throughout this text and extend your knowledge.

*Unit 1 Introduction to marketing planning*

In addition, you should regularly read various journals, such as *Marketing Week*, *Marketing* and *Campaign*, which have international accessibility, particularly *Marketing Week*, through www.mad.com. Other suggestions are *The Economist* and broadsheet papers, in particular the weekend versions and equivalents of *The Financial Times* and *The Sunday Times*. Here you will see a range of useful and relevant examples of how all of the components of marketing impact on everyday business in your own country. One of the most useful resources is *Marketing in Business*, the CIM magazine, where you will find many useful case studies that will consolidate your learning.

As e-commerce plays such a pivotal role in everyday life, you will also find a range of different websites referenced. It is recommended that you visit them where appropriate and in the context in which they have been offered. A useful journal to support aspects of e-commerce in relation to Marketing Planning is *connectis* – Europe's e-business magazine.

### Study tip

As part of your studies you will be continually referring to a range of promotional activities and international references.

To assist you in preparing for the examination you are advised to set up two separate information files. One is for keeping cuttings relating to marketing mix activities, in respect of both consumer and business-to-business marketing. In the second file, you should keep a range of international-based marketing cuttings.

It is recommended that you follow developments closely in two or three countries and record events over a period of time.

These would be particularly useful when answering examination questions that say 'in a country of your choice' or indeed a 'company of your choice'. With a file of cuttings to fall back on at revision time, you have a range of examples to use.

## Approaching the Marketing Planning examination

As already suggested, the examinations are written based upon the very detailed indicative content. Furthermore they are clearly focused on ensuring that you can achieve the specified 'learning outcomes' referenced earlier in this unit. It is vitally important, therefore, that you pay close attention to the requirements of the syllabus and learning outcomes, in order that you can successfully attempt the CIM examinations. Any one element of the syllabus could be tested, therefore 100 per cent coverage must be achieved through your studies.

CIM provide you with a range of exam preparation tools within their website. You will be provided with web addresses, passwords and usernames upon completion of your student registration process. The appropriate website address is www.cimvirtualinstitute.com. In addition to this, you can also use the new Butterworth-Heinemann Revision Cards, which are summary cards for each of your units of study. This will help consolidate your learning considerably in the final revision stages.

The exam paper questions will be mostly practical in nature, in that the questions will ask you to take on a role, possibly solve a problem, write briefing notes, develop an outline plan or devise the basis of a strategy. Many of the questions will ask you to put different concepts from within Marketing Planning into practice.

Questions will be naturally challenging at this level, and will not require you to regurgitate knowledge but to apply it into real-life situations or scenarios. This is a key requirement at the Professional Diploma level. You are about to prove to the Senior Examiner that you can 'do marketing' at an operational management level. Therefore avoid superficial answers and get straight to the thrust of the question.

In addition to the examination, you will also be able to take 'assignment-based assessments'. The assignments are designed to enable you to apply the concepts and theories relating to Marketing Planning in practice. Assignment-based learning allows you to use your own company or one you know well, to develop your assignment and demonstrate your ability 'to do' marketing in a practical and applied way. This book has an appendix specifically related to assisting you with your assignment, and you should refer to it, to ensure you understand the requirements of the process.

## An overview of the strategy and planning hierarchy

### The backdrop to the planning process

In the last two decades, the function of marketing has had an increasing influence upon the strategic development of the organization, achieving a much more favourable position, more on a par with the other business functions. This has been an uphill battle, one that has seen marketing gaining a very prominent position in the 1980s, and subsequently being diluted in the early 1990s as a result of the economic recession. Ever since, marketing as a business function has had to fight back in order to establish its position at the heart of the corporate planning process.

Essentially, the marketing function may play a pivotal role in feeding information upwards, to provide substance, guidance, direction and vision to support the corporate planning process. In turn, the significant work that the marketing function undertakes plays a major role in establishing a vision and mission for the organization, a sense of direction as to where it is heading in the short, medium and long term.

To put this into context, it is necessary to understand and conceptualize the strategy and planning hierarchy (Figure 1.1). This highlights the route that strategy and planning takes from the corporate strategy stage down to the marketing function and through to marketing tactics. For example, it is likely as a marketing director that you will have a significant input to the strategic decision-making process, this is commonly known as 'bottom-up planning'. Your role would include providing the board and the corporate strategy team with appropriate levels of information to support corporate level decision-making. Subsequent to this, you would also have a vital role in taking the corporate objectives and corporate strategy, and translating them into marketing objectives and marketing strategy (Figure 1.1).

Unit 1 Introduction to marketing planning

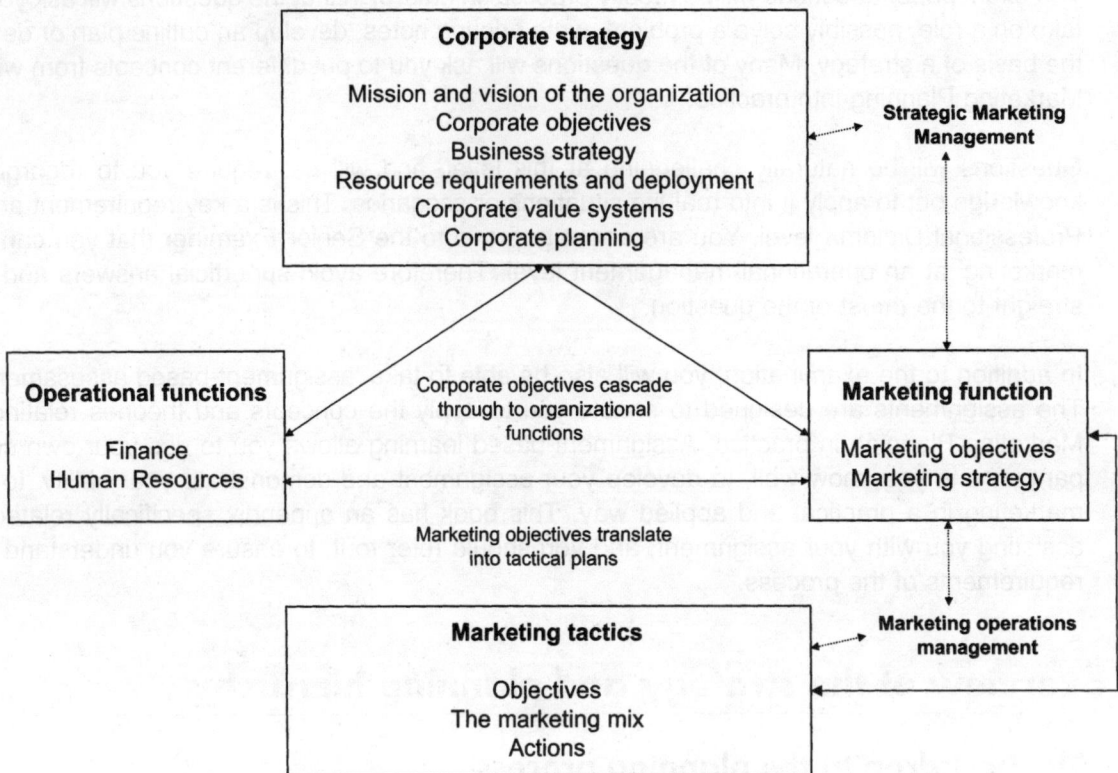

Figure 1.1 Strategy and planning hierarchy

Further down the strategy and planning hierarchy (Figure 1.1), Marketing Planning starts to play a pivotal role in implementing the marketing plans, through a tightly defined marketing programme. This is known as bottom-down planning.

At this stage it is appropriate to consider the various tiers of the strategy and planning hierarchy in a little more detail, in preparation for your studies in Unit 2, 'The marketing audit'.

## Corporate planning – what is it?

Corporate planning starts at the very top of the organization. It provides clearly defined objectives for the organization as a whole, which can then be translated down through the hierarchy to each of the business functions, inclusive of marketing, human resources, finance, and the operations departments. In turn, each of these business functions has responsibility to deliver the overall corporate objectives, meeting the corporate mission and corporate vision of the organization. They will also have a key role in ensuring that corporate values are deployed and understood by the internal market.

While the business functions will vary in nature, it is essential that they each work together, developing an innovative and integrative approach to delivering corporate objectives. No business unit should work in isolation of the other functional units; ignoring this approach could ultimately have a detrimental effect. It amounts to planning in a vacuum.

A good example of this would be a financial services organization. You will be aware that financial services organizations such as 'Egg', First Direct Bank, American Express or MBNA rely heavily upon 'people' in order to provide the required level of service to meet customer demands and expectations. For any of the above organizations to succeed, both the human resources and marketing business functions will need to work closely together to achieve an integrated approach to fulfilling the corporate objectives.

Read the case history below and then undertake Question 1.1.

## Case history

### The Egg that came first

October 1998 saw the Prudential launch 'Egg' – a financial service that was developed and tailored to meet individual needs.

Egg was a new 'brand' development with a new and innovative strategy, with the main focus being on the delivery of this brand via the Internet. Egg was designed with a clear focus on utilizing the new technologies, not just providing an information-based website, but clearly a transaction-based website where customers could manage all of their financial needs wherever they were, whenever they wanted.

Significant marketing research was undertaken and the outcome suggested that Egg would appeal to a core of 15 million people in the UK, particularly young professionals, the well-off older generation and busy younger people.

Egg made its financial services available 7 days a week, 24 hours per day, by telephone, post and Internet. Within days of its launch, the website had received over 1.75 million hits and over 100 000 telephone calls were received. Personal loans were processed in 24 hours and home loans in 48 hours.

The brand name was a great success. By Christmas 1998, Egg had achieved 50 per cent recall of the name 'Egg', rising to 75 per cent by the end of 1999.

Egg have now established themselves as Europe's leading online bank. Today, they have over two million customers. In June 2000 they listed on the London Stock Exchange, so are now 79 per cent owned by Prudential, the leading international financial services group, and 21 per cent owned by their shareholders. They showed profits of some £17.3 million in the first quarter of 2003.

Egg, having a staff of over 2000, are based in three locations in the UK – Derby, London and Dudley – and expanded onto the Continent in November 2002 when they launched in France. Egg say that they always intended to develop into an international company and launching in France was their first step. However, Egg will not break even until 2005, which has led to a cooling of its expansion to the USA.

The Egg brand continues to grow and includes just about every package you could think of, e.g. travel insurance, credit cards and promotional incentives such as unlimited access on the Internet and e-mail or 1 per cent off for all high street purchases. Its promotional activity was considerable, including special offers. Egg's website is www.egg.com – research for information to support your case study answers.

Unit 1 Introduction to marketing planning

> ### Question 1.1
>
> In the case of 'Egg', why would it have been vitally important for the marketing function and human resources function to have worked closely together?
>
> Before commencing this question it would help if you start to think about the role that marketing plays within the organization and what it is that they need to be able to function. You should think about this in the realm of both physical and human resources.
>
> You should then be able to approach this question understanding the linkages between human resources and marketing and how they might be dependent on one another. You will see that there needs to be clear co-operation between the business functions. This ensures that there is synergy between functions, in order that the brand values can be delivered and a sustainable competitive advantage achieved. Defining the service that Egg was to deliver could not be undertaken in isolation, as there was a requirement for a sound infrastructure to deliver the high level services envisaged.

## Marketing strategy – what is it?

In this unit the words strategy and planning often appear linked together in the same sentences. Clearly, however, they are not one and the same, and therefore they must be differentiated.

> *Marketing strategy – a strategy indicating the specific target markets and the types of competitive advantages that are to be developed and exploited.* (Dibb, Simkin, Pride and Ferrell, 2001, p. 656)

> *As a strategy, marketing seeks to develop effective responses to changing marketing environments, by defining market segments, developing and positioning product offerings for those target markets.* (Webster, 1997, from Hooley, Saunders and Piercy, 1998, p. 7)

> *Strategy is the matching of the activities of an organization to the environment in which it operates and to its own resource capabilities.* (Johnson and Scholes, 2001)

On close examination of these definitions, it is clear to see that they have a common thread. That is, marketing strategy should create a sense of vision and direction. Nigel Piercy (2001) states that:

> *Strategy is all about doing best what matters most to the customer.*

and

> *Finding new and better ways of looking at important things to get some leverage for changing the way things are done.*

Marketing strategy provides the basis of a framework for meeting organizational needs and customer wants in an integrative and innovative way. It communicates to the internal market and its external stakeholders the strategic intent of the organization, where the organization is going, to whom it is taking its products and services and how it proposes to achieve a positive competitive market position.

When developing a strategy, the critical success factor is to ensure that the marketing strategy is robust and focuses on building long-term relationships, creating customer value and sustainable competitive advantage. This is quite important to comprehend, as while organizations are subject to constant change, and as a result often work continually on various contingency plans, there should be some consistency in approach. Therefore, a robust marketing strategy is long term, it is strategic in nature and should remain constant. The contingency approach is very much tactical, leading to changes in the marketing mix as a result of changing market conditions.

Piercy (2001) suggests, in his book *Market-Led Strategic Change*, that a robust marketing strategy should have the following characteristics:

- Focus on providing superior customer value, but recognize that innovation offers a sustainable advantage
- Make long-term investments in relationships, with suppliers, distributors, employees and customers
- Be built around 100 per cent satisfied customers based on capabilities and motivation of their people
- Build effective supply chains and IT infrastructure to deliver superior operating performance.

Therefore, the key to success is to build a strategy based on these concepts, added to which an organization must strive to ensure that it implements a learning culture, is open to change and is innovative, with a long-term commitment to developing long-lasting customer relationships. Figure 1.2 represents some of the key components of the fundamentals of marketing strategy.

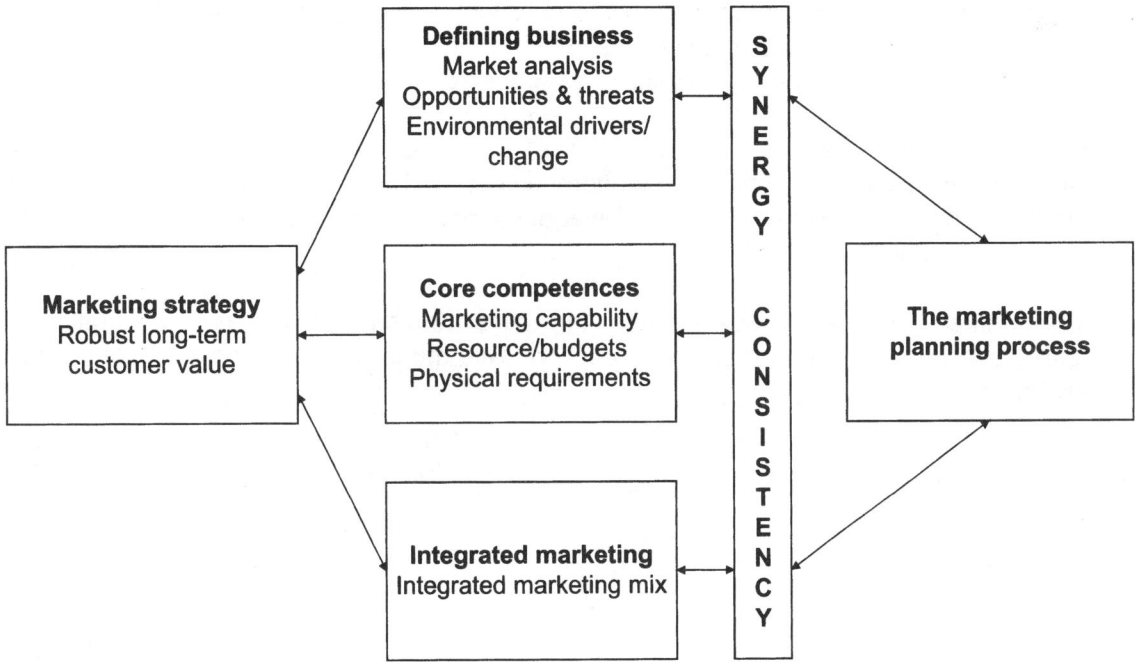

Figure 1.2 The basics of strategy
Source: Adapted from Drummond, Ensor and Ashford (1999)

Essentially marketing strategy should identify specific segments of the market, towards which the organization's marketing activities and programmes might be aimed. It should highlight opportunities to be exploited and explicitly state the objectives required in order that the corporate goals of the organization should be achieved.

Ultimately, strategy should ensure synergy across the whole organization without exception. Critical to the success of any strategy is the need to ensure that all business functions and their underpinning activities are working to the same purpose and design, with a common vision, achieving integration and consistency in approach.

## Planning – what is it?

Planning is an essential process ensuring that the defined strategy may be successfully implemented, and that the infrastructure required in order to meet the corporate and marketing objectives has been set in place. Planning provides specific direction, activities and timetables, and it creates pathways to achieving competitive advantage. Effectively it becomes a programme of events.

More and more organizations today appear to have an increasing emphasis on the importance of planning, and Johnson and Scholes (2001) suggest a number of reasons why this might be:

- Planning provides a structured means of analysing the marketplace, considering the dynamics of it and forcing managers to both question and challenge what they quite often take for granted.
- Planning provides a sense of direction, and can be seen as a means of involving employees in the development of a strategy. This provides an opportunity for employees to take ownership of the overall objectives and the planned approach to achieving them.
- A plan is a good way of communicating proposed actions/activities expected to be undertaken by the organization, in order that it achieves its corporate objectives.
- Having a plan in place provides a sound basis for control, and presents an opportunity to regularly review the organization's progress against objectives.

While there is an emphasis on 'planning' as a key business activity at this stage, your studies will focus on 'marketing planning' at an operational level. Therefore, it is important to highlight a typical marketing planning model at this stage, so that you understand the level for which you are being prepared.

The 'marketing planning process model' in Figure 1.3 clearly illustrates how planning might take place within a typical marketing function. This model will form the basis of your study within Unit 2.

*Unit 1 Introduction to marketing planning*

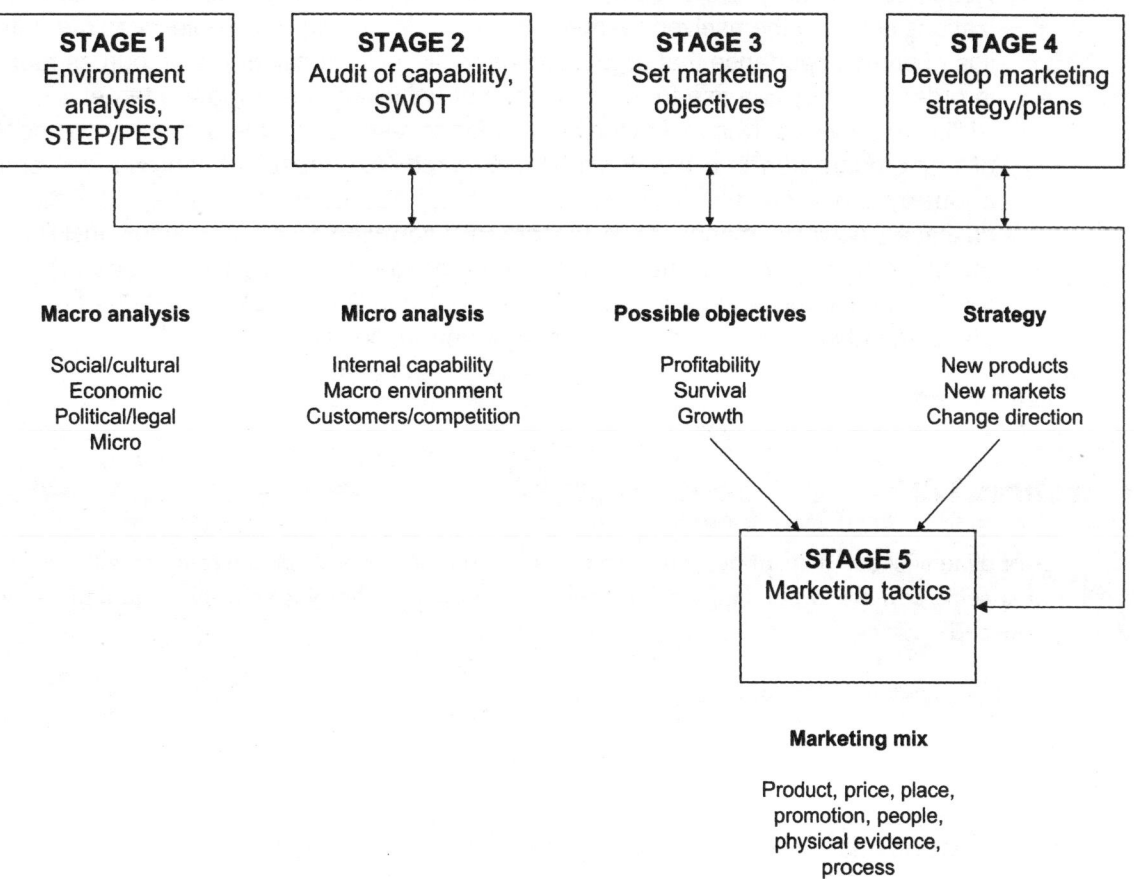

Figure 1.3 The marketing planning process

However, while the focus will be around marketing planning, it is still important to understand the 'bigger picture' of how it all fits together, including the issues and implications of planning.

## Barriers to planning

While planning has many positive facets, it can also create many barriers within the organization. It is likely that the majority of people and organizations have faced considerable change as a result of newly defined strategies and have had to come to terms with some of the major repercussions of this level of change. The most prominent factor related to change is that, almost without exception, it is linked with cost cutting and downsizing.

Drummond, Ensor and Ashford (2003) suggested that barriers to successful planning are:

- The existing culture may not be amenable to marketing plans, particularly if the organization is not marketing-oriented.
- *Power and politics* – All organizations are subject to internal politics and often as a result of this the strategic planning process becomes a boardroom battlefield, where vested interests fight each other's proposals in order to gain resources and status.
- *Analysis not action* – Many organizations waste time and energy in analysing data and developing rationales for action, but ultimately fail to act. A further element of this is 'paralysis-by-analysis', too much information, not enough direction.

- Resources – After years of downsizing, striving for increased efficiencies, many organizations now find themselves resource-starved. When corporate objectives are defined, it is of prime importance that organizations realistically consider the resources required, in order that they can rise to the challenge of achieving the corporate targets.
- Skills are very closely linked to the challenges of resources. One of the key components of any organization is a highly skilled workforce. As a result of the changes brought about by the economic slowdown in the early 1990s, marketing as a function was cascaded down to managers in the organization who were untrained, unskilled and unable to suddenly carry the mantle of marketing that had now been bestowed upon them. An unskilled workforce could hinder significantly the implementation of marketing plans and ultimately reduce service and performance levels overall.

## Question 1.2

Stop for a moment and think about your own organization, or one that you are familiar with. Make a list of specific barriers to planning and the subsequent change that your chosen organization has experienced.

Why do you think these barriers were created?

### The influence of 'change' upon the planning process

One of the most certain factors impacting upon the planning process in any organization is 'change' – change is a by-product of the modern-day world. Planning is now undertaken against the backdrop of constant change, internally and externally. Organizations are challenged to manage through a range of either predictable change or unexpected change, cyclical change or evolutionary change. Either way, the impact upon the organization can be significant, causing a slowdown in the strategy implementation process, or a diversion to develop an unexpected and unanticipated opportunity that it is essential to exploit and promote.

Of course, alternatively, change can mean that strategies and plans are no longer relevant or that they will no longer guarantee the levels of success that had previously been anticipated. One of the most recent examples of this is Marks and Spencer (M&S). In March 2001 they announced the closure of all their international branches outside the UK, marking a change in direction and overall strategy. As a result of a wide range of changes, Marks and Spencer had suffered considerably over the previous 2 years, with market share and associated profits reducing, against the tide of increasing competition in the high street and also on the Internet. However, Marks and Spencer have been successful, through radical change, in turning the business around. Most recently however, Marks and Spencer have struggled again to capture the imagination of the customers, particularly over the period of Christmas 2003. This shows the need for continuous change and a continuous awareness of the state of the market, including customer needs. Part of their response to this is to move to the opening of discrete stores selling only the 'Per Una' range.

In today's rapidly changing environment, understanding the key drivers and forces will be of primary importance if an organization is going to be prepared to respond to these key drivers.

In essence, change means the future is unpredictable, more intense, more competitive, with shorter life cycles, shorter planning cycles and much uncertainty. In an environment where planning is a key activity, the challenges presented by change will intensify.

## Activity 1.1

Taking your own organization, or one that you are familiar with, consider the various changes they have implemented over the past 2 years. Then think about the key drivers of that change – make a list of them.

# Relationship marketing with the wider public and society

In the final stage of this unit, it is important to consider marketing in the broader context of the wider public and society, i.e. carry out the marketing activity in a way that is socially acceptable, ethically driven and is proactively incorporated into the organization's vision, mission, ethos, culture and day-to-day business dealings.

At times ethics and business seem to be mutually incompatible, as we will see in the mini-case study on Exxon in Unit 2 'The marketing audit'. However, social and ethical marketing are a very politically correct element of today's society and business at large. A further example of how a social and ethical issue in the context of 'green marketing' has affected a high volume market is McDonald's. McDonald's has been involved in a number of social and ethical responsibility issues, in respect of the construction of their products and packaging, which they have had to address so as to retain favour with the marketplace. This was a costly exercise and one that was carried out under the spotlight of huge publicity.

Today there are a number of dynamic groups and individuals who engage themselves in social issues, such as human rights and, in particular, green issues. With the introduction of the Kyoto Agreement, there has been a significant impact upon how organizations manage their activities to remain within the framework of reference that the agreement has defined. Failing to redress the balance between where the organization is and where it should be in respect of the Kyoto Agreement has been shown to cause high levels of discomfort.

Recognition of corporate social responsibility (CSR), both as an important part of business behaviour and a key marketing issue, has increased enormously in the last few years. This is because it is not only an issue of ethics but one which has become integral to sustaining the consumer goodwill that feeds sales and profits.

Increasingly people are not just passive consumers insensitive to what is going on around them. The indications are that the upcoming generations are more aware and more likely to buy from companies they see as socially responsible.

Where organizations transgress, as in the case of Esso and Exxon, reputations can be swept away almost overnight, as these and other global corporations have discovered.

The drinks industry is under constant attack and the particular target is alcoholic soft drinks, which took the market by surprise, indeed by storm, in the summer of 1995. In particular, drinks such as Hooch, Lemonheads and Vodka Sauce are the source of constant contention between consumer movements and the brewing industry with regard to the problem of under-age drinking and distinguishing between an alcoholic drink and a soft drink. This has since continued to be a source of contention as there is an increasing number of alco-pop drinks on sale.

## Marketing and social responsibility

Marketers are not blind to criticism. A company knows that if the products it sells are not acceptable to the consumer, then it has problems.

> **Definition**
>
> **Social responsibility** – The obligations and accountability to society of individuals and organizations above and beyond their primary functions and interests.

A further definition is that of CSR. The European Commission in its 2001 green paper Promoting a European Framework for corporate social responsibility define it as 'a concept whereby companies integrate social and environment concerns in their business operations and in their interaction with their stakeholders on a voluntary basis'.

*Corporate social responsibility relates to actions which are above and beyond that required by law.* (McWilliams and Siegel, 2001)

Others see it more simply as 'doing things right' and a matter of good management which takes a holistic view of an organization's role and responsibilities. A poll of 25 000 citizens across 23 countries on six continents showed that perceptions of companies around the world are more strongly linked with citizenship (56 per cent) than either brand quality (40 per cent) or the perception of business management (34 per cent).

### Case history

#### Marks and Spencer

When M&S decided in 2001 that it wanted its food products to contain only free range eggs, it faced a massive task. The company markets around 4000 different products that contain egg or egg derivatives and they are manufactured by hundreds of suppliers. Reaching a point where the company could confidently say that all egg products passing through its chain were free range was no easy task.

The decision was part of a broader business agenda for the company and part of its commitment to animal welfare.

Marks and Spencer category marketer Ray Mak said 'We realize that there would be a cost in the free range commitment but had to weigh it up against where we want to stand as a brand. It was worth the investment.'

Marks and Spencer corporate social responsibilities are:

- Take care and act responsibly in delivering high quality products and services
- Create great places to work
- Help make our communities good places in which to live.

*Unit 1 Introduction to marketing planning*

Manufacturers need to care for consumers in terms of safety. This could involve environmental or health consequences. The social costs and benefits of new products must also be examined. Marketers have to consider their response to, say pharmaceutical products, where the side-effects of new drugs must be researched, and often through contentious methods such as testing on animals.

Marketers must also consider other issues important to social marketing, such as environmentalism, legislation, consumerism and consumer pressure.

The accepted wisdom on the value of CSR is that it achieves the following objectives:

- To meet responsibilities
- To put something back
- To manage impacts on society
- To improve reputation
- To meet government expectations.

## Case history

### Starbucks

Starbucks maintain that CSR runs deeply through the company, by giving back to communities and the environment and by treating staff with dignity and respect.

The company policy points to the following commitments they have made:

1. *Commitment to origins* – by making investments that benefit coffee producer communities and the natural environment.
2. *Protecting the environment* – by promoting conservation in coffee-growing countries and recycling programmes.
3. *In the community* – by making contributions to neighbourhoods where Starbucks have outlets.
4. *Commitment to partners* – by creating a happy work environment where staff are treated with respect.

Some useful websites that you may want to look at to find out more about CSR are:

- Business in the Community – www.bitc.org.uk
- Institute of Business Ethics – www.ibe.org.uk
- Society of Business – www.societyandbusiness.gov.uk.

### Environmentalism – green marketing

Wastage, effluent, emissions of fumes and acid rain have to be taken seriously by manufacturers. Due to the high level of industrialization in the modern world, the environment is under constant threat from global warming. In recent times we have experienced severe weather effects, such as heavy rain, gales and significant flooding. All of this relates to environmentalism and as such means that organizations must in the future consider their strategy in relation to these issues.

Organizations such as NIREX, who dispose of atomic waste, are subject to heavy criticism by environmental groups such as the Green Party and also by the press. Their contact with the consumer is minimal; they deal with industry, hence they are little influenced by the consumer.

## Case history

### Shareholder activism goes Green: corporations increasingly called to account for environmental issues

Frustrated by legislation that is often compromised or not enforced, and legal challenges that can take years to resolve, environmental and social justice groups are challenging corporations head-on through the use of boycotts, direct action and shareholder activism.

Shareholder activism is uniquely suited for a direct approach to corporations since it provides a formal channel of communication between management and shareholders. Shareholder activists use the power of stock ownership to file resolutions, raise awareness, build coalitions and exert pressure to 'create change' from the inside.

While the corporate world sometimes disregards the criticism of grassroots groups, it pays serious attention to its own peer group and financial community.

Shareholder activism has traditionally been organized by religious groups such as Interfaith Centre for Corporate Responsibility (ICCR) – a coalition of more than 300 religious and social investors with $150 billion in stock. Recently, environmentalists have begun to add this tactic to their activist toolbox.

In 2000, Greenpeace received strong support for its resolution asking BP Amoco not to drill in the Arctic and to increase its solar energy programme. The National Wildlife Federation votes in its proxies on environmental resolutions and the Sierra Club initiated shareholder activism through shareholder campaigns in 2002.

Some key resolutions that shareholder activist groups and collaborative groups have undertaken are to influence the environmental practices of organizations such as Coca-Cola, in order that they will recycle elements of their containers, and BP Amoco on global warming and Hershey on genetically modified foods.

For more information see www.asyousow.org or www.socialfunds.com/sa.

*Source*: Lexis-Nexis.

## Legislation

Perhaps one of the most dynamic areas for the major political parties when in power has been the introduction of legislation to protect the consumer. This provides external constraints on business, the most significant being that of government policy itself.

The manufacturer and the supplier have legal duties to consumers and a number of laws have been passed over the years to protect the latter, notably:

- The Trade Descriptions Acts 1968 and 1972
- The Consumer Safety Act 1978
- The Consumer Credit Act 1974.

These are just three of the most important areas of legislation.

# The rise in consumerism

A major element of social responsibility is considering the impact of consumerism. Although consumers have had rights, enforceable by law, for many years, they have not really been effective because of the cost of taking legal action. The consumerist movement is a way of taking agreed action for specific purposes, such as opposing the building of another runway at Manchester or Birmingham Airport, and similar schemes elsewhere.

Such schemes are often associated with local initiatives. One group that is known nationally is the Consumers' Association, famous for the publication *Which?*

The consumer movement is a diverse collection of independent individuals, groups and organizations seeking to protect the rights of consumers.

It may be useful to consider at this stage two definitions of consumerism.

### Definition

**Consumerism** – Consumerism is an organized movement of concerned citizens and government to enhance the rights and powers of buyers in relation to sellers (P. Kotler, *Strategic Marketing for Non-Profit Organizations*, 5th edn, Prentice Hall, 1995).

**Consumerism** – Is a social force designed to protect the consumer by organizing legal, moral and economic pressures on business (D. Cravens and G. Hills, 'Consumerism: A Perspective for Business', *Business Horizons*, 1970, 13, 21–3).

In both of these definitions there is a suggestion of an alienation from business and industry, and a feeling that the consumer's point of view is neglected.

# Social response to consumerist pressure

Companies have responded in many different ways to the consumer movement and the individual consumer. Some have resisted and actively lobbied against consumerist pressure; others have ignored it and gone about their business as if the consumerist movement did not exist. However, evidence from the USA suggests that those companies which reacted to the consumerist movement positively increased their market shares and profits quite substantially, and it is now recognized that most companies have to respond to environmental and social issues and accept the new buyer's rights, at least in principle.

It is quite interesting to consider the differing responses of organizations to social and environmental pressures. Below are some of the responses of businesses:

- *Ignore consumerism* – A reaction that encourages legislation in the marketing area, as companies believe/hope that the consumerism movement is a passing phase.
- *Counter consumerism* – The stronger elements in the business sector will endeavour to resist consumerist pressures by lobbying government. This is really a delaying tactic, as a government wins more votes from consumers than from big business generally.
- *Profit from consumerism* – To respond to consumerist pressures by creating new means of profit is the most acceptable alternative long-term strategy for business.
- *Voluntary adaptation* – This is, in fact, treading the tightrope – meeting consumerist demands, but over a longer period than the government would want. This approach could misfire, indeed backfire.
- *Accept government intervention* – Business has traditionally resisted government interference, but it is now becoming more acceptable, and certain politicians talk of a government/business partnership.

There is one thing, though, that is certain and that is that consumerism is here to stay. Increasingly it demonstrates against the building of more roads or airport runways, and it shows that people have a high level of determination that can no longer be ignored.

The same applies to the 'Green' movement, which aims to preserve the natural order of things to reduce pollution. Quite often the improvement of processes, which is necessary to reduce pollution, is a once-only capital cost and the process runs at lower cost after improvements.

It is clear that the ideas of consumerism and anti-pollution make some sense, even if manufacturers do not like the details of some of the claims, and it is essential to have a policy on these matters.

Reduction of pollution is a social responsibility, and can often be achieved either through factory processes or in lower-cost wrappings, and this, in turn, is a matter which can be used as a topic for favourable publicity.

For many organizations, it would make sense to run a social audit, in the same way that they may run a marketing audit. The difference would be that the results could be used for publicity purposes, either to show existing good practice, or to report progress on matters that need attention.

Most important of all, though, is a declaration of company policy regarding consumerism and social responsibility. When all members of staff at all levels have a clear directive to which they can work, they will feel happier to do the little bit extra that is often needed to work more cleanly. This may look like a matter of ethics and social responsibility, but it will often result in the production of economies and a reduction in selling costs.

## Ethical issues for consumers and marketers

We have very much focused on social marketing, of which ethical marketing is an important part. Taking social responsibility often means being ethical in behaviour. We must briefly consider the importance of ethical issues relating to the role of marketing.

Some of the matters that are highlighted by the consumer movement are often taken up because they impinge strongly on the livelihoods of people who are closely involved with the industry. Farmers have to work the land efficiently and effectively, yet intensive farming methods spoil wildlife habitats. These methods include the growth of GM (genetically modified) crops, even when these crops threaten to upset the ecological balance of the agricultural environment.

Instead of just fighting farmers, organizations such as the Royal Society for the Protection of Birds have investigated a range of activities and produced a book to show farmers how they can benefit from looking after wildlife as well as their crops. The government has found itself with a moral and ethical obligation to consider the impact of GM crops more closely also. In turn, codes of practice or legislation will be introduced on the future inclusion of GM crops in the marketplace and the development of associated food products.

This is probably a more acceptable view of consumerism, but at times there are excessive demands from consumers, who continue to bring the consumer movement into disrepute. Therefore, it is necessary, where appropriate and indeed possible, to have codes of ethics by which industry can operate.

## Ethical implications for the marketing mix

Should a company be quite serious about acting responsibly at a social and ethical level, then it is likely that there may be some adoption of the marketing mix. Key issues in the mix are:

### Product

- Meeting safety standards
- Dangerous products modified or removed
- Ethical issues relating to planned obsolescence should be considered
- No further testing on animals.

### Price

- Consideration given to what is a fair price
- Monopolies and mergers more closely monitored to prevent monopolistic power on prices.

### Promotion

- Ensuring that advertising standards are upheld and not brought into disrepute.

Unit 1 Introduction to marketing planning

## Case history

### 'Swedes urged to re-think advertising policy aimed at children': A case of commercial ethics versus social responsibility

The Swedish EU Presidency was urged by a number of advertising chiefs to re-think its plans for a ban on advertisements aimed at children.

The Culture Minister told a Stockholm Conference that children were a 'special group of society in need of special care and attention' and called for barriers against harmful content.

The Minister insisted that Sweden would press for further discussions to pursue this in the future.

The advertising industry was quick to respond. Andrew Brown, Director-General of the UK Advertising Association, suggested that there was no evidence to suggest that there was a need for binding legislation or a ban.

He went on to say 'Children are not the naïve, gullible and exploited sector of society, who can be isolated from the commercial pressures of the real world, those who believe in bans suggest.'

Within the EU, Sweden and Greece already have bans on advertising aimed at children. Denmark, Ireland, and Flemish regions of Belgium are said to support further restrictions. The UK, Germany and France support the status quo.

### Place

- A duty to ensure that products are available to all, on an equal cost basis
- Environmental transportation concerns are considered.

## Summary

As many markets reach maturity, organizations are working significantly harder to achieve and retain sustainable competitive advantage. The varying dynamics of devising strategies and plans require careful and sensitive management, as the organization, i.e. 'the corporate group' of business functions, seeks to achieve its organizational objectives.

There are many strategic marketing issues that need to be addressed in respect of the future success of an organization and its product/services portfolio. Ideally an organization will need to focus on the brand values, brand statements, customer services, supply chains and, of course, its customers and consumers.

Developing a strategy and associated plans that are innovative, competitive and sustainable is a tremendous challenge. Ultimately the most successful measure of performance is said to be customer satisfaction. Without satisfied customers the organization will struggle to remain competitive and remain at the leading edge in the marketplace, and the challenge will never be fully realized.

According to Nigel Piercy, author of *Market-Led Strategic Change* (2001), you can tell if a company has a strategy and knows where it is going and develops the capability to get there. He suggests 'this is something that stands behind planning and systems and structure – strategy is more fundamental'.

It is therefore clear to see that strategies and plans give focus, structure, outcomes and a planned destiny for the organization. Every organization should have a pathway mapped out that takes it to a state of competitive strength.

In Unit 2 of this book, we look very closely at the setting of appropriate objectives, and the development of appropriate strategies, but prior to looking at this, it is essential to understand the planning framework and where it all fits together.

## Study tip

Nobody will be expecting you to produce a fully fledged strategic marketing plan as a result of study for this module. The learning outcome supporting this module is very focused on providing you with *an understanding of marketing planning at an operational level*. This 'Planning Overview' will have provided you with an insight into the relationship between corporate planning and marketing planning, and therefore the focus of your studies will relate to 'bottom-up' planning, i.e. operational level marketing, where the responsibility rests for the successful implementation of the marketing plan.

Drummond, Ensor and Ashford (2003) describe 'bottom-up planning' thus: 'Authority and responsibility for formulation and implementation of strategy is devolved. Senior marketing managers approve, and then monitor, agreed objectives.'

## Bibliography

Dibb, S., Simkin, L., Pride, W. and Ferrell, O. (2001) *Marketing: Concepts and Strategies*, 4th European edition, Houghton Mifflin.

Drummond, G., Ensor, J. and Ashford, R. (2003) *Strategic Marketing: Planning and Control*, Butterworth-Heinemann.

Hooley, G.J., Saunders, N.A. and Piercy, N.F. (1998) *Marketing Strategy and Competitive Positioning*, 3rd edition, FT Prentice Hall.

Johnson, G. and Scholes, K. (2001) *Exploring Corporate Strategy*, 6th edition, FT Prentice Hall.

McWilliams, A. and Siegel, D. (2001) *Academy of Management Review*, **26**(1), pp. 117–127.

Piercy, N. (2001) *Market-Led Strategic Change*, Butterworth-Heinemann.

**Useful websites include:**

www.cimvirtualinstitute.com
www.wnim.com
www.cim.com
www.connectedinmarketing.com
www.mad.com
www.marketresearch.org.uk (useful links on ethics and code of conduct)

---

Sample exam questions and answers for the Marketing Planning module as a whole can be found in Appendix 4 and past examination papers can be found in Appendix 5. Both appendices can be found at the back of the book.

# unit 2 the marketing audit

## Learning objectives

The main focus of this unit is on the development of the marketing strategy and the overall planning function. The learning outcomes associated with this unit will enable you to:

- Explain the constituents of the macro and micro environmental marketing audit

- Assess the external marketing environment for an organization through PESTEL

- Assess the internal marketing environment for an organization through using an internal audit

- Critically appraise processes and techniques used for auditing the marketing environment

- Explain the role of marketing information and research in conducting and analysing the marketing audit

Syllabus reference: 2.1–2.5

This unit will serve to provide you with some of the analytical tools of the trade for ensuring that sufficient analysis is undertaken and then used to underpin the marketing decision-making process and overall strategy development.

## Introduction

Having worked through the introductory unit, and the overview of the strategy and planning hierarchy, you should now have a good idea about the importance of marketing planning in giving structure and direction to marketing activities.

Principally, in the words of Dibb, Simkin, Pride and Ferrell (2001):

*Marketing planning is a systematic process of assessing marketing opportunities and resources, determining marketing objectives and developing a thorough plan for implementation and control.*

Therefore, the overall purpose of the marketing plan is to create a blueprint, a map, which provides detailed requirements of the company's marketing activities for the future. It serves a number of purposes:

- It provides a pathway along which a company may travel to reach its ultimate destination
- It provides time-lines for marketing activities to be achieved within, e.g. 6 months, 12 months, etc.
- It enables resources to be allocated efficiently and effectively to ensure high levels of performance are achieved
- It identifies strengths, weaknesses, opportunities and threats, all of which can be addressed, exploited and improved upon
- It ensures that the organization is marketing-oriented and customer-focused, ideally striving to meet customer needs, wants and expectations
- It may shape the organizational structure in order to achieve the corporate objective and marketing objectives
- It assists in the implementation and control of the marketing strategy.

Planning is fundamental to the successful implementation of strategy and achievement of objectives.

## Conducting a marketing audit

The marketing audit is of pivotal importance to the planning process, as it provides the backbone analysis that supports both the *corporate and marketing decision-making process*.

Its primary objective is to ensure that the decision-making process is an informed one and that the organization is coming from a position of strength in respect of its knowledge of the marketplace, as opposed to 'planning in a vacuum'.

The audit seeks to provide information on two key aspects of the marketing environment, the external and internal environment, otherwise known as the 'macro' and 'micro' environment (Stages 1 and 2 of Figure 1.3).

Primarily the macro environment will provide information in relation to the external conditions in which the company operates, taking into account the following:

- The wider *political/legal* environment, not just on a local basis, but on a global basis. For example, the European Union, World Trade Organization (WTO), G7 countries, organizations such as NAFTA. (These will be addressed again in Unit 9, 'International marketing'.)
- Key *economic* factors – understanding key economic drivers that affect organizations' ability to achieve high performance and profitability.
- *Social/cultural* issues – this element will concentrate on demographics, population trends, birth rates, and life expectancy, changing lifestyles and family life cycles, the changing role of women.

One of the most significant influences on modern marketing is the rapid evolution of new technologies. *Technological* factors are highly influential in today's environment and they enable high levels of innovation, create factors influencing competitive advantage and have enabled the implementation of more efficient and effective manufacturing processes and a wide range of scientific developments. The most radical change in our time is that of the Internet, the World Wide Web (WWW), the information superhighway, which is rapidly changing the way we all do business, broadening business horizons and opening up new opportunities.

The significance of understanding the macro environment should never be underestimated. Understanding important trends, anticipating change, forecasting the organization's future, measuring the impact of strategies and preparing alternative strategies (contingencies) will all be directed by the outcome of the macro environmental analysis.

The key words are: political/legal, economic, social/cultural, technological; they are the key environmental factors, more formally known as PEST. Other acronyms are used, such as SLEPT. For the purpose of this text we will use PESTEL.

- Political
- Economic
- Social
- Technological
- Environmental
- Legal.

No organization should ever underestimate the powerful force of external drivers within the marketplace, as they can ultimately hinder the success and indeed aid the failure of many organizations. Changing trends in the marketplace have often seen the demise of business. Take for example the ongoing downturn in electronic communications. As competition has intensified over the past months, many major corporations have been cutting jobs in a big way.

A further effect of this downturn in hi-tech industries is that banks are being hit by a meltdown in hi-tech deals. They experienced a devastating slump in business in the early part of 2001 and onwards into 2002, and as a result only 50 per cent of the banking deals normally made were experienced.

However, possibly one of the most devastating events of all time, which had an impact of unprecedented measure, was 'September 11th 2001' and subsequently the Tsunami on 26th December 2004. Whilst we can see that economic downturn had a significant impact upon the economy earlier in 2001, the events that took place in the United States of America did untold damage to many industries and many economies, not least of all the airline industry and the US economy, with tens of thousands of jobs being lost as a result, the impact of which is still being felt. Of course the war in Iraq in 2003 has had a tremendous effect on world stability and the impact upon tourism, for example, is a strong case in point. In terms of the Tsunami, the impact of this event has devastated tourism in some areas for the foreseeable future, for instance parts of Sri Lanka, Indonesia, Thailand and India – this has an impact on countries all over the world and those organizations to sell holidays to exotic locations such as these.

Thinking back to the effects of September 11th, the ongoing effects of terrorism are quite considerable, with the ongoing threats against the UK and the US. In early 2004 a spate of British Airways flights to Washington and Saudi Arabia were cancelled due to impending terrorist threats, this then continued later in the year, with a number of US-bound flights being cancelled due to terrorist threats. Added to the bombings in Bali, Indonesia and mostly recently Madrid, last year on 11th March 2004, much has been done to disconcert the travel industry and cause terrific instability in the tourism and airline markets.

## Case history

**E-booker shares tumble because of war in Iraq**

E-booker shares tumbled 16 per cent in early trading on Monday as the online travel group warned about the 'negative impact' of the war in Iraq.

Dinesh Dhamija, chief executive, admitted the hostilities would have an inevitable impact on sales and profitability in the final days of the first quarter. However, he said, the group was 'confident about our prospects for 2003'.

'After both the first Gulf War and 9/11 our business experienced rapid recovery as European consumers swiftly regained their confidence in booking leisure travel,' he said.

His comments came as the group reported a fall in annual pre-tax losses from £19.3 million to £5.2 million before exceptional items. Including exceptional costs, pre-tax losses of £12.3 million, halved from £25.6 million previously. The basic and diluted loss per share fell from 55.49p to 25.62p for the year.

*Source*: FT.com – March 2003.

---

Again as a result of change in the environment in one industry, a range of industries subsequently have to respond also as the downturn may affect their ability to exploit new opportunities as originally planned. On the other hand the 'micro environment' looks at a range of internal factors, which relate to the elements of the internal marketplace. Typically this will look at issues relating to marketing processes, suppliers, customers, competitors, stakeholders, and integral to this, issues relating to resourcing and financing the future marketing activities of the organization.

Should organizations fail to respond to changing marketing conditions, or underestimate the internal infrastructure that may be required to support the changing marketing conditions, then they may further fail to understand the changing needs of customers. In addition they may also fail to understand their customers' increasing expectations, which ultimately means failure to meet growth and profit-related objectives.

External forces are dynamic, the marketplace is volatile, and changes can be rapid. Today it appears that organizations face new levels of uncertainty, more significant threats, but also major opportunities. The key is being prepared to understand and analyse the market, and indeed respond to key drivers that are forcing such rapid rates of change.

There are two vital activities, therefore, that an organization should be involved in:

1. Environmental analysis
2. Environmental scanning.

Environmental analysis is the process of analysing, assessing and interpreting information collected through the environmental scanning process.

Environmental scanning is the process of actually collecting the information in order that the organization can understand relevant information in relation to external forces and drivers within the marketplace (see Figure 2.1).

| Description | Step |
|---|---|
| Continually scan the environment so that early changes can be identified and acted upon. | **Step 1** Scanning the environment |
| When change has been identified, the pace of change must be monitored so implications of the change are understood, opportunities and threats identified. | **Step 2** Monitoring |
| Forecasting change is difficult, but the information obtained as a result of monitoring should be used to measure the intensity of change. | **Step 3** Forecasting |
| Assess the impact of potential change on meeting customer requirements, and examine what opportunities change could present. | **Step 4** Assessment |

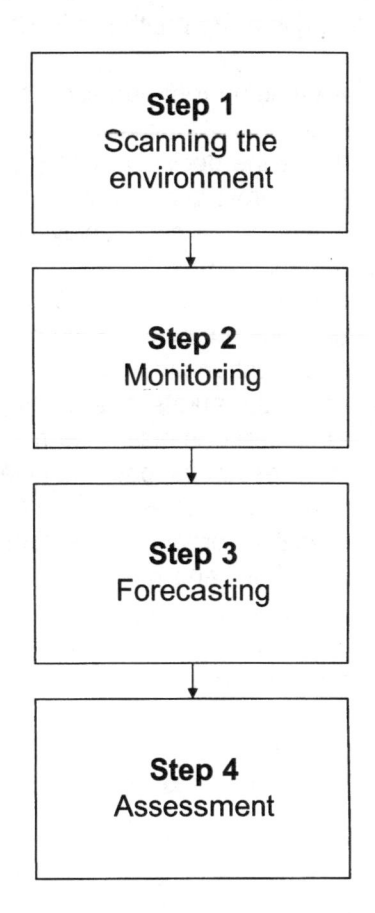

*Figure 2.1* Environmental assessment process

## Assessing the marketing environment

When undertaking an assessment of the marketing environment, there are critical areas of external information that might be useful to consider.

- o *Market intelligence* – Looking at change, potential, competitors and associated marketing activities.
- o *Technical intelligence* – Vital given the rapid evolution in today's technology. An examination of technological developments that would aid and improve production techniques, increasing quality and efficiency, but also allowing innovation and modernization, is essential.
- o *Political/economic intelligence* – Looking at political and economic shifts within the external environment.
- o *Mergers/acquisitions intelligence* – In an era of ever-larger mergers and acquisitions betweens banks, IT organizations, communication networks, etc. it is vital that organizations assess the potential impact and how they might respond to it.
- o *Supply chain intelligence* – What is the position of the supply chain in terms of supplies of raw materials, available resources, etc.

Assessing the marketing environment is a huge task, but of major importance to the future success of the organization.

Unit 2 The marketing audit

## Stage 1 – Analysis of the macro environment

In this section you will now be looking at the components of the macro environment and considering in more depth the issues relating to each element of SLEPT.

There are a number of perceived benefits to the organization in undertaking such an activity:

- It aids the decision-making process and planning process.
- It can provide a sound basis for change and evolution within the organization.
- It provides a clear analysis of competitive activities and an understanding of related market share.
- It enables organizations to anticipate the opportunities that change in the external environment might present.
- Organizations may become more aware of emerging trends and opportunities in international markets that it may be appropriate to pursue.
- Organizations may, as a result of the changing external environment, need to consider their resources, both financial and physical, in order that they may implement relevant change strategies.
- It enables organizations both to foresee and consider the implications of environmental, regulatory and political change and to manage the implementation of such changes successfully.
- It can assist organizations in forecasting potential supply and demand from the open market and from their supply chain.

The list could go on. What is important, however, is that understanding the key components of PESTEL is essential to an organization if it is to cope with change and, most important, respond to it.

### Political

The 21st century is experiencing a new kind of political power that is very broad and very diverse. With increasing moves towards emphasis on globalization, there is more and more influence from global politics and international driving forces. Both national and international governments are increasing their political weight, enforcing greater regulation of a range of industry sectors, in order that customers and organizations alike are protected from irregularities that can bring organizations into disrepute.

Political initiatives both at home and abroad can create many opportunities, while also generating many threats into the political scene. There are political agendas in all areas of business; there is political influence in agriculture, mining and fuels, to name but a few. Take for example the recent Free Trade Agreement between Singapore and Japan, in January 2002. Here two significant political forces in the Far East came together to work out an agreement that would be politically, socially and economically beneficial to the two countries involved.

Additionally, in March 2002 we saw other political forces at work between the USA and Europe as the EU aimed to fight its corner on tariffs introduced by the USA on the importation of European steel.

Key issues might include:

- Increases in taxation, reducing disposable income
- Environmental protection (a social and political issue)
- Employment law
- Health and safety
- Foreign trade agreements
- Stability of political systems (e.g. Middle East).

Political factors can also often impact in a cyclical manner, and the cause and effect scenario sees political influences cross-fertilizing with other elements of the external market analysis, as we can see in the case study of Exxon.

## Case history

### Exxon

The 'Stop Esso' initiative, launched by Bianca Jagger, is seen as a way that 'people' can make a difference, that assertion of consumer power can drive change within organizations.

The National Consumer Council has suggested that 'undoubtedly consumers have the power to influence even a multinational either by causing enough embarrassment or by having sufficient impact on a company's bottom line'.

Exxon has repeatedly declined to sign the Kyoto Treaty, which is designed to cut greenhouse gases in the USA by 5 per cent by 2010. While Exxon has taken this stance, competitors such as Shell and BP have acknowledged the need to combat global warming.

More than 160 governments worldwide have now acknowledged links between fossil fuels and global warming, but in a recent statement Exxon condemned the promotion of scientifically unfounded scare scenarios.

Esso in the UK has suggested that 'we are concerned that the obligations of the Kyoto protocol to reduce emission of greenhouse gases would impose dramatic economic costs throughout the developed world'.

The 'Stop Esso' campaigners, however, insist that they will continue their protest until Exxon contributes towards the global warming issues and endorses the Kyoto Treaty.

Esso, the company that tells the world to 'put a tiger in your tank', could be brought to its knees by environmental pressure groups, who are effectively presenting the biggest demonstration by consumer activists since Barclays Bank were forced out of South Africa.

The biggest consumer boycott of all time was launched in May 2001 and has continued even through until March 2003, seeing Greenpeace and Friends of the Earth trying to force Esso and Exxon to abandon their opposition to the Kyoto climate change agreement. The two pressure groups concerned have 500 000 members in the UK branches alone, which is quite a powerful tool. If their initiative is successful Esso in the UK could experience a reduction in sales of more than £1 billion a year.

Unit 2 The marketing audit

## Question 2.1

What do you consider will be the long-term effect upon Exxon, if they continue to ignore the driving forces of change in the 'oil and related products' marketplace? The demonstrations in respect of Exxon are socially motivated, as a result of political initiative on a global scale. Ultimately, there will be legal, economic, political and social consequences, should they refuse to change their policy to reflect the components of the Kyoto agreement.

### Economic

One of the key influences in any organization is the state of both the local economy and the global economy. There has been talk of economic slowdown in the USA and its potential to create a spiralling effect on economies all over the world. Historically, economic indicators have provided a basis for business cycles to move on to the next stage, effectively 'boom' or 'bust' (Figure 2.2). Obviously the impact of September 11th is a classic example of how economic indicators can be affected by world events.

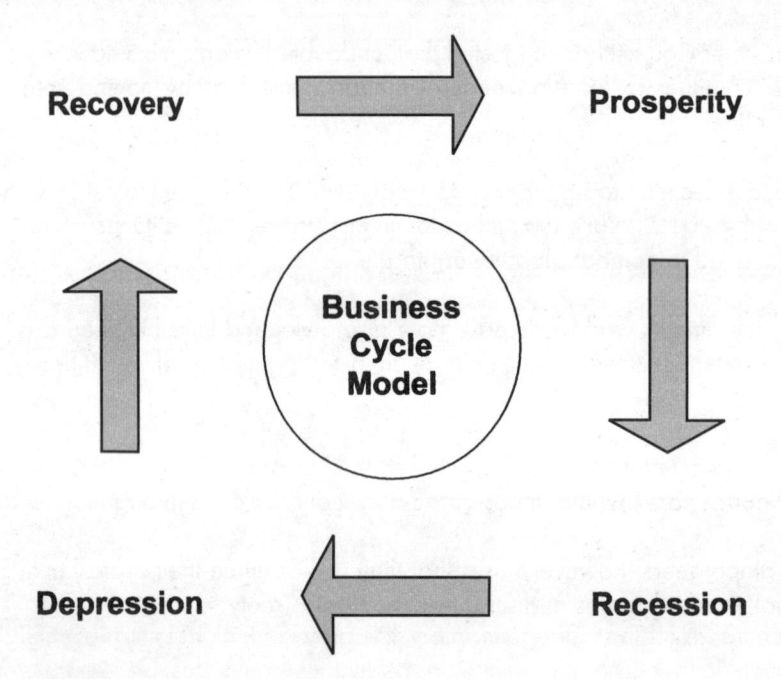

Figure 2.2 Business cycle model

Key component measures of the economy are:

- Inflation rates
- Interest rates
- Income levels
- Resources
- Gross National Product
- Gross Domestic Product
- Employment levels
- *Exchange rates* – currency valuation
- Consumer spending patterns.

As a marketer, it is important to understand economic factors and indicators and also how to use the information to aid your marketing decision-making and planning process.

For example, if there is a fluctuation in interest rates, then it is likely that your organization may be involved in considering increases in costs. Essentially this is like 'cause and effect'; as the interest rate rises, there will be a cyclical effect in the marketplace. The cost of living increases, the cost of borrowing increases and, therefore, the likelihood is that availability of disposable income may drop, reducing consumer spending considerably and thereby influencing a slow-down in market activity.

From the perspective of a marketer it is important to consider closely how to manage this particular element of economic change. You will be encouraged to consider how long it might take for the impact of an interest rate rise to filter through to organizational activity, how long the anticipated rise in interest rates is likely to last, and what might be the competitive responses to this economic change. Furthermore, you need to think about what will be the consumer response to this change and ultimately what it will do to consumer spending power.

The whole area of economic pressure and power is complex, but crucial to understanding the power of buyers and suppliers in the marketplace.

## Social

Understanding the social influences and implications on the marketing environment is of utmost importance, as organizations need to respond to the social infrastructure of their marketplace.

Social factors include issues such as:

- *Demography* – The characteristics of customers, age, sex, class, family life cycle, etc., trends in age distribution.
- *Society* – This reflects upon the infrastructure of society and its attitude towards many issues, i.e. religion, culture, families, the environment, green and ethical issues. (This will also be looked at under 'Environment'.)

## Question 2.2

The population trends for the older generation, 'the grey market', are clearly highlighting that people are living much longer. What potential opportunities could this present to you, as marketing manager for a healthcare products manufacturer?

For example, there has been a serious decline in churchgoing in the UK, which would suggest the demise of the Anglican Church by the middle of this century. There are now fewer 19-year-olds going to church than at any time previously.

In response to the 'Green Issue', vehicle manufacturers such as BMW have been stressing the suitability of their 3 series range for recycling, making them more environmentally friendly cars. This was in response to potential EU legislation that would likely have enforced the recycling of vehicles. BMW responded to this and now has 30 partner recycling plants worldwide. In doing this they have responded to the growing social and environmental awareness of their customers.

Today we find ourselves subject to lively debate and forceful demonstrations about environmental issues. There is an increasing choir of consumer voices raising the stakes in respect of environmentally friendly practices. As there is growing social concern for the environment, the impact of which could be quite major to industry practices today and ultimately upon organizational profitability in the future, organizations are being faced with change programmes as never before. The significance of understanding consumer power, customer needs and wants is critical to organizational success, and therefore failure to react to the outcomes can have a high profile and catastrophic implications in the future. An example of this can be found in the Exxon case study.

- *Culture* – The range of variables relating to culture is extensive, and will be covered in more depth in Unit 9, 'International marketing', but they include:
    - Language
    - Religion
    - Values and attitudes
    - Law
    - Healthcare
    - Education
    - Social organization.

This is possibly the most complex area of analysis that an organization might involve itself in. Values and norms will vary greatly from country to country, and will reflect different social divides.

For an organization involved in exploiting international marketing opportunities this is important to understand, as on occasions significant mistakes have been made by large organizations as a result of their lack of appreciation of the underpinning culture of their host nation.

## Technological

Technology has evolved rapidly over the past 20 years and particularly in the past 10 years. Technological developments have seen improved manufacturing techniques, new and dynamic innovations and increases in efficiency and effectiveness in a way never previously imagined.

However, marketers need to understand the drive for technological change, and the need to go with the flow, to remain competitive. Decisions to improve, change or implement new technological processes must be made in order to meet customer needs and expectations. Principally, if there is a cost-effective method or process that could improve customer service and increase efficiency and effectiveness and add to the bottom line financially, then it should be the focus of serious research and development, in order to pursue the opportunity that technological advances might present.

External or 'macro' market analysis is vitally important to the development of any marketing strategy and associated plan. As a marketer engaged in operational level marketing, you may find yourself very involved in collating much of the intelligence gathered, in order that the decision-making process may be fully informed and responsive to the challenges of the external marketing environment. It will be important to call on previous knowledge gained through Marketing Research and Information, in order that you fully understand the challenges of market scanning and intelligence gathering.

While on occasions you may collect information specifically related to developing strategies and plans, it is equally important to continue scanning the external environment, in order that change may be detected and subsequently responded to in a proactive rather than in a reactive way.

## Environmental

The world is currently in an age where there is growing industrial wastage, discharge of effluent, emissions of fumes and acid rain, all of which have to be taken seriously by manufacturers. Due to the high level of industrialization in the modern world, the environment is under constant threat from global warming. In recent times we have experienced severe weather effects, such as heavy rain, gales and significant flooding. All of this relates to environmentalism and as such means that organizations must in the future consider their strategy in relation to these issues.

There are many organizations whose role is to dispose of atomic waste. Organizations such as NIREX are continually subject to heavy criticism by environment groups such as the Green Party and the press. Their contact with the consumer is minimal; they deal with industry, hence they are little influenced by the consumer.

However, organizations need to become increasingly aware of their environmental responsibilities and aim to ensure that inherent within their corporate mission, vision and strategy, is the need to be environmentally aware, and should position environmentalism as a principle that should be embedded within their overall CSR.

## Legal

In a culture bound by regulatory bodies, legal restraints and an increasing role played by European and international legislation, organizations will clearly need to understand the legislative nature of their own marketing environment and abide by it.

Every organization is bound by controls. For example, there are regulations concerning:

- Monopolies and mergers
- Competitive activities
- Unfair trading
- Consumer legislation
- Trade descriptions
- Health and safety
- Professional codes of conduct (for example, the Chartered Institute of Marketing).

# Stage 2 – Analysis of the micro environment

Analysis of the 'micro' environment is equally important; as a marketing manager you must clearly understand the issues relating specifically to your organization.

For example, you will need to consider the following components:

- Sales
- Market share
- Marketing procedures
- Profit margins
- Sales/marketing controls

Unit 2 The marketing audit

- Marketing mix
- Number of employees
- Financial resources
- Physical resources
- *Production* – capacity and variety.

Each of these factors will in some way affect the organization's overall achievements in terms of the key marketing objectives of meeting both the needs of customers and the organization's profit requirements. In turn this results in the undertaking of an 'internal audit'.

A more simplistic approach to this analysis will be to break it down into the following five key elements:

1. Business
2. Competitors
3. Suppliers
4. Customers
5. Stakeholders.

## Business/marketing function – internal audit

When developing marketing strategies and devising marketing plans, organizations need to consider very closely the internal prerequisites for success.

In this instance, it is essential that organizations develop a strategy that primarily meets the needs, wants and expectations of their customers and that they have the resources and infrastructure within the organization to deliver their promises and meet their corporate and marketing objectives.

Ultimately, a culture appropriate to customer demands must be in place, i.e. a marketing-oriented customer-focused culture, with the customer at the centre of the business, as expressed by the Chief Executive of 'easyJet' in Unit 1.

In doing this, serious consideration should also be given to the 'internal' customer. When a newly devised strategy indicates significant change, then the reactions, attitudes and abilities of the workforce must be considered, managed and adapted to meet the overall objectives of the organization.

In order to achieve this, a tightly defined strategy must be designed, which ensures that management, research and development, production, logistics, physical and financial resources are working to the same end and 'synergy' must be prevalent in the planning process. Without the appropriate mix of resources across the organizational business functions, the corporate goals may not be achieved.

Therefore analysis of each of these functions should be considered. Undertaking a company capability profile is therefore of the essence.

A full audit should be undertaken, with consideration being given to the following factors:

Managerial factors

- Corporate image
- Speed of response to changing conditions
- Flexibility of the organization

- Entrepreneurial orientation
- Ability to attract and retain highly creative people
- Aggressiveness in meeting competition.

Competitive factors

- Product strengths
- Customer loyalty and satisfaction
- Market share
- Use of the life cycle
- Investment in R&D
- High barriers to market entry
- Advantage taken of market potential
- Customer concentration
- Low selling and distribution costs.

Financial factors

- Access to capital when required
- Ease of exit from the market
- Liquidity
- Degree of financial leverage
- Ability to compete on prices
- Capital investment versus capacity to meet demand
- Stability of costs
- Ability to sustain effort in cyclic demand
- Elasticity of price.

Technical factors

- Technical and manufacturing skills
- Resource and personnel utilization
- Strength of patents and processes
- Value added to product
- Intensity of labour to produce product
- Economies of scale
- Newness of plan
- Application of new technologies
- Level of co-ordination and integration.

One way of undertaking this form of analysis is grading these areas from 1 to 5, with 1 being weak and 5 being strong. Clearly any particular element that falls under the level of 3 requires urgent attention, while factors being above 3 demonstrate room for continuous improvement.

This type of analysis is vital to the success of organizations and will ultimately enable you to identify key strengths and weaknesses, opportunities and threats within your own environment.

It is of primary importance to undertake an 'audit' of the actual 'audit process' itself, the marketing objectives and plans and the overall marketing activity including the effective integration of the marketing mix.

Marketing managers will have some responsibility for adopting existing practices and modifying plans, in order that these factors are taken into consideration at the implementation stage.

## Competitors

> **Definition**
>
> **Competition** – Those companies marketing products that are similar to, or can be substituted for, a given business's products in the same geographic area (Dibb, Simkin, Pride and Ferrell, 2001, p. 56).

Very few, if any, organizations exist in isolation of competition. You have already seen, earlier in this unit, some of the effects of competition in relation to the high tech electronics industries, where as a result of intense competition, profits have declined, resulting in massive job cuts across the industry as a whole.

From the perspective of a marketing manager, in order to truly ascertain the full force of the external environment, you must consider the influence of competitive forces upon the external marketplace and your own organization. Therefore a competitor analysis is essential.

There are many components to competitive activity, and in marketing terms competitive strategies can be quite ferocious in attack. From a strategy development perspective you will probably be familiar with terms such as 'guerrilla attacks' and 'offensive attacks', which indicate some of the fighting talk that underpins competitive behaviour.

In order that your organization can respond to competitor attacks, you must be familiar with the profile of your competitors and therefore must analyse their activities and behaviour quite closely.

Ultimately, competitor attacks can provide the basis of significant threats to the successful implementation of the corporate and marketing strategy.

Typical competitor analysis should include a review of the following elements:

- Marketing capabilities
- Technical capabilities
- Management capabilities
- Production capabilities
- Innovation and design capabilities.

Clearly you will need to align your own strengths and weaknesses against those of your competitors in order to identify areas of improvement in your own organization.

One of the key tools for undertaking this is a 'Company capability profile', as previously discussed. You could do this by undertaking a SWOT analysis on your competitor. This is covered in more detail shortly, but as you will see when looking at it, there are possibilities of mapping your own capability against that of your competitors. You could potentially grade each of the components within an element and then grade your own organization against it. Not only would this provide you with a basis of understanding your competitor, but also it would highlight any opportunities to exploit their weaknesses and attack their strengths.

The main focus of most competitive attacks is on price. Competitive warfare today is most prevalent in the retail sector, with intense competition between supermarkets, making high profile headlines on a regular basis. A further example is financial services, where competition in respect of services and products offered continues to intensify on a day-to-day basis.

## Porter's Five Forces – competitive analysis

It is imperative for you as a marketer to have a clear understanding not just of your competitor, but of the nature of the competitive environment, particularly if you are to succeed in developing a sustainable competitive advantage and be able to respond from a position of strength to competitor attacks. The objectives of any organization will relate closely to profit margins, increasing market share, diversification or market penetration. In order that an organization can define the future direction of its corporate and marketing strategy, it is of primary importance that it should consider the nature of the driving forces within the marketplace so as to understand exactly what is shaping the industry. Therefore when undertaking a micro analysis it is important to consider the components of Porter's forces and understand either the potential threats from within the marketplace, or the profit potential of the industry.

Porter's Five Forces model (see Figure 2.3) will be particularly helpful when undertaking a competitor analysis within the existing marketing environment. It provides a framework for an analysis of a range of micro-factors, which enables industry attractiveness to be measured and also helps organizations understand the complexity of the markets in which they operate.

**Potential entrants**

Threat of new entrants

**Barriers to entry:**
- Economies of scale
- Product differentiation
- Capital requirements
- Switching costs
- Access to distribution channels
- Cost disadvantage additional to scale
- Government policy
- Entry-deterring price
- Experience

Bargaining power of suppliers

**Suppliers**

**Powerful if:**
- Few suppliers
- No substitutes
- Industry not important customer of supplier group
- Supplier groups products are differentiated
- Threat of forward integration

**Industry competitors**

**Intense rivalry if:**
- Numerous of similar-sized competitors
- Slow industry growth
- High fixed costs
- Lack of differentiation
- Diverse nature of competitors
- High strategic stakes
- High exit barriers

**(Rivalry among existing firms)**

Bargaining power of buyers

**Buyers**

**Power if:**
- Large proportion of seller's sales
- High proportion of the buyer's costs
- Undifferentiated product
- Low buyer switching costs
- Threat of backward integration
- Seller's product not important to quality of buyer's product

Threat of substitute products or services

**Substitutes**

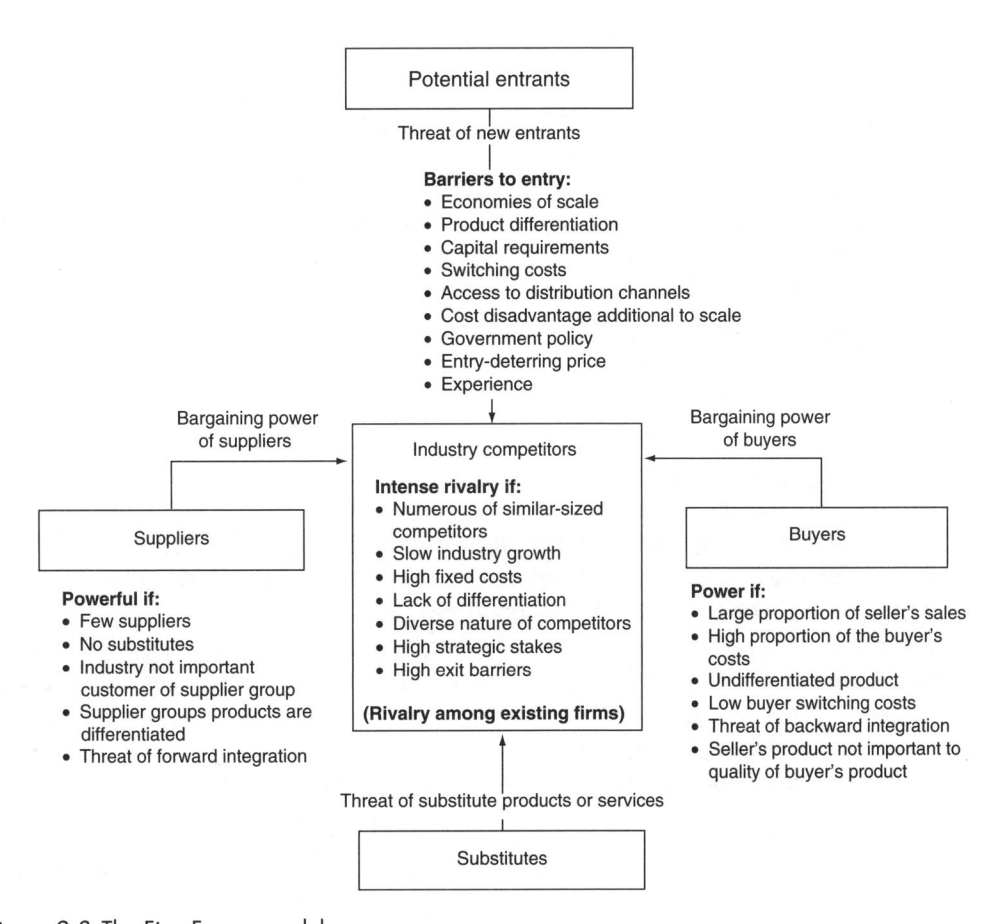

*Figure 2.3* The Five Forces model
*Source*: Adapted from M. E. Porter, *Competitive Strategy*, The Free Press (1980): © The Free Press/Macmillan

## The threat of competitive rivalry

Competitive rivalry within the marketplace is highly intense. Intense competition has, over the years, changed the shape of a number of industries, and as a result there has been an increasing number of mergers and acquisitions to ensure that major players within the marketplace maintain market share and superior positioning. This has been particularly prevalent in the financial services sectors, with a number of mergers between key players in the banking sector, e.g. Royal Bank of Scotland and the Halifax.

We have already seen that competition can take various shapes. Competition can be cut-throat, with ongoing price wars, as have been experienced in recent years in the food retail industry, while at the other end of the scale, competition can appear to be non-existent. However, while rivalry might seem healthy, it can have both positive and negative effects.

Organizations who succeed in competition, possibly increasing market share, through a range of activities, potentially experience a rise in profit. However, the reverse may happen; the organization might increase market share, but at the expense of their profit margins.

Key factors influencing competitive rivalry will be identified when undertaking the competitor analysis as already suggested, but key components might be:

- Stage of the product life cycle (PLC) of competing products
- Use of specialized production techniques
- Liquidity of competitor
- Ability to achieve differentiation and brand loyalty
- Competitor intentions
- The relative size of the competitor
- Barrier of exit from the industry.

Understanding the balance of various forces is critical to ensuring that the organization makes the correct competitive response.

### Bargaining power of suppliers

The key components of this particular element of Porter's Five Forces emphasize the following key points:

- *The strength of the supplier brand* – Is it a brand that all organizations will want to exploit, and will this therefore increase the price of supplies?
- *The source of supply spans only a small number of suppliers* – Limited sources provide the supplier with a supply and demand component in their favour: the more limited the demand, the higher the price they can charge.
- *Switching supplier* – The cost of switching suppliers can be quite high: negotiation of new contracts, establishing relationships and developing trust all cost time and resource. This can act as a deterrent to many organizations, who will want to retain their relationship with their supplier.
- *Substitute products of suppliers* – Are there appropriate substitute products available?
- *Forward integration* – Is there a threat of suppliers establishing their own production facilities?

## Bargaining power of buyers
The bargaining power of buyers is likely to be quite strong in the following instances:

- *Where few buyers control a large volume of the market* – A good example of this might be that larger players in the electrical goods industry can buy large volumes of products based on economies of scale and can pass these reductions on to their customers.
- *Where there are a large number of smaller suppliers fighting for a share of the market* – Again the retail industry would be a classic example of this, particularly in the food sector, i.e. grocery and meat products.
- *The cost of switching supplier is low* – The retail sector and high street are a good example of how customers who are not brand loyal will swap around to gain the best deal. This can happen where the relationship between customer and supplier is not based upon loyalty.
- *The supplier's product is a mass-market product and not necessarily differentiated* – e.g. where there are many variations on the same theme, for example, toothpaste, soft drinks, etc.
- *Strong customer power* – This involves knowledge of the market and where to attain the best deal.
- *Threat of backward vertical integration* – Where the buyer goes back to the supplier, cutting out the middle man.

## The threat for potential entrants
This issue looks at the obstacles to entering new markets:

- *Economies of scale* – Existing organizations often have economies of scale and therefore new entrants will struggle to achieve the same competitive economies in the short/medium term.
- *Access to new distribution channels* – It may be difficult to gain access to the appropriate distribution channels, due to competitive operations and networks in the marketplace.
- *Brand loyalty* – In a brand-loyal market it might be difficult to attract new customers and therefore marketing spend could be quite considerable.
- *Capital investment* – It can be cash intensive to enter into new markets and require high levels of investment – from a competitive perspective, this would actually weaken your initial position, unless you are a cash-rich organization.
- *Competitor retaliation* – It is likely that competitors will follow suit quite closely behind, therefore competitive rivalry could be highly intensive.
- *Regulatory influence* – What is the position in respect of fair competition, monopolies and mergers. The case of Microsoft is a clear example of trying to prevent competitive rivalry.

## Threat of substitutes
- *A new product or service equivalent* – A directly equivalent product, from a differing brand, may have a competitive influence. This is typical of the evolution of 'home brands', e.g. supermarket brands as a substitute in soft drinks, breakfast cereals, etc.
- *A new product replacing an existing product* – For example the DVD player replacing the VHS video player or cassette tapes being replaced by compact discs.
- *Consumer substitution* – Consumer choice can be the basis of a threat, when the consumer is willing to search for substitute products; for example, when the consumer chooses a new kitchen over a new car.

Essentially the Porter framework is an opportunity for the organization to understand the holistic range of driving forces in the micro environment, which they can clearly link to the macro analysis, i.e. the SLEPT/PEST analysis.

From an audit perspective, whereby information is being collected in order that key marketing decisions are made and strategies developed, it will enable the organization to consider ultimately the following factors, that will in turn enable a full SWOT analysis to be developed, to inform the strategy development process.

- What is the likelihood of change in the marketplace, both on a macro and micro scale and what is driving that particular change?
- What is the likely response that the organization can make, in order to retain sustainable competitive advantage in the marketplace – how can they develop their weaknesses and turn them into strengths and their threats into opportunity? Ultimately what is their competitive response likely to be?
- What is the likely response of their competitor in the marketplace – how are the driving forces affecting them, what might be their likely approach – what might it do to their competitive positioning overall?

As a marketer you must consider what the likely response of your organization might be – will it be certain retaliation – will you compete on an aggressive basis, if so what is the likely challenge that you will be presented with?

A further consideration will be what will happen if you fail to act, fail to compete aggressively. What will it do to your market share, your customer base? Will you see a loss of long-term customer relationships, will your brand loyalty be challenged, will your bottom line be challenged?

Reacting competitively does not just mean reducing prices or increasing sales promotions, it means looking at the bigger picture of increased marketing budget, diversification, new product strategies, to name but a few. The biggest failing of many organizations is to attack what is an overt competitive hit by competitors, but to continue blissfully unaware of the competitive activity that is being orchestrated behind closed doors. This will then hit the organization from behind, it will not be ready for the attack, and will then have to develop a reactive marketing approach, as opposed to a pre-emptive marketing strike.

Failure to observe competitive actions will mean inconsistency in competitor attack. Losing sight of the competitor will give them a position of strength and they will ultimately be unpredictable, preventing a continuous competitive reaction from your organization.

Finally, organizations should never be complacent, and as a marketing manager, you should not be lulled into a false sense of security by the continuous monitoring of existing competition. All organizations, without exception, should also be on the look out for new entrants to the markets, who could potentially offer a competitive proposition with the development of the same or substitute products. Therefore, competitive monitoring in line with environmental scanning are critical components of a successful marketing-oriented organization.

## Suppliers

Supplier relationships are a further critical component to the success of any organization. It is of primary importance to many organizations to ensure consistent supplies flowing through in order to meet consistent demand for their products. Therefore, supplier analysis is vital.

This should include a review of the following:

- The basis of the supplier relationship
- The supply and demand components of raw materials
- Supplier innovations
- The relationship suppliers have with competitors
- *Supply record* – i.e. ability to deliver and meet demand on an ongoing basis
- Liquidity and financial stability
- Costs
- Quality
- Warranty provision
- Supply trends
- Any potential change to the supply environment – new entrants.

There is more discussion of supplier relationships in Unit 8, 'Managing marketing relationships'.

## Customers

As already indicated and highlighted in the case of easyJet in Unit 1, customers should be at the centre of any business. Organizations should be customer-focused, meeting customer needs and managing to deal with the evolution of ever-increasing customer power.

It is essential that customers are analysed; we must know who they are, where they are, what they are, what they want, when and how they want it. The sole focus of the marketing effort should be based around meeting customer expectations, the idea being that as an organization you can provide the right product, at the right price, communicated through the right medium and distributed to the right place at the right time.

While undertaking the Professional Diploma, formerly known as the Advanced Certificate – Stage 2 in Marketing your studies will focus on other modules, including 'Market research and information'. Here you will look very closely at the concept of using information about your customers to support the marketing decision-making process. In addition, 'Marketing communications' will focus very much on the psychology of the customer, buyer behaviour, the necessity to understand the strategic importance of the customer, marketing segmentation and market research. Both these modules will underpin the analysis of customers and their buying behaviour.

The important aspect of understanding customers is being able to respond and react and to remain competitive for them, in order that you retain them as customers in the long term.

Ultimately, once customers have been segmented into particular market groups, then they can be targeted with a tailored marketing mix that meets their individual demands.

Once again this will require marketers to ensure that the infrastructure of human, physical and financial resources is in place to underpin the customer experience.

## Stakeholders

The role of stakeholders in any organization seems to have an increasing influence on the way in which organizations can do business. The mini-case study on Exxon highlights how environmental pressure groups actually strive to influence the future direction of the organization overall.

Stakeholders include:

- Customers
- Suppliers
- Shareholders
- Employees
- Financiers
- Wider social community (including pressure groups).

Stakeholder influences and expectation should be understood. In the Exxon case, it would appear that they might have underestimated the potential power of the 'wider social community' and the pressure that they may bring to bear upon the organization. It is vital that the organization understands the balance of power and influence that various stakeholders might have.

For example, in many organizations, shareholders play a vital role in the decision-making process. The pending de-mutualization of Friends Provident, or the merger between the Halifax and the Royal Bank of Scotland, is reliant on the vote of the shareholders for the planned changes to succeed.

In order that your organization can provide the basis for strong relationships with stakeholders, it is necessary to understand the balance of power that they hold so that appropriate marketing mix strategies and indeed marketing communications strategies can be developed to keep them informed of the proposed changes. Effectively, you will need to know how influential they are, and how controllable they are. Currently in the case of Exxon, the demonstrations could do untold damage to the business, should Exxon fail to respond to the treaty while competitors work towards meeting the objectives of it.

For both the 'macro' and 'micro' environment, analysis is essential, as is monitoring and reacting to changes. It is important that organizations are not just reactive, but that they are proactive, managing the components in the 'micro' environment, to provide the basic infrastructure for an organization to meet the demands of its customers and the marketing environment.

There is a key marketing tool that we can use to help us bring the main elements and components of the marketing analysis together. It is commonly known as the SWOT analysis.

## SWOT analysis

A SWOT analysis draws together key strengths, weaknesses, opportunities and threats that have been highlighted as a result of the marketing audit, i.e. the 'macro' and 'micro' analysis and assessment.

SWOT, alternatively known as 'WOTS-UP' analysis, is an important tool in enabling organizations to distil the findings of the audit into a more cohesive and succinct model. It is essential that it is used for this purpose and that it is seen as an addition to the marketing audit, not a replacement (Figure 2.4).

Figure 2.4 highlights some of the issues that you might include within a SWOT analysis and that might have been derived from the marketing audit.

The aim of the SWOT process is to enable you to *convert* weaknesses into strengths and threats into opportunities, by taking remedial action to improve existing situations and plan a programme of ongoing continuous change. Where an organization is weak in respect of a skilled workforce then it is essential that training is identified as a key objective of the internal marketing strategy and that this is underpinned by financial investment and resource.

Unit 2 The marketing audit

When undertaking a SWOT analysis, you should also be aware of the differences between controllable and uncontrollable. Essentially the controllable areas are those relating to internal issues. By and large your organization does have control on 'micro' issues relating to technology, skills, investment, resources, innovations, morale, motivation, etc.

External factors, however, are often uncontrollable, and while you might be able to influence their outcomes you will not be able to control them. When establishing future opportunities and how to improve upon weaknesses, you will be required to work on the controllable variables, i.e. that which you can change.

It is, however, essential to realize that an organization cannot aim to address all of the issues raised within the SWOT analysis and must ideally prioritize the issues appropriately. The SWOT analysis should be used to distil the critical factors that have been identified during the auditing process. Essentially it acts as a summary of the audit and not a replacement for it. Therefore the analysis should aim to identify highly critical areas, in order to focus attention on them during strategy development.

## *Strengths*     *Weaknesses*

**CONVERT** ←———————

|  | **Strengths** | **Weaknesses** |
|---|---|---|
| ***Internal*** | Financial resources<br>Product portfolio<br>Economies of scale<br>Technical capability<br>Management ability<br>Innovative design<br>Profitability<br>R & D<br>Marketing intelligence | Lack of skilled labour<br>High workforce turnover<br>Lack of financial investment<br>Poor internal communications<br>Lack of management commitment<br>Supplier relationships<br>Lack of resources<br>Management weaknesses<br>Over-capacity |
| ***External*** | Global markets<br>Investment opportunities<br>Diversification<br>Technology innovation<br>Internet<br>High quality products | Global markets<br>Competitive activity<br>Competitive investment<br>Supplier desertion<br>Substitute products<br>Market saturation<br>Resistance to change |

## *Opportunities*     *Threats*

**CONVERT** ←———————

Figure 2.4 SWOT analysis

Unit 2 The marketing audit

> ### Question 2.3
>
> Undertake a SWOT analysis of your own organization or one you know well, highlighting the key components of each element. Suggest how you might turn weaknesses into strengths and how you could potentially reduce the threats that affect your organization.
>
> See Answers and debriefing (Appendix 3). As you can see, undertaking a marketing audit is a major task, not only in terms of the volume of analysis to be undertaken and the concepts, elements and components which you are required to understand, but also in ultimately putting the outcome of the audit into the context of strategy development and planning.

A marketer's responsibility might be to ensure that scanning and monitoring of the environment is constant and undertaken regularly. In turn, the outcomes should be used to maximize the potential of the marketing programme and adaptation of the marketing mix should be undertaken. Furthermore, remedial actions have to be taken to overcome any areas of weakness identified that may ultimately reduce the bottom line of the organization.

The marketing audit should not be ad hoc, but planned, co-ordinated, structured and predetermined in nature, context and content. Without key objectives, and a planned approach taken, the marketing audit could be too extensive, too complex and ultimately meaningless, and therefore wasteful in the extreme. The marketing audit process can be costly and therefore a structured approach is an absolute.

## Identifying key opportunities

Having undertaken the planned and objective audit process, you should now be armed with considerable information that will assist you in establishing the potential marketing strategy for the organization to pursue.

A marketing opportunity provides the organization with the opening to venture into new territory, perhaps a new target market, or diversification opportunity, or indeed the opportunity to launch a new product into the marketplace.

The Ansoff matrix (Figure 2.5) provides an opportunity for an organization to think creatively about its future, about how it can take a strength and make it a key success factor or driving force for a successful outcome in the marketplace. Principally the Ansoff matrix allows you to consider a range of four strategic options:

1. Product development
2. Market development
3. Diversification
4. Market penetration.

The Easy Group started off with the core activity of providing low-cost flights into Europe. This is its core business, and with over 18 million passengers a year flying easyJet, the Easy Group needed to establish alternative options in order that the business could grow and expand.

The Easy Group has taken a threefold route. While continuing with penetrating the existing air transport market with low-cost flights, it is also developing the market potential to include greater accessibility of easyJet flights by increasing the number of airports handling easyJet passengers.

While flights are the core business of the Easy Group, a complementary diversification programme has been entered into, in order that a 'travel solutions' package is made available to meet the whole range of customer needs and expectations of both frequent and holiday travellers. The travel solutions business is aimed at both the corporate and consumer sectors of the business.

You can see here that taking the key strengths and opportunities available to it the Easy Group has established a further growth strategy, which includes further market penetration, market development and diversification into new, but compatible areas of the business.

## Products

|  | Existing | New |
|---|---|---|
| **Markets: Existing** | Market penetration (Low cost flights) | Product development |
| **Markets: New** | Market development (Increase number of handling airports) | Diversification (Hire cars, Internet cafe, Hotels) |

*Figure 2.5* Ansoff matrix – 'easy everything' (easyJet)

It is important to consider the basis of Ansoff at this point, by way of illustrating how you can identify core strengths and opportunities and then develop them into potential strategies. However, we will return to this in Unit 3, 'Marketing planning, implementation and control', as we consider the process of developing marketing objectives and strategies and ultimately defining the strategy and developing the plan to underpin overall achievement of objectives.

### The role of marketing information in the planning process

For an organization to implement the marketing concept successfully and take a marketing- and customer-oriented approach to its decision-making, one of the first things it should be doing is to find out a lot of information about its various customers and markets, both macro and micro. It should identify what they need, what they want, what their characteristics are, their buying power and indeed their willingness to buy. In effect, marketing research provides a useful link between the supplier and the customers.

Without information organizations are operating in a vacuum; they are making decisions in an uninformed way and ultimately that holds a serious risk to them, that they may not meet their customers' expectations.

Furthermore, as you saw in the previous units, the world is a volatile place, economically, socially and politically. Organizations have a duty to understand the environment in which they operate. They cannot and should not be insulated from it, but rather be able to respond to it when the time is right. Hence the necessity for scenario building and planning.

In order for organizations to make decisions about future plans, in terms of new market opportunities, international growth, new product development, change of systems and processes, new integrative communications strategies, new technologies, etc. they need information in order to make informed decisions. Informed decisions based upon accurate and targeted information will enable the right decisions to be made and the right markets to be targeted in an appropriate way. In doing this it is likely that the information will serve to provide an understanding of what customer needs are and how customer needs can service the organization's needs for profit and growth.

Table 2.1 identifies the types of information you need in respect of the marketing environment, competition and indeed the marketing mix, which will in turn enable more informed decisions in relation to the planning process to be made.

*Table 2.1* The task of market research – what should it determine?

| Marketing environment | Competition | Product | Marketing mix | Firm-specific historical data |
|---|---|---|---|---|
| Political context: leaders, national goals, ideology, key institution | Relative market shares, new product moves | Analysis of users: Who are the end-user industries? | Channels of distribution: evolution and performance | Sales trends by product and product-line, salesforce and customer |
| Economic growth prospects, business cycle stage | Pricing and cost structure, image and brand reputation | Industrial and consumer buyers; characteristics: size, age, sex, segment growth rates | Relative pricing, elasticities and tactics | Trends by country and region |
| Per capita income levels, purchasing power | Quality: its attributes and positioning relative to competitors | Purchasing power and intentions | Advertising and promotion: choices and impacts on customers | Contribution margins |
| End-user industry growth trends | Competitors' strengths: favourite tactics and strategies | Customer response to new products, price, promotion | Service quality: perceptions and relative positioning | Marketing mix used, marketing response functions across countries and regions |
| Government: legislation, regulation, standards, barriers to trade | | Switching behaviour, role of credit and purchasing, future needs, impact of cultural differences | Logistics networks, configuration and change | |

*Source*: Adapted from Terpstra and Sarathy (1997)

While the research needs to focus on the environment, and the customer, it also needs to focus on the necessary adaptations that might be required to the marketing mix. Therefore, it will be necessary to involve the organization in research that will ascertain the position of the product, and its appropriateness for the market, the threshold for pricing and market sensitivity, and the most appropriate distribution channels.

## Developing a marketing information system

A typical marketing information system (MIS) would potentially look very similar to the one in Figure 2.6, and is something that you will concentrate on in the early part of your studies in Market Research and Information.

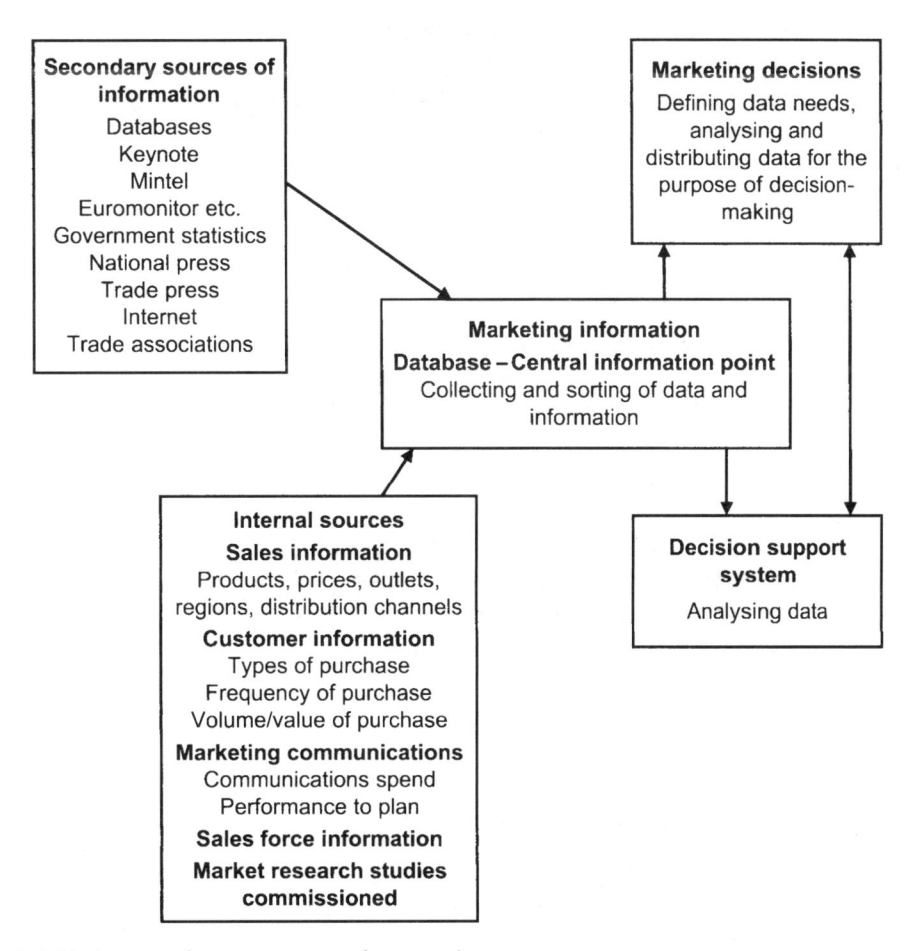

```
Secondary sources of information
Databases
Keynote
Mintel
Euromonitor etc.
Government statistics
National press
Trade press
Internet
Trade associations

Marketing decisions
Defining data needs, analysing and distributing data for the purpose of decision-making

Marketing information
Database – Central information point
Collecting and sorting of data and information

Internal sources
Sales information
Products, prices, outlets, regions, distribution channels
Customer information
Types of purchase
Frequency of purchase
Volume/value of purchase
Marketing communications
Communications spend
Performance to plan
Sales force information
Market research studies commissioned

Decision support system
Analysing data
```

*Figure 2.6* Marketing information system framework
*Source*: Adapted from Brassington and Pettitt (2000)

### Areas for research and information

Below is a more detailed overview of some subject areas that are researched by many organizations, as identified by Adcock, Bradfield, Halborg and Ross in *Marketing – Principles and Practice* (1995). This of course will feed into the grid system in the model above.

(a) Research on markets

  (i) Estimating market size
  (ii) Estimating/studying marketing trends
  (iii) Defining customer/user characteristics
  (iv) Defining characteristics of product markets
  (v) Analysing sales potential
  (vi) Analysing market potentials for existing products
  (vii) Estimating demand for new products
  (viii) Sales forecasting.

(b) Research on products

  (i) Studying customer satisfaction/dissatisfaction with products
  (ii) Comparative studies with competitive products
  (iii) Determining uses for present products
  (iv) Customer acceptance of proposed new products
  (v) Packaging and design studies.

(c) Research on promotion

  (i) Analysing advertising and selling practices
  (ii) Selecting advertising media
  (iii) Evaluating advertising effectiveness
  (iv) Establishing sales effectiveness
  (v) Motivational studies.

(d) Research on distribution

  (i) Location and design of distribution centres
  (ii) Handling and packaging merchandise
  (iii) Cost-effectiveness of transportation
  (iv) Dealer supply and storage requirements.

(e) Research on pricing

  (i) Studying competitive pricing
  (ii) Measuring customer demand
  (iii) Cost analysis
  (iv) Pricing strategies.

(f) Research on sales

  (i) Sales per geographical area
  (ii) Sales per salesperson
  (iii) Sales per product
  (iv) Quarterly sales figures
  (v) Repeat purchase sales figures.

Marketing research provides a useful link between the supplier and the customer by keeping up to date with customer needs and wants.

## Summary

As a result of studying through this unit, you will hopefully have a clear perspective of the importance of undertaking a thorough, structured and objective marketing audit, in order to understand the marketing environment in which your organization operates.

It is of primary importance that both macro and micro factors are analysed and that subsequently a clearly defined strategy is developed based on sound management information. This will allow reliable forecasts to be derived that represent anticipated market share and future potential sales.

While it is essential to understand the macro environment, the micro environmental issues must be addressed so that an organization is well poised to respond to changing market conditions. An organization should analyse in depth the issues related to their internal relationships, customer relationships, supplier relationships and stakeholder relationships and ultimately must be prepared for the demands that each might place upon the organization.

Additionally, it will be of considerable importance to ensure that the organization has the capacity to respond to the driving force of change, by creating an appropriate infrastructure. The infrastructure should be based on highly skilled employees, appropriate levels of financial investment, adequate resources and technological soundness, ultimately ensuring that the customer is at the centre of the business and that the organization is marketing-oriented and customer-focused.

The marketing audit is a vital ingredient of the overall strategy and planning hierarchy and a process that organizations must successfully develop to underpin the corporate objectives and goals.

## Study tip

The December 2003 Examination Mini-Case Study on Starbucks asked students to address aspects of the use of MIS in relation to the marketing audit. Many students failed to address this area and therefore were unable to be awarded available marks. Do not underestimate the importance of collecting information to support the marketing audit and also be able to discuss how it might be used to support the decision-making process.

Additionally, look at the June 2004 case study, to give you an insight into the styles and approaches of exam questions in this area.

## Extending knowledge

A few helpful websites for marketing audit activities:

www.ft.com
www.tradepartners.co.uk
www.ecola.com
www.economist.com
www.asiannet.com
www.cbw.com/busbj
www.dti.com
www.mad.co.uk

## Bibliography

Adcock, D., Bradfield, R., Halborg, A. and Ross, C. (1995) *Marketing Principles and Practice*, FT Prentice Hall.

Brassington, F. and Pettitt, S. (2001) *Principles of Marketing*, Thomas Higher Education.

Dibb, S., Simkin, L., Pride, W. and Ferrell, O. (2001) *Marketing: Concepts and Strategies*, 4th European edition, Houghton Mifflin.

Drummond, G., Ensor, J. and Ashford, R. (2003) *Strategic Marketing: Planning and Control*, Butterworth-Heinemann.

Piercy, N. (2001) *Market Led Strategic Change*, Butterworth-Heinemann.

Terpstra, V. and Sarathy, R. (1999) *International Marketing*, Thomas Learning.

**Useful websites include:**

www.ft.com
www.euromonitor.com
www.europa.eu.int
www.oecd.org
www.un.org

---

Sample exam questions and answers for the Marketing Planning module as a whole can be found in Appendix 4 and past examination papers can be found in Appendix 5. Both appendices can be found at the back of the book.

# unit 3
# marketing planning, implementation and control

## Learning objectives

In this unit, the focus will be on developing marketing objectives and marketing plans. The learning outcomes associated with this unit are:

- Evaluate the relationship between corporate objectives, business objectives and marketing objectives

- Explain the concept of the planning gap and its impact upon operational decisions

- Determine segmentation, targeting and positioning within the plan

- Determine and evaluate marketing budgets for mix decisions included in the marketing plan

- Describe methods for evaluating and controlling the marketing plan

- Explain the role of strategy development in relation to developing marketing share and growth

Syllabus reference: 2.10

This unit will provide you with the basics in order to understand the process of marketing planning at an operational level, and also enable you to develop marketing objectives and plans at an operational level.

## Introduction

In Unit 2, the concentration was on the need to undertake a planned marketing audit, so that we clearly understood the nature and context of an organizations' marketing environment.

Clearly, the marketing audit plays a pivotal role in underpinning both the corporate and marketing planning processes, effectively feeding information from the 'bottom up' in the organization to support the corporate decision-making process.

In this unit, the focus will be on Stages 4 and 5 of Figure 1.3. Next we will move on to look at issues associated with implementation within the organization.

In any organization, there are three key questions to be asked in ascertaining the vision and direction for the future:

1. Where are we now? Stages 1 and 2 – Marketing audit
2. Where are we going? Stages 3 and 4 – Marketing strategy
3. How are we going to get there? Stage 5 – Marketing plan.

## Planning horizons

One of the major considerations expected from strategies and plans is the time horizon. In today's marketing environment, while the ideal is to have a predetermined plan for the long term, in some environments this is becoming increasingly difficult, as we have seen, in particular, in the hi-tech industries.

**Typical planning horizons**

| | |
|---|---|
| Short term | 1–3 years |
| Medium term | 3–5 years |
| Long term | 5 years and beyond |

In many organizations there is an obvious friction between long-term and short-term planning horizons. In the main, short-term planning drives marketing activities at an operational level. However, the real conflict lies in the fact that it is often difficult to establish the impact that short-term objectives might have on long-term strategies. Because marketing is subject to many changes, it is fairly typical for organizations to work on the basis of short-term objectives, short-term budgeting arrangements and short-term resource allocations. Therefore, for objectives to be strategic in nature, they should be developed within a long-term time frame. Obviously, these planning horizons will vary from writer to writer and organization to organization (see Figure 1.3).

## How to take the marketing audit to the planning process

The principal objective of the marketing audit is to provide an indication of potential opportunities and threats that might exist within the marketplace, and ultimately enable the organization to move on to develop their marketing objectives and strategies.

The most effective way of providing a more succinct approach to the audit is to produce a SWOT analysis, which highlights very specific areas that should potentially be addressed through the planning process.

Essentially, the analysis produced in Unit 2 highlighted some of the possible SWOT components that might be an outcome of the audit process, i.e. strengths, weaknesses, opportunities and threats.

To assist the planning process, the SWOT analysis should be substantiated with background information that underpins it and gives considerably more detail on the potential opportunities or even pitfalls that might arise in respect of developing future strategies. This might include a range of internal and external documents: for example, forecasts, company reports, secondary data, competitive information etc.

Making assumptions can be a useful activity so that the organization can conceptualize the potential that a particular opportunity might present or indeed what the effect might be of not exploiting it. An organization might make assumptions based around competitive practices in relation to price levels and promotional activities or perhaps the introduction of a new product range or an addition to the product portfolio. For example, it is possible that launching a new product range will produce an anticipated growth at a rate of 10 per cent per year for 2 years and 15 per cent thereafter.

It is recommended that as few assumptions are made as possible, and that they are based on solid management information attained through the audit process.

## Question 3.1

In what way does the SWOT analysis assist the planning process?

## Stage 3 – The setting of objectives

As a result of the SWOT analysis and any subsequent assumptions made as a result of the marketing audit, the organization is now in the position of considering realistic marketing objectives, i.e. establishing 'where they are going'. It is hoped that these objectives will go a significant way to underpinning and achieving the corporate goals. One of the key issues relating to setting objectives is ensuring their relevance to achieving the corporate vision and mission.

Objectives should be widely understood by the organization and closely related to the organization's financial, physical and human resource capability.

Setting objectives within the organization is central to its overall effectiveness and its ability to achieve high level performance. In the words of Dibb, Simkin, Pride and Ferrell (2001):

> *A marketing objective is a statement of what is to be accomplished through marketing activities.*

An objective is something that you want to achieve and it should have the SMART components illustrated in the following table.

| | |
|---|---|
| S | *Specific* – objectives should be descriptive, succinct and provide clarity throughout the organization as to what is to be achieved |
| M | *Measurable* – objectives should clearly state tangible targets that can be measured in the future |
| A | *Aspirational* – objectives should be challenging but achievable, motivational and not demoralizing |
| R | *Realistic* – objectives should be based on sound market analysis. Financial, human and physical resources should underpin the objectives |
| T | *Timebound* – a timescale should be set against the achievement of each objective in order for performance measurement to be undertaken |

The basis of SMART objectives is that they are simplistic, quantifiable and therefore easier to measure, monitor and control.

## Corporate objectives

In the first instance, many organizations will set corporate/primary objectives. These are expressed in financial terms. For example:

- To achieve 15 per cent return on equity
- To increase operating profit by 25 per cent
- To achieve ROCE of 22 per cent
- To achieve 10 per cent growth in earnings per share.

Profitability on its own is insufficient, as the key principle behind profit is ensuring that the original capital invested is being paid back at a percentage rate every year, so that ultimately the organization can then be more profit-oriented.

## Business non-financial objectives

While financial objectives are vitally important at the corporate level, so are non-financial objectives. For example, we have seen that many organizations have to adjust their strategies and plans in order to survive in a time of intense competition across a number of industry sectors. Therefore functional and operational objectives need to be defined in order that survival is achievable.

*Functional objectives* may read as follows:

- To increase highly skilled element of workforce by 10 per cent
- To increase training provision to the organization by 10 per cent
- To increase productivity by 10 per cent – operations function
- To introduce new technology programme by June 2005.

As a marketer your job is to define marketing objectives to further underpin corporate objectives in order that corporate goals might be achieved.

## Marketing objectives

Marketing objectives in the main are about products and markets only. Do not get confused about marketing objectives being set directly in relation to pricing and advertising. Service levels are the *means* by which objectives are achieved, rather than objectives in themselves.

It is likely therefore that marketing objectives will focus on:

- Increasing sales of existing products into existing markets
- Launching new product ranges into existing markets
- Launching existing products into new markets
- Launching new products into new markets.

Then transfer these concepts into objectives and you may see some of the following quantifiable and measurable objectives. Below is a list of examples highlighting some possible objectives that could be set by an organization:

- To increase sales of the 'X' product range into the existing marketplace by 10 per cent by December 2004
- To launch Product 'Y' into China by October 2004, providing a sales turnover of £5 million by October 2005

*Unit 3 Marketing planning, implementation and control*

- ○ Increase market share of Product 'A' by 20 per cent by June 2006
- ○ To increase customer retention by 30 per cent by June 2005.

## Programme/subsidiary objectives

In particular, these relate to objectives specifically focused around the marketing sub-function, or marketing activities. This is most closely related to the marketing mix. You will note that in the Planning Process model (Figure 1.3), Stage 5 reflects upon the marketing mix. These are more tactical objectives. For example, in this area, you will find specific objectives relating to pricing, the promotional mix, distribution elements or product mix requirements.

Each of these subsidiary objectives is developed specifically in relation to achieving a 'higher' level marketing objective.

For example, where an objective relates to 'penetrating the existing market and increasing market share by 10 per cent', a subsidiary objective might be to drive prices down, therefore a pricing objective may then read 'to reduce prices by 10 per cent to increase marketing penetration by [date]'.

Whilst the focus on setting objectives will be based around 'marketing', it is essential that at a corporate level, objectives are balanced – i.e. that corporate objectives reflect across the whole organization, the idea being that the whole organization integrates, works together, consistently and with synergy, to achieve corporate goals.

Having an understanding of the 'balanced scorecard' approach to setting objectives and ensuring a balance is achieved is important.

## The balanced scorecard

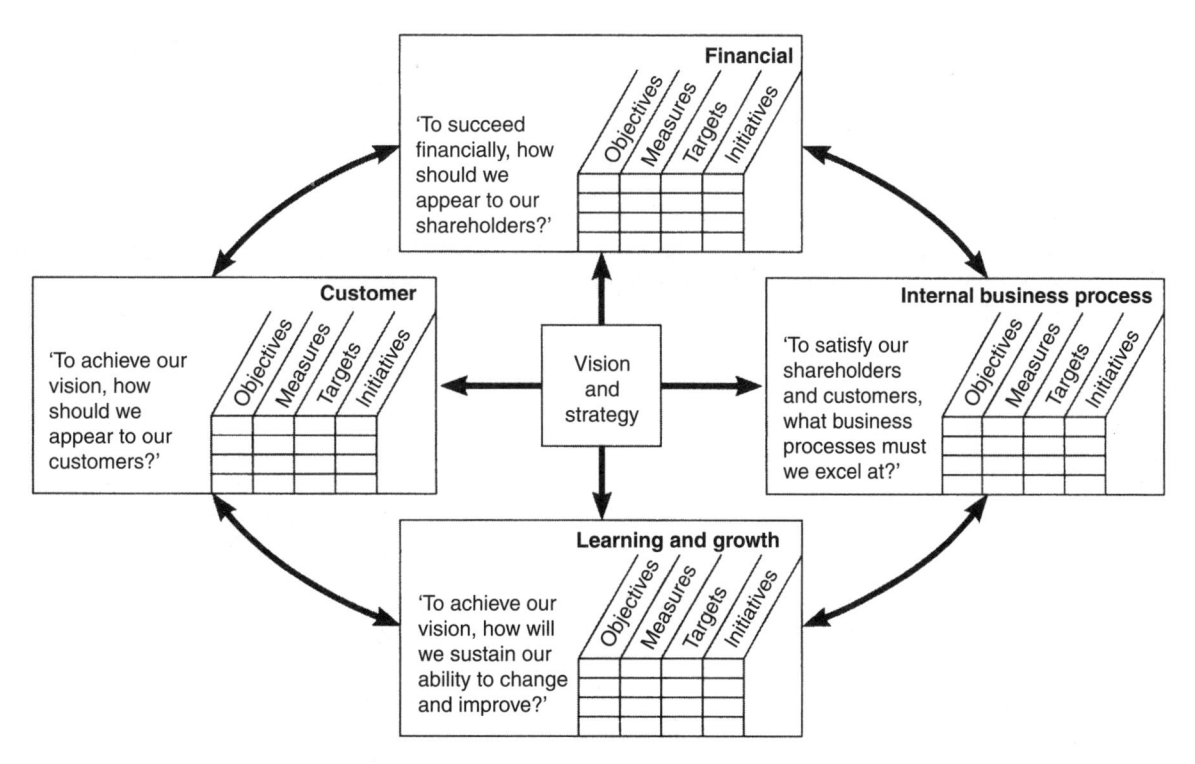

*Figure 3.1* The balanced scorecard
*Source*: Adapted from Kaplan and Norton (1996)

The balanced scorecard (see Figure 3.1) is a management system developed by Robert S. Kaplan and David P. Norton. The balanced scorecard provides a key link between setting objectives and measuring performance. It is a management system that provides a channel whereby abilities and knowledge held by personnel throughout the organization can be used towards achieving long-term goals.

Kaplan and Norton suggested that a balanced set of objectives should be developed and, at the same time, a complementary set of performance measures could be set alongside them.

Primarily, the balanced scorecard is a tool that guides performance and identifies key measurements in four categories:

1. Financial perspective
2. Customer perspective
3. Internal perspective
4. Innovation and learning perspective.

## The financial performance

This closely aligns with the financial objectives you have already seen, i.e. it looks at factors such as those shown in Table 3.1.

Table 3.1 The financial perspective

| Strategic objectives | Strategic measures |
| --- | --- |
| Return on capital | ROCE |
| Cash flow | Cash flow |
| Profitability | Net margin |
| Profitability growth | Volume growth rate versus industry |
| Reliability of performance | Profit forecast reliability Sales backing |

Source: Adapted from Kaplan and Norton (1996) and Drummond, Ensor and Ashford (2003)

Ideally the role of the 'financial' perspective relates to seeing how the business might look in the eyes of the shareholders (i.e. stakeholder influences). The proposed strategic measures subsequently ensure both the success of the organization's strategy and also its implementation overall.

## The customer perspective

Understanding the basis of the customer perspective (see Table 3.2) is vitally important, as this element reflects how the customer might perceive the business, in particular, issues such as relationships, quality, service and performance levels overall.

*Table 3.2* The customer perspective

| Strategic objectives | Strategic measures |
| --- | --- |
| Marketing share | Reflecting the proportion of business acquired in a given market (volume per customer) |
| Customer satisfaction | Monitoring performance criteria such as customer satisfaction index. Mystery shopping |
| Customer retention | Tracking customers, measuring the rate at which the business retains customers or maintains ongoing relationships |
| Customer profitability (value for money) | Measuring the net profit of a customer, segment or target market |
| Customer acquisition | Measuring the rate at which a business attracts new customers |

*Source*: Adapted from Kaplan and Norton (1996) and Drummond, Ensor and Ashford (2003)

## The internal perspective

The internal perspective (see Table 3.3) looks very closely at the implementation of essential internal processes required to meet customer needs and achieve ultimate customer satisfaction. The focus of this particular area will be providing the organization with the specific human resources and physical resources required and the necessary competences in order that customer satisfaction might be achieved.

This area will focus on the functional aspects of the organization:

- Marketing
- Manufacturing
- Logistics
- Quality.

Table 3.3 gives an example of some possible strategic objectives and the potential strategic measures that could be implemented.

One of the key benefits of the balanced scorecard is its ability to ensure that not only objectives are developed, but also associated performance measures, by which an organization can monitor and control its achievement.

*Table 3.3* The internal perspective

| Strategic objectives | Strategic measures |
| --- | --- |
| **Marketing** | |
| Product and service development | Pioneer percentage of product portfolio |
| Shape customer requirements | Hours with customers on new work |
| **Manufacturing** | |
| Lower manufacturing cost | Total expenses per unit versus competition |
| Improve project management | Safety incident index |
| **Logistics** | |
| Reduce delivery costs | Delivered cost per unit |
| Inventory management | Inventory level compared to plan and output rate |
| **Quality** | Zero defects |

*Source*: Adapted from Kaplan and Norton (1996) and Drummond, Ensor and Ashford (2003)

## The innovation and learning perspective

One of the KSF of organizations today is their ability to be innovative and involve themselves in a programme of continuous improvement (see Table 3.4). This should be both in terms of business processes, manufacturing processes, research and development, product development and services delivery.

Therefore it is essential that innovation-led objectives are developed in order that an organization can strive to achieve sustainable competitive advantage in the marketplace.

Furthermore, it is of primary importance that the organization is seen to be a 'learning' organization.

*Table 3.4* The innovative perspective

| Strategic objectives | Strategic measures |
| --- | --- |
| Innovate products and services | Percentage revenue from pioneer products |
| Time to market | Cycle time versus industry norm |
| Empowered workforce | Staff attitude survey |
| Access to strategic information | Strategic information availability |
| Continuous improvement | Number of employee suggestions |

*Source*: Adapted from Kaplan and Norton (1996) and Drummond, Ensor and Ashford (2003)

The balanced scorecard should broaden the horizons of managers, ensuring that they focus on a cross-section of 'balanced' objectives across all functions of the organization, in order that they create 'distinctive' objectives that will enable them to meet corporate goals and ultimately achieve sustainable competitive advantage and customer satisfaction.

Later in this unit we will be looking at barriers to implementation and issues relating to internal marketing, in respect of the planning process. One of the benefits of the balanced scorecard is that it forces management to address a broad range of issues, sometimes issues that they would previously have tried to avoid. It will also force the issues of setting realistic, SMART objectives that can be underpinned by an infrastructure providing the right resources for delivery of products and services to the marketplace.

In Unit 1, we considered the need to ensure that objectives, strategies and plans reflected consistency and synergy in respect of implementation. Effectively, the balanced scorecard would go some way to redressing the balance across the organization, ensuring the successful implementation of plans both vertically and horizontally, cross-functional, top-down and bottom-up.

As you can see, setting objectives is not a simple exercise. It requires dexterity and simplicity at the same time. It requires an understanding of the context of the vision, mission and corporate goals and how they will ultimately be achieved.

# Gap analysis

One of the most significant problems within many organizations is that they use objectives as a basis of forecasting what levels of performance will be, and then turn the objectives into corporate goals, as opposed to setting objectives based on forecasts.

A gap analysis is used to assist the organization with its strategy development process and in simple terms it is designed to illustrate 'where are we now' and 'where do we want to be'.

The analysis undertaken as part of the marketing audit will tell the organization 'where they are now' and then a forecast can be undertaken that shows 'where the organization wants to be'. It is then possible to identify a gap between the two (see Figure 3.2). In other words, it represents the divide that the marketing strategy has to address to allow the organization to meet its objectives by crossing the gap.

The role of marketing is to try to develop attractive propositions that would allow the company to offer desirable added values superior to or not offered by competitors.

Such gaps may be closed by the clever and creative development of a competitive marketing strategy. Such strategies may include developing approaches such as the three generic strategies identified by Porter (1980): these include cost leaders, differentiation and focus.

Cost leadership could be achieved through such areas as economies of scale, linking relationships to profitability and generating costs savings and ultimately developing a cost-effective infrastructure.

Differentiation strategies could include looking at areas such at improving product performance or product perception. Here the organization may look at whether it is the performance of the product or the perception of the product which is most important.

In terms of the focus strategy, the organization will clearly concentrate on a narrower range of business activities. The aim will be to specialize in a specific market segment and derived detailed customer knowledge in relation to this segment.

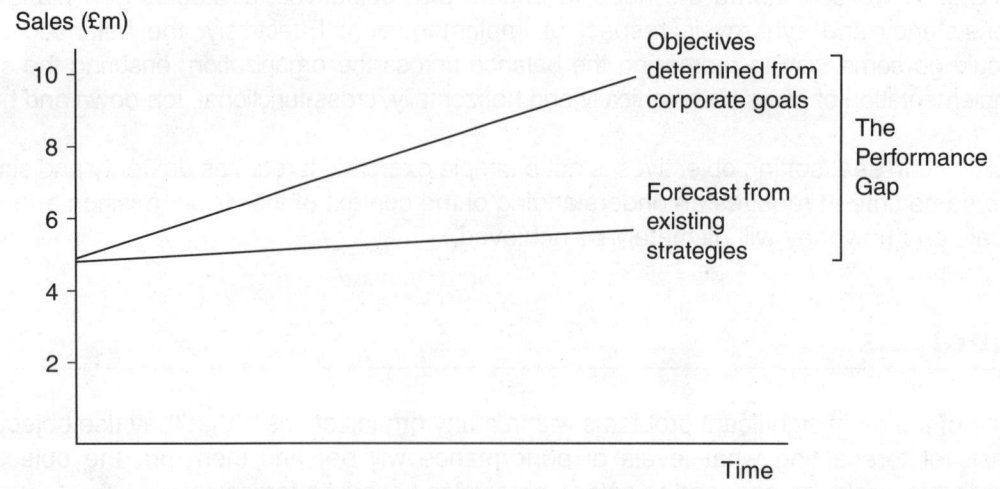

Unit 3 Marketing planning, implementation and control

*Figure 3.2 Gap analysis grid*

## Case history

### Kellogg's Cornflakes

Kellogg's is probably one of the best-known and trusted brands in the world, particularly in the branded breakfast cereals market where it has been in operation in excess of 100 years.

For decades they have been the leading light in the breakfast cereals market, with Kellogg's Cornflakes, in particular, leading the way. But like every other organization in today's volatile marketing environment, they have been subject to intense competition, and threats such as radical changes in market structure and lifestyle patterns.

In the mid to late 1990s Kellogg's saw their market share in the breakfast cereals market reduce from 38 per cent to 32 per cent. In this period of time Kellogg's experienced a reduction in profit from 19 per cent to 15 per cent. Share prices fell, net profit fell and Kellogg's position as number one cereal provider in the USA was overtaken by General Mills. For the first time in decades Kellogg's US leadership had slipped away.

Kellogg's warned shareholders that earnings per share would fall by 15 per cent because of the actions it needed to take to restore market share. The policies they implemented centred on boosting sales, heavy spending on promotional activities, potentially to the detriment of expected profits.

For example, in response to continued loss of market share to supermarket own-label brands, Kellogg's was involved in a serious attack on the UK cereals market, cutting prices simultaneously across its major brands by as much as 12 per cent, and at the same time increasing its advertising budget by 40 per cent.

During that period, Kellogg's entered into a significant retrenchment programme, cutting back on high-salaried white-collar jobs both in the USA and in Europe, essentially providing savings of some $10 million a year.

They diverted the advertising spend into the Kellogg's brand name and moved it away from individual products. As a result of the ongoing difficulties faced by Kellogg's, their then Chief Executive launched a new strategy to '*fill the gap*' between declining market share and long-term planned objectives.

The key elements of Kellogg's strategy included:

- Leadership in product innovation
- Strengthening their position in seven of Kellogg's largest cereals markets
- Accelerating the growth of convenience foods with expansion of markets and distribution channels
- Developing a more focused organization to support the growth strategy
- Continuing to reduce costs.

*Source*: Adapted from *Tales from the Market Place*, by Nigel Piercy (2001).

As you can see from the mini-case study above, Kellogg's could not have continued without trying to redress the balance between what was actually happening and what should have been happening, i.e. the gap. Therefore, a balanced strategy was developed. If you refer back to the balanced scorecard approach, you will notice that a balance of cross-functional issues had been addressed and would be the basis for a consistent, integrated organizational approach to achieving corporate goals.

## Question 3.2

What are the key benefits of undertaking a gap analysis?

## Formulation of the marketing strategy

Now that the objectives have been defined and the gaps identified, it is time for the organization to define, develop and shape the direction they will take in the short-, medium- and long-term time horizons which they have planned within.

The key questions that should be asked in any organization are:

- Where are we now?
- Where are we going?
- How are we going to get there?

Marketing strategy seeks to develop effective responses to ever-changing marketing environments. It does so by defining market segments and then developing and positioning product offerings for particular target markets.

It is of the utmost importance that you have a good foundation in strategy in order to put your marketing planning into context.

## Strategy or tactics?

It is important that a clear understanding of the difference between strategy and tactics is established at this early stage (see Table 3.5).

*Table 3.5* Strategy Vs. tactics

|  | **Strategic marketing** | **Tactical marketing** |
| --- | --- | --- |
| Time frame | Long term | Short term |
| Focus | Broad | Narrow |
| Key tasks | Defining marketing and competitive positioning | Daily marketing activity |
| Information and problem | Unstructured, external, speculative | Structured, internal, repetitive |
| Example | Market growth | Advertising |

*Source*: Adapted from Drummond, Ensor and Ashford (2003)

The constant theme of this text has been the necessity of developing a sustainable competitive advantage. This, of course, will be achieved through the development of appropriate marketing objectives and a marketing strategy, in order to achieve the corporate goals.

Two other key components of the strategy development are the need to achieve a strong market position through potential growth and to have a sound product/market strategy.

The next stage of this unit focuses on how, as an organization, you develop an appropriate mix of marketing strategies to retain the much-desired 'sustainable competitive advantage'.

## Competitive marketing strategy

The marketing audit process should include a competitor analysis. It is important to develop a competitor profile, identifying likely competitive attacks, and have a full understanding of the various forces that will define the shape of the marketplace, through the analysis of Porter's Five Forces. This information, consolidated in the main within a SWOT analysis, will form the basis of your considered approach to developing a competitive strategy.

Michael Porter also defined a Competitive Advantage Grid based upon three generic strategies that enable an organization to closely identify the various competitive options open to them. Typically they would include:

- Cost leadership
- Differentiation
- Focus.

Porter himself suggested that strategy is primarily about creating and sustaining a profitable position in the marketplace. The organization needs to identify the competitive scope available to it, considering the approach to targeting and segmenting the market, and ensure that the organization is operating in a closely defined market.

## Cost leadership

One of the key competitive positions to achieve in a mass market setting is that of cost leadership within your defined industry or sector. The focus of marketing and indeed overall strategic activity at this level will relate to ensuring that a low-cost structure is implemented. In essence the organization will be looking to achieve economies of scale, cost reduction policies, zero defects, minimum expenditure on research and development and very closely defined cost-effective marketing strategies. Therefore, the organization is likely to be process-driven and technologically focused.

The basic drivers of cost leadership, according to Drummond, Ensor and Ashford (2003) are:

- *Economy of scale* – The single biggest influence on cost
- *Linkages and relationships* – Being able to link activities together and form long-lasting customer relationships, inclusive of customer retention programmes
- *Infrastructure* – Factors such as location, availability of skills and government support.

## Differentiation

This particular strategy presents the opportunity to market products or services distinctive from those of its competitors. However, while it might be distinctive in nature, it is only competitive and purposefully different if it ultimately adds value to the overall customer experience.

The product/service should have unique features, characteristics and even benefits. It should enable the organization to achieve a degree of customer loyalty and should ultimately be a competitive response that cannot be challenged directly by any competitor.

The most likely scenario is that as a result of the differentiation it will command a premium price, that will essentially reflect the quality of the brand, design, product and high service levels.

Again Drummond, Ensor and Ashford (2003) suggest that the common sources of differentiation will include:

- *Product performance* – the product's performance can enhance its perceived value from the customer perspective
- *Product perception* – the perception of the product is often different from the performance
- *Product augmentation* – the product can be extended and augmented in ways that will be of value to the customer (we will look at this later under Product Operations).

## Focus

Interestingly the basis of competitive strategy is both cost leadership and differentiation, but instead of competing in a mass market environment, it is more likely to compete in a smaller or narrowly defined area of the market. In particular the focus will be on attractive segments or niche markets. The emphasis of a focus strategy primarily implies that the organization is focusing effort on producing products for a closely defined market. Often the products will be customized, high quality, differentiated and potentially premium priced. For example, specialist clothing, or the high quality car market, e.g. Rolls-Royce, Morgan, etc.

Clearly the more successful the organization is within the niche, the more likely it is to attract attention. Therefore, the emphasis of a focus strategy should be on:

- *Product and service specialism* – Producing highly differentiated, possibly exclusive products to a closely defined target market
- *Geographic segmentation* – Tailoring product/service needs to geographic regions, as long as the markets are commercially viable, based upon size
- *End-user focus* – The focus might be on the end-user, therefore a customer profile might be more appropriate to target than an entire marketplace.

These strategies, while studied in isolation from a student perspective, are very much part of a bigger integrated corporate and marketing picture.

## Question 3.3

What is the significance of differentiation when establishing a sustainable competitive advantage?

## Growth strategies

While Porter offers one approach to identifying competitive strategies, it is also essential to consider Ansoff's approach. The Ansoff matrix was developed to provide linkages between both products and markets. Ansoff proposes four alternative strategies to take the product to market in order that corporate goals and related marketing objectives are achieved.

At the end of the section on 'The micro environment' in Unit 2, we looked very briefly at Ansoff to put the SWOT into context. However, now we need to consider it in the context of defining the marketing strategy, in respect of identifying options available to the organization for growth.

Ansoff's model builds on Porter's generic strategies and highlights the gap the subsidiary objectives relating to the marketing mix are used to fill.

Principally the Ansoff matrix (Figure 3.3) allows you to consider a range of four strategic options.

At the end of Unit 2, there was a brief reference to Ansoff. However, it is now important to consider Ansoff in the context of defining the marketing strategy.

### Market penetration
The basis of the market penetration strategy is primarily to increase sales of existing products in existing markets. If you look at the top left-hand side of the matrix, you can see where this fits. To do this, the organization will need to demonstrate a high level of competitive force; they will need to be price-competitive, promotionally competitive and execute a hard-hitting advertising campaign.

## Products

|  | Existing | New |
|---|---|---|
| **Markets Existing** | Market penetration | Product development |
| **Markets New** | Market development | Diversification |

*Figure 3.3* Ansoff matrix

The focus of market penetration will be on persuading existing customers to buy more of your products. A number of examples highlight this particular practice. Retailers offering store cards, with opening discounted rates of purchase, e.g. open a credit card account today and you will receive 10 per cent discount. The broader scope of this particular strategy is winning customers from other competitors, testing out the power of the buyers, their willingness to change. Therefore part of your strategy might be to create easy transition between the organization and its competitors.

The main problem with market penetration is that while it is appropriate now in some industries, markets are becoming increasingly saturated and therefore competitive intensity at this level is forcing some organizations to revisit their existing strategies. A full and comprehensive marketing audit should identify these emerging issues, and ongoing environmental scanning will enable organizations to take proactive actions in advance of market saturation, rather than waiting for it to happen.

### Market development

Market development is an alternative growth strategy that focuses on the development of new markets for existing products (Figure 3.3, bottom left-hand side of the matrix). The aim will be to open up new geographical regions; target new market segments and find new uses for existing products.

This particular strategy draws on the creative skills of marketers to develop alternative uses for products and then devise creative and dynamic marketing programmes to underpin them. A good example of this would be Timberland Boots. In the main designed for walkers, who stalked the hills and dales, Timberland Boots are now a fashion statement. While existing customers continue to buy Timberland Boots for leisure pursuits, others wear Timberland Boots on a day-to-day basis.

### Product development

Expanding and developing the product portfolio is an essential marketing activity, in order that organizations continue to move with the times and the new and more challenging expectations of their customers, i.e. the power of the customer/buyer. Product development is required to attract existing customers in existing markets to new products, or revamped, redesigned equivalents.

A good example of product development could relate to the car market. On a regular basis most popular brands extend the life cycle of their existing vehicles by giving them either a minor or major facelift. The aim is to maintain existing customers and encourage them to develop customer loyalty traits in order that they will purchase the redesigned and redefined model. Mercedes have recently revamped the Mercedes 'A' Class and also the 'C' Class range, attracting a surge of interest from the existing customer base. One of Mercedes' KSF until now has been their ability to retain customers and develop a long-term relationship with them. Along with Saab, they boast one of the highest customer retention records in the motor vehicle market history.

In an ideal world, a product portfolio would have a range of products that should provide something for everybody. However, this is not always possible.

Product development plays an important role in attracting new customers, opening up new markets and providing many new opportunities, but clearly the main drawback can be the level of investment required. So as a growth objective, it is the one that provides the greatest strain on resources. Here the organization would need to undertake a financial analysis, including a break-even analysis, to measure how long it would take for the new product to break even, should it be launched into the market.

Related marketing activities would clearly need to reflect a strong competitive response, in order that the product is taken to market in advance of similar competitive strikes and before the threat of substitute products arises.

The organization would clearly have to exploit the company name and brand in order that the product is given credence in the marketplace. Therefore the components of success will rely upon a good quality product, associated high service levels, and a compatible promotional and pricing strategy to give it a head start.

### Diversification

Diversification potentially poses the most significant risk to the organization. This strategy is based on diversifying or moving away from the core business of the organization and looking for an alternative or complementary source of income and profit. This often results, in today's market economy, in mergers and acquisitions, as organizations seek to set up compatible business portfolios, increasing their market attractiveness and market share along the way.

This is a high-risk strategy, a move into the unknown, and one that may present threats associated with 'new entrants' in the marketplace: high investment, lack of economies of scale, and difficulties associated with distribution. Again going back to the previous point, one of the benefits of mergers and acquisitions in this sense is that some of the risk is reduced. However, this is an expensive alternative option; for many organizations it is a last resort.

While this puts a negative perspective on the benefits of diversification, there are indeed a number of success stories in the marketplace. Take for example the case of easyJet referred to in Unit 1, to see how Ansoff was used to identify potential diversification for the Easy Group.

One of the principal benefits of using Ansoff is that in addition to contributing to identification of the potential direction to take in relation to developing the marketing strategy, it also focuses the mind of the organization on the future deployment of the marketing mix.

In linking Ansoff back to the SWOT analysis the potential opportunities that face an organization in the future may be identified.

## Market positioning strategies

When defining market positioning strategies, it is not just about product position, it is also about positioning the organization within the marketplace. Now is the time to give the organization a competitive identity. Is the organization going to be a market leader, market challenger, market follower or a market niche?

### Market leaders

Market leaders are extremely dominant and high profile within their industry sector and target marketplace. This marketplace might be local, national or even global. It is likely that they possess significant market share. For example organizations such as Coca-Cola and Pepsi are market leaders in the 'Cola' drinks industry. They possess significant market share within the soft drinks industry.

Positioning the organization as market leader immediately leaves them open for a range of competitor attacks. These attacks are likely to be aggressive in nature, and therefore constant monitoring of the competitor activities should be undertaken in order to pre-empt any potential strikes.

Typical competitor attacks might include market expansion, aggressive and offensive attacks to regain lost market share or even defensive attacks, trying to protect existing market share from a market leader contender. You should be aware that offensive attacks are not just the market leaders attacking, but in essence can be mounted by any industry player in the associated market.

### Market challengers

Market challengers are particularly difficult to compete with, as they are aggressive and will very much strive to take market share. In the main you will find that these organizations are fairly significant, cash rich and well resourced.

Their likely approach will be based around selective targeting of competitors or indeed an attack on the market leader. Armed with the competitor intelligence and competitor profile built during the marketing audit activities, the market challenger will know where to attack to cause the most pain and discomfort to the competing organization. Probably one of the best-known examples of this is the fight between British Airways and Virgin Air. The battle for clawing back market share has been particularly high profile and ongoing for a number of years. It is a battle that is continually fought in the spotlight of media attention. It is a long-term war of attrition, and it will take a long time before any change is evident.

### Market followers

Quite often being a market follower can be more favourable than being a market leader. Being second or third or even lower down the rankings within the target marketplace, can have a number of advantages.

The key to success here is continually 'following the leader': whatever they do, the follower duplicates. Therefore the strategy is somewhat reactive rather than proactive in context. If the prices go up, the follower puts them up. If the market leader approaches a new market then the follower effectively follows on behind.

It is very rare that the follower will challenge the leader in this particular market positioning area, unless they were absolutely sure of success.

### Market niches

As we saw from looking at the generic strategy of 'focus' earlier, niches are known for the ability to specialize and focus on particular market segments. Their aim will be to achieve competitive advantage by differentiating their products and services, and move towards the high level, high quality markets.

When defining a marketing strategy, there are so many components that an organization and you as the marketer must consider. The essence of the message is that strategy development cannot be undertaken in isolation, and therefore, the importance of the marketing audit must never be underestimated or ignored.

The basis of an earlier heading was 'How to take the marketing audit to planning'. Primarily you should never get to the planning process without it. You should be able to see, from the use of Porter's Five Forces, PEST and SWOT, how the information is then transferred into a decision-making pot, out of which a number of potential competitive, growth and market development strategies might be developed and defined.

While the overall basis of the strategic direction has been established, it is equally important to ensure that the specifics of the target audience are clearly understood. As a result of this, marketing segmentation is a crucial activity that must be undertaken, in order that the marketing effort is specifically focused.

## Question 3.4

What are the key benefits of being a market follower?

## Market segmentation and competitive positioning

At an operational level, segmentation, targeting and positioning are often linked together and the terms interchanged regularly.

For a marketer, there are three stages in the segmentation and positioning process, as can be seen in Figure 3.4.

---

**SEGMENTATION**
Consider the basis on which to segment the market
Look at the profile of people and how they break into groups
Confirm the groups are valid segments

---

**TARGETING**
Decide on a target strategy
Decide which segments should be targeted and why

---

**POSITIONING**
Understand consumer perceptions
Position products in the mind of the consumer
Design an appropriate marketing mix to meet customer requirements

---

*Figure 3.4* The process of segmentation

For the time being, however, the concentration of your study will be purely on the principles of segmentation.

### Definition

**Segmentation** – The act of dividing the market into specific groups of consumers/buyers who share common needs and who might require separate products and/or marketing mixes (adapted from Kotler *et al.*, 1998).

### Definition

**Market segmentation** – Identifying the most productive bases for dividing a market, identifying the customers in different segments and development of segment description (adapted from Hooley, Saunders and Piercy, 1998).

The aim of marketing segmentation is to assist the organization to differentiate their product/service offerings to differing groups of customers. It helps describe how marketers can divide up the market into groups of like-minded customers, at the same time as understanding the different characteristics of them and the different demands that they might make.

Marketing segmentation recognizes the differing needs of buyers and a different approach for each segment identified may subsequently be developed. This is then known as target marketing. This has grown in importance to meet the complex demands of the markets.

Therefore building on the existing stages in the segmentation process, the key steps to market segmentation may be as follows:

- *Identify the possible segments within the market* – This will consist of individuals or organizations with similar needs and preferences
- *Gather information on those market segments identified* – To do this the segments need to be accessible
- *Evaluate the attractiveness of the different segments* – They need to be large enough to be viable
- *Ascertain the competitive positioning within each of the target segments*
- *Develop variations on product/service specifications to meet the needs of individual segments*
- *Design the appropriate communications mix to meet the target market demands.*

For a market to be split into segments specific criteria must be met. These criteria clearly relate back to the decision-making process in the previous section.

- Customers must want or need the associated products or services
- Customers must assert their buying power, i.e. money, resources, etc.
- Customers must be willing to use their money and resources to buy products
- Customers must have the authority to buy different products.

## The basis for segmenting markets

Segmenting markets is a complex issue, but is often seen as a critical factor in the successful implementation of marketing strategy.

Segmentation relates to identifying customer groups and their common characteristics. Segments are often formed based upon common customer characteristics, brand preferences and customer attitudes.

## Segmentation of consumer markets

It is important to understand what is often termed the 'classificatory' information and 'background' characteristics of your customer. Customers have two types of characteristics that can be measured; they have objective characteristics, which relate to:

- Demographics
- Socio-economics
- Consumer life cycle
- ACORN
- Media usage.

They also have subjective characteristics, which relate to the 'psychographics'. Psychographics look closely at various personality traits and inventories and very importantly, particularly in the 21st century, lifestyles.

### Geographic segmentation

Geographic segmentation is a popular form of segmentation; for example, geographic regions of television areas are used as a form of geographic segmentation. Geographic segmentation means that the market can be broken down into areas for marketing purposes – into towns, cities, regions, countries, etc. This is particularly relevant with the tourism industry, where particular regions will be promoted as holiday and leisure destinations.

Geographic segmentation is particularly important on a global basis, as there are so many different cultures, characteristics and lifestyle requirements that need to be met. Many organizations will try, where possible, to standardize their product offerings globally, while others may try to tailor global requirements. It will very much depend upon the marketing place and the competitive elements that exist within it.

### Demographic segmentation

One common area of demographics is social class. This is often a contentious issue. Let us look at some of the areas developed by the JICNAR social grade definitions when looking at segmentation (see Table 3.6).

As a marketer you should be able to recognize different market segments for any major product, for example, motor vehicles. There are a number of different cars available to suit the many and varied needs of customers and their lifestyles.

*Table 3.6* JICNAR classification

| Social grades | Social status | Characteristics of occupation |
| --- | --- | --- |
| A | Upper middle class | High managerial/professional |
| B | Middle class | Intermediate managerial/administrative professional |
| C1 | Lower middle class | Supervisory/clerical/junior/managerial/administrative/professional |
| C2 | Skilled working class | Skilled manual labour |
| D | Working class | Semi-skilled and unskilled manual labour |
| E | Lowest level of subsistence | Widows, casual workers, state pensioners |

### Geo-demographic segmentation

Geo-demographic factors are a combination of demographic and geographic variables which suggest that certain groups of people tend to move in circles appropriate to class and occupation, while others may move together relating to lifestyles and geographic factors. There are two particular methods in this area that should be considered, ACORN and MOSAIC.

### ACORN

ACORN (A Classification of Residential Neighbourhoods – Table 3.7) is a classification system which identifies people by geo-demographics. The current ACORN system divided the UK into 17 groups, which comprise of a total of 54 different types of areas, which share common socioeconomic characteristics. The basis of this type of segmentation is recognizing that different residential areas have very different profiles of people within them and therefore the products they may need may vary from area to area. In many instances products may not even be targeted at specific groups as it is not deemed to be appropriate.

*Table 3.7* ACORN consumer targeting classification

| | | |
|---|---|---|
| Category A Thriving | 19.8% | 1 – Wealthy achievers – suburban areas |
| | | 2 – Affluent greys, rural communities |
| | | 3 – Prosperous pensioners |
| Category B Expanding | 11.5% | 4 – Affluent executives |
| | | 5 – Well-off workers, family areas |
| Category C Rising | 7.6% | 6 – Affluent urbanites, town and city areas |
| | | 7 – Prosperous professionals, metropolitan areas |
| | | 8 – Better-off executives, inner city areas |
| Category D Settling | 22.3% | 9 – Comfortable middle-aged, mature home-owning areas |
| | | 10 – Skilled workers – home-owning |
| Category E Aspiring | 13.7% | 11 – New home-owners, mature communities |
| | | 12 – White-collar workers, better-off multi-ethnic areas |
| Category F Striving | 22.6% | 13 – Older people, less prosperous areas |
| | | 14 – Council estate residents – better off homes |
| | | 15 – Council estate residents, high unemployment |
| | | 16 – Council estate residents, greatest hardship |
| | | 17 – People in multi-ethnic low-income areas |
| Unclassified | 2.4% | |

*Source*: Adapted from Dibb, Simkin, Pride and Ferrell (2001)

From the seven overall categories, ACORN can then go on to identify issues relating to behaviour, personality, motives and lifestyle. These are what we termed the 'psychographics'. The 'objective' characteristics of ACORN versus the 'subjective' characteristics of personality, motives and lifestyle, serve to move the organization much closer to understanding the basis of customer needs, wants and expectations.

## MOSAIC

MOSAIC is a classification system which analyses information from a variety of sources. It analyses geo-demographic data including the census (which provides housing, socioeconomic, household and age information), post code address records (to provide housing and special types of address information, e.g. non-residential addresses), the electoral role (to provide composition of households and population movement information) and the CCN files/Lord Chancellor's office (to provide information on credit searches and bad-debt risks).

MOSAIC provides three types of information as follows:

- *Unit postcodes* – A six or seven digit code
- *Census enumeration districts* – Based upon census data, containing about 180 addresses in each district
- *Pseudo-enumeration districts* – Areas created by MOSAIC using a combination of unit postcodes within an individual enumeration district.

Presently there are 58 individual neighbourhood types in the MOSAIC classification system.

### Lifestyle segmentation

Lifestyle segmentation is a very complex area and is based upon the characteristics of psychographics. These are more subjective and less easy to measure than the typical traits of demographics.

The key areas of interest for a marketer would typically be:

- *Social activities* – leisure activities, sport, eating out, holidays, shopping habits
- *Interests* – music, reading, science, history, food, fashion, Internet
- *Opinions* – social and ethical issues, business, politics, culture, education, religion.

Clearly these characteristics will then be linked with demographics, to start establishing a clear customer profile, on which to base segmentation.

### Behaviour segmentation

Behavioural segmentation relates to dividing customers, or indeed organizations, into groups based upon their purchase behaviour, frequency of purchase, attitudes towards the products/services, benefits sought and consumption patterns.

There are a variety of different ways that a market can be segmented. The process of market segmentation involves the following steps:

- Analyse and describe the market segments
- Validate segment choice by testing
- Choose an appropriate strategy for segmentation
- Develop the product or market positioning.

Dividing the market into smaller segments can often present a wide range of new and exciting opportunities for organizations, enabling them to meet more directly a wider range of customer needs, but also enabling them to remain competitive in the marketplace. Segmentation can also allow organizations to respond faster to the changing needs of the customers and also the macro-factors of the external marketing environment.

Market segmentation is therefore essential for successful implementation of marketing strategy. It can help achieve:

- Lengthening of the PLC
- Increased sales and profits
- Capture of some of the competitors' share of the market
- Survival of a small firm operating in a competitive market consisting of large firms
- Effective resource allocation
- Strategic marketing planning.

### Business-to-business and organizational segmentation

The disciplines of marketing in a business-to-business (B2B) context are often quite different and unfortunately the segmentation techniques available to those marketing to individuals are not available to the organizational marketer. However, a particular bonus of business-to-business segmentation is perhaps the more limited size of the customer base.

For business-to-business and organizational segmentation grouping of customers can be as follows:

- Using the Standard Industrial Classifications (SIC)
- By the industry technology, e.g. chemical or electrical, etc.
- By size of organization
- By season purchasing trends
- By geographical location
- By the type of product needed.

Demographics, in a B2B context, assume that organizations operating in similar industries have similar needs and will exhibit similar behavioural traits.

All organizations aim to satisfy their customer needs, whether their customer is an individual or a business. As we have already identified, organizations do find it difficult to totally segment their markets for B2B buying because of the characteristics of the market they operate within.

Therefore, there are five key variables that organizations should consider:

1. The personal characteristics of the buyers
2. Situational factors
3. The organizational approach to purchasing
4. Operating variables – technologies, etc.
5. Demographics.

*Company demographics* have a slightly different approach, and are in the main far less personal. However, they do focus on areas such as company age, location, size and the likelihood of them wanting to change their product specification in the future.

Clearly these factors are highly significant, as they will indicate the volume of purchases, the ordering procedures, accessibility for delivery, etc.

Business-to-business buying should reflect the same considerations as consumer segmentation and the same approach to developing marketing plans and strategies should apply.

Further consideration of this area is included within Unit 10.

## Continuous monitoring of segmentation

As with any element of marketing, segmentation, targeting and positioning should be tightly controlled and monitored, to ensure the information provided has enabled an organization to meet its corporate and marketing objectives.

Should an organization not meet its objectives, then it should review and evaluate segments selected to ensure that the profile of customers is one that matches the benefits and characteristics of the product, or indeed that the correct medium has been selected to get the message to the customer or consumer.

If the segment that has been targeted should prove to be ineffective, then further research should be undertaken, and plans revised and the marketing mix strategy redefined.

Possible examples of segmentation monitoring might include measuring the sales distribution across segments, measuring advertising effectiveness, repeat sales and responses to special sales promotions.

## Achieving segmentation effectiveness

Ineffective marketing segmentation can have lasting effects and be the cause of many lost opportunities. Therefore it is essential that there is clear and perceived value in the segmenting process. It is of primary importance that the appropriate segmentation characteristics are identified and that time is not wasted and investment is not lost in the selection of the incorrect or inappropriate segmenting variables. For example, there is little point in segmenting a homogeneous market, as it does not provide the basis for effective segmentation.

Unit 3 Marketing planning, implementation and control

Therefore the following criteria should be adhered to:

| | |
|---|---|
| Specific | Clearly identified, broken down into a number of meaningful groups |
| Measurable | Each group should be quantifiable in order for the organization to identify opportunities and forecast the future |
| Achievable | The segments themselves need to achieve organizational objectives, they will therefore need to be viable groups and accessible |
| Realistic | What is achievable in the name of segmentation must be realistic in terms of resources, and with a clear indication that customer expectations can be met |
| Timebound | Appropriate segments of the market must be targeted in an appropriate and timely way and in line with the organizational objectives. |

While marketing segmentation can be a very process-driven exercise, it will require a degree of commonsense and perhaps even a number of related assumptions, in order that the market can be closely defined.

Ultimately the benefits of segmentation are significant and they include:

- It allows target markets to be mapped against organizational competences
- It helps identify gaps within the marketplace
- It enables marketers to match the product/service to their customer – a basis of competitive advantage
- It provides an opportunity for mature/declining markets to identify possible growth segments
- The failure to segment can reduce competitive strength.

## Targeting

Targeting is the process that involves evaluating the attractiveness of a range of potential market segments that have been identified in terms of being commercially viable.

### Definition

**Targeting** – The decision about which market segment(s) a business decides to prioritize for its sales and marketing efforts (Dibb, Simkin, Pride and Ferrell, 2001).

Each organization has several options when deciding on which segment specifically to target:

- Organizations could concentrate on making one product for one market and having one marketing plan or programme – this is known as *undifferentiated marketing or even mass marketing*
- The organization could concentrate its efforts on one market but have a number of different versions of each product. This is known as *differentiated marketing*
- Another alternative is to have a product that meets the need of each segment within the market with a specific product – this is known as *target marketing*
- Concentrating efforts on a small and carefully chosen segment, often referred to as a niche and the basis of a '*focus*' strategy.

77

Targeting in essence is where we identify a number of different segments within the market, whereby a sustainable competitive advantage can be built.

In ascertaining the appropriate target market strategy the organization must take into consideration the following six components:

1. Customer needs, wants and expectations
2. *Product market* – size and structure
3. Brand strength and market share
4. Company capability
5. Competitive rivalry
6. Economies of scale – production and marketing.

The organization must, through market research, identify which is the most appropriate target, which they can effectively manage to meet the customer needs and wants, in a cost-efficient and effective way, in order that they can meet the corporate goals of the organization.

Segmentation is not an exact science, and will require a balanced view of market conditions, clear and precise criteria for assessing segmentation attractiveness and an understanding of the key components that will enable successful target marketing.

## Question 3.5

Why is it so vital for an organization to undertake segmentation and targeting activities?

What would be the effect of failing to undertake segmentation and targeting?

### Positioning

Earlier on in this unit, we looked at the concept of market positioning strategies. Here we want to look at the source of positioning, starting with the product.

### Definition

**Positioning** – The act of designing an offer so that it occupies a distinct and valued place in the minds of the target customers (Kotler et al., 1998).

Simplistically, positioning refers to how you present your product or services to the marketplace, it is almost a state of mind, a perception, it is something you as a marketer have to create in the minds of your target audience.

When establishing a positioning strategy there are a number of steps that can be taken in preparing a positioning plan.

- Identify all of the segments within the market
- Decide which segments are the most suitable to target, based upon marketing research information
- Ensure that the organization clearly understands the customer requirements

- o Develop a product or service that specifically meets the needs of the target audience
- o Identify benefits, usage, user category, competitive positioning components
- o Evaluate how the product/service is positioned in the eyes of the target group
- o Identify an image that matches the requirements of the customer
- o Promote the product to the target audience, establish relationships, aim for customer loyalty.

Pivotal to the success of positioning is the ability to differentiate your products and services from those of your competitors.

From a competitor perspective, there needs to be a comparison of competitor positioning, which means that as a marketer you should:

- o Determine competitive positioning
- o Examine the competitive dimensions
- o Determine the customer positions
- o Understand and identify the positioning decision
- o Track the positioning strategy.

This will ultimately enable you to monitor competitor positioning and take the necessary retaliatory action.

Perception is a vital component of positioning strategies and therefore it is helpful for organizations to try to represent the similarities between products or services and try to ascertain what the differences are, in respect of position. The key tool to support this process is a perceptual map (see Figure 3.5).

You will see when looking at the perceptual maps that there are four perceptions to be considered:

1. High price and high quality
2. High quality and low price
3. Low price and low quality
4. High price and low quality.

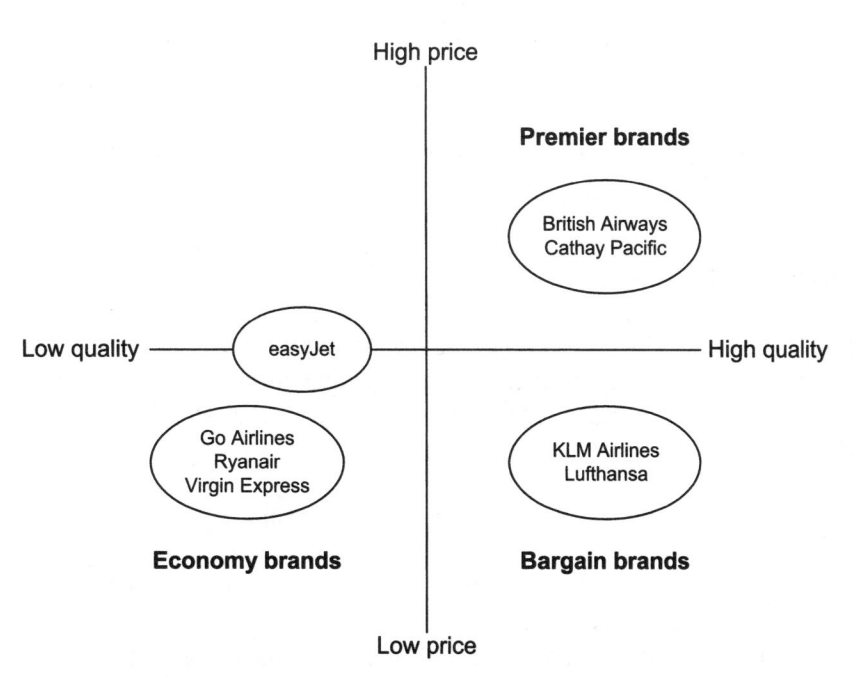

*Figure 3.5* Perceptual positioning map

What effectively happens with a perceptual map is that it represents similarities and differences between products/services and ultimately it highlights where products are similar/dissimilar.

As we can see here, the service offered by British Airways and Cathay Pacific is of a very high standard. The accommodation and service on board in a British Airways flight is aimed at meeting customer expectations at a high level, which is primarily the executive market. British Airways are known for their superior service in executive, business and first-class flights. But obviously this all comes at a premium. Therefore in this instance British Airways have positioned themselves as premier quality, premium priced. Cathay Pacific seek to achieve the same positioning.

At the lower end of the scale, we have MytravelLite, Ryanair and Virgin Express, in addition to easyJet. However, while easyJet position themselves at the lower end of the market, flights to Malaga for example, fall anywhere between £45 and £175, flights from London to Edinburgh fall between £68 and £228, depending upon how far in advance they are actually booked. The further in advance you book, the cheaper the flight is.

Therefore for a 'no frills' brand, they are actually positioning themselves as an economy brand, 'low-cost airline'. However, in reality their positioning is somewhere between economy and high price, which is a slightly confused positioning. Other factors to consider with 'no frills' is the additional expenses customers incur while in flight, i.e. they add on expenses of food, drink. Of course, in terms of positioning, reliability will play a significant factor in the minds of the consumer, in respect of value for money, something for which easyJet received extremely poor publicity during the early part of 2001, through the range of television programmes that focused on a day in the life of easyJet.

Whilst positioning is a positive activity from both a customer and competitor perspective, it is not an exact science. In positioning your organization you are raising an expectation in relation to the level of product or service quality you might offer. The important element of that is achieving the expectations that you have established in the eyes of the consumer.

Plotting on the perceptual map in Figure 3.5 is based upon the perceptions of customers, but it is also useful to consider this from a competitor perspective. Plotting competitor positioning on a perceptual map will enable you to further understand the role and positioning of your competitors, enabling the organization to have a clear understanding of the nature of the competition and, of course, where to attack. However, remember that when you attack, positioning is something that has to be sustainable, therefore in attacking a competitor it has to be more than a short-term activity and part of a longer-term strategy to compete on product and market positioning.

## The positioning alternatives

Perceptual maps should be based upon marketing research, in order that a factual presentation of the information can be plotted, and assumptions made in relation to positioning are as accurate as possible. It is not recommended that you use either expert witnesses or expert judgements, or take the very subjective approach of establishing positions on gut feel.

Ries and Trout (1998) suggest that there are three positioning alternatives available:

- *Distinctive attributes* – Identify the distinctive attributes of the product and service as a source of credible positioning.
- *Fill the gaps in unfilled positions* – Where there is a positional gap in the perceptional map, this may present a business opportunity to exploit.

- *Repositioning* – Changes in consumer behaviour (which are quite frequent) may mean that the PLC could be maturing or going into decline, therefore you might need to reposition your products to attract a different market. Clearly in the instance of the perceptual map in Figure 3.5, there is a space in the high price, low quality quadrant – *but this is not one to fill*. Of course, as a marketer, you would need to consider carefully why the gap might exist. It would be difficult in this instance to actually conceive what would be the benefits of selling a 'high price – economy' product, as it is unlikely that customers will pay for it. Therefore this should always be addressed and the likely gaps that you might wish to exploit are the remaining three.
- Think about alcopops. They were originally aimed at the younger end of the market – 18–25-year-olds. Now they are more sophisticated perceptually and are as popular with 31–40-year-olds. This is a slight repositioning in order to allow for market penetration, i.e. ensuring customer retention for the 18–25-year-old market, but undertaking market development to target new markets, i.e. the 30+ more mature markets, but with the same products.

As part of the segmentation and targeting process, it is essential where possible to closely define the segmentation basis and associate it with the product/service in question. Ultimately, it is then possible to position the product clearly in a defined positioning strategy, in order to meet customer needs and expectations.

## The role of a marketer in positioning

The role of a marketer will be to assist with the definition of positioning, in the context of the market, the brand and the product. As you move through this book, you will come across a number of different tools of the trade that will assist you with ascertaining positions in relation to the brand, for example the Boston Consulting Group Matrix, which will allow you to make decisions in relation to product positioning.

Positioning is all about differentiating your products and brands for your customers: what are the key characteristics and benefits that stand out – that differentiate your product/brands from those of your competitors; what characteristics do your products have that your competitors' may not? The purpose of positioning is to establish a position and perspective of your brands, products and services in the marketplace.

Clearly segmentation can therefore be a complex activity, and should always be objective in nature, i.e. very clearly defined, very specific and very focused. Subjective judgements in relation to the segmentation base and target market may lead to failure to implement any marketing strategy.

According to Hooley, Saunders and Piercy (1998): 'Segmentation and positioning researchers have indeed failed to find a single criterion which will fit all markets, despite the claims of those selling lifestyle segmentation.' Therefore the safest and most reliable way to segment, target and position your markets is through the use of product market data that enables customers to be clearly segmented into smaller groups in order that they might be specifically targeted.

### Question 3.6

You have been asked by your marketing manager to develop a brief statement that clearly explains the positioning of your own company – in no more than 50 words.

## The marketing plan

This section focuses upon conceptualizing the basis of a marketing plan. There are some components that we will only look at briefly within implementation, as they are the source of strategic planning and beyond the scope of the CIM syllabus for this module.

*Table 3.8* Contents of the marketing plan

1. Executive summary
   Key issues, current position, potential overview of the outcome
2. Corporate strategy
   Corporate mission/vision and corporate goals/objectives
3. Macro/micro analysis
   Market assessment
   Current state of the market
   Market trends
   Competitor analysis
   SWOT
4. Marketing objectives
   Financial objectives
   Marketing objectives
5. Marketing strategy
   Segmentation, targeting and positioning
   Marketing strategy
   Marketing programme
   Product, price, place, promotion
6. Implementation
   Key tasks, resources, budgets, contingency plans
7. Monitoring and control
   Basis of the plan and the assumptions made
   Key/critical success factors
   Benchmarking
   Forecasts/costs/revenue

There is no set way in which the marketing plan must be presented. Table 3.8 shows the key headings that you should cover and also the order and sequence that is logical and appropriate. Planning offers you the opportunity to present the future of the organization and its marketing activity systematically, in a way that is meaningful and clearly defined. The basis of this particular plan will provide the template by which the organization will operate in the forthcoming years and will also form the basis of a planned approach to implementation. Furthermore, it will provide the basis for measurement, monitoring and control and it will act as a benchmark of what needs to be achieved, taking the organization from where it is now, to where it wants to be in the future.

## Implementation of the marketing plan

There are a number of key components that you should familiarize yourself with in respect of the implementation of marketing plans. From an organizational perspective, implementation is one of the most challenging activities you will find yourself involved in.

Nigel Piercy (2001) suggests that:

> *The real strategic problem in marketing is not strategy, it is managing the implementation and change.*

New plans, new processes, different approaches are all components of change, and in many situations change meets with opposition and many barriers are therefore erected. You may recall these barriers from Unit 1, and here they are again as a reminder.

- o The existing culture may not be amenable to marketing plans, particularly if the organization is not marketing-oriented.
- o *Power and politics* – All organizations are subject to internal politics and often as a result of this the strategic planning process becomes a boardroom battlefield, where vested interests fight each other's proposals in order to gain resources and status.
- o *Analysis not action* – Many organizations waste time and energy in analysing data and developing rationales for action, but ultimately fail to act. A further element of this is 'paralysis-by-analysis', too much information, not enough direction.
- o *Resources* – This is one of the most contentious issues facing many organizations, as after years of downsizing, striving for increased efficiencies, many organizations now find themselves resource-starved. When corporate objectives are defined, it is of prime importance that organizations realistically consider the resources required, in order that they can rise to the challenge of achieving the corporate targets.
- o Skills are very closely linked to the challenges of resources. One of the key components of any organization is a highly skilled workforce. As a result of the changes brought about by the economic slowdown in the early 1990s, marketing as a function was cascaded down to managers in the organization, who were untrained, unskilled and unable to carry the mantle of marketing that had suddenly been bestowed upon them. An unskilled workforce could hinder significantly the implementation of marketing plans and ultimately reduce service and performance levels overall.

There are some key ingredients that are required and vital for the successful implementation of any marketing plan, and the driving forces of change. They are:

- o Strong and committed leadership
- o A marketing-oriented and customer-focused culture
- o A supportive and effective marketing structure
- o Financial and human resources
- o *Internal marketing* – systems and processes
- o Control and measurement mechanisms.

For a strategy to be successfully implemented, it is therefore important that these areas are managed effectively. If they are not, immediately a range of barriers to implementation will arise and then change becomes very difficult to manage.

Let us look briefly at the importance of each of these factors.

## Strong and committed leadership

You might recall that, in the first unit, there was a reference to 'top-down' and 'bottom-up' planning. In a planning environment, leadership needs primarily to come from the top. A leader therefore must demonstrate commitment at the highest level to the proposed strategy and plans. Leaders need to be effective communicators, motivators and facilitators.

The process of continuous improvement will only succeed if those in influential roles demonstrate their commitment to the process, but also ensure that they equally affect the commitment of their followers. Commitment is not a management function that can be delegated downwards, it has to be shown by actions.

Commitment is difficult to measure but it is likely that the following key factors will be present:

- A vision for the future has been developed
- The necessary resources have been committed
- When solutions to problems are found they are promptly implemented
- Barriers to change within the organization have been dismantled.

While this is a limited list, it is obvious that each relates to potential causes of conflict within the implementation process, therefore committed leadership is imperative to successful implementation of the marketing plan.

There is more to leadership than autocracy or democracy, charisma or inspiration – in the words of Sir John Harvey Jones: *leadership is about making things happen*.

Therefore effective leadership starts at the top, with the vision for the organization, examining closely the needs of the market, creating, exploiting and capitalizing on opportunities for the organization, at the same time as ensuring that it achieves competitive advantage.

## Marketing-oriented and customer-focused culture

The 'marketing concept' in the words of Kotler *et al.* (1998):

> *Holds that achieving organizational goals depends on determining the needs and wants of target markets and delivering the desired satisfactions more effectively and more efficiently than competitors do.*

Reflecting on the different facets of marketing you have already examined, it is clear that marketing is increasingly dynamic and if you and your organization are going to succeed then you need to ensure that you take into most serious consideration the expectations of your customer.

Organizations will need to be marketing-oriented, which means that there must be a clear focus throughout the whole organization on the customer needs and wants and how these needs are met constantly.

Marketing orientation consists of five key facets:

1. Customer orientation
2. Competitor orientation
3. Integrated functional co-ordination
4. Organizational culture
5. Long-term profits.

To enable the marketing concept to continue to evolve and for marketing orientation to develop within organizations, organizations, big or small, should pay serious consideration to the following:

- Create customer focus throughout the business
- Listen to the customer
- Define the nature of the organization's key abilities, i.e. what they are good at
- Target customers precisely
- Manage profitability
- Make customer value the guiding star
- Let the customer define loyalty – how many times they may wish to repeat business
- Measure and manage customer expectations
- Build customer relationships and loyalty
- Commit to continuous improvement
- Manage the marketing culture.

For culture change to be implemented successfully, the following components must be at the forefront:

- Innovation must be highly valued
- Leadership must be an activity not just a function
- Shared values and rewards
- A learning organization
- Empowerment.

Ultimately, change in the context of marketing should be planned, consistent and incremental.

Strategy implementation can be a complex period full of conflict and recriminations. Cultural change must create something that did not exist before. The careful crafting of the 'internal marketing plan' may ease the situation.

## Internal marketing

It is clear from everything we have seen so far that change is the one factor that is here to stay. It is also evident that the implementation of a new corporate strategy and indeed a new marketing plan may also require change within the organization.

The basis of internal marketing is focusing on the relationship that exists between the organization and its employees, often couched in terms of the 'internal customer'. It has been suggested on many occasions that the successful implementation of the marketing plan hinges upon treating internal staff like 'customers', hence the link with the internal customer.

### Definition

**Internal marketing** – The application of marketing internally within the company, with programmes of communication and guidance targeted at internal audiences to develop responsiveness and a unified sense of purpose among employees (Dibb, Simkin, Pride and Ferrell, 2001, p. 731).

Nigel Piercy (2001), suggests that:

> *Marketplace success is frequently largely dependent on employees who are far removed from the excitement of creating marketing strategies.*

Therefore it is highly important that the internal marketing programme bridges the information gap between the strategy development team through to technical engineers, customer services staff, production and finance, to name but a few, so that essentially they are fully informed about the direction of the organization.

Internal marketing plays a pivotal role in ensuring that the organization is marketing and customer-focused, the components of which have already been discussed in the previous section. It is based upon a programme of communications externally that ultimately demands a positive response from the employees, i.e. buy-in and commitment to the newly formed strategy and planned changes that are due to be implemented.

One of the critical success factors of internal marketing is its ability to break down the various barriers to planning that were evident earlier in this unit. Its prime objective is to ensure that a more positive attitude is formed towards the organization and its vision and that productivity, effectiveness and efficiency will increase.

Internal marketing can go a long way to achieve the two key factors important to planning: 'synergy' and 'consistency'. These factors will come from a workforce in tune, integrated and committed to achieving the corporate vision.

Successful implementation of an integrated market plan will be based upon employees understanding the concepts and philosophy of the organization and that they will understand the mission and corporate goals. It may enable employees to feel part of the organization, responsible for its achievement.

One of the key components of an internal marketing programme is therefore communication. Internal marketing is, as suggested earlier, a communications programme. There are a number of steps that an organization can take in order to achieve internal synergy and employee co-operation:

- Creating an internal awareness of the corporate aims, objectives and overall mission
- Determining the expectations of the internal customer
- Communication to internal customers
- Changes in tasks and activities
- Internal monitoring and control.

As with the external marketing plan, the internal plan ultimately needs the same components:

- Internal vision
- Aims and objectives
- Internal marketing strategy
- Segmentation, targeting and positioning
- Marketing programme to include all elements of the marketing mix
- Implementation
- Monitoring and control of the success or failure of execution.

It is as important to segment your market internally as it is externally, as the basis and the focus of the message will need to be tailored to the particular audience, potentially fitting their contribution and that of their departments into the context of the proposed change.

The key aim of the marketing plan must therefore be the successful motivation and retention of the internal customer in order that the organization can meet the needs of the external market. The marketing mix will be the tools with which to achieve it.

Later on in this book in 'Place promotions', we will be looking at 'Managing marketing relationships' and we will examine this particular area in a lot more depth, looking at the techniques involved in internal marketing. Ultimately if internal marketing is implemented effectively it will have something to offer in achieving the level of strategic change the organization may want.

### Question 3.7

What is the importance of communication to the 'internal marketing process' and why?

## A supportive and effective marketing structure

For a marketing strategy to be successfully implemented it will rely on an infrastructure to be in place that will deliver the corporate goals in an efficient and effective way. The sign of a good leader is one who ensures that the organization is structured in a way that gets the job done.

Therefore it is essential that you are fully aware of the different ways of organizing the marketing activities.

Typically the structure of the organization might be functional, territory-based or product-based.

### The functional organization

The functional organization (see Figure 3.6) typically defines each of its business functions, from which each functional unit will have a management line of control established. In terms of marketing it is likely that this is headed up by the Director of Marketing, down to a range of functional specialisms including sales, product development and market research. This will allow for the marketing team to work on an integrated basis, undertaking a range of marketing activities on a day-to-day basis.

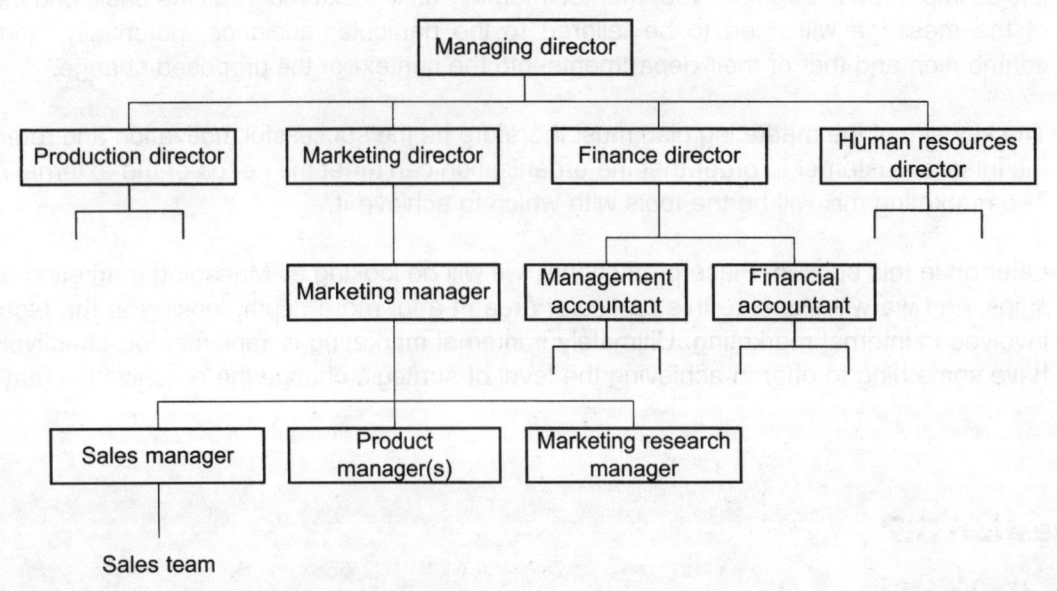

Unit 3 Marketing planning, implementation and control

*Figure 3.6* Departmentalism by function

## The territory-based organization

This is quite a useful structure for organizations who trade internationally, or particularly in the retail sector, where there may be independent marketing activities undertaken in each territory (see Figure 3.7). However, this is formally known as decentralized management. This is where the business management functions are devolved to the regional centre of activity, whereby they will be responsible for their own 'territory' budget, resources and marketing activity, albeit still in line with meeting the corporate goals and objectives.

This is more typical of large organizations, and where cultural differences are significant enough to perhaps require a different approach.

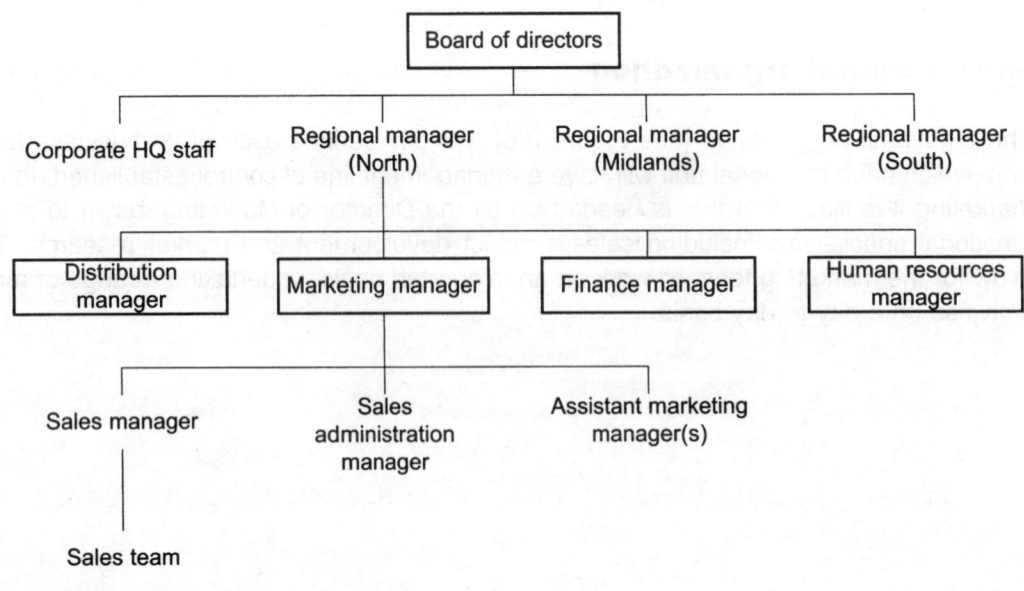

*Figure 3.7* Departmentalism by territory

## The product-based organization

Organizations such as Philips, Pepsi, Coca-Cola, Lever to name but a few, work on a product-based structure (see Figure 3.8), whereby different brands and products are managed as separate business units. Each brand is individually accountable for its own performance, although it is still aligned to and responsible for meeting the overall corporate goals. In a product-based organization, product managers will have responsibility devolved down to them and be expected to ensure that their particular brand and product range delivers in line with corporate expectations.

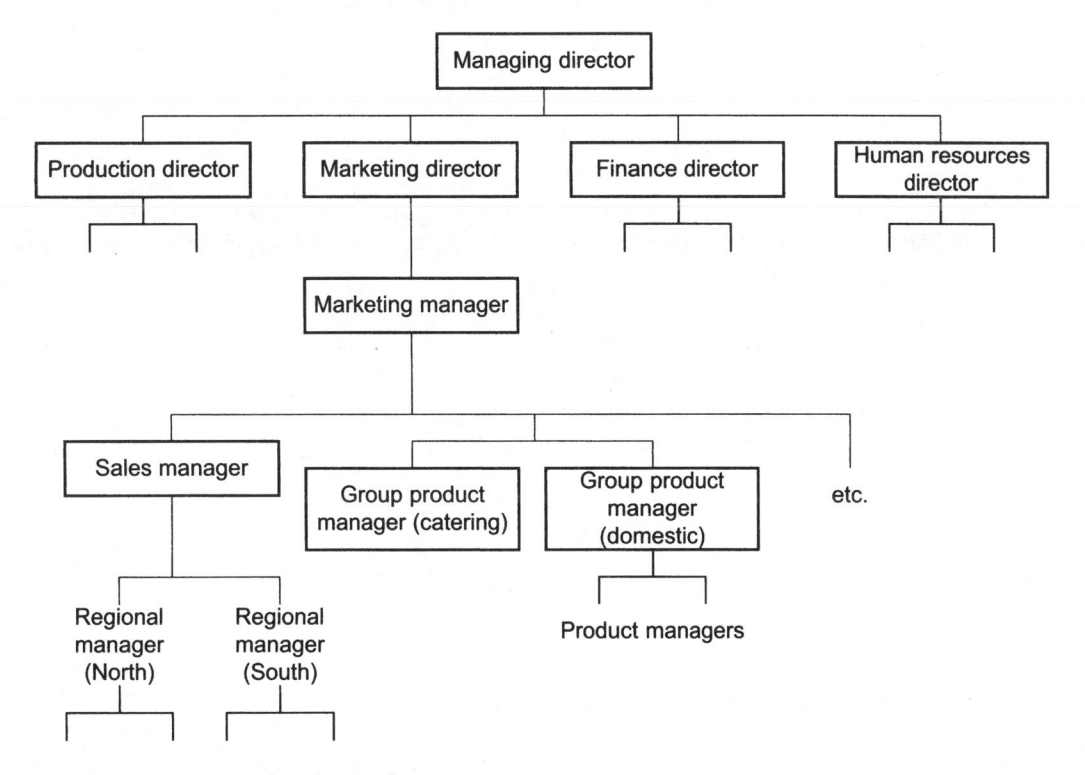

*Figure 3.8* Departmentalism by product

Other organizational structures include *matrix management*, whereby the responsibility of the marketing manager can potentially cut across all business functions. As the role of marketing has evolved over time, it encroaches more and more on other business functions in order that an integrated and co-ordinated approach is undertaken to achieve the corporate goals.

*Customer-based structures* are also quite prevalent, particularly in organizations involved in financial services, whereby customers and products might be linked together and therefore the organization is run in such a way as to be able to ultimately manage and retain customers.

Whatever the structure of the organization, it is vitally important that the lines of communication are clearly defined, in order that from an internal perspective employees clearly understand the purpose and direction of the structure and ultimately their contribution overall.

> ## Insight
>
> ### Changes to Royal Mail's Marketing structure
>
> Royal Mail Introduces New Marketing Structure
>
> Royal Mail's Marketing Director Paul Rich is introducing a new structure, to align his team more closely with the company's sales force. The move is to enable more effective and customer-driven development of products and services as the company's marketplaces become increasingly competitive.
>
> The review of Royal Mail's marketing structure has led to five new areas covering products, sectors, brand, commercial policy plus pricing and value-added solutions. A director for each area will report directly to Rich.
>
> The new team will be responsible for all Royal Mail branded products and services, including special stamps and philatelic products, international services and logistics where marketing was previously carried out within separate business units.
>
> Paul Rich said: 'The new roles provide a renewed focus for us and bring all Royal Mail branded products and services under one marketing roof. This will give us a far more cohesive, integrated and customer-focused approach. This is all part of competing effectively by making sure that we are developing and selling products and services that precisely match our customers' needs and offer best value in our marketplaces.'
>
> *Source*: Adapted from www.royalmail.com.

## Financial and human resources

One of the key successes of good vision and leadership is the ability to produce the resources to get the job done. By resources we mean the money, the people and the place, in which the marketing activities can be successfully implemented.

Today resources appear to be one of the most scarce commodities in the workplace and quite often one of the key barriers to implementation. This is a result of resources actually being budget-driven. However, when strategies are being defined and planned, resource implications must be considered as part of the overall process.

For the organization to function it needs people and finance, so for the marketing strategy to be successful it is of primary importance to ensure that the whole infrastructure is in place.

### Human resources

From a human resource perspective, it will be essential that the organization has the appropriate mix of management and technical skills required for implementation of the marketing plan. A team of multi-skilled marketers will be critical to successful implementation. You will learn about this within Effective Management for Marketing, where you will look at issues relating to being an effective marketing manager, appropriate recruitment, selection and team-building strategies.

As a marketing manager you will have responsibility for managing the marketing team, ensuring the implementation of the process, through the successful management of tasks.

## Financial resources/budgets

The processes of strategic planning and budgeting are very closely linked. In real terms, having a budget means that you are able to execute and implement a very carefully laid plan in a very controlled way, as budgeting is probably the most common control mechanism of any planning process.

When developing a plan and setting a budget, often the full picture of the situation can be unclear. This may be as a result of missing or inaccurate information. But in any case, the budget allocation process will ensure that an indication of the resources required to make the plan work is considered, together with the financial implications of the plan. Much of the information formulated within the budget is based on forecasts, and there is an important difference between the two.

From this a budget will be defined. The budget is a financial plan demonstrated in quantitative terms. It is likely that the budget will show volumes as well as values, over a set period of time, which in most organizations is 1 year. Budgets may be prepared for the various activities undertaken by the firm or they may be for products, locations and organizational functions, such as marketing, sales, administration, research and development, production, etc.

In setting a budget, you have a control mechanism, a tool to quantify plans, co-ordinate activities, highlight areas of critical importance and assign responsibilities.

According to Drummond, Ensor and Ashford in their book *Strategic Marketing* (2003), budgeting seems to highlight two key points. First, they suggest that budgeting is about resource allocations and secondly, budgeting is a political process, hence the need for negotiation and bargaining, to secure the resources necessary to achieve the proposed plan.

Effectively what we are seeing is that a budget must be prepared to allocate resources in order to achieve marketing objectives. It should contain estimates of costs of implementing the plan; costs of each functional area of the organization; and, in respect of marketing, costs of research, advertising, sales and other promotional mix activities.

A budget is effectively a financial plan of action, for an identified period of time. It is essential that the budget be developed in line with both corporate and marketing objectives. For the purpose of sales and marketing, it may include a number of project areas that have been planned for a year ahead.

It is important to understand that a plan is effectively worthless without any control element. Control will be achieved by comparing actual figures against budget figures, and the variance can then be calculated.

Budgeting can play the role of a motivational tool, when managing people who are involved in marketing activities. While organizations should be customer-driven, in many instances they are budget-driven and achieving objectives, within time and within budget, is a key motivational factor, for which personnel are often rewarded.

Budgeting must not be carried out in isolation from corporate objectives or other business functions, otherwise the budget becomes ineffective, as it does not take on the realism of the situation and what can be effectively achieved corporately. This could result in lack of focus or direction.

Budgeting is critical for measuring both the performance of the organization and of individuals. Budgeting and performance can play a very significant role in personnel appraisal processes, where the budget versus the actual can be the basis of an individual achieving their employment objectives for the period. Within the organization as a whole, the same applies. It is critical that sales and production targets are met, and the only realistic way in which this can be measured effectively is by measuring actual performance against budgeted performance.

From this you will see that human and financial resources are essential to the successful implementation of the marketing plan and provide the basis of a benchmark of performance.

Typical budgetary methods include:

- *Bottom-up budgeting* – This is where the budgeting process is fed and developed from within the organization and where the activities happen. Here managers will prepare detailed budgets for activities that will aid the achievement of the corporate objectives. This information is then fed into the global budgeting process and considered in the round of budgetary decisions.
- *Negotiated budgeting* – Negotiated budgeting is, as it sounds, a process of budget allocation by negotiation and can often appear a little like objective and task approach budgeting (see below). Here it is likely that the marketing manager will have to negotiate expenditure based upon income forecasts in order to execute the marketing plan.

Negotiated budgeting does have a place within the organization, but more in relation to ad hoc projects, where it is possible to bid for a pot of money for extraordinary activities. However, as an overall method for budgeting it can be arduous and also rather political as it can be open to the self-interest and self-fulfilment of individuals as opposed to the greater good of the organization.

- *Objective and task approach budgeting* – This is a common approach in marketing fields, where the budget is allocated specifically on the necessity to achieve output, i.e. to achieve objectives. The marketing team will need to clearly define the tasks that will be undertaken to achieve the objectives and specify clearly the resources required. Based upon this, budget may or may not be allocated. In some instances this can be very like zero-based budgeting.
- In relation to evaluating the effectiveness of this model, it is important to realize that much of the detail is spurious. There is no justification for the market share target or the objectives for awareness, trial or gross rating points. Different assumptions would give very different budgets and there is no criterion in the model for preferring one assumption to another.
- *Incremental budgeting or historical* – This type of budgeting is often based on the provision of an incremental rise in budgets year on year, in line with predicted growth in the forthcoming year, or indeed achieved growth in the previous year.

However, this approach can be somewhat restrictive in terms of creating space for new activities, or indeed, should sales be in decline, it will be difficult to achieve the investment required to generate future growth. Some organizations are unable to increase on the previous year's expenditure and they often work on the basis of using the 'same as last time'.

- *Percentage of sales method* – This is a well-known method particularly relevant to the contribution from the overall budget to marketing communications. It works on the basis of a percentage of the previous year's sales being allocated to marketing communications activities for the forthcoming years. However, should sales fall the contribution from the budget falls with it, at the very time there is a greater requirement for increased expenditure to recover falling sales in order to meet targets.

There is no rationale for the percentage chosen, other than perhaps tradition and there is no effort to consider whether or not a higher or lower amount would be more profitable.

- *Competitive parity* – This approach is based on spending the same percentage as competitors within the industry. This gives managers the illusion of safety in numbers; that the collective wisdom cannot be far wrong. However, there is little rationale for this approach. Clearly organizations differ in their marketing opportunities and profit margins, so that significant divergences should exist in the market. Those with better products and higher margins should spend more.
- *Judgement methods* – More recently techniques have been developed to elicit formally the judgements of managers most directly involved about the future of the business. Managers are asked to judge what sales level will be attained with no advertising support, advertising at half the current level and advertising at 50 per cent more than the present level. Putting together the consensus estimate allows a projection of the optimal level of expenditure. This is a promising approach in that managers are forced to use their judgement and experience in a rational manner. The downside is that the method is only as good as the collected wisdom of those participating in the exercise.
- *Experiment and test* – This is particularly relevant to isolating the effects of advertising. Here the organization may run an experiment whereby one region of the country gets a higher level of spending than others. Company sales then give an estimate of the incremental effect of advertising. Whilst such approaches may give insights, they again run into a host of practical problems. How representative is the test and the test area? Is everything else similar across the regions? Has the experiment lasted long enough to judge any long-term effectiveness? Therefore this approach is limited and can be difficult to get an objective outcome for the appropriate level of advertising expenditure.

What you will find is that often organizations operate on a combined budget approach, using a hybrid of methods to suit the nature and scope of their business. It is not unusual for an organization to allocate 90 per cent of its budget specifically but to withhold 10 per cent for special, contingency projects, all of which may be negotiated or managed on the objective/task-based method.

### Study tip

Question 2 within the December 2003 examination paper focused on budgeting, being able to recommend, justify and evaluate various budgetary methods. It is important not just to know what the budgeting methods are, but also which ones are most appropriate for any given situation. For example, it has been highlighted that 'percentage of sales and judgemental' methods of budgeting are appropriate for setting advertising expenditure, but both have their drawbacks, as shown above. Therefore be prepared to answer questions in relation to this. It is something that you as operational marketing managers should be able to address.

## The control process

The final component of the planning processes that it is necessary to comprehend is the need to control.

In order that the goals of the organization are met, continual monitoring of the business functions within the organization must be undertaken.

Monitoring and control effectively contains four key activities:

1. Development or adjustment of marketing objectives
2. Setting of performance standards
3. Evaluation of performance
4. Corrective action.

In Figure 3.9 you can see the planning cycle, which includes two lines of arrows, each line pointing in opposite directions. The purpose of this is to highlight the importance of planning, which is going in one direction, i.e. forward and onward, and control, which is continually going backwards and checking what has happened so far and essentially establishing whether the plan reached its targets step by step throughout the process. If the targets are not being met, then clearly the planning process may need to be revised.

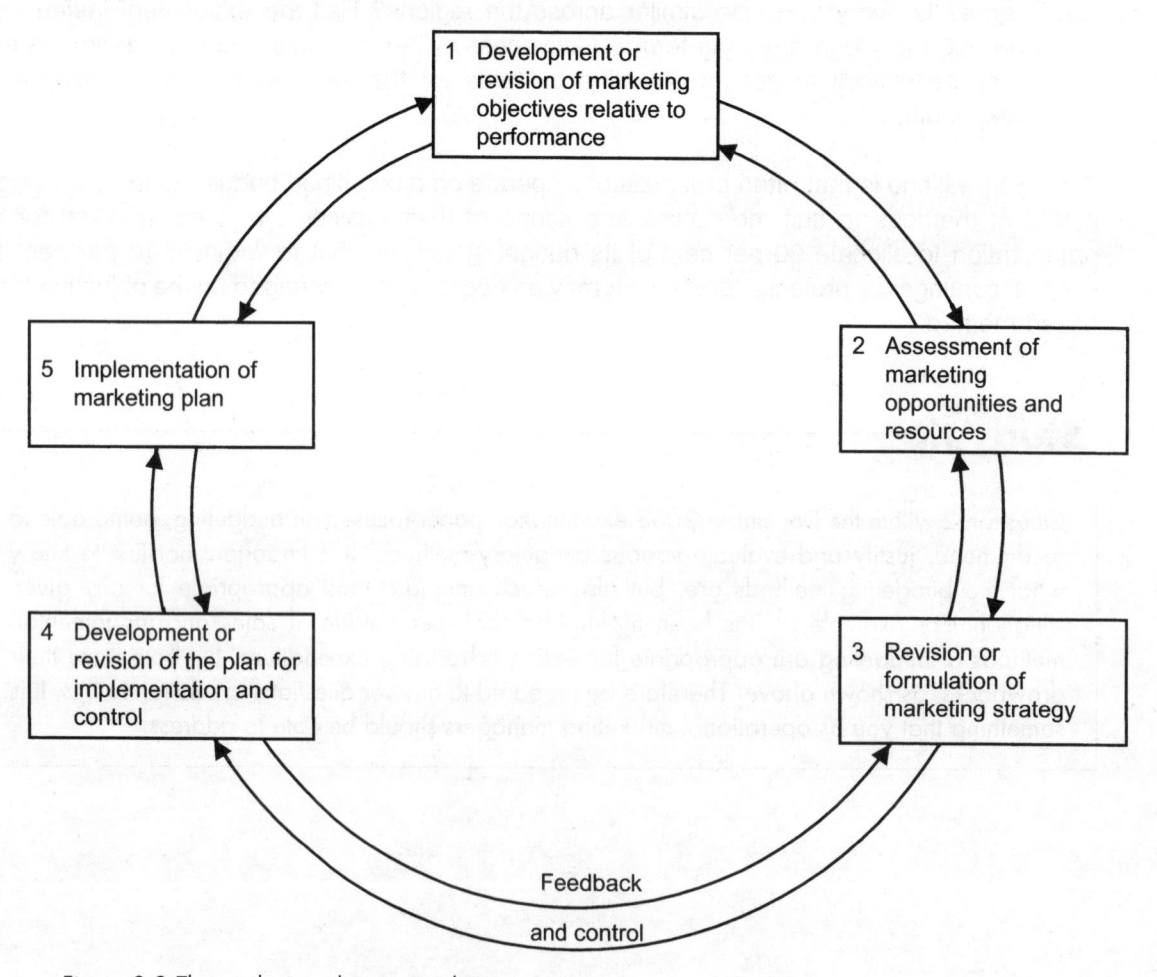

*Figure 3.9* The marketing planning cycle

The first stage in the process after setting the objectives, by which performance will be measured, is setting performance standards. *Performance standards are principally the level of performance against which actual performance can be compared.* In the main, performance standards are presented in the form of budgets. The sole purpose of this will be to ensure that the amount of money given over to expenditure is not exceeded and that the proposed targets for income and profit are actually achieved.

There are a number of techniques that can be employed in this area, but basic and generic principles apply. There are a number of organizational methods of measuring performance overall, such as *performance appraisal/evaluation* which includes measurement and control of staff performance. This consists of reviewing performance, giving feedback and counselling if necessary.

In addition to this there is *benchmarking*, which ensures that the organization develops an ongoing process of measuring processes and achievements against key performance indicators, such as competitors and best practice standards.

Monitoring and measuring performance is a critical element of business and therefore every organization must find effective ways of ensuring that plans and budget appropriations are met, or revised accordingly, and that they underpin the corporate, business and marketing objectives.

As control is an important part of the planning process, it is critical to manage it in a way that is transparent and meaningful. Therefore for the purpose of ease, it is likely that the budget will be broken down into a number of smaller areas, often termed *cost centres*. For each of these, planned income and expenditure are monitored and compared with the actual results.

In many organizations, each function, i.e. marketing, personnel, production, becomes a cost centre. Splitting the budget on this basis enables an overview of how each division is performing against the plan and where the variances lie, giving an opportunity to identify each variance and potentially move towards a contingency plan if necessary, depending on the cause of the variance.

For example, typical headings on a monthly or annual budget report would be as shown below:

INCOME BUDGET – Marketing and sales division

| Income | Actual year | Month | Budgeted amount | Variance under | Variance over |
|---|---|---|---|---|---|
| Sales | | | | | |
| Interest earned | | | | | |
| Sales commission | | | | | |
| Licence fees | | | | | |
| Royalty payments | | | | | |
| Property rentals | | | | | |
| **Total income** | | | | | |

Unit 3 Marketing planning, implementation and control

EXPENDITURE BUDGET – Marketing and sales division

| Income | Actual year | Month | Budgeted amount | Variance under | Variance over |
|---|---|---|---|---|---|
| Sales | | | | | |
| Rent | | | | | |
| Advertising | | | | | |
| PR | | | | | |
| Sales promotions | | | | | |
| Travel | | | | | |
| Sales commission | | | | | |
| **Total expenditure** | | | | | |

## Variance analysis

One of the main things that control is likely to expose is constant variances from the planned budget. For example, when your sales are planned for £300K for the first quarter and they are only £200K in this session, then this is a variance from the actual budget.

Variance analysis is commonly used along with budgetary control. What it seeks to do is to compare the planned budget and then the variance is examined in order for the difference between the two to be established. It is a little like looking for a cause and effect.

Variance analysis is not confined to price or volume either. It can include variance on profit achieved, budgeted costs and change in potential market size.

The key to this control tool is to be fully aware that very often variance in budgets is inevitable and can mean that changes to the existing plan, be they contingency or fully fledged changes, are for the duration of the plan.

## Budgetary control

In essence, budgetary control involves financial control of the whole business through a system of budgets. It consists of:

- Preparation of budgets
- Measuring actual performance
- Comparing actual results with budget results
- Taking corrective action if necessary.

Other methods of measurement and control might relate to *customer satisfaction surveys*. These may be carried out at peak points during the control process or monitored on an ongoing basis. It is essential that the organization identifies whether or not they are meeting customer expectations, needs and wants, and if not what remedial action might be required.

*Brand awareness* is a further example of measuring marketing effectiveness. You may recall in the case of Egg and easyJet, that brand awareness was one of the KSF, in particular the speed at which brand awareness increased.

Both these measures are vital to the measurement of the organization's performance. High levels of customer satisfaction and brand awareness are vital to the achievement of corporate goals. Should there be a decline in either of these key areas, then the organization may have to take remedial action, particularly at the marketing mix level.

## Benchmarking

In the words of Drummond, Ensor and Ashford (2003), benchmarking is defined as follows:

> *A systematic and ongoing process of measuring and comparing an organisation's business processes and achievements against acknowledged process leaders and/or key competitors, to facilitate improved performance.*

Benchmarking is about demonstrating a commitment to continuous improvement and showing that the organization is a learning organization, willing to learn from past mistakes and also past successes and develop an approach to best business practice.

In essence benchmarking falls into three categories:

1. *Competitive analysis* – Reviewing on an ongoing basis competitor activities in order to learn from their success
2. *Best practice* – Here the organization should involve itself in reviewing the best way of undertaking activities across the whole of the organization
3. *Performance standards* – Ensuring that targets are either met or surpassed.

# Effectiveness of the marketing mix

Other units of this text focus closely on marketing mix operations, and how to plan and implement the marketing mix taking an integrated approach. Therefore understanding key components of measuring the marketing mix will be essential in the long term. Some of the potential performance standards might be based upon price, whereby the effects of a particular pricing policy will be measured.

Organizations such as easyJet now combined with Go will frequently undertake promotional activity to generate interest and awareness in the brand. It will be vital, therefore, to monitor the response to the promotional campaign, in order that future successes or failures are identified in relation to the marketing mix.

# Competitor performance

Many of these factors are internal analysis components. It is therefore essential that while monitoring your own performance you also continually monitor that of your competitors. This can be done through scanning the press, but also from obtaining financial information in relation to their performance.

Typical competitor comparisons will be based upon the original financial factors relating to their organization, such as the financial objectives provided in Table 3.1. Going back to the capability profile will allow you to monitor the performance of your own organization against your competitor quite effectively and again will also highlight the need for pre-emptive or reactive strikes.

For an effective control process to be implemented, the marketing manager should consider ways of developing and maintaining effective marketing control processes.

Information is the key to monitoring and measuring marketing success effectively. The quality, quantity and speed of information will be critical.

The control process should be designed to enable a flow of information that will quickly allow a marketing manager to identify the difference between the planned and actual performance, i.e. the variance, and therefore the manager should be able to make informed decisions about any possible remedial changes. Should control procedures trigger a change in the overall plan, or even part of the plan, the full implications of the change must be carefully considered and, ultimately, carefully communicated.

Effective marketing control therefore hinges on quality, quantity and speed of information. The biggest single factor that inhibits the control process is that areas such as environmental changes, time lags between marketing activities and their outcomes and, more seriously, the cost of marketing activities, are often difficult to determine. This means that careful budget monitoring and control is essential.

## Corrective action

Implementation of marketing strategy very rarely goes directly to plan, as external driving forces, time-lags, competition and economic downturn may all change the pace at which the organization's growth can be achieved.

As a result of this many organizations will have to take varying forms of corrective action. In the main this is required when a performance standard falls below what is termed a 'tolerable' level. For example, if sales are in decline at an unsustainable rate, then corrective action may have to be taken.

Corrective actions can take the form of:

- Revised forecasts
- Revised sales targets
- Increased advertising
- Competitive responses
- Price reductions or increases
- Repositioning of products
- Marketing development strategies.

These are only a few, but it gives you an insight into the potential for change, in extenuating circumstances, when the organization can effectively no longer 'tolerate' the market conditions.

This probably brings us back to a key learning point in respect of setting objectives, developing strategies and plans. Objectives always need to be achievable, and it may be that in many instances the reason for the failure to meet performance standards is the lack of realism in the original objectives set, and perhaps failure to resource the implementation programme satisfactorily.

## Summary

This has been a particularly extensive unit, focusing on the broad range of issues associated with planning. However, you are reminded that while you have been provided with an insight into the notion of marketing planning, the basis of Marketing Planning is to look at marketing at an 'operational' level. In the text we have looked closely at:

- Taking the marketing audit to the planning process
- Setting different types of objectives
- Segmentation, targeting and positioning
- Strategy development
- Implementation of the marketing plan.

The influence and importance of marketing planning must never be underestimated; it is vital to the success of the organization. There is endless academic writing in relation to this subject area, but while many are a slight variation on a theme, there is a core at the heart of planning that never actually changes. It is very important to read around the subject wherever possible and gain a real insight into the major driving forces behind the planning processes and what makes planning such a vital activity.

## Study tip

Operational level marketing will focus quite clearly on involvement in the marketing audit, preparing the audit for strategy development, and thereinafter providing information to support the decision-making process, that ultimately culminates in the development of the marketing mix programme.

At an operational level, you will be expected to define, based upon the key strategic marketing objectives presented to you, a marketing strategy and tactical marketing plan, i.e. define a marketing programme based upon the marketing mix.

## Extending knowledge

### Recommended reading

You may find it useful to read Chapters 21–23 of *Marketing: Concepts and Strategies*, 4th European edition by Dibb, Simkin, Pride and Ferrell (2001).

## Bibliography

Dibb, S., Simkin, L., Pride, W. and Ferrell, O. (2001) *Marketing: Concepts and Strategies*, 4th European edition, Houghton Mifflin.

Drummond, G., Ensor, J. and Ashford, R. (2003) *Strategic Marketing: Planning and Control*, Butterworth-Heinemann.

Hooley, G.J., Saunders, N.A. and Piercy, N.F. (1998) *Marketing Strategy and Competitive Positioning*, 3rd edition, FT Prentice Hall.

Kaplan, R.S. and Norton, D.P. (1996) *The Balanced Scorecard*, Harvard Business School Press.

Kotler, P., Armstrong, G., Saunders, J. and Wong, V. (1998) *Principles of Marketing*, FT Prentice Hall.

Piercy, N. (2001) *Market Led Strategic Change*, Butterworth-Heinemann.

Piercy N. (2001) *Tales from the Marketplace*, Butterworth-Heinemann.

Porter, M. (1980) *Competitive Strategy*, Free Press.

Ries, A. and Trout, J. (1998) *Marketing Warfare*, McGraw-Hill.

**Useful websites include:**

www.cim.co.uk
www.cimvirtualinstitute.com
www.revolution.haynet.com
www.marketing.haynet.com
www.ft.com
www.acnielson.com

---

Undertake Question 2 from the June 2004 Examination paper to be found at the end of this text. Additionally undertake Question 2 from the December 2003 paper. Attempting these questions will help you prepare for the examination, in the likely event that such questions should arise in the future.

# unit 4
# promotional operations

## Learning objectives

Introduction to promotional operations in the context of the marketing mix

This subject area has been divided across two units: the theory of communications and the practice of communications, i.e. 'promotional operations'.

The syllabus elements directly relating to this unit are as follows:

o Explain how strategy formulation and decisions relating to the selection of markets impact at an operational level on the planning and implementation of the co-ordinated marketing mix

o Explain the role of branding and its impact on the marketing mix decisions

o Describe methods for maintaining and managing the brand

o Explain how the marketing communications mix is co-ordinated within the marketing plan

Syllabus reference: 3.2, 3.3, 3.4 and 3.10

## The marketing mix in the context of marketing planning

The marketing mix is a set of tools that provides the basis of implementation of the marketing plan. The promotional tools provide the means by which an organization communicates with potential and existing customers about their products, services, distribution outlets and overall prices.

For many organizations, the marketing mix provides a basis for the organization to develop its marketing strategies, plans and tactics. They will take the marketing mix and develop a marketing strategy that will enable them to meet customer needs, be highly competitive both in terms of proactive and reactive competition and allow them to differentiate on brand, products and services and position themselves successfully against competitive equivalents.

The principal approach to marketing should be based around three key ingredients, i.e. integration, co-ordination and communication. This applies to the design and development of the marketing mix as well as every aspect of the planning process, with synergy and consistency as critical success factors to the overall implementation of the plan.

The marketing mix cannot be developed in a vacuum or in isolation of the other elements. For example, an organization cannot develop a quality, value-added product/service without due consideration to the cost of the product and how they can charge that to the customer. Organizations will then have to give due consideration to how they will distribute it. Then of course, how do they communicate with their customers to inform them of the existence of the new product or service?

For a truly marketing-oriented, customer-focused organization it is of primary importance to understand the impact of each element of the marketing mix upon customers and their perspectives of the organization.

In order to provide a clearer understanding of customer responses and reactions to the marketing mix, it is useful to consider the key components of the 7Cs model as shown in Figure 4.1.

| Organizational perspective of the marketing mix | | Customer perspective of the marketing mix |
|---|---|---|
| PRODUCT | = | CUSTOMER VALUE |
| PRICE | = | COST |
| PLACE | = | CONVENIENCE |
| PROMOTION | = | COMMUNICATION |
| PHYSICAL EVIDENCE | = | CONFIRMATION |
| PEOPLE | = | CONSIDERATION |
| PROCESS | = | CO-ORDINATION AND CONCERN |

*Figure 4.1* The 7Cs of the marketing mix

This model provides you with a framework of reference when identifying customer expectations of the organization's marketing mix. For example:

o The customer does not buy the product/service, but the value that the product/service provides
o The price of the product/service is not the customer issue, but how much it will cost them
o What is important to the customer is not the method of distribution, but the convenience of the product for purchase
o The customer perspective is not the promotion but how the messages are communicated to them
o The customer is not concerned with the surroundings or physical evidence, but wants confirmation of their assumptions
o Customers are not concerned with people involved in providing services, but that consideration is provided when purchasing
o Customers are not concerned with the process, but that efforts are co-ordinated to meet their requirements.

It might appear that the main focus of the 7Ps is very much on the services aspect of marketing, however, it is becoming extremely clear that more and more products and services are integral and reliant on one another. What is important is the 'customer experience' – this will require a co-ordinated approach to some or all of the marketing mix elements simultaneously and not in isolation.

# Profiling marketing segments for promotional activities

It has already been suggested that segmenting markets in relation to promotional activities can be a complex process. However, whatever the range of variables that the organization uses in order to establish target groups of customers, it is essential that they establish a clear understanding of the characteristics of the individuals within the group before ultimately defining their make-up.

> **Definition**
>
> **Profiling** – Profiling is the task of building up a fuller picture of the target segments (Dibb, Simkin, Pride and Ferrell, 2001).

Profiling is achieved by taking a group of what is commonly known as descriptors, based around traditional segmentation criteria, i.e. demographics, geographics and socio-economics of the target group, and seeking to understand how these descriptors match against the variables established to identify customer needs and wants. The idea is that while some of the customer base might have matching demographics, their socio-economics might differ and result in differing customer needs. It is essential that you profile customers in this way, to highlight as many similarities as possible, in order to maximize the potential impact of a fully co-ordinated marketing mix.

A good example of this would be the motor vehicle market. While most 30–45-year-olds possess a car, the needs associated with the car will differ significantly. Therefore in the context of promotional needs the targeting of cars in the upper range, such as high level specification Mercedes or BMWs, might require a different promotional mix to those who are looking for a low-cost family saloon. Typical profiling strategies will ensure that the differences between target groups are identified to maximize the potential of the promotional mix.

This then allows for very specific targeting in promotional terms, and allows the organization to define its approach on either a mass media basis, or indeed a concentration strategy or even a focus strategy approach to promotional activities.

# Push and pull strategy

Prior to moving on to look at the intricate detail of the promotional mix, and how the promotional tools are used to implement the marketing strategy, it is essential that you understand the nature of 'push and pull' strategies.

## Push strategy

This is where the manufacturer effectively takes the decision to concentrate their communications effort on the members of the distribution channel, i.e. the wholesaler and retailers. This means that the wholesalers may possess a significant amount of stock that they need to move on from a particular manufacturer and therefore they in turn promote the products to the end-user and customer.

The basis of this strategy is that the manufacturer is promoting directly to the suppliers, and the products are, therefore, pushed down the line by the different members of the channel. By the same token, the promotional activity is also pushed down the line in parallel with the product. In this instance it is highly unlikely that the manufacturer will therefore have any direct contact with the customer.

### Pull strategy

This strategy operates in contrast to the push strategy, in that it requires the manufacturer to create demand for the product through direct communication with the customers. From here it is likely that the retailers might identify and perceive the demand for this product and that it is essential in the interest of serving their customers. They might then demand the product from their supplier/wholesaler. This effectively sees the product being pulled up the line by consumer demand, i.e. the consumer is pulling it to market and being pulled by the manufacturer.

However, on this occasion it is likely that the promotion and communications activity will be working in the opposite direction from the product, and therefore the communication relates to pulling the product to market, effectively developing a strong consumer demand.

Of course, in reality, manufacturers will involve themselves in both push and pull situations, in order to assert as much influence as possible on the supply chain and the customer.

## Promotional operations and the planning framework

```
Corporate business objectives
            ↓
    Marketing objectives
            ↓
     Marketing strategy
            ↓
  Communications objectives
            ↓
   Communications strategy
            ↓
    Advertising objectives
            ↓
     Advertising strategy
         ↙       ↘
Creative objectives    Media objectives
      ↓                     ↓
Creative strategy      Media strategy
```

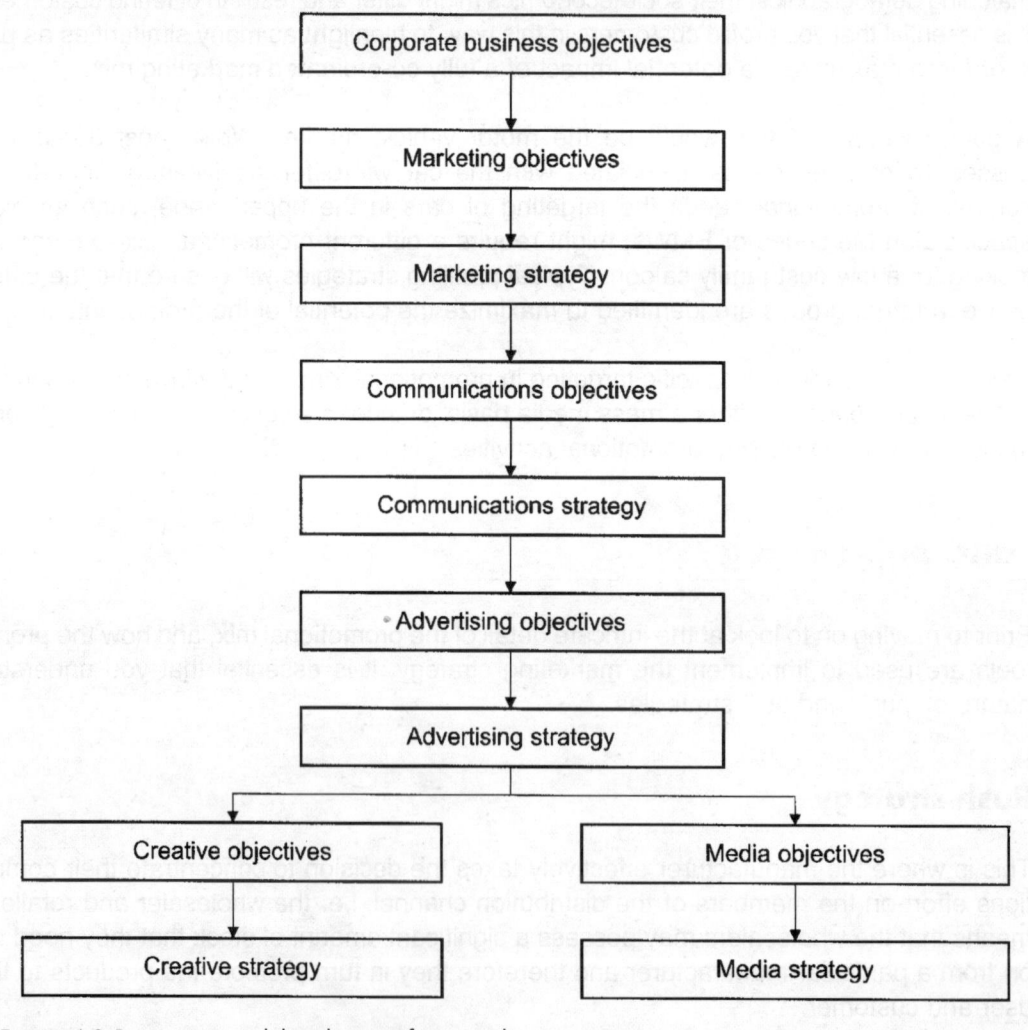

*Figure 4.2* Promotions and the planning framework

It is important to understand the role of promotional operations and the role it plays in terms of the implementation of the overall marketing strategy. Figure 4.2. provides an insight into where promotional operations will fit into the planning hierarchy.

# Aims and objectives of the promotional communications process

You will probably by now realize that the process of product adoption is a high level objective – for any component of the promotional activity and the promotional mix. Therefore it is essential that you translate this into five key communication effects:

| | |
|---|---|
| Category needs | The perception and understanding of the actual customer needs |
| Brand awareness | The ability of the consumer to identify and associate with a particular brand and differentiate from another brand |
| Brand attitude | This relates to the consumer's particular observations, view and perceptions of the brand – cognitive beliefs |
| Brand purchase intention | Once the category needs have been identified, the brand purchase intention follows |
| Purchase facilitation | The purchase activity needs to be facilitated by the organization, by ensuring that the product is available at the right price and the right place – this in essence is the manifestation of the co-ordinated marketing mix. |

These aims break down into a number of more specific promotional objectives that the promotional operations activity will seek to achieve in order to meet the corporate goals and marketing objectives and also to ensure successful implementation of the marketing strategy.

Possible communications objectives will therefore include:

- Clarification of customer needs
- Increasing brand awareness
- Increasing product knowledge
- Improving brand image
- Improving company image
- Increasing brand preference
- Stimulating search behaviour
- Increasing trial purchases
- Increasing repeat purchases
- Increasing word-of-mouth recommendation
- Improving financial position
- Increasing flexibility of the corporate image
- Increasing co-operation from the trade
- Enhancing the reputation with key stakeholders
- Building up management ego.

*Source*: Based on Delozier (1976)

Ultimately, any activities that you undertake as part of the promotional operations process will therefore be aiming to achieve one or more of the above promotional objectives, reflecting very much the nature of the key marketing objectives and strategy.

The critical success factors associated with achieving the aims of the promotional communications process relate to targeting specific customer groups through a clearly defined profiling process.

In the same way that short-term and long-term objectives are an issue within the marketing strategy framework, so are they in terms of promotional activity, as the promotional strategy will be shaped and determined by those objectives. However, it is likely that much of the promotional activity will be based on short-term activity, but in the context of the broader picture of the long-term achievement of goals.

You will realize from the above considerations that branding is an essential part of the strategy development process, both from a generic perspective but also from a promotional operations perspective, therefore understanding the strategic implications of branding and how to manage the brand is an essential component of your learning.

# Branding

*A successful brand is an identifiable product, service, person or place, augmented in such a way that the buyer or user perceives relevant, unique, sustainable added values, which match their needs most closely.* (De Chernatony and McDonald, 1998)

A brand is a highly powerful tool, because it provides a balance of functional benefits and performance values. The term 'brand' is used to describe the 'personality' of a particular company's products. The brand concerns use of design, colour, typography, the quality that brand portrays and the actual identity of a product or service as the customer sees it. The brand is not just a name, the brand is a multi-functional concept.

There are many well-known brands throughout the various segments that have built up reputations as providers of good quality produce or services. For example, Nokia, Coca-Cola, Nike, Reebok, BMW are all well-known brands of reputable quality.

Branding is of primary importance to the organization, as it provides the organization and its product portfolio with an identity, something that people can associate with. It is essentially the key to successfully differentiating the organization and its products from the competition. However, to develop a successful brand will require a considerable investment in both time and money, an investment, which if properly planned and managed, should reap significant rewards.

The brand plays a number of roles from an input perspective, output perspective and time perspective.

Brands are complex, but ultimately they rest in the minds of customers as a basis on which to identify with a product, quality and image that is portrayed (Table 4.1).

*Table 4.1* Different brand interpretations

| Input perspective | Output perspective | Time perspective |
| --- | --- | --- |
| Logo | Image | Evolving entity |
| Legal instrument | Relationship | |
| Company | | |
| Risk reducer | | |
| Positioning | | |
| Personality | | |
| Cluster of values | | |
| Vision | | |
| Value added | | |
| Identity | | |

*Source*: Adapted from De Chernatony (2001)

These points realistically need little explanation. However, it is essential that you are aware that the input perspective relates to everything that is put into the brand to actually make it a brand and, from the perspective of the organization, what are the inputs that make the brand successful. This means the way in which the brand is managed, i.e. the resources required to ensure that the brand is of significant value, both rationally and emotionally, to the customer.

From an external perspective, the brand will be perceived and interpreted by the customer: how it impacts upon the customer, motivates them, fulfils them and actually achieves some purpose for them.

'Time-based' is something of a radical component in branding. How long is a piece of string, some might say, but it is indeed an important factor. It may appear that some brands, such as Ford for example, might go on into perpetuity. However, this would be a complacent and dangerous strategy to follow; one with likely catastrophic results.

## Brand values

Brand values are often difficult to define. However, they represent KSF of the organization and its products. Rokeach (1973), in *The Nature of Human Values*, suggested that:

> *A value is an enduring belief that a specific mode of conduct or end-state of existence is personally or socially preferable to an opposite or converse mode of conduct or end-state existence.*

Values are essential in any organization, both from the internal perspective, where values will define the basis on which the organization does business, but also from the external perspective, where values essentially become meaningful and often the source of 'added value'. For example where quality is a value, quality is a perceived benefit to the customer.

Brand values, therefore, become the basis of an organization being perceived as different. However, while they might form the basis of differentiation, the organization must be clear as to why they arrived at these values in the first place, and what they might mean to the future vision of the business.

As a customer it is likely that you will be drawn to brands that hold values compatible to your own personal ones, and by the same token employees are often drawn to organizations that are associated with core principle values very much in line with their own.

Where are values formed? Values are formed as a result of a range of influences on each individual from childhood through to adulthood. Key influencers in our lives, parents, peers, and colleagues, form them. A value is a belief, something we believe in, see as important, and allow to shape and form our behaviour.

As a result of the key components that define values, organizations therefore are challenged to specifically develop values that are akin to their customer groups, their target markets, which makes the segmentation process all the more complex. However, not only is the segmentation process complex, but the expectations of the organization in the minds of the customers as a result of their brand values are highly demanding and need careful planning.

An excellent example of brand values is that of the Virgin brand. Richard Branson declared that the qualities associated with Virgin are:

- Quality
- Innovation
- Value for money
- Fun
- A sense of challenge.

These are more formally known as a cluster of values. These core values will, therefore, be at the core or heart of whatever Virgin do in the future. If they continue to extend the brand, as they have done on many occasions before, these values should continue to be the core of all of the businesses, not just exclusively one.

Branson used five values to demonstrate the ethos of his organization, five being an appropriate number and sufficiently challenging to deliver.

Many organizations develop brands for an external perspective and with the 'external' customer in mind. However, more and more organizations are moving towards making the brand values the focus point of the whole business, both for internal customers and external customers; actually making them a core rather than peripheral activity.

## Core and peripheral values

While developing and defining corporate values is an essential activity, there are two levels of values which a company can focus on.

*Core values* are those values that the brand will always uphold, regardless of the external drivers of change, which are here to stay. On the other hand *peripheral values* are those that are of secondary importance to the brand, and those that might change with market forces and conditions. Therefore, while quality might always be a core value, a peripheral value might be related to an activity or service level that the organization changes in line with market forces.

In essence, establishing brand values provides a robust basis for ascertaining appropriate behaviour on the part of the organization. Values contribute in part to the vision and mission of the organization and ultimately establish a culture based upon which the organization can do business, meet customer needs and actually make a difference to customer experiences and customer achievements.

## Brand loyalty

One of the benefits of defining corporate values is that there can be a brand association between the customer and the organization. This brand association can often be the basis of a long and loyal relationship. Brand loyalty is a hot topic in today's competitive environment, with significant pressure on brand switching to gain market share from competing organizations.

In achieving brand association the brand should be tightly targeted and assist customer achievement, so that brand loyalty and customer retention can be achieved.

Brand loyalty, brand preference and brand recognition are objectives of branding and form the structure and basis upon which brands are developed. However, in this context there is a significant difference between brand recognition and brand preference. Brand recognition is a measurement of customer awareness: the case study on Egg in Unit 1 or easyJet both make reference to the level of brand recognition.

The more important measures of success will indeed be brand loyalty and brand preference; they will form a very vital part of the brand planning process.

## Question 4.1

What are the long-term benefits of building brand loyalty?

## Brand planning

Planning in relation to brands is an essential activity, as it determines the future behaviour of the organization and provides a SMART basis on which the organization is to operate. Planning ensures delivery of brand values and the whole brand experience to the marketplace.

Typically there are long-term and short-term objectives relating to the brand, as with any other marketing activity. Long-term objectives are often perceived as being particularly stretching on the part of the organization, where they form part of the greater vision for the future. For example, back in the 1960s, IBM set themselves a brand objective of 'reshaping the computer industry' while Boeing set a long-term brand objective of launching a commercial jet aircraft, which they ultimately achieved through the launch of the Boeing 707, bringing jet travel to the commercial market.

Short-term objectives, however, relate to the more immediate future, whereby sub-sets of objectives need to be defined to underpin the longer-term vision. Therefore, they will relate to ways of achieving the long-term goals. For example, Boeing determined that they would:

- Be the airlines' first choice
- Show strong profitability and meet investors' expectations
- Have a global network and a global outlook
- Delight customers.

In many ways, brand planning will be quite a strategic role. However, it is useful for you to be aware of the implications of brand planning, as in a product management role or marketing management role, responsibility will lie with you in terms of the overall implementation of the plan and the tactical activities involved.

## Brand strategies

It is important at this early stage to examine closely the importance of brand naming strategies for naming products and services across the organization. The focal point for decision-making in relation to brands is on the emphasis an organization wishes to place on creating a 'distinctive' offering in the market against the weight it wishes to place on the origin of the product or service.

There are several options open to the organization, which we will now explore.

## Corporate brands

This is where organizations would use one corporate name across all products, for example organizations such as Heinz do this. Individual products carry a descriptive name under the corporate umbrella of the Heinz brand, for example Heinz Tomato Ketchup, Heinz Soups and, of course, Heinz Baked Beans. The linking of these products by the use of the name Heinz enables the organization to create a strong overall image, whilst at the same time potentially creating economies of scale in marketing communications and distribution. Clearly this is an advantage to organizations such as Heinz.

However, in their book *Strategic Marketing: Planning and Control*, Drummond, Ensor and Ashford (2003) suggest that there is a clear danger and on some occasions disadvantage in this approach in that if there is a problem with an individual product the reputation of all of these products may suffer. A clear example of this would be the Mercedes A Class, where back at the early stage of its launch it became known for a variety of problems relating to its stability on the road.

Other brand naming strategies include:

- *Multi-branding* – Manufacturers introduce a number of brands that all satisfy very similar product characteristics. For example, in the detergents market Procter and Gamble have several brands all fulfilling the same purpose. It also means that anyone trying to enter the market for the first time would have to launch several brands at once to compete. Again there are many advantages and disadvantages associated with this approach. For example, an advantage is that this approach allows for individual differentiation of the brand and also allows products to occupy different positions in the same market, i.e. premium and discount brands from the same company. However, this is countered by disadvantages.
Disadvantages for multi-branding include factors such as each brand requires a separate promotional budget in order to promote it and sell it effectively. However, a side point here is that, of course, these products are therefore dependent on the market containing enough potential to support more than one brand.
- *Company and individual brand* – Unilever used to practise a multi-brand approach with its washing powders but has been moving closer to the strategy of linking a company name to an individual brand name. Their products now have Lever Bros as a high profile endorsement on individual brands such as Persil and Surf.
The main advantage of this approach is that the product can clearly be supported by the reputation of an existing corporate brand while at the same time the individual characteristics of the specific offering can be emphasized. However, this is countered by two clear disadvantages.
First, the product failure has the potential to cause some damage to the company brand and secondly, the positioning of the company brand constrains decisions on quality and pricing of individual products.
- *Range brand* – Some organizations use different brand names for different ranges of products, in effect creating a family of products. Ford has done this to an extent, using Ford for its mass-market car range and Jaguar for the upmarket executive car range. Volvo, Ford's latest acquisition, has its own distinct brand values to appeal to a particular market segment and therefore will become another brand family for the Ford Group. Of course there are some advantages and disadvantages of this approach. For example, an advantage would be that the strength of the brand would be conveyed

across all of the products in the range and that promotional costs are spread across all of the products in the range also. However, this is countered by any new product failure damaging not just the discrete brand, but rather damaging the range; also positioning the brand constrains decisions on quality and pricing for individual products.
- *Private brand* – This is better known as the distributor's own brand. An organization may decide to supply private brands, in particular retail brands. In this case the private brand is owned and controlled by the distributor who will make decisions regarding the product's position in the market. The distributor is likely to use company or individual brands for its products. The advantages of this are that the promotional spend by the producer is quite small and this therefore enables them to concentrate on gaining cost efficiency through volume production. However, the downside is that marketing decisions then tend to be controlled by the distributor which can then remove the producer from direct contact with the market.

## Brand threats

Brands are no exception when it comes to threats from external forces, as attacking a brand, particularly a well-known brand, can reap rewards in terms of high levels of publicity, as in the case of British Airways and Virgin and indeed Camelot and Virgin. But it can also actually impact upon marketing share.

Typical threats therefore include:

- *Competition* – This component has just been covered. Brands do need to protect themselves against high levels of competitor threat. The key to success in overcoming brand threats is to ensure that the branding strategy relates to uniqueness, differentiation, robust corporate identity and strong core brand values.
- *Brand names* – The key threat here is the potential misuse or copying of brand names. Some organizations use brand names in order to heighten awareness of their brand, or to give it a comparable position with another brand. For example, Kleenex is a brand of paper handkerchiefs (i.e. paper tissues) in the UK, while in Iran, if you wish to purchase a box of tissues, it does not matter what the brand name is, tissues are known synonymously as 'Kleenex'. Therefore, in Iran, this has diluted the power of the actual Kleenex brand and its associated product.
- *Copyright* – A major infringement of intellectual property rights is the use of trademarks, designs and logos that have been legally protected against misuse and copy. If they are not legally protected, then other organizations can use them and benefit from them.

## Managing the brand

Branding is an absolute minefield; and is a subject in its own right. We have only touched upon some of the generic issues associated with branding. Branding is a core activity, a differentiating activity and one that enables the organization to establish a corporate identity and a vision based around clearly defined brand values.

To ensure that the brand is successful and there is synergy between the branding strategy and the remainder of the product, and the marketing mix, it is essential that the brand be carefully managed.

### Successful brands

> **Key points**
>
> **To create a successful brand a company must:**
>
> - Make quality a priority
> - Offer superior service
> - Get there first
> - Differentiate its brands
> - Develop a unique positioning concept
> - Support the brand
> - Deliver consistency.
>
> *Source*: Adapted from Dibb, Simkin, Pride and Ferrell (2001).
>
> These key points set the tone of the role of brand management, which is essentially based around building an effective brand that will ultimately support the corporate goals and marketing objectives.

The focus of any marketer's role is based upon creating an awareness of the brand and its associated values to the customer, monitoring consumer reactions and meeting their needs.

> **Study tip**
>
> Branding was an inherent theme in the December 2003 Marketing Planning Examination Paper. In Question 3A students were expected to differentiate between Corporate and Product Branding. Therefore it is important to understand the range of brand naming strategies and the advantages and disadvantages of a range of approaches.

## The promotional mix

The promotional mix will now be the heart of this unit, whereby we will be looking at how it is used in a direct way in order that the organization can communicate with its various target audiences.

### Tools of the promotional mix

The tools of the promotional mix are deliberately selected for their ability to attract customers, fulfil their desire for information and ultimately persuade them to adopt the products. In this unit, we will be looking specifically at advertising, sales promotions, public relations, direct and interactive marketing communications, sponsorship and personal selling.

Choosing the ultimate promotional mix is a complex task, that requires skill in creatively matching the profile of the customer and the target group with a promotional mix that will essentially attract them to the product. Of course the complexity of the exercise will differ based upon the market. Certainly from a B2B perspective, it is highly complex given the number of people involved in the decision-making process.

It has been suggested on a number of occasions that the key to success in implementing the ultimate promotional mix is understanding customers and their characteristics, something that is a consistent theme to implementation of communications and promotional objectives.

However, the success of any promotional campaign will impinge upon the co-ordinated approach to using the promotional mix.

## Co-ordinated marketing communications

Co-ordinated marketing communications is growing in impetus and importance in marketing today as more and more organizations realize the importance of taking a more structured, ordered and integrative approach to their marketing communications activities.

In the simplest form, it involves the integration and cohesion of all elements of the marketing mix. A campaign that is co-ordinated is planned, it is uniform in terms of its design, and it shares a Unique selling proposition (USP) and communicates the same message in a co-ordinated way. By combining more than one element of promotion, the message that is communicated is more powerful.

For example, Walkers Crisps have been involved in implementing a co-ordinated campaign. This has been both on TV and poster advertising. In addition to that, they are developing a consistent approach to advertising, using key personalities to identify with their products. As a result of this, Walker's market grew by 21 per cent, while the crisp market generally rose only by 11 per cent.

Customers require a variety of different communication and promotional activities to fulfil their need to know about products and services and then to purchase them. So while this course is predominantly about advertising, you must consider the need to integrate and co-ordinate all of your marketing and communications/promotional activities.

Communications plans can only be successfully developed if the key factors within the marketing plan are clearly defined, identified and developed.

According to Chris Fill, in his book *Integrated Marketing Communications* (1999):

> *Co-ordinated marketing communications cannot be achieved just by saying the same message through a variety of tools; the marketing mix is also a strong communicator.*

Co-ordinated communications are mostly likely to occur when organizations attempt to enter into a co-ordinated dialogue with their various internal and external audiences. The communications tools used in the dialogue and the message sent should be consistent with the organization's objectives and strategies.

Co-ordinated marketing communications often means different things to different people, but in the main the view is that it should embrace the marketing mix, the promotional mix, internal communications and all those who contribute to the overall marketing communications process. This means that PR, advertising, direct mail, trade promotions, consumer promotions, packaging, point-of-sale signage, brochures, literature, merchandise, websites and sponsorship all have their own individual role, but all achieve the corporate and marketing objectives for the brand.

There are a number of driving forces at work encouraging the growth in co-ordinated marketing communications. From the organizational perspective, there is the need for improved efficiency, rapid growth in global marketing, co-ordinated brand development and competitive advantage and the organization's drive to provide direction and purpose for the brand.

From the market-based perspective, drivers include better-educated audiences, cost of media and greater amounts of information – 'message clutter', competitor activities, growth in relationship marketing and the growth of networks, collaborations and alliances.

Communication-based drivers include technological advances such as the Internet, databases, new segmentation techniques, message effectiveness, more consistent brand images and the need to build brand reputations to provide clear identities.

As we move on it is essential that while you look at each element of the promotional mix in isolation, to understand its role in the promotional operations process, you should also look at ways of maximizing the mix potential by integrating it and aligning it with other promotional tools in order to optimize the marketing effort.

## Advertising

Advertising is one of the most influential forms of communication within the promotional mix, and the one that perhaps has the most impact upon our everyday lives. It does not matter where we go during a day, it is likely that we are bombarded either by radio, billboard, TV, cinema or by banner advertising on a regular basis.

### Definition

**Advertising** – Advertising is a paid form of non-formal communication that is transmitted through mass media such as television, radio, newspapers, magazines, direct mail, public transport vehicles, outdoor displays and the Internet.

It is likely that advertising will serve a number of purposes in terms of communicating with both individual and organizational customers. It is used to meet a number of specific marketing and promotional objectives as you have already seen, but its main emphasis is to inform, persuade and remind customers to purchase products and services.

Ideally advertising is used to promote products and services, but it is also a source that creates long-term images and perspectives of the organization. It is likely that there have been a number of adverts that stick in your mind, that have impacted upon you in a direct way, created an image and perception in your mind.

Take for example 'Orange Tango' – being 'Tangoed' became a way of life for young people for a long time as a result of the orange coloured man running around and slapping an unsuspecting person in the face. It is probably one of the most successful advertisements in achieving 'recall'.

## Advertising objectives

You will see later in this unit where advertising objectives actually come into play, and how they break down into different categories. Advertising objectives should be SMART in the same way that marketing objectives are SMART and they should relate directly to achieving the marketing objectives overall. It is therefore likely that advertising objectives will reflect some of the following components:

- Promoting product, organizations and services
- Stimulating demand for products
- *Competing* – offensive/defensive advertising
- *Increasing sales* – growth
- *Educating the market* – brand and product awareness
- *Increasing the use of product and services* – market development
- *Reminding and reinforcing* – market penetration
- Reducing fluctuations.

For example, a typical advertising objective could be to increase sales by 10 per cent from £500K to £550K by the end of June 2004. A further example, perhaps as in the case of Egg or easyJet, is to increase brand awareness from the existing 70 per cent to 100 per cent within 12 months to June 2005.

However, there is a fine line between advertising to create sales and advertising to create awareness and each of these will require a different approach in order to achieve the long-term goals of the organization.

It is quite clear that one of the key tools of the promotional mix to support the sale of products is advertising. This is particularly so for consumer-based products, where advertising serves to create an awareness of the product, its characteristics, its image and buying habits.

A good example to demonstrate how consumer-based products interact with advertising is chocolate. A low involvement, low unit-price bar of chocolate would not, of course, warrant an investment in personal selling to the millions of consumers who purchase it on a day-to-day basis. In this situation it is much more likely that the emphasis would be through some form of advertising, or even sponsorship through advertising. Sponsorship-based advertising is becoming increasingly common, with organizations such as Cadbury sponsoring the UK soap opera *Coronation Street*, for example.

It is critical that you understand the impact of advertising and the role it plays on the product, and the link between the advertising campaign and the different stages of the PLC. However, it is also important that first you understand the appropriate media and their characteristics and how they can be used.

## Question 4.2

Why is it important to define advertising objectives?

Unit 4 Promotional operations

# Advertising and the marketing mix

Advertising is used to support many elements of the marketing mix, but in most instances the product and brand are the key focus to advertising activities.

Advertising for both distribution and retailing is very much related to the 'push' and 'pull' strategies that we discussed earlier. In essence an organization at this stage may be developing a strategy related to increasing the number of outlets it has, e.g. a marketing objective may have been set to increase the number of retail outlets by 15 per cent within a 12-month period.

Advertising will be focused on encouraging retailers to stock their products. In this situation, advertising will be very closely linked to a high level of promotional activity to support the advertising and give an incentive for distribution outlets to stock their products.

A good example of this is electrical wholesalers, who are encouraged by organizations such as MK, Mitre and Crabtree to sell their products on to electrical retailers. They will therefore advertise in trade media and quite possibly offer incentives for wholesalers to carry stock.

A push strategy would often include a range of personal selling, trade (sales) promotions, advertising and direct marketing, in addition to public relations.

For a retail outlet, a pull strategy would be developed. The key to developing this is to create an awareness of the brand and its associated product and encourage customers to purchase from them.

Advertising on this occasion will take several forms, such as TV, radio, press advertising and possibly a big poster campaign. Clearly the level of advertising will be based on the budget available both through the manufacturer and the retailer.

Quite often in retailing situations some promotional support will be available from the manufacturer, such as various brochures, point-of-sale display materials and merchandising support. Again this is very relevant with the sale of electrical goods. Organizations such as Philips or Electrolux offer keen incentives to their retail outlets and distributors to sell their products.

As a marketing communications planner you will need to undertake the following activities in this area:

1. Liaise with channel members to ensure that stock is available
2. Be aware of the needs of the channel and how and when they need communications support
3. Provide consistency for all communications
4. Ensure that all members of the channel support and are empowered by the message the advertisement seeks to deliver.

## Repositioning through advertising

Taking a more strategic perspective, advertising can also be used to reposition a product and redefine it in the mind of the customer. Quite often this happens in response to competitive pressures and therefore both aggressive and defensive advertising is likely to be used in order to improve or at least sustain a competitive position.

Positioning is the definition of how and where the brand is going to compete: what particular virtues does the product possess, what are the benefits it offers and when can it best be used?

The most likely approach to this would be opening up new segments of the market to operate within, either based on a benefit usage or possibly geographical or demographic segments.

Ultimately, the brand repositioning will need to provide an even stronger point of differentiation for consumers. Advertising must represent how the brand is meant to fit into its market. It must represent the truth about the brand and offer benefits that are strong enough to encourage customers to buy.

### Advertising and its influence on price

The role of marketing communications is informing the target market about the price of a product or service offering. This can be undertaken through advertising in addition to the other elements of the promotional mix, e.g. personal selling, promotions, etc.

There will be many instances when buyers will be concerned with the price of their purchase. However, they may not consider the price in isolation, indeed you will most likely consider it in respect of the product, its size, shape, smell, colour and overall benefits.

Organizations must be aware that price can in fact inhibit purchase of products and services for many people and therefore a pricing strategy needs to be reflected in the communications undertaken by an organization. The customer/consumer has thus a clear understanding of the cost impact upon them.

Price issues will vary from product to product and target group to target group, but the prominence that price receives will depend upon a number of factors:

- Target group
- Level of involvement
- Attitude to risk
- Complexity and technical nature of the product/service
- The importance of price to the decision-making process.

Therefore with this in mind, the design of an advertisement and its emphasis on price will be based on the target audience, positioning of the product and the competitive position the product has in the marketplace.

### Question 4.3

In what way does advertising support the other elements of the promotional mix?

## Sales promotions

Sales promotions traditionally are complementary to advertising. They are used to reinforce and encourage customers to trial the product and then to purchase. Sales promotion provides a range of short-term tactical measures to induce sales of particular products or services. Its aim is to provide extra value to the product or service, creating the extra impetus to purchase products that we might not normally buy.

> **Definition**
>
> **Sales promotions** – A range of tactical marketing techniques designed within a strategic marketing framework to add value to a product or service in order to achieve specific sales and marketing objectives.

Sales promotion should be part of a planned approach and very much an integral part of the marketing communications planning framework. It should be planned and executed in parallel with associated advertising and possible public relations campaigns.

Marketers will therefore rely upon sales promotions to enhance the performance of other components of the promotional mix. Again this reinforces the nature of a 'co-ordinated marketing communications' approach to promotional activity.

The main aims and associated objectives of sales promotions are usually:

- To increase brand and product awareness – attracting new customers
- To increase trial and adoption of new and existing products
- To attract customers to switch brands and products from competing organizations
- To level out fluctuations in supply and demand
- To increase brand usage
- To increase customer loyalty
- To disseminate information
- To encourage trading up to the next size or the next range – particularly pertinent to the car market.

If you were to align this in respect of the hierarchy of objectives it might look like this:

| | |
|---|---|
| Marketing objective | To increase market penetration by 20 per cent |
| Advertising objective | To reinforce product and brand to existing customers |
| Sales promotion objective | To encourage repeat purchase of products and brand loyalty |

To achieve sales promotion objectives a number of promotional techniques must therefore be considered.

## Sales promotion techniques

There are a range of sales promotion techniques that can be used to achieve each of the above aims and objectives. Typical techniques in both sectors will include:

- Money-off vouchers/coupons
- Buy one get one free
- Customer loyalty bonus schemes
- Twin packs
- Bulk buying
- Discounts

- Try before you buy
- Cash rebates
- Trial-sized products
- Prize draws
- Competition codes
- Point-of-sale displays.

## Trade promotions

Earlier on we looked at the nature of the 'push and pull' promotional strategies, whereby manufacturers are looking to encourage their wholesalers and retailers to take their products and effectively 'take them to market'.

As a result of this process, trade promotions are often based around ensuring that product penetration is achieved. However, in order to achieve product penetration the incentive levels often have to be quite high, as product penetration is likely to be contrary to the typical 'volume stock traffic' aims of the wholesalers.

It is likely that manufacturers will encourage organizations to *increase their stock levels* in order to gain some level of commitment to increase sales potential in the marketplace, but also perhaps with the view of gaining some kind of supply chain relationship, with priority given to one particular supplier.

Alternatively, there is intensive competition for *increased shelf space* within retail outlets. The greater the incentive provided by the manufacturer, the more potential there is for greater shelf-space in the retail outlet. 'White goods' products are often at the heart of this scheme, with particular brands securing more floor space or shelf space than some of the lesser brands. There is the potential in this situation for a joint promotional activity between the manufacturer and perhaps the retailer to give incentives for a greater number of sales, from which both organizations will clearly benefit.

Good trade promotions, i.e. a good 'push strategy' highly incentivized, backed up by appropriate merchandising and appropriate advertising, may be advantageous. Alternatively, policies such as sale or return are also a good incentive and ultimately reduce the financial risk involved.

*Seasonal fluctuations* are often problematic to both manufacturers and suppliers, and therefore it might be that through a range of sales promotion activities incentives to buy the products outside the typical season could be achieved. The likely nature of these would be to involve the manufacturer in both the push and pull strategy context, in line with both consumer and trade promotions.

*Competitor response* sees sales promotion being used as a tactical weapon to dilute the impact of competitor activities. Therefore during the launch of a new competitor product, it might be that the focus of trade activity relates to creating high barriers to entry for the trade in order to sustain your market share in the wholesale community.

Specific methods might include:

- Allowances and discounts
- Volume allowances
- *Discount overriders* – based upon retrospective performance, e.g. on a quarterly or annual basis
- Free merchandise
- *Selling and marketing assistance* – cooperative advertising, merchandising allowances, market information, product training
- Sales contests
- Bonus payments.

## Retailer to consumer sales promotions

The key aims and objectives of this process will be to increase sales through a range of promotional techniques, as you can see below:

- *Increase in-store trade and customer traffic* – the use of coupons and money-off vouchers
- *Increase frequency of purchase* – discounted promotions for next purchase
- *Increase in-store loyalty* – through the use of storecards and rewards systems
- *Increase own brand sales* – encourage customers to purchase own brand products through a range of sale promotion incentives such as trial packs, in-store demonstrations, etc.
- *Achieve consistent demand* – reduce fluctuations, provide sales promotions in particular time bands to encourage a more consistent approach to shopping.

## Manufacturer to consumer sales promotions

This relates to the 'pull' strategy, whereby the manufacturers take responsibility for creating awareness and demand in order to pull products up through the supply chain to the customers.

Typical sales promotion activities might include:

- *Encouraging trial* – samples, gifts, trial drives of vehicles, allowing customers to decide for themselves
- *Disseminating information* – information packs on a door-to-door basis, perhaps closely linked with a direct marketing campaign (again utilizing the co-ordinated marketing communications approach)
- *Trading up* – encouraging customers to trade up from their existing models, a typical activity of car manufacturers and white goods manufacturers.

The list of promotional activities is endless, but the important issue from a promotional operations point of view is to ensure that demand for the products is continuously stimulated and is consistent with the marketing plan.

We will look at the impact of sales promotions on a B2B basis later in the text.

## Customer loyalty schemes

Ensuring that customer loyalty is achieved is a major focus of promotional activity (Table 4.2).

*Table 4.2* The 11Ps of loyalty marketing

| | | |
|---|---|---|
| 1. | Pricing | Be customer-specific |
| 2. | Purchases | Make product-specific offers |
| 3. | Point flexibility | Occasionally offer double points |
| 4. | Partners | Develop alliances with retailers |
| 5. | Prizes | Weekly draw for cardholders |
| 6. | Pro-bono | Allow customers to convert points to charity donations |
| 7. | Personalization | Direct mail, specifically targeted at the customer |
| 8. | Privileges | Invite cardholders to special events |
| 9. | Participation | Invite best customers to take part in new schemes |
| 10. | Pronto | Generate offers at point of sale |
| 11. | Proactive | Use information to predict/pre-empt customer behaviour |

As with advertising, a planned approach must be undertaken and programmes tightly managed. Therefore the typical planning process will include:

- Identification of the target market.
- Sales promotion objectives versus budget appropriation.
- Identification of both cost of communication for the sales promotion campaign, but also the actual cost of the campaign, i.e. the 'fulfilment cost' – the cost of actually hosting the campaign in terms of postage, free gifts, etc. – effectively the cost of the promotion to the organization. Obviously this should be looked at in association with the ultimate benefits in the longer term.
- Implementation – the same applies here as to the advertising programme, but clearly the promotion will probably run in parallel with the advertising programme, therefore issues relating to timescales, drip and burst style promotions, etc. will apply.

It is essential that whatever your promotional objectives are, the appropriate sales promotional activity is applied in the right context. Figure 4.3 highlights possible solutions to meeting PR objectives that might enable you to select the most appropriate method to meet your organizational needs.

| Objectives | Mechanics | Immediate free offers | Delayed free offers | Immediate price offers | Delayed price offers | Finance offers | Competitions | Games and draws | Charitable offers | Self-liquidators | Profit-making promotions |
|---|---|---|---|---|---|---|---|---|---|---|---|
| Increasing volume | | 9 | 7 | 9 | 7 | 5 | 1 | 3 | 5 | 2 | 1 |
| Increasing trial | | 9 | 7 | 9 | 2 | 9 | 2 | 7 | 7 | 2 | 1 |
| Increasing repeat purchase | | 2 | 9 | 2 | 9 | 5 | 3 | 2 | 7 | 3 | 3 |
| Increasing loyalty | | 1 | 9 | 0 | 7 | 3 | 3 | 1 | 7 | 3 | 3 |
| Widening usage | | 9 | 5 | 5 | 2 | 3 | 1 | 5 | 5 | 1 | 1 |
| Creating interest | | 3 | 3 | 3 | 2 | 2 | 5 | 9 | 8 | 8 | 8 |
| Creating awareness | | 3 | 3 | 3 | 1 | 1 | 5 | 9 | 8 | 8 | 8 |
| Deflecting attention from price | | 9 | 7 | 0 | 7 | 7 | 3 | 5 | 5 | 2 | 2 |
| Gaining intermediary support | | 9 | 5 | 9 | 5 | 9 | 3 | 7 | 5 | 1 | 1 |
| Gaining display | | 9 | 5 | 9 | 5 | 9 | 3 | 7 | 5 | 1 | 1 |

Each square is filled with a rating from 0 (not well matched) to 10 (very well matched). Use it as a ready reckoner for linking your objective to the mechanics available.

*Figure 4.3* Solutions to PR objectives
*Source*: Adapted from H.T Cummins (1990) in Worsam (2000)

## Question 4.4

What are the most likely sales promotion alternatives open to a manufacturer when trying to attract consumer attention?

## Question 4.5

How do you perceive that sales promotions add value to the process of advertising?

# Public relations

Publicity and public relations are often interrelated and seen as companions within the promotional mix. Indeed publicity is often deemed to be part of public relations activities and certainly seems to happen as a result of PR. However, let us be clear on the differences:

- *Publicity* – is information, news, communications in relation to the organization, transmitted through a range of different media.
- *Public relations* – is a planned and sustained effort to establish and maintain goodwill and mutual understanding between an organization and its target publics.

The role of public relations is to look after the nature and basis of the external relationships between the organization and all stakeholder groups. It is aimed at creating a sustainable corporate brand and an overall company image within the marketplace.

The definition of public is:

> *Any group with some common characteristics, with which an organization needs to communicate. Each public poses a different communication problem, as each has different information needs and requires a different kind of relationship with the organization, and may start with perceptions of what the organization stands for.* (Marston, 1979 as quoted in Brassington and Pettitt, 2000)

Public in the main consist of:

- Customer groups
- Local and central government
- The general public
- Financial institutions – investors/shareholders/borrowers
- *The media* – TV, press, radio (locally and nationally)
- Opinion leaders/formers
- *Internal marketplace* – employees, trade unions, employee relations bodies
- Potential employees.

## Aims and objectives of public relations

Typically PR aims and objectives will closely link to the following:

- To create and maintain the corporate and indeed brand image
- To enhance the position and standing of the organization in the eyes of the public
- To communicate the organization's ethos and philosophy, and corporate values
- To disseminate information to the public
- To undertake damage limitation activities to overcome poor publicity for the organization
- To raise the company profile and forge stronger, lasting, customer and supply chain relationships.

Public relations, as with all other elements of the marketing mix, requires a planned approach and plays an important role at a strategic level. It is also subject to strategic level objectives. For example, the launch of a new model by Mercedes Benz will be subject to a significant PR campaign running in parallel with significant advertising and direct marketing, perhaps on a local level by the local dealerships. Therefore PR becomes a high-level communications objective and it is critical that it is subject to the same intensity in respect of targeting specific groups of the public.

### Marketing versus corporate public relations

While publicity is a sub-set of PR, public relations is not a sub-set of marketing – although that is how it is often portrayed. Public relations is very important to marketing, but its role is far broader and of primary importance to corporate level activities in terms of marketing communications.

The public relations practitioner will often report directly to the board, probably to the chief executive officer and/or the chairman. He or she will be very concerned with corporate identity and will be establishing a corporate communications policy, which will include the equivalent of a positioning statement.

If this is the case, it must follow that marketing communications strategy is determined to a great degree by the public relations strategy. Here again is the influence of co-ordinated marketing communications. PR is a companion to virtually all elements of the marketing mix, and without the level of publicity raised through PR activities, many of the other promotional mix strategies may not be as successful.

From a marketing perspective, it will be used to meet marketing objectives and will support them by continually raising awareness, raising the profile and enhancing other marketing activities.

At a corporate level, PR is part of the long-term relationship-building strategy implemented by the organization to remain close to all components of the public. However, it does have a contingency use, with a short-term tactical benefit, in that it is used to respond to certain unpredictable or unexpected events, such as fatal accidents, disasters, etc. We will look at this a little later in the unit under 'crisis management'.

## Public relations and attitude change?

The whole basis of public relations is to continually reinforce a positive attitude towards the organization in the minds of the public, therefore for PR to be successful it has to change a range of negative attitudes into positive attitudes (see Figure 4.4).

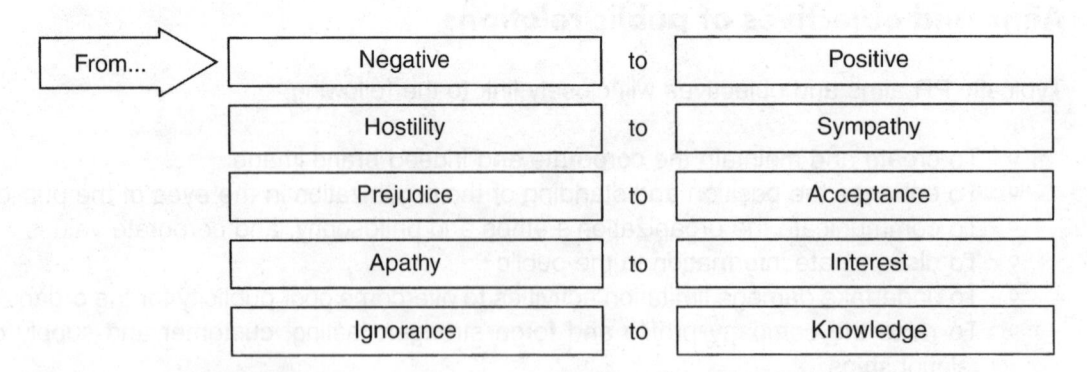

| From... | to | |
|---|---|---|
| Negative | to | Positive |
| Hostility | to | Sympathy |
| Prejudice | to | Acceptance |
| Apathy | to | Interest |
| Ignorance | to | Knowledge |

*Figure 4.4* Attitudinal change
Source: Adapted from Worsam (2000)

In order to undertake this level of attitudinal change you will require a clear and specific understanding of the nature and breakdown of the market in which you operate, both from a customer perspective and from a media perspective.

# Public relations techniques

It has already been identified that PR has two roles, one which is a long-term developmental role, and one that reflects the need to have contingency activities in place. From a marketing operations perspective, you need to understand when to use which particular public relations technique to optimize the level of 'positive publicity' the organization can deliver.

Typical techniques include:

- Press releases
- Press conferences
- Publications
- Advertising
- Media relations
- Events
- Annual reports
- Lobbying
- Internal PR.

During your studies for Marketing Communications, you will find that you learn much more about how these sources of information are used effectively in a co-ordinated communications mix.

## Internal PR

We looked at the importance of internal marketing in Unit 3, which highlighted the importance of developing a structured and meaningful communications process in order to win over the confidence of the workforce and gain support for strategy implementation and the associated change. Internal PR plays a vital role in respect of this communication and while they are part and parcel of the overall public, the workforce requires a more tailored and organizational approach.

The likely emphasis of internal PR will be based around keeping people informed, avoiding cloak-and-dagger style internal politics. Should a successful PR campaign be implemented internally, then motivation and attitude levels might appear to be more positive within the organization.

Particular techniques included in this area will relate to journals, newsletters and internal briefings.

It is likely that on some occasions internal PR will be based around 'crisis' style PR, perhaps announcing redundancies, changes in management structure, disaster, etc.

When selecting the appropriate public relations technique it is essential to ensure that you undertake an assessment of three criteria:

1. *Suitability* – It is vital to ensure that the techniques chosen are targeted and therefore appropriate to the target market, in respect of tone, content and style; that the appropriate medium is chosen, which again meets the profile requirements of the customer base; of primary importance will be the necessity to establish the level of influence and impact the actual technique will achieve.
2. *Feasibility* – As with any other promotional activity, PR will be restricted by a budget – therefore any activity or programme of activities will need to come within the required budget. Particular considerations will relate to resourcing the programme both

physically, financially and from a human resource perspective. Ultimately it is important to establish whether the programme is considered achievable and realistic.
3. *Acceptability* – Are the activities chosen acceptable to the organization as a whole, are they appropriate and in keeping with the corporate identity? An assessment of alternative sources of PR should also be undertaken to ascertain which is the most acceptable approach to achieving the desired level of publicity.

## Question 4.6

In what ways do public relations complement other elements of the promotional mix?

## Direct and interactive marketing

Direct and interactive marketing must be one of the most rapidly evolving and changing areas of marketing communications and promotional activities. Key driving forces of change relate to:

- Changing dynamics in demographics and lifestyles
- Increasing competition
- Customer power
- Fragmentation of the media
- Increasing costs of media
- Emerging distribution channels
- Changes in market information (EPOS, smart cards, etc.)
- New technologies.

One of the key drivers of growth is the massive movement in technologies, including the rise of databases, improving analytical systems, developments in phone technologies and the information superhighway.

Added to these, it would appear that in today's marketing environment organizations know more and more about their customers. Their profiling and research techniques are far more sophisticated, making direct marketing an excellent tool for very specifically targeted communication campaigns.

These drivers are the common denominator in almost all change strategies; therefore direct marketing is not an exception to the rule.

The use of direct marketing by an organization effectively demonstrates that the organization has taken a decision to avoid dependence on marketing channel intermediaries and has also decided to deal with customers in a highly targeted way. This of course has implications for the level of marketing and management information that a company may need to obtain and retain in the future.

Direct marketing has in the past been viewed as a very tactical approach to meeting marketing objectives, and like sales promotions and PR has been used as part of both an ongoing programme of marketing communications and promotional activities. However, in cases of emergency, i.e. in crisis or indeed in competitive response, direct marketing has proved to be a useful tool.

As a marketing tool, direct marketing evolved from the mail order business and now it is seen as another compatible element of the promotional mix that supports and underpins the marketing communications activity and can often be found conveying the good news of sales promotions.

However, over the years direct marketing has come under fire as 'junk mail' and has also been found to be the source of 'confusion marketing'. In addition to this, direct marketing has been subject to considerable change due to the Data Protection Act and therefore the introduction of issues such as permission-based marketing has had a tremendous impact upon the future shape of direct marketing.

### Definition

**Direct marketing** – An interactive system of marketing which uses one or more advertising media to effect a measurable response at any location (Institute of Direct Marketing).

While this is quite a broad definition, it does however, identify some of the key component characteristics of direct marketing. For example, it provides the basis of the relationship, which is defined as interactive, being a two-way relationship between the organization and the customer. At the customer's location this could be via phone, fax, e-mail, Internet, post, to name but a few. However, whatever the nature of the communications and wherever and whoever they go to, it is essential that as with every other form of the promotional mix, there is an underpinning and SMART set of quantifiable objectives.

## Objectives of direct marketing

Direct marketing performs a number of tasks, depending upon which element of the promotional mix it might work in parallel with and support.

The aims and objectives of direct marketing might include:

- Increasing direct mail order levels from new and existing customers
- *Dissemination of information* – provision of information to aid customer enquiries and support the adoption process
- *Generation of sales leads* – to increase the number of sales leads and ultimately influence a rise in sales income
- *Generation of trial leads* – to increase the number of customers willing to trial the product, to influence the process of adoption and influence a rise in sales income.

The aims and objectives of direct marketing can be achieved in a number of ways, and can often play a pivotal role in enhancing the selling process, by way of providing sales leads, that might directly result in a sale.

Furthermore, direct marketing objectives can be achieved through techniques such as direct mail, direct response advertising, telemarketing and the Internet, all of which are aimed at increasing sales leads and increasing sales turnover.

# Database marketing

For an organization to really optimize its effectiveness in relation to building and developing long-term customer relationships, it is essential that they secure as much relevant information as possible about their customers and retain it in a database system. This in turn provides an opportunity to create closely defined profiles in order that a tightly defined targeting exercise can take place.

> *Database marketing is the application of digital information collected about current and/or potential customers and their buying behaviour to improve marketing performance by formulating a strategy and building personalized relationships with customers.* (Chaffey, Mayer, Johnston and Ellis-Chadwick, 2000)

As information technology plays such a tremendous role in day-to-day business operations, it is increasingly likely that databases will be built to collect information from customers accessing websites. Databases are essentially known as the 'brains' behind the website, which enables a high level of customer profiling and personalization to take place.

Typical consumer information for database building might include:

- Name
- Address
- Occupation
- Geo-demographic profile
- Psychographics profile
- Previous contacts
- Previous responses
- Frequency of purchase
- Purchases made
- Value of purchases
- Type of purchases
- Media responsiveness
- Promotional responsiveness.

*Source*: Dibb, Simkin, Pride and Ferrell (2001).

However, many underpinning database systems have failed as yet to achieve the level of sophistication required in developing appropriate data-mining opportunities. In addition, unless the site is a transaction-based website, i.e. where customers actually carry out a transaction online, it can be difficult to glean sufficient information about the customers to develop the typical profile basis you might prefer.

A further consideration in database marketing currently is that where databases are highly sophisticated, organizations do not understand how to use the information and put it through the data-mining process.

One of the key benefits of a good database, whether it be based on information gleaned from websites or through other sources, is that it forms the basis of the relationship and how it might be maintained in the future. While databases aid relationship management, database marketing does not constitute relationship marketing, in fact it only provides the means by which the relationship might be maintained.

# Direct marketing techniques

Direct marketing provides significant scope for communicating directly with customers, and can cut across just about any promotional activity as part of the co-ordinated marketing communications activity, and is not used exclusively for the consumer (B2C) market. It is also used very much in the business (B2B) market. However, it has been a central component of marketing strategies in the consumer market for years.

## Direct mail

Direct mail has probably been the most used form of direct marketing over the years, but it is probably the one subject to the most abuse.

Direct mail is widely used in both consumer and business/organizational markets to target customer groups directly. The financial services sector is a classic example of the use of direct mail. Even with the Data Protection Act, it is likely that some households receive as much as one piece of direct mail per day, in relation to mortgages, pensions, insurance, offers of credit cards, to name but a few.

There are many advantages associated with using direct mail, such as targeting. Targeted campaigns can include working on a basis of either geographic segmentation or geo-demographic segmentation. This level of segmentation combined with the level of knowledge that exists in relation to market segments means that targeting can become a very exact science.

Other advantages include:

| | |
|---|---|
| Personalization | Being able to personalize direct mail where appropriate |
| Response rates | If targeting is exact and appropriate to customer needs, response rates can be quite high. However, if targeting is not tight, there can be as little as 5 per cent response |
| Flexibility | Levels of flexibility available in direct marketing can provide much scope for an interesting and creative campaign. It allows for phased postage, delayed mailing, inserts, different size and frequency, to name but a few benefits associated with flexibility |

However, when developing a direct mailing, you must ensure that the information you have is accurate, that customer groups are profiled and then targeted specifically and that the content matches the needs, wants and expectations of the group. This process will be assisted through the database marketing process, and ultimately the information collected will provide a greater insight into the customers and their buying behaviour. The mailing will only be as good as the marketing research information that underpins it.

When purchasing a list externally, it is essential that you ensure the list provides you with relevant and up-to-date information, and is inside the data protection limits, defined in the Data Protection Act.

There are a number of organizations now that specialize in the development of appropriate automated mailing lists:

- *Dun and Bradstreet* – they offer 48 list options
- *Wyvern Direct Response* – based around occupational groups such as accountancy, medical practitioners, hospital contacts
- *Wise and Lovey* – website address http://www.mailing-labels.com

It is expected that more and more online automated mailing lists will become available to keep abreast of the changes in technology and the direct marketing sector.

On a less positive note, when looking at the effectiveness of direct mail, consider these facts. In 1997 over 3.7 billion pieces of mail were sent out, and over 100 million were marked 'return to sender', with another 80 million so badly addressed that they were unable to be delivered.

It is essential that, for any list you are purchasing, very clear criteria have been developed in relation to:

- Relevance of the list in relation to the target market
- The source and ownership of the list
- The level of detail in the list
- Frequency of updates
- Whether the list is of enquirers, purchasers or respondents
- Frequency of purchase
- Level of accuracy.

## Direct response advertising

This is another form of direct marketing and appears in the standard broadcast and standard print media.

Principally it is different from other forms of advertising, as it actually demands a response, by giving a website address, telephone number, or a coupon for a personal visit. This is becoming a popular approach in direct marketing and is growing continually as advertisers try to gain greater value from their advertising experience.

The targeting for direct response advertising is probably a little less scientific than direct mail, and relies much more on an assessment of the average reader or viewer profile than a prepared mailing list. However, the information collected can be used as a database for other forms of direct marketing in the future.

More and more organizations are involving themselves in direct response advertising in order to optimize their expenditure in advertising.

# Telemarketing

We have touched upon the issue of personalization, and how through the use of database marketing we can glean enough information to personalize organizational approaches to customers. However, the difference between telemarketing and other methods of direct marketing is that it is truly a personal approach, whereby there is a direct personal contact, which provides the basis for an interactive relationship between the organization and the customer.

While the personal approach is preferred and is seen as a way of getting closer to the customer, customers can find this approach rather intrusive and are somewhat resistant to embracing deeper and more meaningful relationships with organizations that they might purchase from.

Telemarketing, like other components of direct marketing, should be a planned, highly targeted and controlled activity that will both create and exploit a direct relationship between customer and seller using the telephone.

Telemarketing provides the organization with significant scope as telephone rental and ownership is very high, with over 80 per cent of households possessing them across the European Union. The telephone is a particularly powerful communications tool, which gives you direct access to new and existing customers in a flexible environment, i.e. wherever they are.

Telemarketing also provides the scope to be used for customer service initiatives and customer satisfaction surveys, as well as the basis for developing the existing customer relationship overall.

## The scope of telemarketing

- To generate sales leads
- To screen leads prior to following-up
- To arrange appointments for sales representatives
- To direct sales
- To encourage cross/upward selling
- To provide dealer support
- To manage and service accounts
- To undertake market research
- To undertake test marketing.

*Source*: Brassington and Pettitt, 2000.

As regards promotional and marketing operations, it is clear that telemarketing plays a pivotal role in:

- Increasing sales levels
- Supporting customers
- Increasing levels of customer service
- Providing technical support
- Information gathering
- Credit control.

One of the key disadvantages of telemarketing is the cost. It is a costly exercise, where few economies of scale can be charged. However, many financial services organizations are given very tough limits in terms of varying sorts of telemarketing in order that economies are achieved, but unfortunately this can be to the detriment of the long-term relationship with the customer.

A key factor of telemarketing as a direct marketing tool is that volume is rather limited in comparison with other direct marketing techniques. While a typical telemarketing representative might make between 30 and 60 calls per day, an equivalent piece of direct mail could actually achieve a significantly greater proportion of contacts.

Telemarketing, while having many qualities, is probably one of the least effective direct marketing mechanisms. It is certainly one of the least cost-effective, it is personally intrusive and does not achieve the necessary volume of hits on a day-to-day basis.

## Case history

### 46 000 Oregonians subscribe to 'No Call' list to stop unwanted telemarketing calls

The Oregon No Call list makes it easier for consumers to prevent unwanted telephone call solicitations to their homes. After consumers add their telephone number to the list, their privacy is protected and the responsibility rests with telemarketers to leave them alone.

The No Call list was created as a response to the Senate Bill 915, passed in the USA in 1999. The list is also designed to address the growing problem of telemarketing fraud, which costs the US consumers some $40 billion annually.

No phone call – no fraud! The list gives consumers a way to fight back and regain control of their telephone privacy.

*Source*: Lexis-Nexis.

## Question 4.7

How can direct marketing complement advertising and sales promotions?

# Sponsorship

> *Sponsorship is the provision of financial or material support by a company for some independent activity ... not usually directly linked to the company's normal business, but support from which the sponsoring company would hope to benefit.* (Wilmhurst, 1999)

Sponsorship is a two-way mutually beneficial partnership between an activity being sponsored and the sponsoring organization. It works on the premise that association largely affects image and that the sponsor may exchange money and/or goods or services in kind in return for the association that sponsorship provides.

### Sponsorship objectives

Typical sponsorship objectives may include:

- Increasing brand awareness
- Building and enhancing corporate image
- Raising awareness of brands related to products restricted in advertising through various legislation, such as alcohol and cigarettes.

There are two perspectives to consider in sponsorship, the perspective of the organization being sponsored and that of the sponsor. Both parties will need to consider if the alliance created as a sponsorship arrangement is one that is required by the existing image of the organization and will enhance overall organizational credibility. They will also need to consider how relevant the association would be between the two parties and how both will benefit. The sponsor will need to consider what exposure will be gained as a result of the sponsorship and how similar or dissimilar the target audiences are to their own.

## Types of sponsorship

The main types of sponsorship include the following:

- *Programme sponsorship* – for example, *Inspector Morse*, Beamish Stout. Typically this is used at the start of a TV programme, during the interval and at the end. The cinema and major films often form the basis of sponsorship alliances. There has been a massive boom in TV sponsorship and the opportunity is providing broadcasters with a valuable new revenue stream as money from spot advertisers is no longer as plentiful.
  A decade ago broadcast sponsorship was worth £1 million in the UK. In 2001 it was worth in the region of £85 million, with TV sponsorship increasing by as much as 25 per cent in the first quarter of 2001. (*Source*: lexis.nexis.com)
- *Arts/sports sponsorship* – for example the Carling Premiership. Carling sponsor the Premier Football League in England. Events sponsorship is expensive but can be very high profile and potentially the most cost-effective way of getting increased brand awareness.
- *Sponsorship of other events* – for example exhibitions, festivals and opening ceremonies. These are again high profile, and are sometimes very useful forms of sponsorship for smaller businesses that wish to raise their profile locally.
- *Sponsorship of individuals or teams* – Mercedes Benz sponsor the British tennis player Tim Henman and Siemens sponsor Formula One motor racing.

## Role of sponsorship

Sponsorship can provide a more cost-effective means of reaching your target audience, but the design, content and message are much more controlled. From a corporate perspective and PR perspective, sponsorship raises the profile of the organization and its corporate values, and in some instances can really bring the brand name and corporate image to centre stage.

Advertisers are being drawn in by the opportunity to convey their brand values by clever association with programming that is in keeping with their product and the desired company image.

Many organizations succeed in ensuring that as part of the sponsorship deal their name is an integral part of the overall event, for example the 'Benson and Hedges Cup'.

However, while sponsorship may appear to be a good idea, it is essential that, like all other elements of the promotional mix, it clearly fits a need and will enhance the possibilities of directly achieving predetermined marketing objectives.

Sponsorship offers vast opportunities for the organization in terms of the value-added perspective of merchandising, public relations activities, improved stakeholder relationships, and highlighted ethical and social values. The benefits are quite considerable.

Unit 4 Promotional operations

However, a number of key factors should be considered prior to taking the decision to proceed with sponsorship arrangements:

- What *relevance* does the particular sponsorship arrangement have in terms of the match between the two organizations and the potential target audience? For example, it is clear that when Carling Black Label sponsor sports events it will bring in additional sales of both drinks and cigarettes, both during and after the event, as support for sport is effectively linked to both of these habits.
- *The period of impact* – How long before and after the event will the sponsorship profile last for? Is the event a one-off or a sequence of events?
- *The uniqueness of the sponsorship agreement* – From a competitive perspective it will be essential that the agreement with the sponsored individual or organization allows the brand, market and competitive position to be differentiated in a unique way. In some situations this level of expectation is not achievable, but if the fit of the organization and the sponsorship deal is good, then high profile sponsorship might be achieved.
- *The level of spin-off promotions is also essential* – For example, the importance of a co-ordinated approach between other elements of the promotional mix will be essential to maximize and optimize cost-effectiveness of particular high profile events. Here advertising, merchandising and promotional incentives may be a particular match for the promotional mix.

Therefore, for successful implementation of a sponsorship strategy, it is necessary to clearly define the position of sponsorship and ensure that it is fully representative of corporate and marketing communications goals and effectively integrates sponsorship with other elements of the promotional and marketing mix.

## Marketing through sport

The European Sponsorship Association (ESA) is the voice of the sponsorship industry across Europe. It was formed in 2003 from the ISS and the European Sponsorship Consultants Association (ESCA). It is made up of the leading sponsors, consultants, rights holders, suppliers and professional bodies working within the sponsorship industry. ESA provides information and expertise on all types of sponsorship activity including sport, broadcast, the arts, music, environmental and charity.

European Sponsorship Association is committed to developing all aspects of the sponsorship industry. The ESA advises the EU in Brussels on matters relating to sponsorship and works very closely with the EU on a number of legislative issues. Training and education programmes, sponsorship seminars and conferences are all key areas which have been developed over the years. The ESA Annual Congress is attended by the leading practitioners and professionals within the industry and is recognized as the leading Congress in its field.

Social and networking opportunities are also key elements of ESA's work. The association also works closely with educational establishments developing career programmes and professional qualifications. If you would like to find out more about ESA and the opportunities to join the association, please turn to the 'Membership' section. Cussons Imperial Leather won the 3rd ESA European Sponsorship Award, which recognizes the outstanding sponsorship programmes in Europe by inviting the winners of leading national sponsorship awards to compete at a European level. This year's award was endorsed by MEP Viviane Reding, European Commissioner for Education and Culture.

The 130 delegates at the ESA Congress heard presentations from the four award finalists from Ireland (AIB Grassroots sponsorship), Netherlands (Eiffel Basketball Programme), Sweden (Assa Abloy in the Volvo Ocean Race) and the UK (Imperial Leather).

Imperial Leather's Commonwealth Games sponsorship campaign qualified for the finals by winning the Hollis Sponsorship Awards for Outstanding Sponsorship of the Year and the UK Sports Industry Sponsorship Award.

The decision was made by Congress delegates voting and a panel of sponsorship experts, headed by the ESA Vice Chairman, Helen Day who commented: 'Cussons Imperial Leather's campaign showed excellent use of different marketing disciplines to fully exploit a sponsorship opportunity. The planning and execution which went into the campaign was outstanding as indeed it needed to be in order to dominate in the way they did in a multi sponsored event such as the Commonwealth Games.'

http://www.europeansponsorship.org/pressDetail.asp?id=3

Check out the following website – http://www.europeansponsorship.org.

## Personal selling

In the context of promotional operations it is important that you have a clear overview of how the personal selling process can both be compatible with other elements of the marketing mix and also enhance the effectiveness of the marketing mix.

Personal selling is one of the biggest sectors of business within the UK, with UK organizations employing some 766 000 sales professionals, yet it can appear to be one of the most disorganized and disjointed components of the marketing mix.

### Definition

**Personal selling** – An interpersonal communication tool which involves face-to-face activities undertaken by individuals, often representing an organization, in order to inform, persuade or remind an individual or group to take appropriate action, as required by the sponsor's representative.

When preparing a marketing communications plan, the role of the sales department will usually include some form of personal selling objectives. Particular emphasis will include an analysis of the specific responsibilities associated with personal selling, the role of personal selling overall and how it will influence and enhance other elements of the marketing mix.

It is a known fact that personal selling is the most expensive element of the marketing mix. It is resource intensive, time ineffective, contributing little or no economies of scale, with high contact costs and customer maintenance costs. However, it is probably one of the most effective methods of influencing decision-makers to the stage of adoption. At a strategic level the balance of personal selling versus other more cost-effective methods of the marketing mix must be considered in order that the target market receives the most relevant approach to meet its information-based needs.

Sales force activity will be subject to a number of associated sales objectives that will directly relate back to the marketing objectives, and will be predetermined in order that the organization can optimize and maximize the potential impact of the personal selling team in association with other promotional activities.

## Sales force objectives

Sales force objectives will not all relate directly to increasing income. They may also relate to cost saving, customer relationship management and developing new leads.

Therefore typical sales objectives could be:

- To increase sales turnover by 20 per cent within a 12-month period
- To reduce the number of clients with minimum viable order levels at the end of a 12-month period
- To reduce the cost of sales by 10 per cent within a 6-month period
- To increase the number of distribution outlets by 15 per cent in a 12-month period.

Often personal selling goals are misunderstood and are assumed to be about an increase in sales, where actually personal selling goals will be about increases in overall revenue and profitability. Profitability might be improved by an increase in minimum order levels in order to achieve economies of scale.

Personal selling is a vital role within the organization, but it underpins a range of other promotional activities that it can only achieve through the appropriate level of sales and marketing support and with the appropriate tools of the trade.

It is essential from a marketing and promotional operations perspective that the sales team is kept briefed of any changes to the product portfolio, services mix or any essential information that might either enhance or inhibit sales team performance. As a marketer you therefore have a responsibility to support the sales team in a range of ways in order that they can open and close a sale effectively and efficiently.

- *Provision of market information to support the selling process* – customer and competitor intelligence
- Provision of potential leads from the market scanning process
- *Client history* – database information about purchasing behaviour, purchasing trends, frequency and value of orders
- *Financial reports* – Dun and Bradstreet reports, annual reports, etc.
- Provision of a range of appropriate promotional materials that include company history, product portfolio, services mix, financial package, support packages, etc.
- *Sales aids* – product samples, service packages, demonstration equipment
- Provision of promotional plans in order that sales staff can co-ordinate their call plans in line with particular promotional initiatives
- The provision of promotional incentives, merchandising, etc.

## Summary

One of the key objectives of any promotional operational programme will be to ensure that, ultimately, potential customers adopt the product offering and are converted to the brand, in a way that can establish long and loyal relationships in years to come.

One of the critical success factors of implementing the promotional operations plan will be the degree of synergy and integration that exists between each of the promotional mix elements. It is clear that the mix elements are indeed complementary. Some are more effective and efficient in terms of targeting volumes, while others have a key strength in developing customer relationships in the long term. Ultimately the key success factor for any promotional mix will be its ability to meet the marketing objectives and bridge the successful implementation of the marketing strategy. Promotional planning in complete isolation of the marketing plan could be untargeted and a waste of valuable resources.

At an operational level you are likely to be involved in the development and implementation of promotional plans. Therefore you will need to clearly identify the direct objectives, relate them back at all times to the marketing plan, and undertake a co-ordinated approach to promotional mix tools. When studying for Marketing Communications, much of this will be presented in more detail and will focus you on the finer details of developing a co-ordinated marketing communications mix.

## Extending knowledge

### Recommended reading

For this unit a more in-depth approach is found in Chapters 15–17 of *Marketing: Concepts and Strategies*, 4th European edition by Dibb, Simkin, Pride and Ferrell, 2001.

In addition to this, you should be looking at Mad.com or purchasing *Marketing and Marketing Week* in order to keep abreast of various promotional mix activities.

## Bibliography

Brassington, F. and Pettitt, S. (2000) *Principles of Marketing*, Thomson Higher Education.

Chaffey, D., Mayer, R., Johnston, K. and Ellis-Chadwick, F.E. (2000) *Internet Marketing*, Prentice Hall.

De Chernatony, L. (2001) *From Brand Vision to Brand Evaluation*, Butterworth-Heinemann.

De Chernatony, L. and McDonald, M. (1998) *Creating Powerful Brands*, Butterworth-Heinemann.

Delozier, M.W. (1976) *The Marketing Communications Process*, McGraw-Hill.

Dibb, S., Simkin, L., Pride, W. and Ferrell, O. (2001) *Marketing: Concepts and Strategies*, 4th European edition, Houghton Mifflin.

Drummond, G., Ensor, J. and Ashford, R. (2003) *Strategic Marketing: Planning and Control*, Butterworth-Heinemann.

Fill, C. (1999) *Integrated Marketing Communications*, Butterworth-Heinemann.

Fill, C. (2003) *Marketing Communications*, Butterworth-Heinemann.

Rokeach, M. (1973) *The Nature of Human Values*, Macmillan.

Wilmhurst, J. (1999) *The Fundamentals of Advertising*, 2nd edition, Butterworth-Heinemann.

Worsam, M. (2000) *Marketing Operations*, Butterworth-Heinemann.

---

In addition to looking at some sample exam questions and answers for the Marketing Planning module at the end of this book, undertake Question 3 parts (a) and (b) from the December 2003 paper, as well as referring again to the mini-case study in the June 2004 paper, in particular Question 1(b).

# unit 5
# product operations

## Learning objectives

This unit will be focusing on the role of the product in implementing the marketing plan and will therefore focus on product operations. The learning outcomes associated with this unit are:

- Explain how a product or service portfolio is developed to achieve marketing objectives

- Explain the new product development process (including innovative, replacement, re-launch and imitative products) and the role of innovation.

Syllabus reference: 3.5, 3.6

## Product operations

While the basis of this unit will reflect product operations, it is in line with the syllabus that you are reminded of the nature and purpose of the product, its components and the PLC. You may have already studied for Marketing Fundamentals, where you will have covered some of the basics of the product; however, this is a useful form of revision and will also look at some additional elements of the product.

The product is the core of the marketing mix and is the basis of meeting customer needs and wants with the benefits and features that the product might offer them. From an operational perspective, should the product fail to live up to expectations then ultimately its failure will impact upon the achievement of the marketing objectives and will likely weaken any competitive strength that the organization might possess.

The product poses enormous challenges to many organizations and in turn the marketing function. The product is at the centre of the decision-making process and ultimately the adoption and exchange process that essentially links the organization and its customers together. The product is the component that gives the customer the benefits and possibly experience they have been looking for.

A product is a tangible item purchased by a customer and designed to meet their needs and wants. However, while the customer does purchase a product, what they are actually purchasing is the *benefits* that the product has on offer.

Primarily, the product is the acid test of whether or not the organization fully understands the nature and disposition of the customer and their actual needs and wants.

## Unit 5 Product operations

At this point it is advisable to ensure that the differences between products and services are clearly understood, as services will form the subject of another unit in this book.

> **Definition**
>
> **Product** – A product is a physical good, service, idea, person or place that is capable of offering tangible and intangible attributes that individuals or organizations regard as so necessary, worthwhile or satisfying that they are prepared to exchange money, patronage or some other unit of value in order to acquire it.

A service is an intangible item. When you buy a service, it differs from a product in that it does not result in the physical possession of anything. Essentially you purchase an experience, something that is not consistent and cannot be reused or taken away.

As marketers, what we need to do is to market these benefits to the customer, as the purchase of benefits is critical to the customer experience. Products are described as having three characteristics:

1. Physical
2. Functional
3. Psychological.

Physical characteristics such as shape, size, colour, etc. can change according to the function of the product. For example a hairdryer could be black with a curved handle, difficult to hold. A functional characteristic could be the speed at which the dryer works and the number of varying heat settings it has.

The psychological characteristics are unique. This is concerned with the customers' values and expectations relating to the product or service. If the hairdryer provides a professional finish to your hair and you feel good about yourself then you are likely to be pleased with all of the three key features. If it gives you a good style from drying, but it is difficult to hold then it might have a psychological effect, in that you may not wish to purchase another one.

Benefits are key to the success or failure of a product and to assist you in understanding how the product evolves, you need to realize that the product can be broken down into smaller elements (see Figure 5.1).

Potential product

Augmented product
(the extended product)

Tangible product
(the actual product)

Core Product

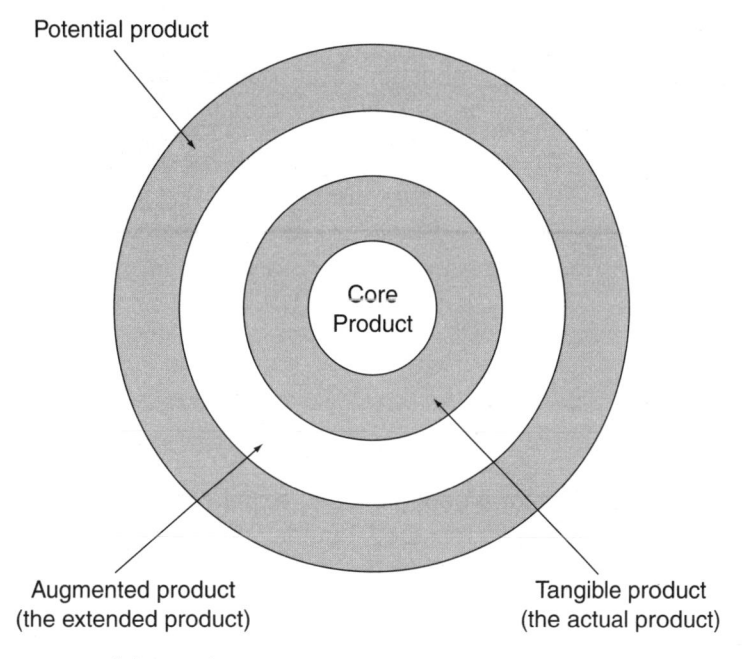

*Figure 5.1* The anatomy of the product

The *core* is as it sounds the centre or heart of the product. The core product provides a very basic function. It is usually seen as the no-frills version of the product; it should deliver the desired benefits effectively. The core product then provides the basis for the next level.

The *tangible/actual* product relates to making the product a reality. The product becomes a real product, with real characteristics and benefits that can then be communicated to the customer to encourage purchase.

The *augmented* product is the core/tangible product with a number of add-on extras which makes the product more marketable and enables organizations to be competitive. These extras do not directly affect the workings of the product as it can exist without them, but they add value to the product in the long term. For example, a car with leather seats: it does not matter whether or not the seats are fabric or leather, what is important is that you can sit on them to drive. The third level is the *potential* product. This means that the company must be responsive to the marketplace and to the change that continues to take place within it, and therefore the organization and the marketer will need to consider what the potential product will be like in the future. The car market is a classic example of this. No sooner have they launched a new model than they are working on the launch of the replacement product. The continuing future development of the product is a strategic issue and will be reflected in the overall strategic direction of the organization.

## Question 5.1

Using the concept of the model in Figure 5.1, explain how BMW might build from the core product through to the augmented products.

## Product classifications

Part of your role as a marketing manager at an operational level will be to categorize the products manufactured by your organization so that you can ascertain issues relating to features, benefits and functions. Then you can contribute to the development of an appropriate integrated promotional mix.

There are three categories:

1. Durable
2. Non-durable
3. Service product.

### Durable
Products that are durable last for a period of time, e.g. a car, stereo system, washing machine, etc. Eventually they will have to be replaced, but they do have a steady life cycle appropriate to the product.

### Non-durable
Non-durable products are different in that they can only be used a small number of times, or even only once. They do not have a durable lifespan, e.g. food, drinks, printing paper, disposable contact lenses or disposable nappies. Many of these products are known as FMCGs – fast-moving consumer goods.

### Service products
Services are intangible – you have nothing physical at the end of the service experience, e.g. holidays, hairdressing, personal banking/financial services.

These three classifications then break down into smaller groups as follows:

- *Convenience products* – These are frequently purchased products, such as food, drinks, petrol, etc.
- *Shopping goods* – These goods are those that customers will shop around for, comparing and contrasting value in terms of benefits versus brand and price.
- *Speciality products* – These possess unique characteristics that customer/consumers will look for. The likelihood is that they will have very specific ideas and expectations of the products and alternatives would not be considered as appropriate. There will also be much emphasis on the brand, e.g. cars – Porsche, clothes – Calvin Klein.
- *Unsought goods* – This area is particularly interesting and relates to customers not really wanting this product, but who ultimately could be persuaded to purchase through strong marketing and effective promotions and communications. For example, air circulation systems in the home, air conditioning units.
- *Business products* – This is quite a substantial area as it really relates to any products that support and enable the business function to take place.
- *Process products* – These goods ultimately become part of the producer's own products.
- *Plant and equipment* – These products are exactly as they sound: they are the fabric of the organization, the equipment and machinery that are needed to enable manufacturing and productivity to take place. Clearly in today's technical age there will be a huge amount of computer-aided technology that will enable a higher level of competitive design with more technical detail and capability than ever before.
- *Supplies and services* – Here you are looking at the things that make the world go round and make business happen. All of the supplies and support that service organizations need come under this heading – maintenance and repair, financial services, cleaning services, etc.

Being a product manager in a marketing context will be a very challenging and complex role. Your aim will be to develop a product that is compatible with the existing product portfolio, meets customer needs and wants and forms part of the overall strategy in line with both corporate and marketing objectives.

## Product management

### Creating a product range

One of the key functions that you will undertake in a marketing role is assisting in the creation of an appropriate portfolio of products, i.e. a product range. This means that an organization will have a range of products that they sell, either similar or even diverse products. The better and more appropriate the range of products the more likely they are to sell them. Take, for example, many 'white goods' organizations, which sell a range of products from TV and washing machines to kettles.

Within the product range there is a *product mix*, which is the portfolio of products an organization sells. This can be broken down into three areas. This really relates back to the circular diagram, the anatomy of the product, earlier in this unit. In simple terms it means that a manufacturer will start off with a core product and will then build on that product, or the idea of it, to build a product range.

The *product line* is a group of closely related products; e.g. Colgate offer a number of various toothpastes, but they are all marketed as Colgate–Palmolive in terms of TV advertising and overall marketing.

The *product mix* is the total portfolio of products that a company has on offer. For example, Cannon manufacture a variety of photographic products; this would then be their total product mix. Procter & Gamble also have a very broad range of products from medically related products through to soaps, soap powders, etc.; this would be their product mix.

When considering the product mix, organizations must establish the breadth and depth of the product mix, the depth being how many products are within a product line, e.g. how many different types of toothpaste are under the Colgate–Palmolive brand, as opposed to the breadth of the product, relating to how many product lines Colgate–Palmolive make, e.g. toothpaste, soaps, etc.

As part of the strategic planning process, the organization should reflect on their existing product range to ensure that their products fit with one another, are compatible and continue to meet the needs of increasingly powerful and vocal customers. Therefore, a decision will be made at a strategic level whether or not to launch new products, withdraw existing products and to extend or decrease the life cycle of a product.

As the product is at the heart of the organization and the reason for its overall existence, this is a serious decision that must be undertaken in an informed way, with a structured analytical approach, understanding customers, market forces, key drivers and factors influencing change. Much of this information will be provided through the marketing audit process, where both the macro and micro audit will likely identify critical issues associated with the product mix.

Unit 5 Product operations

# The product life cycle

The PLC (see Figure 5.2) is probably one of the best-known concepts in the whole theory and practice of marketing as a business function.

Every product has a life cycle. It doesn't matter what the product is, it has an existence, sometimes a planned existence – sometimes even planned obsolescence.

The PLC is an invaluable tool in providing an insight into a common pattern of industry sales, one that might be helpful in ascertaining the expected life of products within the product portfolio. One of the big failures of many businesses has been the failure to recognize a product's ability to exist and to operate at a competitive level.

The marketing mix will vary at each stage of the PLC. As you saw in Unit 4, different types of promotional activities are required to underpin particular points in the cycle. A PLC can effectively be extended or decreased according to particular marketing activities that are undertaken. This could be achieved by product modifications, product repositioning, re-branding and market development, to name but a few possibilities.

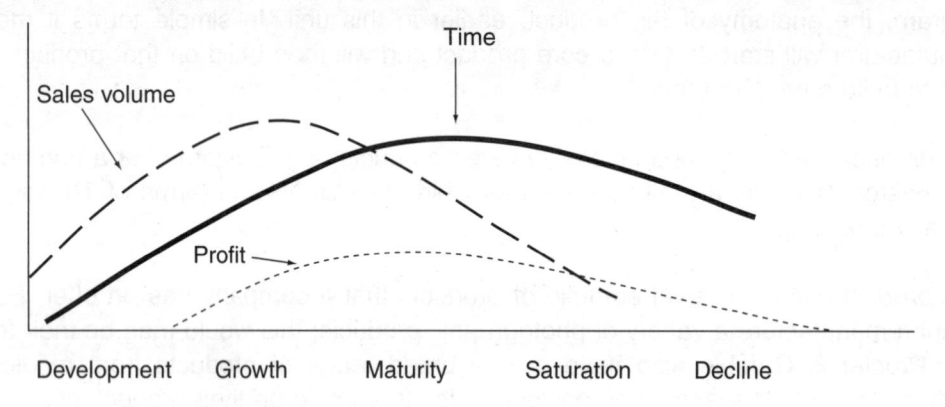

*Figure 5.2* The product life cycle

New markets can often mean that new uses for the product have been identified. This can extend the product for a considerable period of time.

One common factor across all industries in relation to the PLC is that different products have different time horizons; some extend forever, and others will decline and become obsolete very quickly.

## Development

Figure 5.2 illustrates the various stages involved in a product's life cycle existence. A product is in the development stage when market research, product development and marketing testing activities are undertaken. Development costs are high and sales volume will be low, income levels will be non-existent.

## Growth

The product then passes through a growth stage when it is received positively and sales volume increases rapidly. Development costs start to be recovered and costs per unit decrease as production quantities improve. Some profit may appear to be emerging; this will of course vary between organizations based upon the nature of the products and the level of investment required.

## Maturity/saturation

The product becomes fully developed and the initial needs are satisfied. Its success will be dependent on repeat purchase. It is likely that competitors will appear in the market. As the market becomes saturated, sales will slow down and profits will start to decrease.

## Decline

It is very likely that during the decline stage of the life cycle sales will eventually decline and it will be too expensive to maintain the product.

Figure 5.2 illustrates a typical PLC curve. However, in practice, product life cycles can be short, long and of various shapes, depending on various curves. For example, fashion products come into play very quickly and also drop out of the market very quickly as the next fashion comes on board.

At each stage of the PLC the marketing activities and communication activities will change. For a new product launch, the message will be creating awareness, introducing the product to the market. The saturation stage will probably include incentives and promotional activities to encourage customers/consumers to keep purchasing the product.

By the time you get to decline the organization should be ready to launch a new product and therefore the message will be to complete the cycle of the existing product in preparation for the new product. A good example of this would be the car market. Often car prices are decreased significantly to clear existing stock, to make way for the latest model.

However, the PLC does have some limitations. There is a significant danger that organizations might have an over-dependence on the life cycle, meaning that a temporary drop in sales might actually indicate the need for early withdrawal from the market, and be wrongly interpreted as an early decline.

One of the most inhibiting factors of the PLC is that in the real world the PLC is flexible and will change rapidly depending on demand and the activity within the external marketing environment. The change in demand could be based around government policy, competitive activity, technological advances, etc. The changes can be quite sudden and then misunderstood.

The PLC is a very difficult area to manage but organizations should understand that:

- It is dangerous to rely too heavily on one product for too long
- Product life cycles must be tightly managed and continually monitored
- While there might be a predetermined cycle that defines the direction that a product might follow, it does not always take into account the unexpected and the unforeseen external driving forces, technological changes or competitor activity, and can therefore be seen as a little inflexible
- A product portfolio should undergo ongoing review and identify products that should be discontinued or products that should be modified.

On a more positive note, it does aid planning and enables organizations to set key objectives relating to new product development, to when to launch products and to when it may redesign products or even make them obsolete. The PLC has several advantages when used as a planning tool.

- It is a very valuable tool as it helps demonstrate the various stages in the product's development
- It helps forecast potential future demand

- It reminds us of the fact that all products have a limited life
- Profit levels are not constant but change throughout a product's life cycle in a way that is, to some extent, predictable
- Products require different marketing programmes at different stages of their life cycle.

It is important to understand that not all products go through the stages as described above. For example, a product may be developed and launched and may not be successful and therefore declines before it has the opportunity to grow or mature.

Later in the unit you will be spending some time looking at the management of the PLC to provide you with an insight into some to the marketing challenges, both at strategic and operational level. It is essential that the PLC is examined in this context in order to highlight potential tactical level activities that a product or marketing manager might be involved in.

# Managing the product life cycle

Product operational planning in the context of Marketing Planning is concerned with the tactical activities that underpin any particular product-based objectives, such as product development, product line extension, product differentiation and product positioning.

This level of operational planning should without exception underpin the strategic marketing process, exploiting marketing opportunities and growth strategies in an ever-changing environment.

One of the challenges of product management is that a massive growth in innovative products, competitive activity and market saturation will find organizations presented with fewer and fewer opportunities. Therefore, the management of the PLC is an essential activity, in order that every opportunity available can be exploited and the life cycle is extended. Sales will thus be optimized and profit potential maximized.

## Marketing strategy for growth

With new and innovative products it is very likely that product sales could grow at an unprecedented rate. At this stage in the PLC the competition may see and anticipate the rapid rate of growth and enter the market with their version of the product. It is likely that the competition will be highly aggressive, with high levels of advertising and sales promotion activity as they strive to gain their market share by incentivizing customers to switch brands.

As a product or marketing manager, it will be necessary for you to monitor these reactions very carefully and feed back into the strategic marketing process, in order that remedial action can be taken. It is more likely that the actions taken will be of a more tactical nature, principally striking back at the competition. However, in many instances, a strategic decision may have been made much earlier on the product offering, either by extending the product line or by differentiating the product offering.

Targeting of customers may need to be much more tightly defined as each of the competitors strives for market share. Increasing variations on a theme may be required in order to fully differentiate the product offering from that of the competitors.

Typical strategies at this stage will include an increase in push strategy activities by the manufacturer in order to gain preference with suppliers and retailers and command a higher proportion of supplier preference, and pull strategies, targeting more and more distributors, effectively saturating the market where appropriate with your own products.

As indicated in Unit 4, advertising activities will change to include brand awareness and brand benefits, aiming to position the products suitably in the minds of the customer.

In respect of the pricing element of the marketing mix, if growth is rapid then it might be expected that return on investments (ROIs) will also be achieved at an early stage, or that there is significant payback to reduce the price of the products. However, it might be that an increase in sales and volume might also generate economies of scale that could also enhance the possibilities of price reduction.

Price sensitivity may be an issue at this stage depending upon the products, but with more and more substitute products entering the market, it is likely that price will be a critical issue that will need careful management. Pricing will be positioned to sustain market share, and continue the life cycle as long as appropriate.

## Marketing strategy for maturity

Managing the PLC through maturity throws up some interesting dynamics. It is likely that once a product has reached maturity, new products and modified products are running closely behind. It is probable that in this instance enough modifications will be made to differentiate the product suitably in order to reverse its position in the cycle, back towards a growth trend. This is a common policy of car manufacturers who are known historically for changing the light settings, bumper shapes and perhaps superficial features to enhance the look of the car, in line with customer expectations. In doing this, it is likely that the life cycle of the car will be extended. Modifications will reflect three particular categories: quality, functional and style modifications.

Segmentation and positioning become an issue, as customers' expectations change and become more diverse. It is a possibility that marketing development and market penetration strategies could be pursued simultaneously, maximizing profit potential.

Other typical activities might include cost cutting, intensive promotional opportunities and repositioning or even re-branding.

## Marketing strategy for declining products

It is likely that the product has declined to such a stage that profitability has been significantly reduced and is probably non-existent. More innovative products and more up-to-date versions of the same will have replaced the product. The fall may have been predicted, or it might have been forced. However, where possible the decline of the product in the life cycle should be carefully managed.

The organization has a number of potential choices available at this stage:

- *Obsolescence* – Remove the product from the portfolio altogether and replace it
- *Repositioning* – Identify new uses for the product and new markets; position it differently in the minds of the existing and potential customers.

Obsolescence is increasingly common as a result of new technologies. In the last 20 years we have seen the demise of the record player for the CD player and the video player will ultimately decline to be replaced by the DVD player.

In respect of distribution, high levels of promotional activity might encourage customers to continue to purchase and assist distribution channels in moving the stock over for replacements or new products. It is likely that a number of distributors will remove themselves from the channel for a period, or even be removed, in order to maintain profitability.

Depending upon the product, again price sensitivity may be an issue. In the car market it is usual that the price of cars that are in decline is ultimately reduced to clear them once the new replacement models are launched.

Advertising at this stage will be limited, but as already indicated, some level of promotional incentive may still be offered to speed up the decline and obsolescence process in order to release the stock.

Making a product obsolete and actually deleting it from the portfolio also requires some careful management. It is suggested that there are three key ways of deleting a product from the market:

1. *Phase it out* – A natural process, whereby the product strategy does not change until the product has sold out. It is expected that no attempt will be made to revive the product or change it. The Ford Escort was phased out in favour of the Ford Focus.
2. *Run it out* – Increase and intensify the marketing effort in order to effectively clear out stock.
3. *Drop it* – If retaining the product is eating into company profits, and it is being retained at a cost, it is likely that the organization will drop the product immediately and end its PLC.

As already suggested, a lot will depend on the product itself, the circumstances, i.e. is it a natural deletion, a forced deletion, is there loss of face and an effect on competitive positioning? These factors will all impact upon the approach to production deletion.

## Question 5.2

You are one of a team of product managers for a large motor vehicle manufacturer. You have been asked to prepare a briefing paper on the possible marketing activities that might be involved in sustaining a mid-range vehicle at the maturity stage of the PLC for a further 3 years.

## Product portfolio planning tools

You should now understand that while the PLC has its own set of limitations, it is still a critical planning tool which helps focus the organization on the future of its product portfolio.

It is of primary importance that organizations continually monitor and control how their products are doing in the marketplace, what products are in growth and what products are in decline. To assist with this process many organizations use what are formally known as portfolio matrices.

Probably the best-known and most established matrix is the Boston Consulting Group matrix, known as the BCG (see Figure 5.3). Its main purpose is to provide a framework for considering future market growth for both products and services.

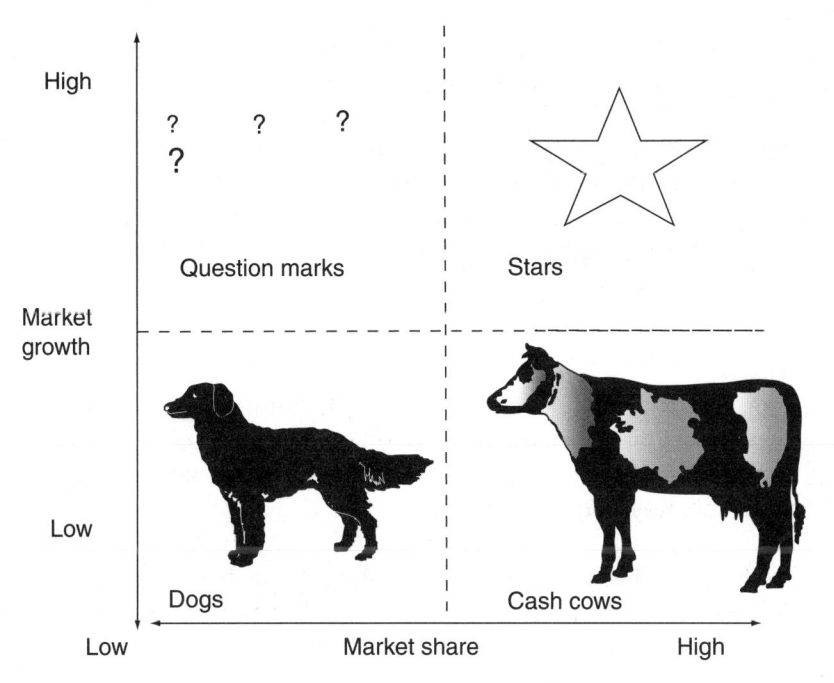

*Figure 5.3* The BCG matrix
*Source*: Adapted from the Boston Consulting Group, 'The Product Profolio', *Perspectives*, August (1970)

## The BCG matrix

The BCG matrix has two key dimensions associated with it, namely the level of growth in the product's market, and the product's market share in comparison to that of its competitors.

Market growth is an imperative to many organizations, as it presents an opportunity in the marketplace for extension, expansion and innovation. However, in low growth markets, it is more about survival of the fittest, as competition is highly intensive as each competitor strives its own portion of a much smaller market potential.

Each of the four quartiles of the BCG offers an indication of potential opportunities or even potential decline in market share.

### Stars
Principally, stars are products that command high levels of market share, with good potential for growth in the future. Key components are:

- The product has moved to a position of leadership in a high growth market
- Income needs are high in order to maintain market growth and keep competitors at bay
- The product generates a large amount of income
- As long as the market share is maintained, the product should become a cash cow.

### Cash cows
Cash cows are essentially products that have a dominant share of the market, but with little potential for growth, effectively having reached a level of maturity. Key components are:

- The product has a high market share and a low level of market growth. Stars become cash cows when the market rate begins to fall.
- The term 'cash cow' comes from the principle that products generate considerable money but use little cash.
- Economies of scale are strong.

### Question marks
Question marks, alternatively known as problem children, are very much as they sound. They are principally products that have a small market share of a growing market. However, they are often subject to high levels of investment in order for them to achieve any significant growth in market share overall. Key components are:

- The product has a low market share in a high growth market
- Considerable investment is required in order to keep up with market developments
- If trying to improve competitive position, levels of investment required are high
- The 'question mark' arises over whether one needs to invest or divest in a market.

### Dogs
The position of 'dogs' in the BCG is typically one of low market share, with no real potential for growth. This can often be an indication that the product is nearing the end of its current life, and should be potentially considered for repositioning or deletion from the product line. Key components of dogs are:

- The product has a weak market share in a low growth market
- A low level of profit or a loss would be typical in return
- Very often dogs take up more time in terms of management than can be justified, so phasing out of the product is likely to be considered
- Strategically, the issue is whether or not to hold on to the business.

From a marketing perspective, the BCG enables the organization to classify the company's products into four clear categories that will, in the main, shape their place in the future marketing strategy. While principally this is a planning tool, which should be used in the strategy development stages, it is important that it is clearly linked with the product in the context of product operations. This is because it will be part of the marketing manager's role to continually evaluate the performance of the product within the marketplace, and to contribute to inform the planning process of the potential growth and market share of the existing product portfolio.

Both the PLC, which we looked at in the previous section, and the BCG matrix have a number of attributes (see Figure 5.4) that will be tremendously helpful in planning for product involvement in the marketing strategy.

Typical outcomes from analysis undertaken through the BCG matrix will be the identification of new opportunities for product development potential, the need for repositioning of products or the need for deletion of products. In terms of potential marketing strategy, the BCG will assist in defining how growth objectives might be achieved through product-based activities.

|  | *PLC* | *BCG* |
|---|---|---|
| Planning strengths | Five-stage view<br>Easy to understand | Focus on SBU or products<br>Allows variety of planning approaches<br>Can be quantified<br>Allows prediction |
| Planning weaknesses | Historical only<br>No predictive capability<br>Not quantifiable | Circle sizes may not reflect true benefits<br>Likely to distort true picture as visuals are simplistic<br>Quadrant position dependent on management decision, not objective data |
| Control strengths | Can suggest possibility of need for action<br>Provides a useful visual shorthand | Relative market share shown<br>Accurately reflects position<br>Can be current or future based<br>Encourage forward planning |
| Control weaknesses | Totally useless<br>Imprecise and inaccurate<br>Not quantifiable | Little value in stable markets, but has been developed into models which are useful |

*Figure 5.4* Strengths and weaknesses of the PLC and BCG

## The General Electric Matrix (GE matrix)

There are a range of alternative models, such as the GE matrix, or market attractiveness business position model (Figure 5.5); however, this is more of a strategic level model. This model indicates levels of market share on the same basis and will ultimately be able to indicate high, medium or low levels of market attractiveness. In using this, organizations will be able to potentially establish market attractiveness and different levels of growth, which will indicate the need either to invest and grow or divest and harvest.

## Shell Directional Policy Matrix

This model takes a similar approach to the GE matrix, in that both have cells that contain policy recommendations for their business. For example invest, divest or grow. However the Shell Directional Policy Matrix (see Figure 5.6) does focus on ascertaining the potential suitability of market segments versus the capabilities of the organization, so identifying all levels of market attractiveness.

Unit 5 Product operations

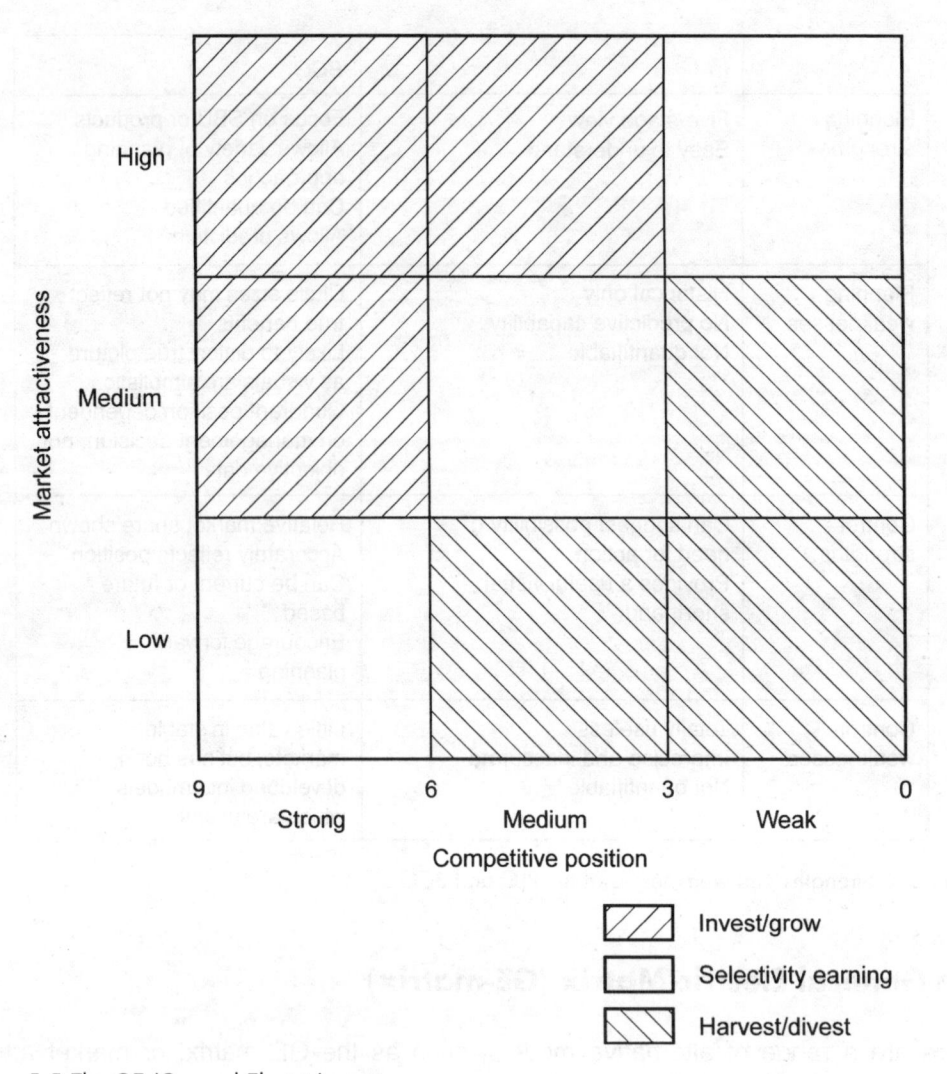

*Figure 5.5* The GE (General Electric) matrix

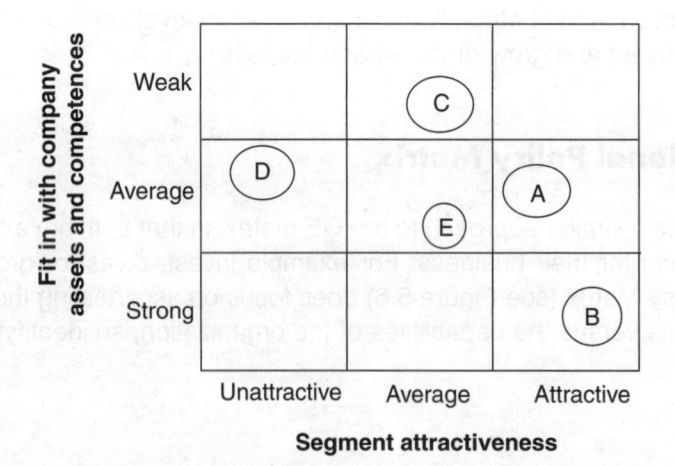

*Figure 5.6* Shell Directional Policy Matrix

The organization must establish whether entering a particular segment is both consistent with their long-term aims and objectives, and it does not matter how tempting or attractive the segment looks, it should be resisted. If not, then the organization wastes both management and time resources and is diverted away from the core goals of the enterprise.

An organization should enter segments that allow it to exploit current assets and competences, or will allow capabilities to develop into strengths. Therefore the Shell Direction Policy Matrix can be adapted to enable it to analyse market segment opportunities against corporate strengths.

This provides the basis for products/services to be analysed and their overall position with respect to the PLC determined. It shows whether there is the scope for growth and expansion, or whether phased withdrawal is required.

As you move forwards onto the Postgraduate Diploma in Marketing the technicalities of how to use the GE and Shell Directional Policy Matrix become more evident.

## Question 5.3

As a marketing manager using the BCG matrix, what information would you expect it to provide you with, and how might you use it?

# New product development

Product development is one of the possible outcomes of the marketing strategy development process, determined by the outcomes of the marketing audit and the use of the BCG and the Ansoff matrix.

It is a known fact that new products and new ideas are far more appealing to some customers than others.

New product development is a highly expensive process that requires massive amounts of time and investment and thus a clear understanding of the rationale for production development is needed (Figure 5.7). Therefore a number of critical questions should be answered:

- Has a customer need been identified?
- Has the analysis from the BCG shown that the potential market is large enough to generate sufficient revenue, ROI and profitability.
- What is the level of resource required – does the company have the R&D expertise, technological ability and innovation required for new product development in the 21st century?

The basis of the answers to these questions will come from producing a formal method for assessing new product ideas – the 'new product development process' – where the feasibility and viability of future development is likely to take place.

**Number of new product ideas**

- Idea generation
- Screening new ideas
- Business analysis
- Product development
- Test marketing

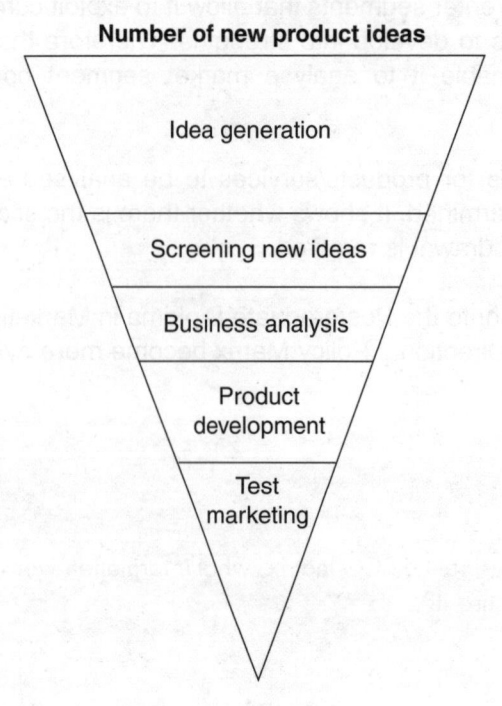

*Figure 5.7* The new product development process
*Source*: Lancaster, Withey and Ashford (2001)

Before moving forwards to look at the new product development process, it is important to consider the type of product that you are going to develop.

| Type of product development | Nature of product development |
|---|---|
| New world/Innovative | The focus of this model of NPD is on technical development and often incurs a high/risk return which can often revolutionize or create markets |
| New product lines or additions | Such products can be (i) new to the provider as opposed to the market place or (ii) be additions to the product ranges already on offer |
| Product revisions/replacements | Replacements and upgrades of existing products. Changes may be aimed at generating cost reductions – no perceived change in performance but more economic production of the product |
| Reposition | Aim to diversify away from existing markets by uncovering new applications, uses or market segments for current products |
| Imitative products | Copycat products produced by others, but where there is a market for many alternative and competing versions |

*Source*: Adapted from Drummond, Ensor and Ashford (2003)

## The new product development process

### Idea generation

The formal process begins with the generation of new ideas. These can come from a variety of sources. A company's own R&D department will be working on new ideas all the time. Innovations can also come from the customer service department, where staff and customers can be encouraged to come forward with ideas. The sales and production departments are another important source. All ideas are listed and submitted to the new product team, where they will be considered. Effectively, a number of people can be involved in this process, both internally and externally to the organization.

## Screening new ideas

Once the ideas have been assessed for their initial viability, it is necessary to devise a method of screening these so as to reduce them to a manageable number that are considered to have real prospects. A series of potential KSF, which research has shown are desirable to the consumer and to the company, will have been identified. In the 21st century, with the continuing rapid growth of ICT, and substantial databases, it is possible to closely match the characteristics of your products to consumer needs.

By clearly identifying the characteristics of your customers, it is possible to identify relevant market segments and niches to which marketing activities can be targeted.

Having identified the different segments, it is likely that they will have different needs. As a marketer, you need to establish the difference or differential between your products and services and those provided by your competitors.

The new ideas can then be compared so as to establish a short list of those that fit most closely to these criteria. Some of the factors that will come under consideration are raw material availability, production, distribution and the effect on sales of other products. Robust research programmes should inform the product design and development process. The characteristics identified against the potential benefits on offer should provide a basis of designing the perfect product solution.

## Product development

At this stage in the process it is likely that the first prototype will be developed in order that the product is taken from conception to reality. The costs involved in this particular element are phenomenal. One of the key issues of product development will be to ensure that the investment in product design will create a new, innovative product that will achieve sustainable competitive advantage in the future. Therefore good sound design principles will provide the basis for competitive advantage in the marketplace.

From a technical perspective, it is likely that the key activities will relate to fine tuning both from a performance point of view and also in relation to ensuring that customer expectations will be delivered.

The product will have been technically designed and specifications drawn up in preparation for the manufacturer in advance of any full-scale production. However, the decision to launch is a critical factor and will require high levels of business and analytical skills, in order that full-scale production can be implemented.

## Concept testing

The next stage, known as concept testing, is to determine whether the new product is likely to appeal to customers. A sample is often made up with varying forms of packaging and often company employees are asked for their opinions. Focus groups are frequently recruited at this stage. The beauty of concept testing is that it makes it possible to gauge consumers' reactions before the company has incurred heavy costs in production runs.

Packaging is also part of the concept testing and with revolutionary technology a range of packaging options can be designed and form part of a virtual concept test. This is an evolving process.

Packaging, like the product, will provide a basis for differentiation and competitive advantage, therefore it is equally important to concept test the packaging in line with the product.

## Business analysis

At this stage, the company has to consider the financial viability of the new idea. Research and forecasting techniques are used to determine the likely level of demand. A cost analysis will examine not only direct production costs but also capital investment and marketing costs and even new personnel. Profitability can then be established in terms of 'break-even' and rate of return analysis.

## Test marketing

The purpose of test marketing is to gain consumers' reactions in an area that has been selected for the test. These are often television areas, such as Tyne Tees, which are considered to be representative of the total market. The test allows the company to evaluate sales and distribution prior to a full-blown launch. Any problems or flaws in the product or its promotion can be identified and made good before the continued rollout.

## Launch

Assuming the test market operation has proved successful, then the product can be launched nationally. Production capacity will have to be increased to cope with the anticipated demand. The promotional campaign can be extended to national media and further distribution channels enlisted. Having an existing distribution network will improve the chances of success.

## Case history

### EarthShell debuts biodegradable hot beverage cups

EarthShell® Corporation is a technology company and innovator of a revolutionary development in food service packaging. Their business model is to license technology to leading manufacturers of food service disposables who will manufacture, market and distribute EarthShell Packaging® to quick-serve restaurants, food management companies, the U.S. government, universities, leading retailers and more. It is specifically designed with the environment in mind, from the beginning to the end of its PLC – and beyond.

Patented, innovative technology allows us to combine simple, abundant, renewable materials, such as limestone and starch, into a material that, like leaves and grass, is 100 per cent biodegradable and recyclable through composting. The result is a line of high quality, new-to-the-world food service packaging that is environmentally preferable and price-competitive to paper and plastic alternatives.

EarthShell have developed cups that are designed to meet or exceed the performance of other disposable hot-cup products currently available while offering the unique environmental attributes associated with other EarthShell products.

EarthShell's initial product development focused on plates, bowls, hinged containers, the recently-announced new sandwich wraps and now, cups for hot beverages. Following product testing, the company will provide more details regarding product availability and other significant characteristics of its first entry into the cup market.

In keeping with the company's mission, hot cups from EarthShell are designed to have unique environmental advantages when compared to traditional hot cups made from polystyrene foam and paper.

EarthShell packaging, made from a composite material consisting primarily of natural limestone and renewable starch, is environmentally preferable from start to finish. When compared to traditional packaging, it uses less total energy and results in low greenhouse gas emissions.

EarthShell packaging is strong and provides good insulation, biodegrades when exposed to moisture in nature and is recyclable through composting.

EarthShell packaging is designed to be cost and performance competitive, compared to other foodservice packaging materials, and also to provide environmental advantages.

www.EarthShell.com

*Source*: Lexis-Nexis.

### Study tip

The December 2003 Marketing Planning Examination asked questions about various forms of innovation and the new product development process. However, the students were asked to apply models of innovation and the NPD model to an organization. Although the question was quite specific about this, many students provided a purely theoretical overview, with little or no application, or use of example. Therefore, please ensure that you can take these processes beyond theory. Practise now by applying aspects of this unit to your own organization!

## The product adoption process

Another imperative is that you clearly understand the basis of decision-making units (DMU), how they are structured, and what active role they play in the decision-making process. This assists you as the marketer to know more about the basis of profiling and targeting specific influences in the decision-making process.

### The consumer decision-making unit

Decision-making for the consumer is not exclusive to one person, it can involve a wide range of influences and influencers (see Figure 5.8). The DMU is a term used to describe the various people or members involved in the decision-making process. It is useful marketing information to know how many people (and who) are involved in the decision-making process. The various people in the DMU will have different roles in decision-making.

```
┌─────────────┐  ┌─────────────┐  ┌─────────────┐  ┌─────────────┐
│  Personal   │  │Psychological│  │  Economic   │  │   Social    │
│ influences  │  │ influences  │  │             │  │ influences  │
│             │  │             │  │   Price     │  │             │
│ Demographic │  │ Perception  │  │  Delivery   │  │Roles and family│
│  Situation  │  │  Motives    │  │  Payment    │  │ Reference   │
│ Involvement │  │  Learning   │  │   Sales     │  │   groups    │
│             │  │  Attitudes  │  │  Service    │  │Social classes│
│             │  │ Personality │  │             │  │             │
└─────────────┘  └─────────────┘  └─────────────┘  └─────────────┘
```

**Consumer buying decision process**

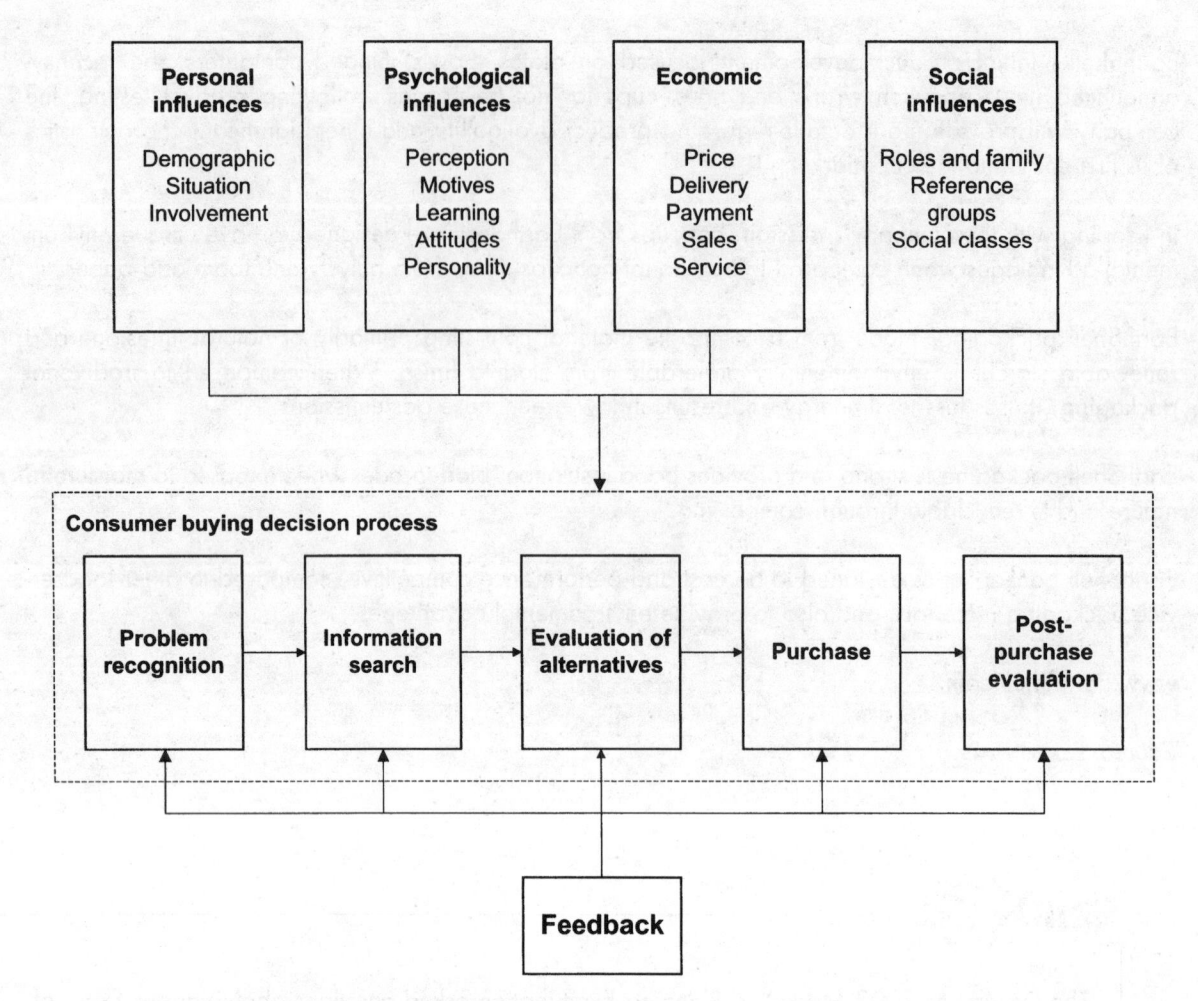

```
┌──────────┐   ┌──────────┐   ┌──────────┐   ┌──────────┐   ┌──────────┐
│ Problem  │──▶│Information│──▶│Evaluation│──▶│ Purchase │──▶│  Post-   │
│recognition│  │  search  │   │    of    │   │          │   │ purchase │
│          │   │          │   │alternatives│ │          │   │evaluation│
└──────────┘   └──────────┘   └──────────┘   └──────────┘   └──────────┘
```

**Feedback**

*Figure 5.8* Possible influences on the decision process
*Source*: Adapted from Dibb, Simkin and Ferrell (2001)

There are four consumer buying roles that must be considered:

1. *The initiator* – Is the person who effectively identified the problem, i.e. the need to buy the product or service. The initiator will most likely suggest the need to buy this product to other people.
2. *The influencer* – Is the person or people to whom the initiator will likely turn for advice and guidance on the purchase. This could be a family member, a friend or an expert in the area. A good example could be the purchase of a personal computer for the home. This is quite a significant purchase and one that involves a lot of technical detail. An influencer could guide you on the mechanics of the PC and the functions you may need it to perform for you.
3. *The decider* – Is the person who will give the go-ahead to purchase the product. This could be the initiator or the influencer. This person will decide what to buy, how much to pay, where to buy it from and what additional service or warranty requirements may be needed.
4. *The buyer* – Is the person who makes the purchase, the individual who then gets involved in the exchange process between the customer and the organization.

There are a number of models that represent the way in which a range of promotional activities within the promotional mix seek to persuade customers to purchase. A somewhat aged model, known as AIDA and designed in 1925 by Strong, developed stages which advertising may go through to attract the customer's attention. Then in the 1960s the hierarchy of effects model was developed by Lavidge and Stiner. This represents the process by which advertising was thought to work and assumed that customers may go through. After that, in 1978 McGuire developed a further model known as the Information Processing Model.

Figure 5.9 demonstrates the phase each of these models takes a customer through to engage their attention towards the product.

These are three commonly used models, which in essence have common denominators, each one trying to ensure that they optimize the possibility of the customer actually adopting their chosen product.

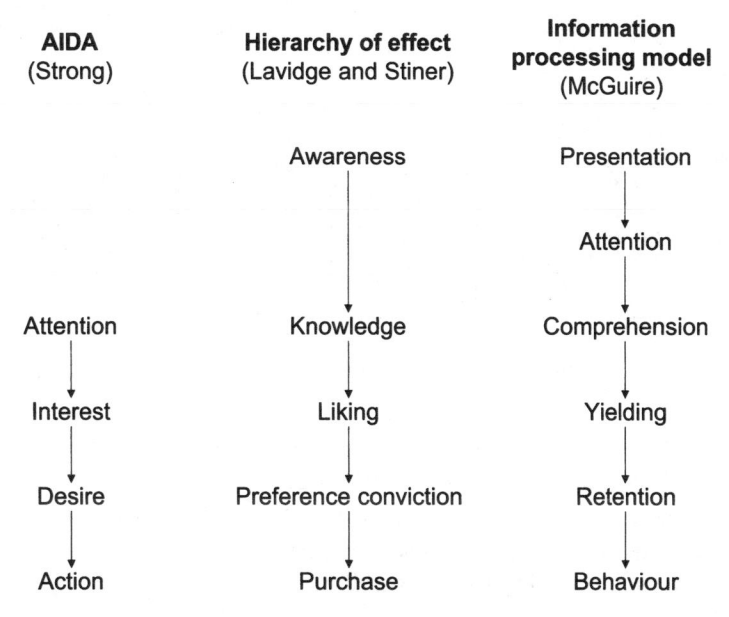

| AIDA (Strong) | Hierarchy of effect (Lavidge and Stiner) | Information processing model (McGuire) |
|---|---|---|
|  | Awareness | Presentation |
|  |  | Attention |
| Attention | Knowledge | Comprehension |
| Interest | Liking | Yielding |
| Desire | Preference conviction | Retention |
| Action | Purchase | Behaviour |

*Figure 5.9* Adoption models

There are other models, such as DAGMAR, which works on the basis of:

- Action
- Conviction
- Comprehension
- Awareness
- Unawareness.

Alternatively there is also the adoption model, which again is very similar to the above with the key components relating to:

- Awareness
- Interest
- Evaluation
- Trial
- Adoption.

In respect of promotional operations, they are to focus the minds of those involved to prioritize and order the various communication objectives against the different stages in the decision-making process. This is necessary in order that the organization exploits every available opportunity to attract the customer's attention with the ultimate objective of securing a purchase.

A further consideration in relation to adoption in respect of communications is that of the process of diffusion and innovation. It is essential that great care is taken over the rate at which sales occur, the speed at which they occur and the level of market penetration that occurs, as this will determine the nature and longitude of the communications plan.

For a new product to be successful, it must first be bought or adopted by individual customers, households and organizations. Diffusion occurs only once acceptance of the product spreads in the marketplace. The diffusion process follows a similar shape to the PLC curve (see Figure 5.10).

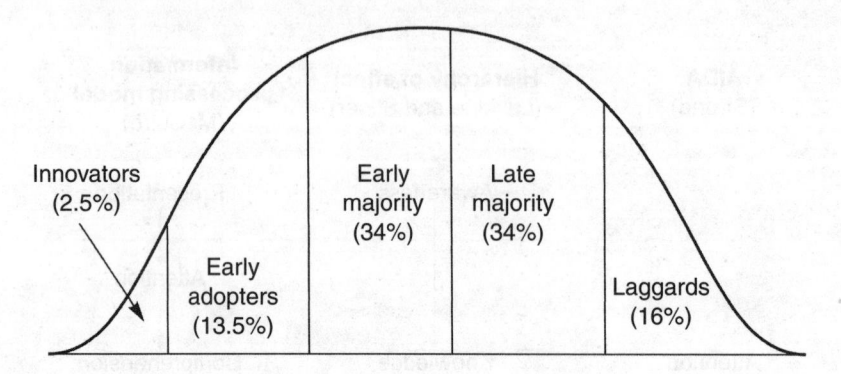

*Figure 5.10* Innovation and diffusion process

It is likely that innovators are probably those who are in the 'B' range of social class as suggested in JICNAR (see Unit 3). As innovators, they may speed up the process of diffusion through their actions and potentially by word of mouth. Clearly this will then need to be supported by a range of other communications tools in order that the opportunity to speed up the diffusion process is optimized and exploited.

The key to successful diffusion will be to target innovators precisely for their characteristics as innovators. From there it is likely that you will continue to target each of the groups, until ultimately you have targeted them all. Each group will require a different approach, a different communication, as they have different lifestyles, different habits, differing attitudes and be subject to entirely different influences.

Everett Rogers identified several different categories of people, based on the ease with which they adopted new products.

## Innovators

These are people who will buy simply because the product is new. This is not a good indicator of a product's future potential.

## Early adopters

This group are those who are willing to try new products before they have achieved widespread acceptance. They are often regarded as opinion leaders in their own circle. Acceptance by this group is essential for any new product.

### Early majority

The early majority are a cautious group and will only adopt the new product once it becomes socially acceptable. Acceptance by this group will determine whether the product will gain widespread acceptance and succeed as a mass-market product.

### Late majority

This group are even more risk-averse than the early majority. They will only consider adopting the product after they are sure that they are going to like it. At this stage, the product is well established.

### Laggards

The laggards are those who resist the new product and may never adopt it. They are generally timid and cautious by nature.

The categories of adopters will vary according to the product. For instance, innovators are not always the same people in each market. Some people may be early adopters in the telecommunications market but laggards in new organic food. Having knowledge of adopters is very important and careful targeting of this group with launch promotional material such as direct mail will help the launch to be a greater success.

Despite all this effort, it is reckoned that only 10 per cent of new products are successful.

## Targeting decision-makers

We looked at market segmentation and targeting within Unit 3, 'Marketing planning, implementation and control'. To remain competitive and cost-effective for both marketing and promotional operations, it is critical to profile and target your audiences and hence communicate with them very specifically, ensuring that all messages are relevant at that particular point in the decision-making process. It is also important to ensure that the messages are meaningful in a way that will pull decision-makers towards the product and a long-term loyal relationship.

However, targeting decision-makers at the right time can be a very complex process, particularly in a B2B setting. It is therefore of primary importance that you ensure that all communications, at each stage of the decision-making, and for meeting each element of the overall marketing strategy, are specifically targeted and provide the basis of synergy and consistency in terms of the overall implementation.

### Case history

#### Black and Decker

Black and Decker developed three distinct product ranges, each one targeted to different channels. They used the Quantum brand at the heavy DIY end of the market, Black and Decker for major multiples and De Walt aimed at trade buyers and contractors. Different promotions and incentives are made available to each target market.

Unit 5 Product operations

## Summary

The product is the very core of what the organization is about; the product is the purpose. The product on its own is worthless, but carefully managed, branded and packaged, the benefits it provides and the satisfaction it will achieve are the key factors to its overall success.

The main aim of any organization should be to create products that customers need, want and expect, always ensuring quality, innovation, customer delight and value is at the core of their strategy development and business activity.

It is of primary importance that the organizations create a differential between themselves and their competitors, through the successful planning implementation of a brand and product strategy, that places them in a uniquely differentiated and competitive position.

However, the critical success factor in establishing product and brand success is ensuring that an integrated approach is taken toward the utilization of the marketing mix. This will be a marketing imperative.

Marketers are becoming increasingly aware of the speed of change, resulting in shorter life cycles, faster levels of innovation, rapid speed of products to market, accelerated diffusion and excessive competition.

With the added impetus of global marketing and new technologies, product development, product innovation and robust product planning are providing the most significant challenge of the 21st century – where do we go from here?

## Study tip

Product-based questions are highly likely within every exam. Questions will be framed on the basis of being part of the overall marketing mix, or on an individual basis. You will be expected to take an integrated approach to the managing of the marketing mix, and while being able to understand key marketing elements in isolation, it is essential to look at them as integrated also.

You will be expected to have some understanding of branding applications, product development, product portfolio matrix models and of course the PLC. The questions will put you in the position of a marketing manager, product manager, or even brand manager, therefore you will need to look at these subjects in an applied way.

In the June 2000 paper alone, there are four questions that have some bearing on this particular unit, emphasizing its significance.

## Extending knowledge

### Recommended reading

As with all other units, the purpose of this text is to consolidate your more extensive learning, providing you with an overview of the key elements. Therefore additional reading is recommended in order that you supplement your learning significantly.

Chapters 8, 9 and 10 of Dibb, Simkin, Pride and Ferrell, *Marketing: Concepts and Strategies*, 4th European edition (2001).

## Bibliography

Dibb, S., Simkin, L., Pride, W. and Ferrell, O. (2001) *Marketing: Concepts and Strategies*, 4th European edition, Houghton Mifflin.

Fill, C. (2003) *Marketing Communications*, Butterworth-Heinemann.

Lancaster, G., Withey, F. and Ashford, R. (2001) *Marketing Fundamentals*, Butterworth-Heinemann.

---

Sample exam questions and answers for the Marketing Planning module as a whole can be found in Appendix 4. Please undertake Question 5 – June 2004 Examination Paper and Question 5 in December 2003.

# unit 6
# price operations

## Learning objectives

In this unit you will be focusing on the importance of pricing operations, and the implications and impact of pricing.

The syllabus elements for this unit are:

- Explain pricing frameworks available to, and used by, organizations for decision-making
- Describe how pricing is developed as an integrated part of the marketing mix.

Syllabus reference: 3.6 and 3.7

## Introduction

The focus of this unit on pricing operations is to allow you to consider the role of pricing within the marketing mix, the importance of price and its overall influence, and the considerations when setting pricing objectives. Furthermore, it is essential that you consider how flexibility in the role of pricing must be delivered in order to develop a marketing mix designed for sustained competitive advantage.

One of the key differences about price is that it is the only element as such that generates income rather than having a cost base to it. It is the determinant that focuses on maximizing revenue in order to meet profitability objectives and goals determined by the organization. Price is not just about generating revenue for the organization, it is about creating a better environment and a more effective long-term relationship with the customer. It is about placing a value on something, be it a product or service.

Value has to be perceived by the customer in order that the required revenue is generated. Customers do not just want products to be cheap or reasonably priced, they expect a certain level of value for money. That means that the product needs to be a certain level of quality, demonstrating that value in a clear and transparent way.

A marketer's involvement in pricing is necessary to ensure that price does reflect the product offering, i.e. the quality, the benefits and the functionality. Furthermore, the pricing strategy being implemented must match the expectations of the customer. Setting a high price is only acceptable if offering high value.

While price is seen to be possibly the most flexible element of the marketing mix, it is probably the most difficult to manage and it has to reflect the state of the market on a continuous basis.

Due to the intensively competitive nature of the marketplace today, price is the most changeable element of the mix. It has to respond to economic changes, competitive activity, customer demand and cost of materials, costs of distribution and a number of other key market drivers.

The role of the marketing manager in relation to pricing is sometimes rather ambiguous in many organizations and the waters become muddied between marketing and the accounting/financial arm of the organization in trying to maximize profitability. Sadly, in a less market-oriented organization, price setting will often be undertaken in a vacuum without considering the influences and implications of pricing and without realizing that considering price alone is not enough.

In many instances setting prices is a thankless task. If it is too cheap, the customer thinks it is too good to be true and asks the question 'What's wrong with it?'. If the price is too high, customers may not want to buy it. If organizations do not get the price right the rest of the marketing mix could potentially be wasted; therefore the mix depends on the right product at the right price!

It doesn't matter who the organization is, or what it does, what matters is to understand that price does not stand alone, it interacts with the whole organization and the other 6Ps. Price is very visible; therefore it has to present 'value' to the customer.

## Price perception and the customer

In the introduction it was stated that price is the value placed upon either a product or a service. For the marketer, developing a marketing mix that is appropriate to customer needs and understanding the implications of it will be critical.

Having developed and communicated the nature of the marketing strategy, the organization is effectively signalling a whole range of information, perceptions and values about the product, its characteristics, benefits and performance. Ultimately, putting a price on a product raises expectations. It is then up to the customer to decide if it meets their needs or matches their perception.

Understanding the implications of price means understanding customer behaviour, motivations, culture, attitudes, values and perception. Of course, market segmentation does offer some answers to these questions, but it does, needless to say, leave price as the hot potato of the marketing mix.

Price is often perceived as being constant, but unfortunately it will change, both in reality and in the minds of buyers depending upon how their circumstances change. Constancy is one thing that price does not necessarily present. With supply and demand indicators changing, as demands of raw materials and components vary, competitive intensity and product rarity, price can change drastically.

## Perspective of price and the organization

Price is the only element of the marketing mix that generates revenue for the organization. Everything else about the organization relates to a cost. Therefore pricing is the opportunity to gain some ROI or return on capital employed, meeting profit objectives and looking at growth opportunities from profits year on year.

It is, however, essential that the organization always considers the price from the perspective of the customer and then relates it to demand. The price that is charged is very much based upon the supply and demand factor of the market, the supply being the availability of the product and the demand based around how many people in the market actually want it. This is often a good starting point for the organization in establishing its potential pricing strategy.

## Pricing in relation to demand

You should now be aware of the link between product quality and price and how price can be sensitive to the perception of the customer and how they see value for money. However, pricing is more complex than this. Pricing has to reflect a number of influences, demands and key drivers, and therefore pricing is subject to the following:

- The subjective beliefs of customers with regard to different pricing
- Competitors
- Quality.

It is necessary to predict the impact of price changes on consumers, distribution and on your competitors. Prices need to mirror the degree of demand for a product in a given market.

Different pricing strategies are relevant at different stages of the PLC in line with the relative costs involved. Generally speaking, price decreases in time in line with the decrease in costs involved.

This concept is known as price elasticity. This is a term used to explain that, generally speaking, demand will decrease as prices increase and that supply will increase as prices go up. Elasticity in demand is the term used to explain that price changes in line with the volume sold.

## Influences on price

One key activity of the marketer through both marketing research and the audit process is to understand the key influences upon pricing.

Pricing is a complex area to manage, if only taking on board the internal considerations such as the running costs of the organization, development costs, overhead costs, the organization's objectives and its corporate mission. But to add to the internal complexities, there are a significant number of external considerations an organization must be aware of.

Organizations have to be very responsive to the state of the market environment, and responsive to the range of factors already discussed, such as competition and demand.

While an organization has to be responsive, it also needs to manage the uncertainty. The 21st century seems to have given the market higher levels of uncertainty than previously experienced. To this end organizations need to endeavour to understand a range of factors relating to the external environment. Figure 6.1 highlights the factors affecting the pricing decisions of the organization.

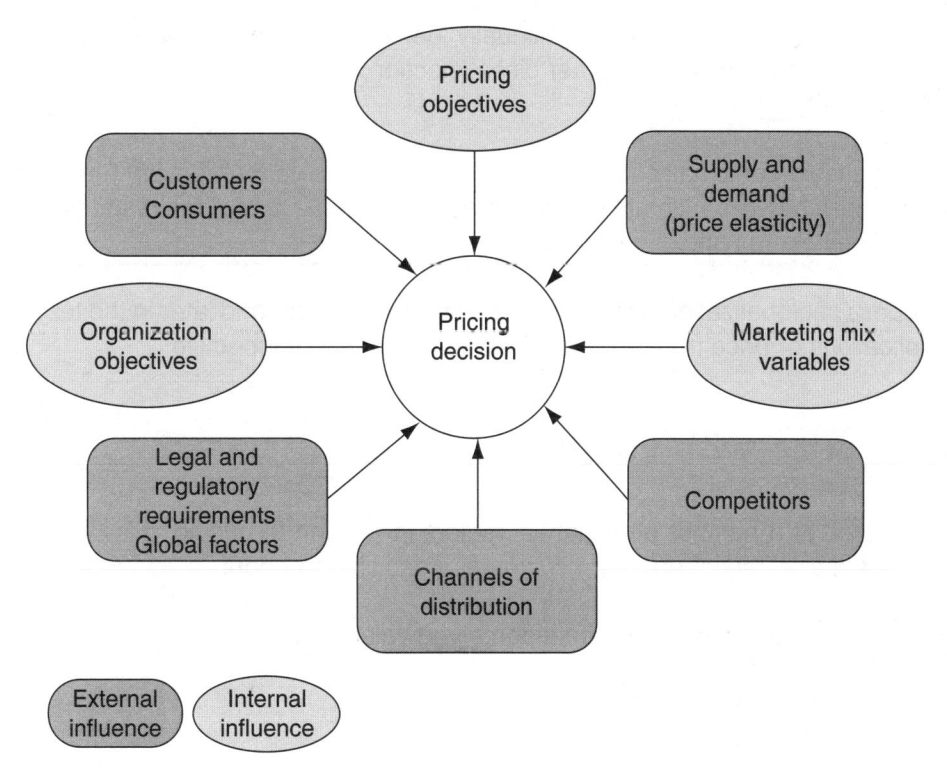

*Figure 6.1* Influences on price

## Question 6.1

On what basis do external market forces influence the price charged for a hotel room?

One of the most prominent headlines from autumn 2000, and an issue still going strong, has been the significantly high fuel prices and vehicle taxation in the UK and indeed some parts of Europe. Consumers, it would appear, have been subject to ever-increasing fuel prices and are continually threatened with the £4 gallon of petrol and the 90p litre. However, more recently, this threat has eased and the price of fuel has reduced significantly.

However, there is still much concern in relation to fuel prices and consumers are continually angered by the threat of high fuel prices, particularly as some of the big oil producers, such as Shell, BP and ESSO, have been announcing considerable annual profits. However, while profits are being made on a global scale through other business opportunities, the influence of supply and demand factors in the oil production markets is eroding profits made in the UK. This coupled with the high levels of taxation invoked by government finds the UK oil market subject to high costs and high demands, a balance that appears very difficult to manage.

Recently, legislation in respect of transportation has also had a significant impact upon costs, not least because of the vehicle emissions ruling. The higher the emissions, the higher the tax burden. The higher the tax burden the higher the cost of distribution is to the consumer. In many instances, the cost of distribution is over 50 per cent of the total cost of the product. In the UK and much of Europe, customers have been subjected to a number of disputes as distributors try to gain the upper hand in achieving price reduction.

In the UK there has been much discussion about new types of transportation taxes, such as tolls on UK motorways during peak travel times.

The issue of high priced fuel is continually pertinent to many organizations, impacting on external influences such as customer dissatisfaction, government intervention and the actions of various WTO.

Marketers should continually be alert to the power of the various driving forces in the marketplace and how they can ultimately, through asserting their power, command changes in pricing structures and overall prices charged.

The process of globalization is also having an effect on price, and later in the text we will look at the implications of price from an international and global perspective.

## Correlating price with value

Having looked at a number of influential factors in relation to pricing, it is clear that perceived value has a major impact upon the customer's decision to adopt.

Some of the typical factors that affect perceived value are:

- Life cycle of the product
- Product benefits and functionality
- Quality
- Prestige and status of the brand
- Ease of use
- Value-added measures
- Differentiation
- Packaging
- Service and technical support
- Competitive alternatives (substitutes).

While these are just some of the factors affecting value, clearly it is a prominent issue. Principally the customer will be paying a price in exchange for 'perceived value and benefits' and therefore the price has to be representative of the overall deal. Essentially these factors start to form the basis of strategic price determinants.

There is a basic rule in pricing, that you price your product or service at the level that your customers expect to pay for the quality you are delivering. This does not just mean that high quality justifies high price, nor does it mean that high price means high quality. What it does mean, however, is that the organization has to justify the price that it charges.

### Question 6.2

The value proposition, i.e. perceived value, is of vital importance when determining a price. How might you use other tools within the marketing mix, such as product and promotion, to justify the value proposition?

# Strategic pricing determinants

Before setting pricing objectives, it is important to consider the determining factor of pricing, i.e. the key influences in relation to ascertaining the correct pricing positioning and pricing objectives for the organization.

## Demand as a determinant

As a marketing manager, you will most likely be responsible for collecting various data that, through analysis, will identify the forecast levels of demand for products within the marketplace.

Demand relates to customers actually wanting to purchase or even needing to purchase particular goods or services. The likely scenario is that the higher the demand for the product, the lower the price and the lower the demand for the product, the higher the price.

The basis of this scenario is that the higher the demand, the more likely the organization is invoke economies of scale, and from there it can pass on its cost savings to the customer, thus lowering the price. However, whilst it is likely that reduced costs can be passed on to the customer, organizations must be aware of the impact this move will have on the supply and demand scenario.

It is important to realize that this strategy may not always be appropriate as in many markets demand needs to be controlled in order to avoid a situation of its spiralling out of control, which in turn could cause a great deal of instability within both the organization and the industry. Therefore, whilst organizations aim to pass on cost savings to customers, there may be a limit to how much they are likely to do this, in order to avoid an unmanageable and uncontrollable increases in demand. This approach would of course avoid early saturation of the market, and enable organizations to exploit future opportunities relating to supply of further similar or associated products.

The lower the demand, the less likely it is that economies of scale will be achieved, therefore likely costs of raw materials and related products will be higher, therefore the cost of the product will be higher.

Forecasting demand can be quite a difficult process, but once potential demand has been established, the price can be set accordingly. Forecasting demand will provide an insight into potential for growth; high levels of growth would potentially mean high levels of demand.

While demand is important, issues relating to elasticity in demand need to be answered. As a marketer it will be part of your role to undertake a range of exercises relating to ascertaining the level of demand and how fluctuations in price might increase or decrease the demand.

The likely findings of this exercise will probably highlight that marginal increases in price are unlikely to affect demand and therefore if they do not affect demand, demand is inelastic. However, if a significant increase in price is implemented, demand could potentially drop dramatically, therefore highlighting elasticity in demand and probably a fickle market.

As an example, if an organization reduced prices by 25 per cent, but as a result only saw a 5 per cent increase in sales, demand would be deemed inelastic. On the other hand, should the 25 per cent price reduction invoke a 50 per cent increase in sales, then price would be elastic. This highlights a degree of market sensitivity at a certain level in respect of price (see Figures 6.2 and 6.3).

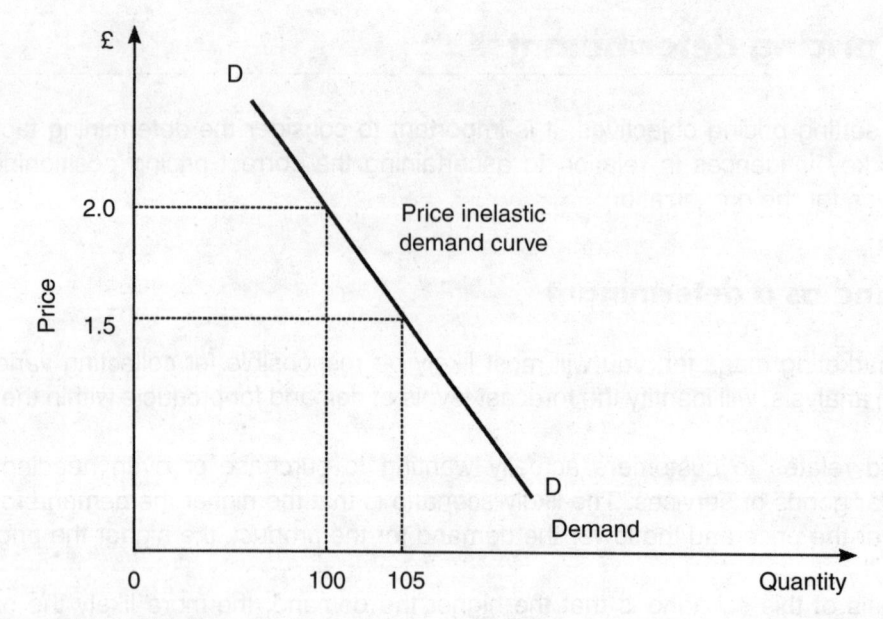

Figure 6.2 Inelasticity of demand

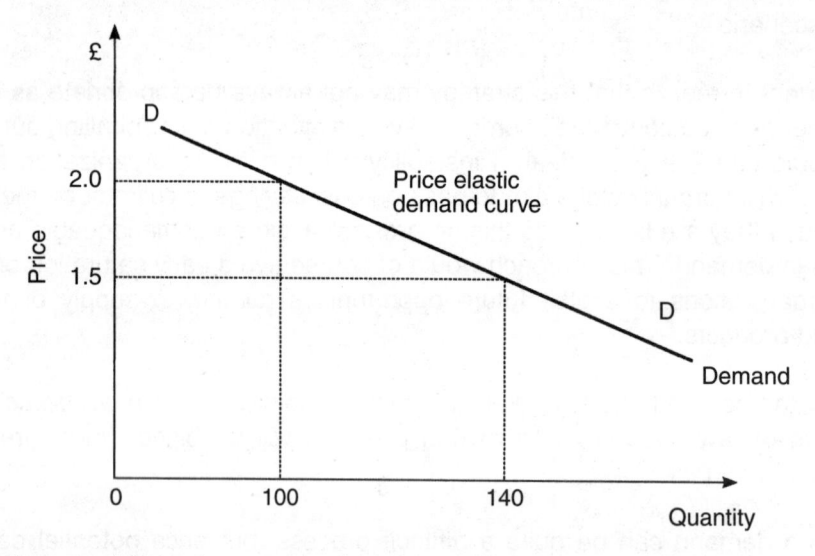

Figure 6.3 Elasticity of demand

## Price sensitive markets as a determinant

One of the most FAQs in marketing today is 'Is the market price sensitive?' or 'How price sensitive is the market?'. The volatility of the marketing environment currently dictates that organizations should maintain an awareness of the price sensitivity issues within the market.

In order to be able to balance price sensitive issues and address them fully, it is essential that the organization defines some key indicators that will ultimately signal to them the level of sensitivity that exists.

Some of the key indicators to observe are:

- How frequently is the product purchased?
- How essential is the product?
- How much does the product cost?
- What are the competitor alternatives within the market?
- What else can the customer's money be spent on?
- What is the effect of quality on price?
- What are the issues relating to stock/inventory?

Drawing anything conclusive from an analysis of the above points may prove to be rather difficult and will be the result of some quite complex analysis. However, the flexibility that surrounds pricing strategies will ultimately provide a basis for a well-balanced pricing strategy that will possibly provide perceived value, a robust competitive response and the level of profitability required.

A word of caution however: while price sensitivity is an issue, customers do not always make their purchasing decision based upon price, and on occasions it will be quite the contrary.

Understanding levels of price sensitivity in association with demand will help the organization ascertain the most appropriate pricing strategy in order to retain some form of consistency in demand, to avoid significant fluctuations.

## Competitors as a determinant

On a number of occasions, the significance of the levels of intense competition has been mentioned. Competitive response profiles for each competitor are essential in managing price competition.

It has already been established that competitor activity also plays a leading role in the price of products for the customer. In the 21st century, price wars are commonplace. Price cutting is used to increase demand, improve market share and beat off the competition. Supermarket wars are a prime example of this. Cost cutting, special offers and reward cards are all part of the war to gain market share. However, Nigel Piercy (2001) suggests in his book *Market Led Strategic Change* that price wars are both dangerous and contagious.

Customers are responsive to price cutting, as long as the perception of brand and product value remains unchanged. However, all organizations are forced to consider feasibility and viability of their marketing activities and corporate goals. Should the competition continue to intensify and profit margins continue to narrow, the infrastructure of the organization may have to change radically to remain competitive.

The pressure on organizations to be involved in competitor price is significant. Some of the key influences on price wars are:

- Customers no longer equate low price with low quality
- Saturation of some markets
- Price is a good tool to attack competitor weaknesses
- Undercutting the competition is the only way to compete successfully and make an impact
- The perception of reduced price and increased value is attractive to customers
- Part of the retail sector culture is to implement ongoing sales promotions.

Price wars create a vicious circle. For example, over the past 2 years or so there have been significant supermarket wars. As ASDA (Wal-Mart) has reduced its prices on the 'roll-back system', Sainsbury and Tesco have followed suit with alternative promotions and have come up with appropriate strategies to detract from the cost cutting in the competitor organization. The mobile communications and personal computer market is another very visible example of this type of behaviour.

In order to manage the demands of competitive intensity and its impact upon price, there are a number of options open to organizations to pursue, they include:

- Matching the price of the competitor
- Reducing the price below that of the competitor
- Implementation of further price changes. This may include additional reductions in further product lines
- Introduce new promotional incentives – 2 for the price of 1, get 25 per cent free, free delivery, etc. However, you must be aware that promotional incentives are often only a quick fix to what is a long-term problem.

Price affects market share; therefore organizations must take action to avoid losing volume of market share. This then comes back again to elasticity in demand and price sensitivity issues. Issues relating to market share will of course be detected through the use of portfolio planning tools.

## Case history

### Pharmacies price war

When the Restrictive Practices Court ruled in favour of lifting price controls on over-the-counter drugs the UK's leading supermarkets quickly moved to slash prices on a range of branded medicines like headache tablets, vitamins and flu remedies by up to 50 per cent. As a result of the knock-on effect on independent pharmacies, it is widely believed that many will go out of business.

Even some of the larger operations say they will pinch. Shares in Boots fell 6 per cent on the news of the ruling and the company said the decision would knock £15 million off profits within a year.

Because many of the independents rely on the margin gained from over-the-counter drugs, it was estimated around 15 per cent would go out of business because of the decision.

*Source*: Lexis-Nexis.

## Question 6.3

What appears to be the overall impact of competitive pricing in the 21st century?

## Product positioning and product life cycle as a determinant

Pricing will affect demand in many situations, and therefore issues in relation to product perception, product position and the stage in the PLC will be of the essence when designing appropriate pricing strategies. If you refer back to Unit 5 on 'Product operations', issues relating to price and profitability in the PLC are addressed.

## Debtors and creditors as a determinant

Issues relating to liquidity, credibility, payment terms and cash flow will all influence the basis of pricing strategies. Pricing strategies will reflect largely the financial management of the company and will need to link closely to their key performance indicators.

## The break-even analysis

The point at which an organization will become profitable will be one of the most important components of the decision-making process. Feasibility, viability, return on capital employed, will all be linked to ascertaining the break-even point. Break-even charts can be extremely useful in evaluating proposals for new products or projects designed to improve profitability. They are based on the marginal approach and, being visual, produce an impact which figures alone rarely achieve.

This can be illustrated in a simple graph – see Figure 6.4.

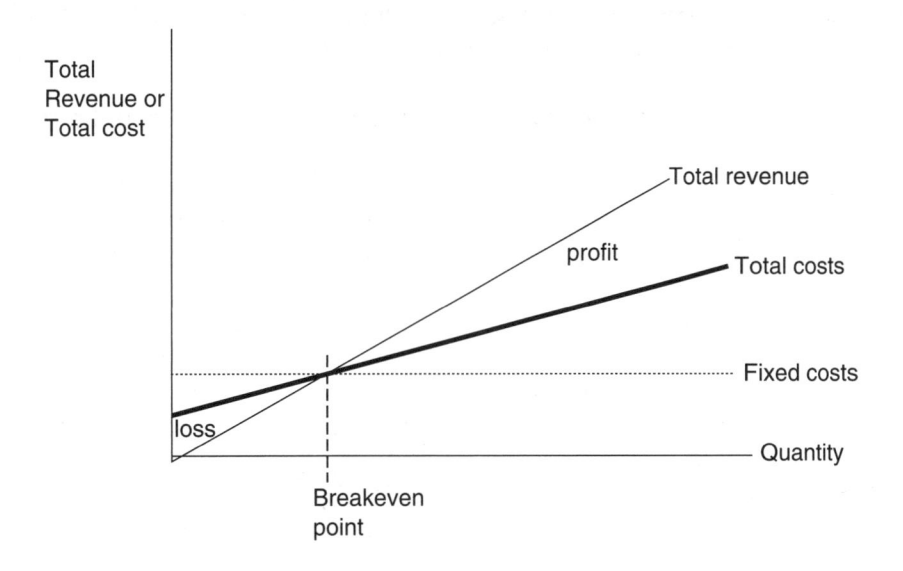

*Figure 6.4* Break-even analysis

Break-even analysis involves looking at the break-even point of different price levels.

The break-even costs can be calculated simply as follows:

Break-even point = Fixed costs/(Price per unit − variable costs per unit)

*Fixed costs* are those costs that are constant; for example property rental, permanent fixed salaries, car fleets, etc.

*Variable costs* are those costs that change based upon the amount of products manufactured, the cost of raw materials, temporary labour.

Add the two together and you get the total cost of production.

This is the starting point for actually setting the price for many organizations. They would then go on to consider how their price should sit within the marketplace, taking into consideration the factors we have already discussed, i.e. the key influences on price both internally and externally.

To obtain an accurate price, it is essential that the organization establish an accurate cost.

As part of your studies within Management Information for Marketing Decisions, you will undertake the physical working out of break-even analysis.

While break-even analysis is an essential component of determining price and future approaches to pricing strategies, you should be aware that in essence, break-even will be a strategic decision. You as the marketer will be responsible for implementing the break-even objectives. However, it is essential that you understand the basic principles of using such models, in order that you clearly understand the basis of how the organization establishes pricing objectives.

## Marginal costing and pricing

It is a given in pricing that sales revenue must at least cover the overhead costs before profit can be achieved. Therefore revenue should cover production, distribution and marketing costs and most likely make a contribution to the overall fixed costs of the organization.

Should a price be determined to recover the variable costs only, then the recovery is at the margin.

As a marketer you will need to establish what the marginal cost is of producing one or more additional units, in order that you ascertain the most cost-effective number of units to manufacture to achieve profit.

# Pricing objectives and strategies

Primarily, pricing objectives are set by companies in order to maximize sales revenue over and above costs in order to achieve profit.

Pricing objectives therefore reflect the basis of achieving profitability:

- *To achieve return on investment* – To ensure sufficient sales revenue to cover all associated cost bases and to pay back initial investment costs.
- *To maximize profits* – Companies who struggle to compete and have low market share may need to charge high prices to maximize profits.
- *To maximize sales revenue* – This will relate to setting prices at a level that will maximize sales turnover – more formally known as penetration pricing.
- *To achieve product quality leadership* – The basis of this objective will relate to providing the best quality product in the market in order to differentiate itself against its competitors, but will charge more than the competitors.

- *Market skimming* – Is where a company sets a high price to capture those customers who are willing to pay more for a product. Essentially this is more crudely defined as skimming the cream off, or targeting the top tier of the market. These people are likely to be the innovators, first in line in the adoption and diffusion process.
- *Survival* – Is as it sounds, generally setting objectives that ensure survival in a highly competitive market. Therefore the aim is to generate enough income to cover all costs, potentially working on a break-even basis in order to stay in business.

One of the greatest challenges of pricing and the marketing mix is to define pricing objectives that allow for the achievement of gaining market share, achieving profitability, providing technical leadership, innovation and quality leadership. Balancing this ship can be very tricky.

As with all other components of the marketing mix, pricing objectives must be clearly defined in line with meeting the overall marketing objectives and corporate goals. The role of pricing will be to integrate fully and support all the other elements of the marketing mix.

## Question 6.4

Explain why it is vitally important that pricing objectives reflect the marketing objectives and marketing strategy.

## Strategic pricing

Two of the pricing objectives are highly strategic and will closely reflect the basis of the marketing objectives. It is therefore essential to understand the key characteristics of price skimming and market penetration.

When a new product enters into the market, it is likely that either one of these strategies will be adopted in order to aid market entry but, at the same time, to gain early ROI.

*Price skimming* has the following features:

- There is a relatively high price per unit
- It is a good strategy to apply to new products and services with little price sensitivity (the development stage of the product life cycle)
- The price can be dropped when a market comes into existence
- The market can be segmented easily
- Profit is made on a per unit basis.

*Price penetration* has the following features:

- It offers a low price per unit
- Price penetration is used when a large volume of the market share is involved
- Profit is made through volume sales
- Price penetration applies to 'me too' type products (copies of other market leading brands)
- Low price is aided by high promotions.

The two strategies above are key to ensuring supply and demand at a strategic level. But there is a tactical level of pricing that also needs to be considered.

## Tactical pricing strategies

Whatever pricing objectives the organization adopts, it will be important to define the appropriate strategy in order that they are achieved.

The development of appropriate pricing strategies will not only focus on the methods of costing, but also on the integration of pricing within the marketing mix. It will take into consideration external and internal influences as they have been described earlier in the unit.

Tactical pricing provides the basis for the implementation of the marketing plan and its price-based objectives.

There are options to consider here:

- Marginal pricing
- Quantity discounts
- Differential pricing
- Cost-plus pricing
- Demand-based pricing.

### Marginal pricing

This involves:

- Offering a special price
- For a limited time period only
- Profit is still made.

An example here might be the introduction of a new consumer product to the market, e.g. a new drink at a special price for an introductory period of time that is limited. The customer might be motivated to trial the product at the cheaper price and may at least temporarily move from the brand they use currently. In saying this, there is research to prove that more often than not the majority of customers return to their own existing brand preference once the promotion has ended.

### Quantity discounting

This involves:

- The principle that manufacturer prices are at their cheapest when large quantities are produced (economies of scale)
- Money is received quickly
- Removing chances for the competition (in encouraging bulk purchase)
- Adding benefits for the customer.

A good example of this would be the purchase of print cartridges from the stationers. If a high usage or minimum purchase for a set period can be guaranteed then the customer may consider bulk purchase to obtain additional discounts. As the stationer does not have to store the materials for as long, it makes storage easier to manage and potentially reduces costs.

## Differential pricing

This involves:

- High fixed costs
- The relevant application of seasons and timings
- Benefit to both the producer and the consumer.

Differential pricing strategies set different prices for different markets, a point picked up earlier in this unit, and also within 'Product operations'.

The leisure industry is an example here. During the week many hotels charge very high corporate rates, e.g. £150.00 per night, room only. At the weekend many of the same hotels have weekend special offers of £150.00 per weekend, per person, for dinner, bed and breakfast. Therefore differential rates are charged for corporate booking than for leisure booking. This strategy underpins the continuous use of hotel rooms throughout the season, but uses different pricing strategies for different target markets.

Other factors involved are:

- Geo-demographics (i.e. geography and demographics) – where perhaps because of remoteness of a town, the cost of distribution is higher
- The same products or services being sold in the same position at different prices geographically.

A good example is possibly the price of eating out. Within the UK there is a considerable price differential based upon geographical location. A further example related to earlier discussion is the price of petrol, which is considerably higher in more remote locations than in the main towns and cities.

## Cost-plus pricing

This involves:

- Covering the overhead costs, plus a percentage on top, to meet marketing/profit objectives.

Cost-plus pricing is usually used for projects that are more difficult to cost out, or actually take a long time for completion. It is also a useful pricing tool while markets are volatile, because you can always change the percentage on top of costs, and adjust it to meet market demands.

Cost-plus pricing is a simplistic approach which determines the cost of manufacture, plus a specified percentage above the price in line with the organization's requirements, which will ultimately achieve the selling price.

## Eight stages to establishing a price

To summarize the key principles of pricing and to put your learning into a more practical context, Dibb, Simkin, Pride and Ferrell (2001) suggest that there are eight key stages to determining or establishing a chargeable price (see Figure 6.5).

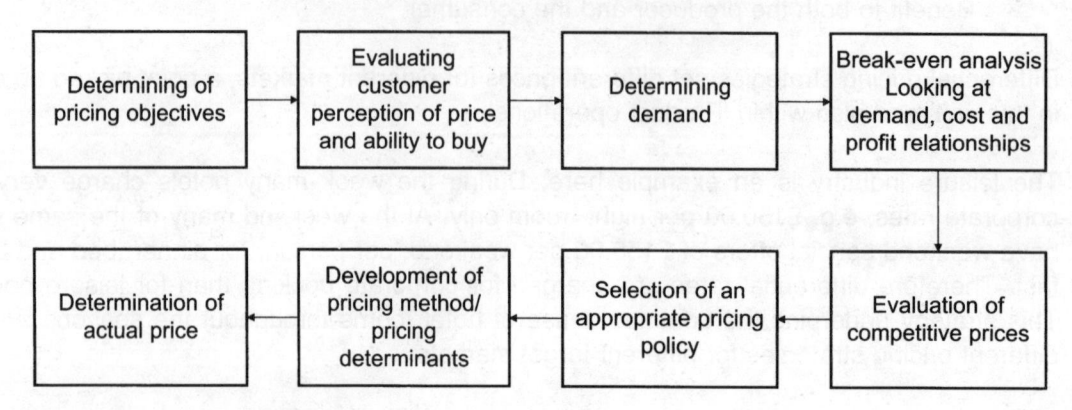

```
Determining of        Evaluating customer         Determining        Break-even analysis
pricing objectives → perception of price    →    demand         →    Looking at demand,
                      and ability to buy                              cost and profit
                                                                      relationships
                                                                           ↓
Determination of  ←  Development of       ←   Selection of an    ←   Evaluation of
actual price         pricing method/          appropriate            competitive prices
                     pricing determinants     pricing policy
```

*Figure 6.5* Stages for establishing price
*Source*: Adapted from Dibb, Simkin, Pride and Ferrell (2001)

## The route to setting higher prices

As a marketer you will always be challenged to identify a potential route for charging higher prices, as it is unlikely that profit goals will allow for the sustainable continuance of low prices. Some of the points to consider in doing this are as follows:

- The strength of the customer relationship built by the salesforce – how does this impact upon the ability of the organization to negotiate higher prices?
- Is the perceived value, i.e. the value proposition, enough to give the organization competitive advantage?
- Does the marketing segmentation strategy highlight where some target groups are more or less price-sensitive than others?
- How might the branding strategy allow for several price positions to be upheld in the market?
- Are there any opportunities for skimming the market – price skimming?

### Summary

The price element of the marketing mix leaves marketers aiming to achieve the ultimate blend of price, quality and perceived value. A balanced marketing mix will ensure the customer is getting the right product in the right place, at the right time, for the right price.

Customers are very fickle today and clearly understand that they have significant choice, and indeed power, in the marketplace and that they have significant influence upon supply and demand.

Prices will vary according to what people are prepared to pay in different situations. Different prices might also reflect what customers can pay or are prepared to pay. However, from a management perspective, you are challenged to consider whether price is simply what the customer will pay, or a more flexible marketing tool than just that.

In order to understand the influence of price on the customers and competitors, a marketer must understand the need for significant ongoing research into the state of the external environment and the activities of competitors and gain a key understanding of buyer behaviour and expectations.

The critical success factors in relation to price are to maintain the organizational objectives, yet endeavour to remain sensitive to the needs of the customers, ensuring that you can address their long-term needs, including the further development of new and innovative additions to the product range and lines. The key to price is to link the product quality with clear indication of value for money from the organization to the customer.

Pitching the price at the right level may be the difference between profit and loss or survival and failure, as pricing will reflect the long-term profitability and market share. Therefore, in order to achieve a marketing-oriented approach to pricing, the organization should take into account a broad range of factors:

- Marketing strategy
- Value proposition
- Price-quality relationships
- Competitive pricing
- Costs
- Ability to negotiate higher prices
- External market forces
- The effects of globalization
- Product line pricing.

### Study tip

The basis of pricing in the context of Marketing Planning relates to understanding the concepts of pricing, the implications of pricing and possible approaches to implementation of pricing strategies in line with the corporate goals and marketing objective. The technicalities of pricing are covered in Management Information for Marketing Decisions, which is where you will learn the actual basis of calculation. Therefore from an exam perspective it is likely that you will discuss potential pricing strategies, discuss influences on price and some of the strategic determinants.

In the exam, pricing is invariably included as an integral part of the marketing mix, with some individual pricing questions appearing on some, but not all, papers.

Question spotting and question prediction is a dangerous game, therefore always be well prepared, ensuring that you have a full knowledge and understanding of the subject in preparation for providing good robust answers.

## Extending knowledge

**Recommended reading**

Recommended reading for this unit again comes from Dibb, Simkin, Pride and Ferrell (2001), Chapters 18 and 19. This will provide you with a very broad perspective of pricing. You will find these chapters very useful again when you study for Marketing Research and Information, as they explain some of the basis of the calculations required.

### Bibliography

Dibb, S., Simkin, L., Pride, W. and Ferrell, O. (2001) *Marketing: Concepts and Strategies*, 4th European edition, Houghton Mifflin.

Piercy, N. (2001) *Market Led Strategic Change*, Butterworth-Heinemann.

---

Sample exam questions and answers for the Marketing Planning module as a whole can be found in Appendix 4.

# unit 7 place operations

## Learning objectives

Place operations highlights the importance of distribution as a key factor in achieving the ultimate marketing mix. It is the final component and relates to ensuring that customers are able to gain access to and purchase their chosen product.

This unit reflects the same principal learning outcomes as the other marketing mix units, in terms of understanding the need to integrate the marketing mix tools and achieve effective implementation of plans.

From a place perspective, the indicative content reflects the following:

- Determine the channels of distribution and logistics to be used by an organization and develop a plan for channel support.

Syllabus reference: 3.9

## Introduction

It is a known fact that without distribution 'place' the best product or service will not be delivered and the marketing mix will break down and fail. It was once said that the 'place' was one of the most powerful elements of the marketing mix, as it is the one way that we can both reach and actually service the customer.

Distribution is seen as a component part of the product. Therefore, in order to achieve total satisfaction, customer service will play an essential part in the overall achievement of customer satisfaction, retention and a sustainable competitive advantage.

Distribution works on two key principles:

1. It organizes the exchange process through distribution
2. It organizes communication.

Place plays a pivotal role within the marketing mix, and the key to success will be its successful integration within it, ensuring that customers get their products at the right place and at the right time. This will involve a range of alternative marketing activities based around promotion, price and the actual product design and packaging.

Distribution plays an important role, primarily because it ultimately affects the sales turnover and profit margins of the organization. If the product cannot reach its chosen destination at the appropriate time, then it can erode competitive advantage and customer retention.

An additional factor now facing distribution is the power of the buyers. As buyers we are becoming increasingly impatient, not wishing to wait for our products for any period of time. Therefore, if distribution is a significant player in the decision-making process the consequences of an inadequate distribution strategy may be catastrophic. There is an expectation in relation to delivery, in the same way there is with product and price. The combined package provides an expectation in the mind of customers and it also influences their overall perception of the value proposition.

Distribution provides many extensive new business opportunities and is currently at the centre of a range of strategic alliances, mergers, acquisitions, joint ventures and licensing agreements. In addition to this, the emergence and explosion of the Internet and other information communication technologies has put distribution on track to be one of the most lucrative business propositions of recent years.

Distribution requires a high degree of management skill, synchronization and integration with the overall organization, as it will be one of the major components in achieving a sustainable competitive advantage. Controlling the flow of products between the manufacturer or producer is no easy task, and as pointed out above, failure to control the flow effectively could decide the level of success you might enjoy in the marketplace.

## Influences on distribution

Distribution is subject to a key set of influences in the same way as the other elements of the marketing mix. It is subject to external driving forces, internal forces and of course the forever-increasing power of the customer. Influences on place operations will therefore include:

- Fuel prices
- Environmental legislation
- Taxation
- Transportation choices
- National/global transportation infrastructure
- Nature of product and product characteristics – perishability, etc.
- Packaging
- Product life cycle
- Changing lifestyles
- The emergence of ICT
- Customer expectations
- Level of complexity in customer buying behaviour
- Competitive strategies
- Production targets
- Demand
- Market size
- Contribution towards costs
- Marketing mix components
- Customer services
- Technical support.

The list is tremendous and some of the factors have significant influence on the cost of distribution. Already in many organizations distribution claims up to 50 per cent of the product costs, which is a considerable amount to absorb when designing appropriate competitive pricing strategies.

Logistics management plays a significant role in dealing with some of these influences and managing through them, in taking decisions such as appropriate order quantities, delivery methods, channel lengths, frequency of delivery, stock and inventory considerations, customer care and customer satisfaction. Each of these elements of logistics management will have a huge influence in achieving a balance between price and profitability.

### Question 7.1

In what way do you think changing lifestyles have impacted on and influenced distribution strategies?

## Marketing issues for distribution

Marketers need to be aware of the implications of distribution in respect of marketing. Distribution is ultimately about providing a service, a service of delivery to the customer, essentially getting the product from A to B. Therefore, there are some principal marketing issues that should be addressed.

The main marketing issue relates to channels. It is essential that you understand that the successful management of the supply chain will be achieved through selecting, motivating and controlling distributors and distribution outlets. However, if you reflect back on Porter's Five Forces, you will see the difficulty that faces any marketer in achieving that, as the power of the supplier can be quite significant.

The other key component of successful distribution is meeting customer expectations in respect of delivery and service promises the organization might make. Think back to the importance of the value proposition. How does it position your business in respect of meeting delivery promises throughout the length and breadth of the distribution channel? The implications of achieving this will be a logistical challenge.

In order to achieve this wish list, a closely designed integrated marketing mix will need to exist. It will be essential that the underpinning support required by the distribution channel be in place in order to adopt both push and pull strategies in the marketplace.

## Distribution channels

The distribution channel consists of a group of individuals or organizations that assist in getting the product to the right place at the right time. They enable the manufactured products to flow from the manufacturer to the end-user in many different ways.

Because of the nature of the marketing environment and the growth in international trade in what is termed the 'global marketplace', distribution can often be very involved, with a number of varying groups playing a key role in moving the products around.

Those groups are known as marketing intermediaries; they are really the middlemen. Intermediaries play a key role in ensuring that the manufacturer's target market is a group of very satisfied customers. Their role is to make sure that the product is available just when the customer wants it and from the place in which they want to purchase it.

Unit 7 Place operations

Within each distribution channel there are a number of different levels and different links, which will of course vary from channel to channel. However, as everything changes over time, the channels are predictably becoming shorter and shorter, with more and more people choosing to cut out the middleman in order to reduce costs and become more competitive.

The choice of channel is a strategic decision in the main and will have implications across the corporate organization in the way in which it does business. It most definitely impacts upon quality programmes, corporate development processes and, very importantly, resources.

## Channel members

Intermediaries play a very important role within the distribution channel and the supply chain. In the main there are organizations such as transportation companies, merchants, agents, wholesaler, warehouses, retail outlets, to name but a few. Let us look at a brief overview of the function of each of them.

### Wholesalers

Wholesalers are the middlemen at the early end of the distribution channel. It is very rare that they will sell directly to the end-user. They will buy products from the manufacturer, store them within their warehouses and sell the products on to the trade. This means that the wholesaler takes financial responsibility for the products; in fact they take legal title and physical possession of them. Producers will likely support the marketing activity through various push and pull strategies in order to ensure market demand increases.

### Retailers

As a result of the technology revolution, the retailer is now not just on the high street but on the superhighway, the Internet. This is having a significant impact upon distribution, as you will see later in this unit.

The role of retailers is essentially the final stopping point for the product prior to its sale. Their role is to manage the transaction in which the buyer resolves to make their purchase decision and then the actual purchase. They will often act as the broker of information, the link between the customer and the producer, and the source of the customer relationship management.

Retailers have a highly prominent position in the channel and therefore potentially have the most challenging role in actually securing the transaction.

They may require considerable technical support, customer services backup, stock ordering facilities, technological systems underpinning the sales process, information and merchandise.

### Distributors/dealers

Distributors and dealers are groups of intermediaries who are associated with stocking products for manufacturers and selling them on, including after-sales service and credit facilities. For example, when you purchase a Hotpoint washing machine, you may buy it from one of the big retailer outlets such as Comet or Currys; you may also buy an extended service warranty. The warranty does not come directly from Hotpoint nor from Comet, but from a third-party distributor.

Dealers are slightly different in that quite often they will specialize in selling one particular brand; for example, car dealerships are often associated with the manufacturer and therefore they sometimes sell on to the end-user, and the channel is somewhat shorter.

### Agents/brokers/facilitators

Agents and brokers, as a general rule, do not take physical possession of the goods, but act on behalf of the manufacturer to sell their goods. Their main purpose is to bring buyers and sellers together. This is particularly common within international trade, where organizations do not necessarily have a physical presence.

### Franchisee

Franchising is quite a common form of making a product available in the marketplace. The Body Shop was well known at one stage for franchising activities, as are Kentucky Fried Chicken and McDonald's. Franchising means that the franchisee holds a contract to market and supply a product or service that has been very strictly designed and developed by the franchiser. The franchiser will most likely have strict terms and conditions on store design, store layout and contents sold within the retail outlet.

### Licensee

This is very similar to franchisee. The licensee pays royalties on sales or supplies to the licensor. The licensor is more often than not the manufacturer of the product.

### Merchandiser

Merchandising relates very closely to retailing. Merchandisers are responsible for store displays relating to different products. For example, most supermarkets now sell CDs in store. Many of the suppliers of the CDs employ merchandisers to go into the store to check supplies and set up promotional displays.

## Why use intermediaries?

Due to the intensity of competition currently being experienced, many organizations are faced with cost reductions, resource reductions and often as a result, restructuring. So why, in the circumstances, should we continue to use intermediaries. What is the rationale that lies behind it?

Whilst distribution is highly expensive, naturally, there are a lot of add-on costs, such as those associated with marketing, administration, packaging, order processing and receiving and making payments. For an organization to undertake all of these activities will be quite costly.

Take the example of a producer with a network of links, a combination of retailers, wholesalers, agents and merchandisers. The network consists of 10 key buyers, who then distribute out to another 10 buyers; there are then 100 links in the network. The physical and logistical management involved might be horrendous. The costs will also be inextricably linked to the size of the network and the management exercise.

Therefore, the rationale behind the use of intermediaries in circumstances such as this is to invest in them and their activities in order that they take on the responsibility for marketing and administration within their network, further pushing the products out into the market. This may be a good value proposition to the suppliers, if the intermediaries are provided with some form of incentive such as heavy discounts or even profit-related returns.

Of course, while the financial benefits are significant, there are other benefits also, and other ways of adding value in the range of the customer-supplier relationship. The basis of these benefits can be segmented into three different groups (Figure 7.1).

**Logistical value**
Stock
Sorting
Breaking bulk
Transportation

**Transactional value**
Financing
Training
Information
After sales

Value added logistical services

**Facilitating value**
Shared risk
Marketing
Administration

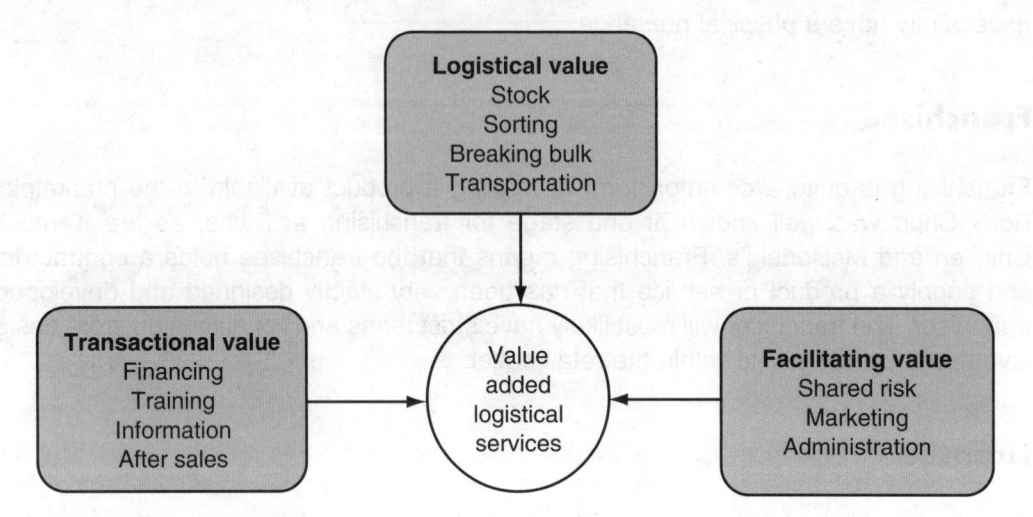

*Figure 7.1* Valued-added services
*Source*: Adapted from Brassington and Pettitt (2000)

It is likely that in a large distribution network, channel members may have to perform a number of these value-added business functions in order to support their own organizational objectives. Should a manufacturer agree to supply an intermediary with their products, it may include securing a commitment from them to market their products appropriately to the target markets. Table 7.1 provides a more detailed basis of how the above value-added services might be undertaken.

*Table 7.1* The role of the intermediary

| Category of marketing activities | Possible activities required |
|---|---|
| *Marketing information* | Analyse information such as sales data. Carrying out research studies |
| *Marketing management* | Establish objectives, plan activities and manage. Co-ordinate financing, risk taking. Evaluate channel activities |
| *Facilitating exchange* | Choose and stock products that match buyers' needs |
| *Promotion* | Set promotional objectives, co-ordinate advertising, personal selling, promotions, etc. |
| *Price* | Establish pricing policies, terms and sales |
| *Physical distribution* | Manage transport, warehousing, materials handling, stock control and communication |
| *Customer service* | Provide channels for advice, technical support, after-sales service and warranties |
|  | Facilitate communication, products, parts, credit control, etc. Maintain relationships between manufacturer and retail outlets, and customer/consumer |

*Source*: Adapted from Dibb, Simkin, Pride and Ferrell (2001)

## Question 7.2

Explain with examples how the use of intermediaries can prove cost-effective in an organization.

## The distribution channel and the customer

There are many variations in respect of the distribution channel structure (see Figure 7.2), however, should intermediaries be deemed as appropriate in the business environment, the following channel structures would be available to you:

1. Passing of goods and services direct from the manufacturer to the consumer
2. Passing of goods and services via a retailer and then on to a consumer
3. Passing of goods and services from the manufacturer via a wholesaler and then directly on to the consumer
4. Passing of goods and services from manufacturer via a wholesaler, then on to a retailer and subsequently on to the consumer
5. Additionally, the manufacturer can distribute the products and services via an agent to a wholesaler and then follow the routes shown in points 3 and 4.

Quite often the types of channels of distribution used by organizations will depend upon the structure of the market, the size of the market, the complexity of the market and the geographical dispersion of the market, among other factors.

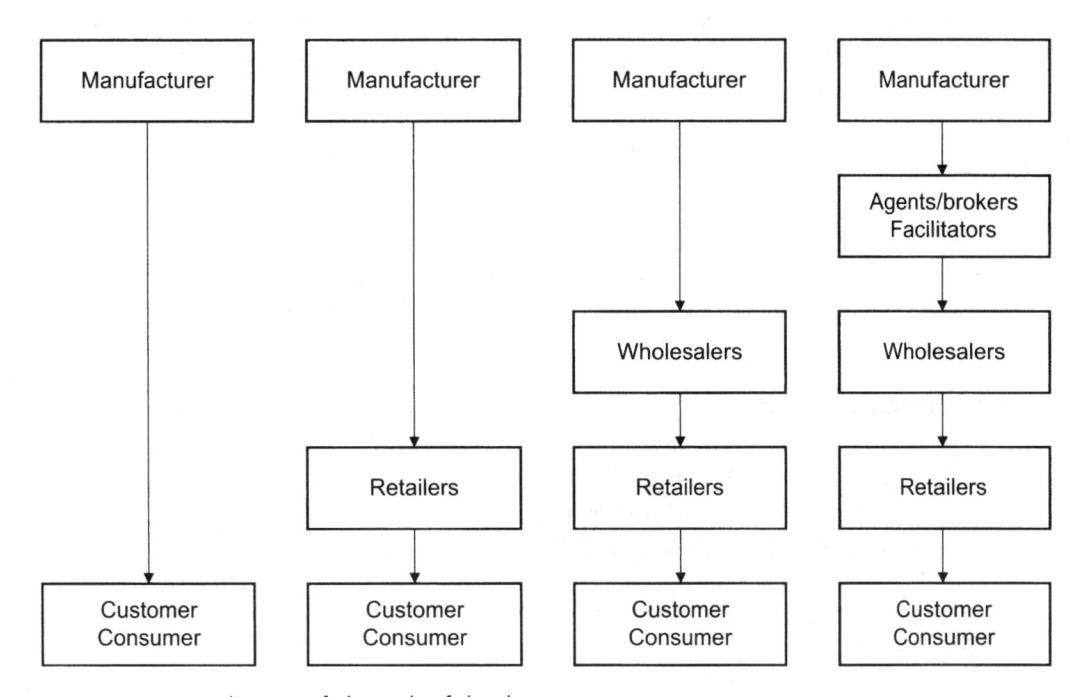

Figure 7.2 A typical range of channels of distribution

## Selecting the channels of distribution

For a manufacturer to select a channel, they must consider the most appropriate one to meet their customer needs. They must consider the following:

- What are the product characteristics and how do they affect methods of distribution?
- Who are their customers?
- Where are their customers?
- What are their customer requirements?
- How, when and where do they want to buy their products?
- What are their competitors doing by way of distribution?
- What is the cost of distribution?
- What are the legal and regulatory constraints of distribution?

These are important issues and require significant levels of analysis in order to gain an understanding of the situation. Clearly some of these questions will form the basis of the marketing audit. Ideally the marketing mix has a clear focus on achieving customer satisfaction and achieving the profit objectives of the organization.

As competition is so aggressive in the marketplace, organizations will always look for new and improved ways of distributing their products. At the same time, retail outlets seem to be concerning themselves with providing as much as possible for the customer to save them going elsewhere, and obviously with the ultimate aim of securing a significant market share and increased profitability.

Supermarkets have moved away from just supplying food-based products to include fashions, music, electrical goods, cosmetics, etc. All of this is focused on meeting all of the above distribution factors. With the recent takeover of ASDA by the American owned Wal-Mart, this kind of service provision is likely to grow and include an even broader range of products.

## Intermediary selection criteria

There are two perspectives of intermediary selection, the strategic perspective and the operational perspective: strategic in relation to looking at the 'bigger picture' and 'operational' looking at the ability to implement the strategic marketing plan and distribution strategy.

### Operational criteria

- Knowledge of local markets
- Appropriate premises and equipment
- Technological systems and processes
- Customer convenience
- Product knowledge and expertise
- Payment facilities
- Sales force structure, size and effectiveness
- Efficient customer service infrastructure.

### Strategic criteria

- Plans for growth and expansion
- Resource capacity and future development

- o Quality assurance processes
- o Management ability
- o Innovative
- o Willing partnership
- o Levels of loyalty and co-operation.

### Applying these criteria to international supply chains

Later on in this text in Unit 9, there is some brief consideration of the implications of developing international marketing channels and supply relationships. However, it is important to note at this time that the application of the above criteria can be considerably more complex in international markets due to issues relating to cultural differences, i.e. the way in which organizations do business, structure themselves, commit themselves to relationships. Additionally, there are issues relating to resource requirements and fulfilment, i.e. does the international intermediary have the necessary resources and infrastructure to sustain a long-term supplier relationship.

It is a known fact that sometimes international intermediaries can be more fickle and establishing long-term supplier relationships based upon partnership loyalty and co-operation can be somewhat difficult to achieve, particularly when competitors offer preferential trade promotions to attract them away. Actually being able to tie an intermediary into a single supplier relationship can therefore be quite difficult.

One of the critical features of a channel network is to ensure that the country market analysed possesses channels which will provide the necessary services. Inherent within this will be the necessity to check financial stability, storage capacity for sufficient quantities of products, supply chain and distribution networks and whether the firm might invest in a dedicated network in order to supply the market.

Channel members tend only to be interested in closely defined or preferential supplier partnerships when high sales and high margins are available, and that they will contribute towards the competitive success of the company.

With a good distribution network established, co-ordination and control will need to be established. This task, even in a small firm, can be complex and must include ensuring that consignments and shipments arrive on time, that distributors are notified, that appropriate promotional mix activities are being undertaken and that the required financial reporting is in place. This will obviously include comparisons between budgeted and actual sales made and so on. Obviously with the increased used of telecommunications and LAN computer networks the control and co-ordination and distribution across different countries are very difficult tasks.

## The balance of power within the distribution channel

The balance of power within the distribution channel is an interesting concept to consider. As each party has its own set of objectives to pursue and its own agenda, fitting in with a partner organization can potentially cause conflict. Who then holds the balance of power? Is it the manufacturer because they have the products available for market? Or the intermediary, who may decide they do not want to sell on the product to retail outlets? Or is it the retailers themselves, who will decide on the most appropriate brand to sell to their customers?

Channel co-operation is critical and channel members need to be united in their destiny. They should share information, agree to be directed to the same target markets and together maximize efficiency.

Often a channel leader will be identified to enable a co-ordinated effort of all parties in the marketing channel. Without co-operation the member objectives or the channel's objectives will not be achieved.

To become a leader within the channel, the channel member must want to direct and influence the channel's overall performance. To do this the channel leader must have significant power and driving force in order to succeed. To gain power in the relationship, the organization will likely be a significant size, with major resources. It must be expert in its field, and have the respect of the other channel members. It must be able to punish or reward other channel members effectively to get what it wants.

The channels will perform most effectively when they co-operate, co-ordinate and integrate their activities. Should they divert their gaze from the ultimate goal at any stage the channel will go into conflict and their effectiveness could be challenged and competitors could seize their opportunity to deflect customers to their products and markets.

## Channel strategy

There are three types of market coverage:

1. Intensive
2. Selective
3. Exclusive.

*Intensive distribution* means that as many available outlets as possible hold this product, e.g. chocolate, newspapers, bread, etc. Intensive distribution will mean convenience to the customer and increased customer satisfaction. The sale of groceries in petrol and service stations is an example of how intensive distribution has grown.

Key characteristics include:

- Maximum number of outlets covered to maximize availability
- Target outlets in as many geographical regions as possible
- Consumer convenience products
- High number of purchasers
- High purchase frequency
- Impulsive purchase
- Low price.

*Selective distribution* is different in that some products are only available from some outlets, e.g. electrical appliances, certain brands of clothes and fashion products.

Key characteristics include:

- Medium level of customers – but likely to be significant
- Less intensive distribution of outlets
- Retailers may require specialist knowledge
- Shopping based products
- Medium number of shoppers
- Purchase is occasional
- Purchase is more likely to be planned
- Medium price.

*Exclusive distribution* is where possibly only one outlet in a certain geographic area supplies a product. This method of distribution usually relates to speciality products, e.g. special cars, specialist clothing, etc. Often exclusive distribution is relevant to niche products.

Key characteristics include:

- Relatively few customers
- Limited retail outlets
- Close retailer/customer relationship
- Speciality products
- Infrequent purchase
- High involvement and planned purchase
- High price.

## Question 7.3

You have been asked by your manager to recommend and justify the most appropriate distribution strategy for a new palm-top product, which is a portable keyboard that can be plugged into the palm-top enabling it to be used as a mini-PC.

## Vertical channel integration

An easy definition of vertical channel management, as quoted by Hill and O'Sullivan (1999), is:

*A distribution system where two or more channel members are connected by ownership or legal obligation.*

A further definition is:

*A marketing channel in which a single channel member will co-ordinate or manage channel activities to achieve efficient, low-cost distribution, aimed at satisfying target market customers.*

When you look at the varying distribution channels illustrated earlier in the unit, and you see the varying organizations involved, you will appreciate that in today's environment organizations, for reasons of economies and profit objectives, are becoming very interrelated.

A prime example of this would be a supermarket such as Wal-Mart, which is likely to service its own supermarket stores from its own network of central warehouses. This means that they own their own warehouses and their own logistics company.

This method of distribution ensures profit maximization is achieved across all areas of the business, with utilization of resources across the board. In doing this, the organization benefits from income vertically up and down the supplier/manufacturer chain. This particular strategy would invoke the demise of the middleman as the manufacturers endeavour to buy them out to service their own functions in-house wherever possible.

However, the vertical marketing system then undertakes the complex task of managing all associated management functions and all of the marketing mix activities in-house, which means that the marketing activities are much more closely related and integrated, and often therefore much more effective. These areas include:

- Product design and development
- Branding
- Pricing
- Promoting
- Stock control and storage
- Merchandising
- Transportation
- Retailing
- Customer services
- Finance/credit
- Warranties and guarantees.

## Horizontal channel integration

Horizontal channel integration is easily defined:

*The combination of institutions at the same level of channel operation under one management.*

This means that organizations that exist at the same level in the channel, e.g. the retailer level of the channel, may integrate with another organization by actually purchasing it. For example, there have been a number of significant mergers and takeovers within the mobile communications network, supermarkets (e.g. ASDA and Wal-Mart, Kwik Save and Somerfield) and the financial services sectors.

In this situation one business will purchase another business, either in the same field or in a similar one, they will re-brand it, but pool resources such as marketing activities, marketing research, advertising, databases, personnel, distribution and warehousing. The net effect is that organizations can extend their market share both nationally and globally, while reducing their overhead costs significantly, but increasing their effectiveness, making them more competitive overall.

## Physical distribution management

Physical distribution management (PDM) is the term used to describe the management of every part of the distribution process. PDM can be contracted out to a specialist or is best developed as a specialist function within the organization. It is the process which ensures that the correct product gets to the correct customer within a given timescale, as cost-effectively as possible.

Part of PDM would include being aware of what your competitors are offering, as suggested above. Elements for consideration would include:

- Costs involved
- *Methods of transport* – road, rail, plane, shipping, etc.
- Routes used
- Stock, storage and stock control

- Protection and delivery of stock
- *Timing* – a key element
- Evaluating the effectiveness of methods of distribution and being aware of other alternatives.

Distribution is an integral part of the marketing mix. With the right distribution strategy in place, that is with the right mode of delivery, the right speed of delivery to the appropriate place of purchase, customer satisfaction can be significantly increased. Failure to deliver these practical points will result in the loss of orders and income to the company and long-term customer loyalty will decline.

The key objective of PDM is to find the most cost-effective way of meeting customer needs in relation to purchasing their product, whoever they are and wherever they are.

Physical distribution management includes the following functions:

- Customer services
- Order processing
- Materials handling
- Warehousing
- Stock/inventory management
- Transportation.

The key success factors of PDM include all elements of the marketing mix:

- *Product characteristics* – how do they affect delivery requirements?
- *Packaging* – can the product be transported?
- *Pricing* – how much does distribution add to the cost of the product?
- *Promotional campaigns* – creating an awareness of the product and where and how it can be purchased.

Timing is a critical element of PDM, as many companies work on the delivery of materials and components on a *Just in Time* basis (JIT).

JIT is just as it sounds; it means that the manufacturer of products, or the supplier of raw materials, must deliver the necessary materials or components as and when required. For example, a window manufacturer, who makes windows for office buildings, will be making windows to order and will be required to deliver them at certain periodic times in the construction of the building. Because storing glass and the metal or plastic structures is difficult, the organization will deliver as and when the office block construction company needs it.

The concept of JIT was developed to encourage maximized efficiency of manufacturing. The process will reduce the storage space requirements, which is a direct cost saving to the organization, but it also means that the organization will only pay for the materials when they have taken delivery of them, rather than in a bulk order at the beginning of the contract. Both save significant amounts of money, which means that the cost savings can be passed on to the customer, making products cheaper to purchase.

JIT is very much linked to quality applications and improvements. Should the organization take a mass delivery of a component, and leave stock standing around, it could be damaged or problems with the delivery may not be discovered until it is too late. Therefore, quality assurance controls and measures can be implemented as the components are dispatched which then aids the quality improvement process. This then enables organizations to work towards zero defects, which means zero wastage of time and materials, which means cost-effectiveness and quality improvement and ultimately a higher level of customer satisfaction.

Within the retail sector, JIT plays the same sort of role. You will note that retail outlets very rarely run out of standard stock products, because they have good stock control processes and systems that enable JIT delivery of those stock items.

Most retailers now work with electronic point of sale systems (EPOS). EPOS registers your purchase at the point of sale, i.e. the payment checkout. The product is scanned into the computer as sold and the computer automatically registers this as a stock reduction. When the stock reduction reaches a certain minimum level, the computer automatically generates a message to place a stock order for that particular product to be in store by a certain delivery date.

The EPOS system allows retailers to monitor frequency of purchase of certain products, which then enables them to forecast demand of their stock products. This in turn helps them plan for their stock requirement and come to appropriate agreements with their suppliers on delivery and storage requirements.

## Push and pull strategies

The way in which products make their way to customers is a critical consideration to marketers. The push element relates to distribution and how personal selling links the supplier to the customer, pushing the product out to the market.

On the other hand the pull strategy is very heavily reliant on advertising, packaging and sales promotions directly aimed at the consumer, effectively pulling them or attracting them to the product, encouraging them to purchase and forge a lasting relationship.

The huge growth in Internet marketing and direct marketing has really speeded this process up, with promotional incentives. For example, Marks and Spencer are now giving discount vouchers to M&S storecard holders to encourage them to make additional purchases. Next Directory offers free delivery or 20 per cent off orders over £100.00. These are pull strategies. There has been a significant rise in pull strategies as a result of the surge in Internet-based shopping. It shortens the distribution channel and makes the response times quicker.

Key factors influencing push strategies might include:

- Levels of economic and financial stability
- Need for economies of scale
- Mature or saturated markets
- Consumer credit restrictions
- Political instability
- Intense competition
- High operating costs
- Indications of low market growth.

Key factors influencing pull strategies might include:

- Levels of economic and financial stability
- Innovative culture
- Underdeveloped retail infrastructure for the products
- High investment potential
- High levels of market growth
- Social stability
- Political stability.

As a marketing manager you will need to understand the importance of supporting onward suppliers in order to maximize economies of scale, associated profitability and benefits of a robust channel strategy.

## The impact of the Internet on channel decisions

Distribution is currently subject to a fast pace of change as a result of the huge growth in ICT, and the majority of manufacturers and distributors have clearly been considering the above points in association with the new channel alternative of the Internet. Manufacturers and suppliers are being forced to reconsider the traditional routes to market that exist in favour of the Internet.

### Insight

#### Internet consumer expenditure in the Netherlands

By mid-2002 there were 7.7 million regular (more than once per month) active Internet-users. The number of active Internet-users is still growing. The growth percentages are lower now than 1 year ago (currently 5 per cent as against 6 per cent half a year ago). The number of online purchasers among active Internet-users is still growing. In the first half of 2003 circa 2.8 million Internet-users made at least one online purchase.

In the first half of 2003 Dutch online consumer purchases increased by 36 per cent to €575 million. During 2001 the online sales share of the total retail trade sales (*Source*: CBS) amounted to 0.65 per cent. By 2002 this had increased to 1.11 per cent (retail trade turnover in 2002 was €82.7 billion). This means that even in 2003 the share of online sales is still gaining ground over off-line sales.

#### Online consumer purchases

#### Market development

Purchases amount to €424 million were made during the first half of 2002. This means that €151 million more was sold via the Internet during the first half of 2003. The total online shopping market grew by 36 per cent during the first half of 2003. In comparison with the second half of 2002, the market has grown by about €62 million, which is a 12 per cent growth.

The growth in the online shopping market is partly due to an increase in the number of shoppers who have bought something online during the past half-year; this group is continuing to grow and has increased by 24 per cent to 2.8 million online shoppers. One year ago this figure was 2.25 million shoppers. What can be seen is a reduction in the number of online purchasers who have purchased something for the first time via the Internet, from 410 000 to about 300 000 first-time shoppers.

On average each online shopper spent €205.00 during the first half of this year, an increase of 9 per cent in comparison with a year ago (€188.00 per online purchaser). The higher expenditure per consumer is mainly the result of greater average expenditure on travel (in view of the summer season), the absolute turnover growth in such sectors as clothing and electrical consumer goods and the arrival of new sectors such as online insurance. The growth in 2003 is explained by an increase in the number of online shoppers and a higher frequency of ordering (from 164 to 185 orders per on-line shopper). In addition, the average total annual expenditure per online shopper has risen (from €188 to €205 per online shopper).

The travel sector is by far the largest sector in turnover: online turnover amounted to €235 million during the first half of 2003; it is true that the increase is leveling off relative to past years, which is the logical consequence of the large absolute magnitude. The growth in other more 'traditional' online market sectors, such as clothing, electronics, hardware and software, music and books is also leveling off.

| Market development | 1998 | 1999 | 2000 | 2001 | 2002 | 2003 |
|---|---|---|---|---|---|---|
| | | | (in million euros) | | | |
| January–June | | 53 | 130 | 226 | 424 | 575 |
| July–December | | 94 | 181 | 301 | 513 | |
| Total | 41 | 147 | 311 | 527 | 937 | |

*Source*: Blauw Research/Thuiswinkel.org, September 2003

**Growth percentage online consumer expenditures**

**Growth percentage**

In comparison with the first half-year of 2002, the market for online consumer expenditure (Internet as sales channel) has grown by 70 per cent (in comparison with a growth of 87 per cent in the first half of 2002). This gives a growth percentage of 78 per cent for 2002. In view of the size the market has currently reached, one would actually expect a drop in the growth percentage. Nevertheless, the opposite has taken place, which makes the growth noticeably high.

| | 1998 | 1999 | 2000 | 2001 | 2002 | 2003 |
|---|---|---|---|---|---|---|
| | | | (Growth percentage) | | | |
| January–June | 600 | 318 | 145 | 74 | 87 | 36 |
| July–December | 473 | 230 | 92 | 66 | 71 | |
| Average | 507 | 257 | 118 | 70 | 78 | |

*Source*: Blauw Research/Thuiswinkel.org, September 2003

**Market share online consumer expenditure**

**Market share**

The travel sector is by far the largest sector in turnover: online turnover amounted to €235 million during the first half of 2003; it is true that the increase is leveling off relative to past years, which is the logical consequence of the large absolute magnitude. The growth in other more 'traditional' online market sectors, such as clothing, electronics, hardware and software, music and books is also leveling off.

| Turnover according to market sector | 1998 | 1999 | 2000 | 2001 | 2002 | 2003 |
|---|---|---|---|---|---|---|
| | | | (in million euros) | | | |
| Travel | 16 | 36 | 90 | 209 | 365 | 235 |
| Hardware, software | 11 | 51 | 82 | 97 | 143 | 68 |
| Clothes | 2 | 5 | 13 | 34 | 54 | 40 |
| Entertainment | | | | 55 | 85 | 45 |
| Electrical white goods | 0 | 6 | 35 | 54 | 96 | 60 |
| Foods etc. | | | | 38 | 86 | 43 |
| Miscellaneous | 12 | 49 | 91 | 40 | 107 | 83 |
| Total | 41 | 147 | 311 | 527 | 937 | 575 |

Source: Blauw Research/Thuiswinkel.org, September 2003

Entertainment: books, music, home-entertainment software, DVD, video; Foods a.o.: foods, personal care, home and garden.

www.thuiswinkel.org

Other trends in the Dutch market relating to the Internet and Home shopping are also quite interesting, with a massive increase in home shopping in 2004.

**Home shopping versus retail trade in Holland** (*in billion euros*)

| | 1999 | 2000 | 2001 | 2002 | 2003 | 2004 |
|---|---|---|---|---|---|---|
| Retail trade total | 72 | 75 | 80 | 82 | 81 | 40 |
| Non-food | 43 | 45 | 48 | 49 | 47 | 22 |
| Food | 26 | 27 | 29 | 30 | 31 | 15 |
| Home shopping | 1.23 | 1.52 | 1.84 | 2.19 | 2.5 | 1.3 |

Source: CBS, Thuiswinkel.org, September 2004

Once again, during the first half of 2004, a larger proportion of the total home shopping turnover was realized via the channel of the Internet. The half-yearly investigation by Blauw Research, in co-operation with Thuiswinkel.org shows that during the first half of 2004 consumers spent €775 million on products and services via the purchasing channel of the Internet, an increase of 35 per cent in comparison with the first half of 2003.

Total Internet sales in the Netherlands are expected to exceed €1.5 billion during 2004.

**Home shopping** (*in billion euros*)

| | 1999 | 2000 | 2001 | 2002 | 2003 | 2004 |
|---|---|---|---|---|---|---|
| Home shopping total | 1.23 | 1.52 | 1.84 | 2.19 | 2.5 | 1.3 |
| On-line shopping | 0.15 | 0.32 | 0.53 | 0.94 | 1.24 | 0.775 |

Source: Blauw Research, Thuiswinkel.org, September 2004

During the first half of 2004 the growth in retail trade sales dropped to –3.2 per cent. Developments are such that sales within the home shopping sector have been growing rapidly since 1999: in 2003 the Dutch home shopping market rose by more than 14 per cent to €2.5 billion. This increase is largely thanks to the rapid increase in on-line consumer spending.

**Home shopping versus retail trade in Holland**
(*increase in comparison with previous period, in per cent*)

|  | 2000 | 2001 | 2002 | 2003 | 2004 |
|---|---|---|---|---|---|
| Retail trade total | 5.0 | 6.4 | 3.0 | −3.0 | −3.2 |
| Non-food | 5.3 | 6.4 | 2.9 | −5.8 | −4.4 |
| Food | 2.7 | 6.6 | 4.7 | 1.5 | −1.0 |
| Home shopping | 24 | 21 | 19.3 | 14.3 | 5 |
| On-line shopping | 118 | 70 | 78 | 32 | 35 |

*Source*: Blauw Research, CBS, Thuiswinkel.org, September 2004

The impact of the Internet on the financial services sector has been significant, with many customers now banking online. This has seen a significant reduction in the number of personnel working for financial services and in the future it will have an incredible impact on the role of the very popular call-centres.

The last few years have seen a complete change in distribution trends, often leading to the demise of many middlemen. A good example of this is the leisure industry, which now trades products and services directly to the end-user through the Internet and TV's CEEFAX and FASTEXT, in particular the sale of holidays, flights, rail travel and hire cars on the Internet. In addition to this, the evolution of response-based advertising, influenced by the increasing growth of digital TV, will take on a new dimension with the growing harmonization between the Internet and digital technologies.

## Case history

### The newest airline on the block!

MyTravelLite is the new low fares airline from the MyTravel Group, the UK's largest and most respected travel company. As a company they are committed to driving down costs so that they can provide you with the cheapest possible flights between local UK airports and mainland Europe. What's more, they are adding new routes all the time. They believe their competitors are right to be worried!

Although price is, as you would expect, the most important consideration, they also work hard to make booking and travelling quick, and very easy.

MyTravelLite think that customers will find their website extremely quick and easy to use. Needless to say, the website is totally secure and customers should have no concerns about entering credit card details or other personal information. What's more online bookings include a £2.50 discount per one way flight per person.

Although they don't offer frills – they don't believe customers want them – their fleet of new generation Airbus A320s are more comfortable and spacious than the Boeing 737s typically offered by other so-called low-cost airlines.

> Another way in which they make travel cheaper and easier is not to issue tickets. All customers need to do to check-in is turn up at the airport with your passport.
>
> They are very aware that when travelling abroad the chances are high that customers will want to organize far more than just flights. MyTravelLite have therefore negotiated special deals on extras such as hotels, car hire, parking and insurance, and their website includes quick links to our partner companies supplying these services.
>
> MyTravelLite follow in an increasingly long line of 'no-frills' airline providers and who are singularly having a dramatic effect on the travel industry as more and more customers opt to make their own online flight arrangements.
>
> www.mytravelLite.com

The potential business benefits of the Internet are endless. The following list provides an insight into the views of 300 executives from across Europe (Chaffey, Mayer, Johnston and Ellis Chadwick, 2000).

At a strategic level:

- Improved corporate image
- Improved customer service
- Increased visibility
- New market growth opportunities
- Lower overall business costs.

At an operational level:

- Speed of transactions increased
- Management of information improved
- Increased service levels to customers
- Removal of time constraints
- Removal of distance constraints
- Ability to complete transaction electronically
- Access to full competitive arena
- Opportunities for new revenues
- Cost-effectiveness
- More effective/closer relationships with business partners
- Improved understanding of customer requirement.

Almost without exception each of those benefits impacted upon the process of distribution.

In the long term it is clear that the Internet has serious implications for both marketing and channel structures. Intermediaries will no longer be the typical agents or brokers, but they may be search engines such as Yahoo!, Google, Excite, AltaVista or Infoseek – they will be formally known as cybermediaries.

The market will be full of virtual sellers, financial intermediaries, forums and user groups and evaluators. What we will see is more formally known as disintermediation, which through the Internet will give organizations the opportunity to sell directly to their customers.

Other structural changes might include customer relationships being more short term, as customers become more fickle and are shaped and directed by market forces, and essentially the impact of the Internet on the supply chain can be used to improve the quality of service delivered through to the end customer.

Ultimately, the basis of many business and marketing plans will reflect the nature and scope of the Internet as a distribution channel, reaping both tangible and intangible benefits. While the world of the Internet has suffered a temporary blip, the one thing that is sure is that it is here to stay.

## Question 7.4

What do you understand by the term disintermediation and what are the overall benefits?

## Evaluating channel effectiveness

It is essential that having selected an appropriate distribution channel and intermediaries, their efficiency, effectiveness and performance are continually managed.

Key performance and evaluation measures include:

- Regular reviews
- A forum for problem review and solution
- Monthly, quarterly and year sales data analysis
- Average stock levels
- Lead and delivery times
- Zero defects
- Customer service complaints
- *Marketing support* – achieving marketing objectives, level of marketing activity, sales promotions, distributor incentives
- Spot-check of distributions further down the supply chain
- Annual performance audit.

From an Internet perspective typical evaluation methods of marketing effectiveness might include:

- Number of leads
- Increased sales
- Customer retention
- Increased market share
- Brand enhancement and loyalty
- Customer service.

These are just some of the performance evaluations that you might implement. However, the tone and commitment to the distribution partnership will determine how much of this information should be provided in management reports, and the timings. Should the relationship be of a different nature, and perhaps the producer has less leverage, then some of the information required for performance evaluation could be significantly harder to come by.

## Summary

The process of distribution is costly, complex and logistically challenging and will often involve many different groups of people or organizations. Right through the 1990s and continuing on into the new century, there has been a significant shift in distribution patterns, including the ongoing demise of many traditional middlemen. More and more organizations are merging, developing alliances and utilizing and pooling resources where possible, always looking at ways in which they can be more cost-effective, and expanding into broader geographical, in fact global markets. As the external marketing environment is so competitive, organizations have to find ways of increasing their market share and, obviously, increasing profits for shareholders.

Selection of the appropriate channel can give organizations the competitive edge over others by reaching customers in new and more innovative ways, particularly with the increasing use of the Internet.

Developing relationships between suppliers and customers is the essence of long-term customer loyalty. Should the marketing mix break down as a result of poor distribution strategy and management, then customers will go elsewhere.

Physical distribution management is a phenomenal task; it is complex, costly and critical. It has many facets, but its key role is getting the products to the customers, when and where they demand them.

One thing all organizations should bear in mind is that it is highly unlikely that customers will 'beat a path to their door'. The marketplace is vast and so is the amount of choice. Ensuring your product is visible when it should be will be one of the keys to marketing success.

## Study tip

Distribution is raising its profile as a serious business function aided by the rapid evolution of e-commerce. You should be prepared to answer questions about any aspect of place operations. You should already be familiar with the basics of distribution in areas such as types of transportation and the roles of the various intermediaries through studying for Marketing Fundamentals, undergraduate studies or experience.

The concentration will be on the operation level of the subject, rather than a strategic level. Therefore it is likely that distribution-related questions will be about tactical implementation of distribution strategies that underpin overall marketing objectives and corporate goals.

## Bibliography

Brassington, F. and Pettitt, S. (2000) *Principles of Marketing*, Thomson Higher Education.

Chaffey, D., Mayer, R., Johnston, K. and Ellis-Chadwick, F.E. (2000) *Internet Marketing*, Prentice Hall.

Hill, E. and O'Sullivan, T. (1999) *Marketing*, Longman.

**Useful websites:**

www.euromonitor.com
www.forrester.com
www.which.net

---

Sample exam questions and answers for the Marketing Planning module as a whole can be found in Appendix 4 and past examination papers can be found in Appendix 5. Both appendices can be found at the back of the book.

# unit 8 managing marketing relationships

## Learning objectives

The basis of this unit is to briefly focus upon the importance of managing marketing relationships effectively in order to maximize customer retention opportunities. This is also very much the focus of the Marketing Communications module and therefore the aim is to underpin the learning undertaken in that module.

- Explain the importance of customer relationships to the organization and how they can be developed and supported by the marketing mix.

Syllabus reference: 3.11

The key to success within any marketing environment will be the realization that managing marketing relationships is crucial to long-term customer loyalty and customer retention, as is the necessity to manage each market differently in order to optimize customer relationships and the associated benefits.

## Introduction

In the majority of situations the basis of any type of relationship that is established is the way in which the supplier creates expectations. In creating expectations, you determine the nature and tone of the relationship and essentially you form and define customer behaviour in response to your organization and its product or service offerings.

The balance of optimizing customer relationships is a difficult one to manage, as quite often concentrating efforts on one customer or group of customers means that another customer might be neglected, ultimately to the detriment of the organization.

Pleasing the customer, creating customer satisfaction, seems to become a greater challenge almost daily, as organizations strive to achieve some form of competitive advantage. Customers become more demanding, assert their buyer power, and their expectations are continually rising, all the time making the value proposition more difficult to achieve.

With the growing influence of a number of key driving forces through SLEPT factors in the market, managing the marketing relationship is becoming a more turbulent affair. Every concept of every relationship now appears to demand more of the organization. The role of stakeholders, the growing influence of social responsibility and ethics, and internal marketing factors are now squeezing organizations from every angle, in order that they please all of the people all of the time.

The emphasis is now on knowing your markets, knowing your individual customers, being able to address them directly. Thus having 'an electronic footprint' of them is essential if you are to establish a robust long-term relationship with them.

Ignoring the issues of managing relationships will ultimately leave organizations and marketers in a very vulnerable position.

One of the main reasons that organizations will, however, start to make positive moves towards managing marketing relationships is in order to maximize their effectiveness by retaining existing customers rather than focusing consistently on new customers. Long-term relationships provide the basis of consistency, synergy and achieving satisfaction. The long-term profitable benefits to the organizations will be considerable. For example, a 5 per cent reduction in customer defections can improve profitability by an excess of 25 per cent.

## Relationship marketing

### Definition

**Relationship marketing** – is to establish, maintain and enhance relationships with customers and other parties at a profit so that the objectives of the parties involved are met. This is done by mutual exchange and fulfilment of promises (Gronroos, 1994). Relationship marketing refers to all marketing activities directed towards establishing and maintaining successful and relational exchanges (Morgan and Hunt, 1994).

The fundamental principle upon which relationship marketing is founded is that the greater the level of customer satisfaction with a relationship – not just the product and service – the greater the likelihood that the customer will stay with and be retained by the organization.

For relationship marketing to succeed in any organization, there will need to be a cultural shift, as discussed in Unit 3 on 'Marketing planning, implementation and control', away from the old transactional style of marketing to the more dynamic and rewarding basis of relationship marketing.

## From transactional to relationship marketing

A more conventional approach to marketing has been the old transactional marketing, whereby the functions of marketing, customer services and quality have been separate entities within the organization. However, the disintegrated approach to marketing meant that the potential to optimize marketing relationships was being lost, as the lack of co-ordination between the three functions gave way to a fragmented approach to achieving customer satisfaction. Ultimately and in many instances this started to prove problematic with many organizations, as they found they were suffering lack of market share compared with the more relationship-focused business.

There are therefore a number of significant differences between the concepts and contexts of transactional and relationship marketing, as illustrated in Table 8.1.

*Table 8.1* The shift in relationship marketing

| Transactional focus | Relationship focus |
| --- | --- |
| Orientation to single sales | Orientation to customer |
| Discontinuous customer contact | Continuous customer contact |
| Focus on product features | Focus on customer value |
| Short timescale | Long timescale |
| Limited emphasis on customer service | High customer service emphasis |
| Limited commitment to meeting customer expectations | High commitment to meeting customer expectations |
| Quality is the concern of production staff | Quality is the concern of all staff |

*Source*: Payne, Christopher, Clarke and Peck (1998)

Principally the key difference in the management of the relationship is that the basis of it will be a long-term relationship, a long-term view achieving long-term customer loyalty.

In order to establish and construct a relationship programme, or indeed a relationship chain, there are four factors that the organization will need to concentrate on, each of which we have covered in other units:

1. Defining the value proposition ('Product operations' Unit 5)
2. Identifying appropriate customer value segments ('Marketing planning, implementation and control' Unit 3)
3. Designing value delivery systems ('Place operations' Unit 7)
4. Managing and maintaining delivered satisfaction (all units).

For an organization to succeed it is of course essential that the value proposition meets the expectations of the customers, that the expectations in their minds meet those in the mind of the supplier and that there is little scope for customer uncertainties, a concept that you will come across in selling. Therefore, the value proposition needs to fill any gaps in expectations.

Market segmentation has been a continuous thread throughout: the more closely defined the target markets, the more likelihood of success. The more you know and establish in the relationship with your customers, the closer you get to delivering what they really want, again closing the expectations gap.

In Unit 4 'Promotional operations' some time was spent on the definition of value: establishing values, core values and peripheral values. For relationship management to work, defining the method of actually delivering that value will be essential. This will include a range of delivery systems and channels, and these should be appropriately tailored to the customer needs. Of course, with the growing influence of digital marketing and service technologies, it will make it far easier for you to perhaps support a diverse range of customers. However, a word of warning, you should be aware of the fact that while it gives you strength to manage customers, so too does it give a competitor strength. The switching process from one company to another can often be fast and painless.

Because the quality and strength of customer relationships is vital to the survival and profitability of all organizations, it is essential for competitive advantage to be sustained, customer loyalty to be achieved, and the process of delivering customer satisfaction to be clearly defined, to avoid any potential gaps in customer perception of the value proposition and their expectations.

## Unit 8 Managing marketing relationships

While this seems quite broad, with every group of customers or each individual customer these are core issues in sustaining the relationship. This applies to the context of each customer group that will be the focus of this unit. It is, therefore, essential that at this stage you actually have an understanding of how broad that scope can be.

# The scope of marketing relationships

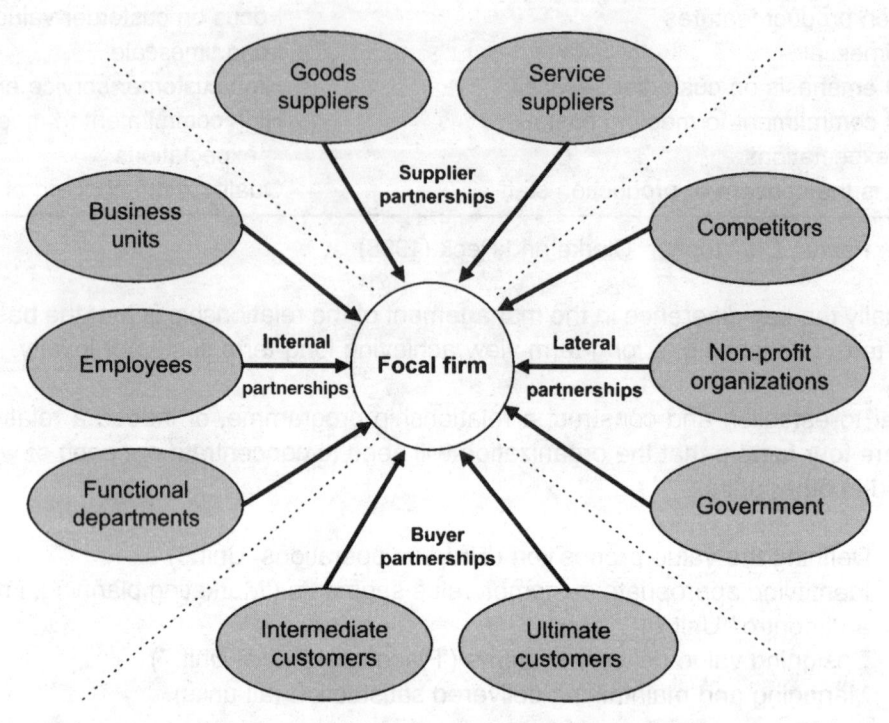

*Figure 8.1* The scope of relationships
*Source*: Adapted from Morgan and Hunt (1994)

The scope of managing marketing relationships is significant (see Figure 8.1), stretching as it does across four key groups: customers, suppliers, internal markets and stakeholder markets, each defined in terms of relationship marketing partnerships.

In addition to this, the scope broadens once more, as you look at managing marketing relationships in the broader context of business sectors:

- Organizational markets
- Service markets
- Not-for-profit markets.

Each of these particular elements is the focus of other units in this text, where some issues pertaining to relationship management are discussed.

However, in brief, the critical issues relating to each market sector are:

- *Organizational markets* – Require high levels of relationship management due to the intensity and time dimensions of the process of purchase. The market is essentially less fickle and more rational, which provides the basis of establishing closer links. Closer links mean working towards gaining preferred supplier status. The basis of achieving this will ultimately mean long-term supplier/buyer relationships, effectively putting a relationship on a strong footing.

Essentially relationship marketing is about collaborative relationships, working together optimizing opportunities and maximizing potential.

- *Service markets* – Relationship marketing in the context of services is the major imperative, as at the core of any successful service delivery will be the relationship between the service provider and the service consumer. Never before has the power and strength of that relationship become so relevant. The whole basis of its success rests upon the key factors of relationship marketing, as defined in Table 8.1:

    - Continuous customer contact
    - Focus on customer value
    - Long timescale
    - High customer service emphasis
    - High commitment to meeting customer expectations
    - Quality as a concern to all staff.

- *Not-for-profit markets* – Relationship management is the critical success factor and should be the core of these markets. In order for charities, for example, to succeed they need to establish long-term relationships so that they can sustain three key factors:

    - *Donors* – The givers of money and equipment to support their work
    - *Volunteers* – The people who give time and effort and avoid company overheads
    - *Client* – The users of the charitable service – the charity needs to gain trust, understanding and often long-term relationships in order to undertake the work at the heart of their organizations.

## Question 8.1

Think about the scope of your own organization or one you know well, and make a list of groups of individual customers with whom you have relationships – you might be surprised at the balance of the group.

## Planning for relationship management

A marketing relationship does not just happen, evolve or emerge, it has to be planned. As with all other aspects of marketing, it requires a structured approach to ensure that relationship marketing does maximize business potential, provide the basis of profitability, and create sustainable competitive advantage, through robust and long-term customer, supplier and stakeholder relationships.

In order to plan for relationship marketing, there needs to be an understanding of some key factors: customer loyalty, the dimensions of quality, building trust and the basis of continuous improvement.

## Customer loyalty

To achieve customer loyalty is highly challenging, as it looks at the loyalty of all customer groups that are involved in the relationship marketing process. For relationship marketing to be truly implemented and part of the business culture, it has to focus on all customer groups.

We have already established that relationship building is a long-term process, and in order for customer loyalty to be achieved, there are a number of key identifiable stages that the relationship moves through. This is more formally known as the 'Relationship marketing ladder' of customer loyalty (see Figure 8.2).

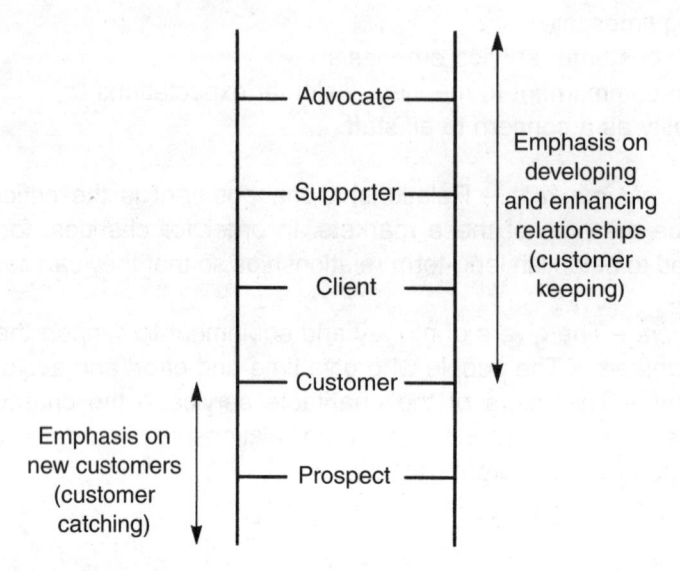

*Figure 8.2* The relationship ladder
*Source*: Adapted from Payne, Christopher, Clarke and Peck (1998)

The ladder highlights the process from targeting the customer, to adoption, to developing the relationship from customer to long-term client. From here it is then essential to encourage them to become both a supports and advocate of the company, in order that they can become marketing tools, on your behalf. Thus you not only retain them, but also use them to grow your market.

The recent addition to the ladder is that of partnership. In the organizational marketing context, partnership is a very positive stage to move towards, in order to secure optimization of opportunities to be exploited to the benefit of both the supplier and buyer organizations.

Customer loyalty, however, has two dimensions: long-term loyalty, which is the basis of a true relationship marketing scenario, and false loyalty. This will essentially be driven by a number of key factors:

- Limited completion of the task
- High switching costs
- Proprietary technology
- The attraction of some loyalty scheme.

The key objective in this context, therefore, will be to actually switch the power base of loyalty to a more long-term relationship and indeed partnership.

Customer loyalty, of course, is very interlinked with brand loyalty, which was discussed in the unit 'Product operations'.

## The key dimensions of relationship marketing

In the 'Industrial/business-to-business and services marketing' unit you will look at the basis of services marketing, that is to ensure that quality is at the core of the business and the relationship with customers.

Therefore, there are some key dimensions upon which an organization must deliver in order to provide a basis for a relationship.

- *Reliability* – Ability to perform the promised service dependably and accurately
- *Responsiveness* – Willingness to help customers and provide prompt service
- *Assurance* – Knowledge and courtesy of employees and their ability to inspire trust and confidence
- *Empathy* – Caring, individualism and attention to customers
- *Tangibles* – Physical facilities, equipment and appearance of personnel.

In order for the relationship to be established, the quality gap must be filled, i.e. the difference between the customer expectations and the organizational perception of what is being delivered.

## A relationship based upon trust

Morgan and Hunt suggested three dynamics to trust within a relationship (see Figure 8.3).

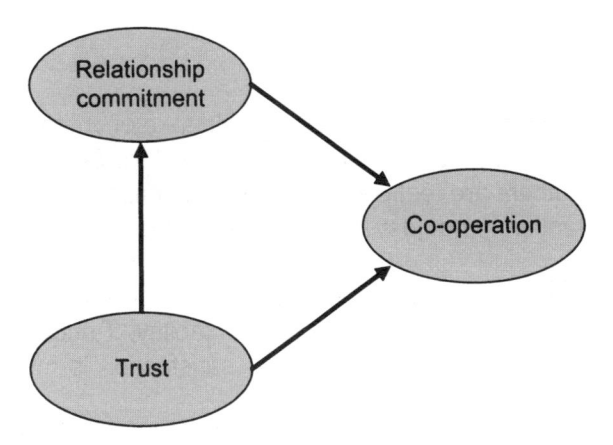

*Figure 8.3* What builds trust?
*Source*: Adapted from Morgan and Hunt (1994)

These are three quite simplistic components that would form the basis of any relationship, personal or business. The basis of trust provides the opportunity to develop a relationship that includes co-operation, leading to relationship commitment. While principally they should be the basis of relationship marketing aims and objectives, typically these three components can often be overlooked, perhaps assumed or even ignored. However, in Figure 8.4 you can start to see the benefits of building a relationship on trust, as you can save on relationship termination costs, gain many benefits and look towards a relationship based on shared values. Opportunistic behaviour will be a great benefit of partnerships in a relationship management context.

Communication is an absolute, as the more inward and outward-bound communication that exists, the more you will find out about the customer, their needs, wants and perhaps their competitive experiences, all of which will only serve to strengthen the basis on which you might operate.

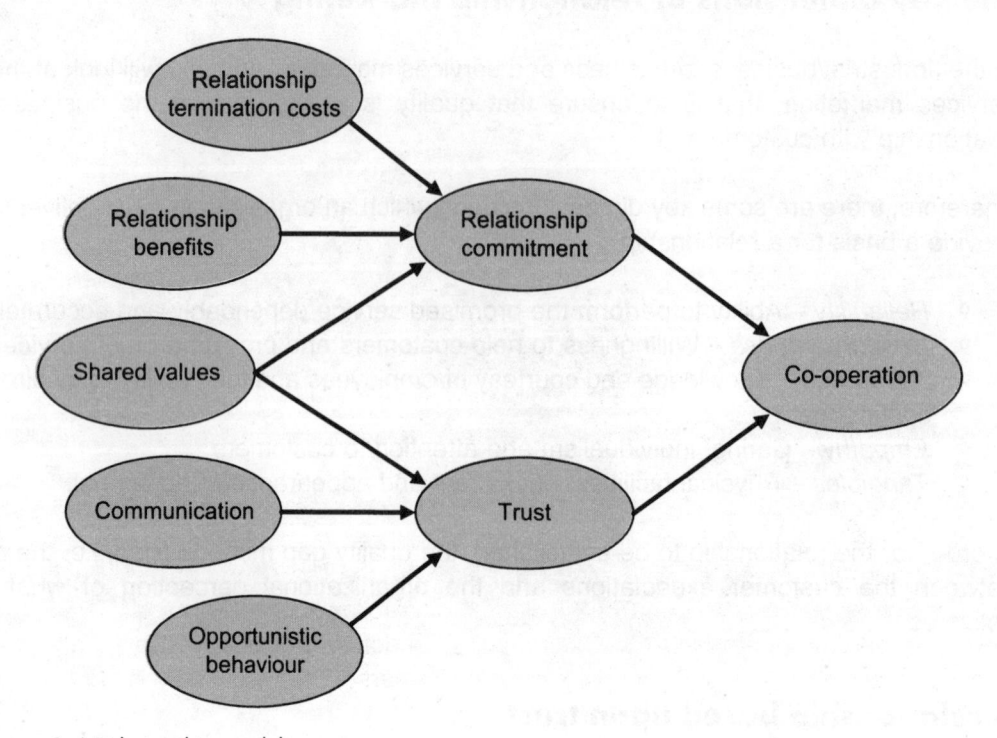

*Figure 8.4* Relationship model
*Source*: Adapted from Morgan and Hunt (1994)

## Customer retention management

The most simplistic view that any organization could take of customer retention management is that the way to keep customers is to keep them satisfied. Some organizations think that this means zero defects, others are realizing the increasing importance of this and are really looking at ways in which retention is not just a concept but a reality.

Payne *et al.* (1998) have developed a number of techniques for measuring customer satisfaction and essentially linking them directly to profitability. Principally what they are doing is measuring customer retention, where customer satisfaction is measured at the rate at which customers are kept.

Payne *et al.* suggest that a retention rate of 80 per cent means that, on average, customers remain loyal for 5 years, whereas a rate of 90 per cent pushes the average loyalty up to 10 years. And as the average life of a customer increases, so does the profitability to the firm.

They go on to suggest that long-term established customers are more profitable for six reasons:

1. Regular customers place frequent, consistent orders and, therefore, usually cost less to serve
2. Long-established customers tend to buy more
3. Satisfied customers may sometimes pay premium price
4. Retaining customers makes it difficult for competitors to enter a market or increase their share

5. Satisfied customers often refer new customers to the supplier at no extra cost
6. The cost of acquiring and serving new customers can be substantial. A higher retention rate implies fewer new customers need to be acquired, and they can be acquired more cheaply.

Here you see some of the benefits alluded to within Figure 8.4, so therefore a relationship based on trust can gain commitment and co-operation, with all of the other add-ons as previously discussed.

## Customer retention in consumer markets

In consumer markets, customer retention schemes are in the main focused around loyalty cards. Most people on average will have at least five loyalty cards on the go at any one time.

Loyalty cards became highly popular in the mid to late 1980s as the intensity of competition began to rise in the supermarket wars, closely followed by banks and credit card companies. For example, the American Express Blue Card gives you a penny back for every pound you spend on their card, at the end of the year. Boots followed suit with their loyalty card, which proved to be very beneficial to the customer. With double points and special offers, the Boots card has been branded as a success by its customers.

The latest example of this type of loyalty bonus is the 'Nectar' card sponsored by Debenhams, Sainsbury's, BP and Barclaycard. After getting off to a rather rocky start due to issues relating to website registrations, and the crashing of the Nectar website, the Nectar card has become one of the recent success stories in consumer retention markets. See the overview of the Nectar card launch and the basis upon which it operates, with sponsoring organizations working together to achieve customer loyalty.

## Case history

### Nectar cards

In March 2002 Sainsbury's, launched one of the most success loyalty arrangement packages ever to be offered to consumers, in conjunction with a number of key sponsors, launched its new customer loyalty card known as Nectar. This is a new type of reward card – one which lets you collect points at more than one place, rather than using lots of cards in different shops. So now it's easier for you to earn more points than ever before. And the more points you have, the more *rewards* you'll be able to enjoy.

All you have to do is hand over your Nectar card whenever you shop at Sainsbury's, Debenhams and wherever you see the Nectar sign at BP*. You can also earn points every time you use your Barclaycard*. And if you pay with your Barclaycard at Sainsbury's, Debenhams and BP you'll earn two lots of points! You can also earn points when you shop by phone or on the Internet*. And from time to time you'll be able to earn bonus points to boost your total ... which means you could enjoy even more great rewards.

When you pay at the till at Sainsbury's, Debenhams or BP your Nectar card will be swiped and any points added to your account. When you pay by Barclaycard anywhere in the world your points will be added to your Nectar account each month (once you have registered your Nectar number with Barclaycard). Shop with your Barclaycard at Sainsbury's, Debenhams or BP and you'll earn two lots of points.

> Once you've collected enough points for the rewards you want, whether it's free meals, great days out, flights abroad, cinema tickets – the choice is yours. You can even use your points to save money at Sainsbury's or Argos.
>
> In recent time Nectar provision of loyalty arrangements has extended to include many more companies than the ones discussed earlier in this package, which is a key indication of the success that the Nectar card has achieved.
>
> New companies include:
>
> o Ford
> o Vodaphone
> o E-bookers
> o Threshers
> o Adans
> o Magnet
> o Brewers Fayre
> o Beefeater.
>
> To see all others log-on-to
> http://www.nectar.com/earnpoints/viewSponsorStart.nectar?pageValue=1

## Customer retention in organizational markets

We have already touched upon some of the issues relating to this within this unit, and will develop the issues relating to customer retention management in other contexts later in the book. However, there are five basic principles that an organizational market should consider:

1. *Technical support* – Providing added value to clients in industrial markets.
2. *Technical expertise* – Providing expertise in design and engineering can be a USP of the organization and add to the value proposition.
3. *Resource support* – Ensure that a range of versatile resources are available to support the relationship, that are cost-effective and efficient, and that could ultimately see the development of an alliance when business opportunities are presented (the basis of partnerships).
4. *Service levels* – These appear to be of growing importance and will relate in particular to time, delivery and product quality.
5. *Reduction of risk* – Giving as much insight into the product proposition as possible through exhibitions, trial use, product delivery guarantees.

## Customer retention in not-for-profit markets

The basis of customer retention in not-for-profit organizations is covered in some depth later in the book.

Essentially one of the key considerations is that marketing activities in not-for-profit markets need to be very focused at each of their customer groups, as we ascertained earlier, those being donors, volunteers, client/users.

It will be essential that the charity understands their target markets and segments them exactly, as each of them will manifest different customer retention characteristics, particularly as their personal reasons for charitable involvements will be very diverse.

Key relationship marketing issues will include:

- Analysing acquisition and retention costs
- Managing customer retention and customer acquisition activities concurrently
- Recognizing how emphasis needs to be placed on all markets in order to achieve the success the objectives demand
- The need to have adequate information sources about each of the customer groups.

Of course within the not-for-profit sector there are some far broader strategic issues that typical organizations will grapple with, such as the challenges of the functions of management and marketing, developing and understanding the basis of market segmentation strategies and finally the scope of their mission, which in many instances can be huge.

All in all, the challenges of both relationship and retention management in the context of marketing are quite daunting.

## The marketing mix for customer retention management

As you will be beginning to conclude, the foundation of success in managing marketing relationships and customer retention marketing is the value proposition. Therefore, it is essential that the use of the marketing mix as a key set of tools be optimized in order to have maximum impact upon the customer base, meeting their expectations and retaining them and your competitive advantage.

Therefore, the following marketing mix suggestions should be considered. They relate back to, and build on, your studies in other units.

### Product extras

- *Product and service augmentation and innovation* – guarantees of standards and service levels, preventive maintenance
- *Customizing the offer* – relationship building
- Cross-selling other products in the product line or portfolio.

### Relationship pricing

- Price incentive for increased customer spend and perhaps customer share
- *Price sensitivity* – what are the issues with price sensitivity – is it a relationship issue?
- *Perceived value* – the value proposition versus the price.

### Specialized distribution

- *Priority customer-handling* – e.g. British Airways offer Executive and Standard check-ins
- *Pre-view evenings* – Marks and Spencer House of Fraser, Laura Ashley – typical tactics in relationship marketing
- Exclusive or selective distributors
- Multiple accessing options, i.e. the Internet, retail outlets, direct marketing.

### Reinforcing promotions

- Sales-force responsiveness
- *Loyalty schemes* – reward cards, membership benefits, sales promotions, magazines
- Tailored direct marketing.

## Managing internal marketing relationships

> **Definition**
>
> **Internal marketing** – Can be defined as 'marketing by a service firm to train and effectively motivate its customer contact employees and all the supporting services to work as a team of people to provide customer satisfaction' (Kotler et al., 1998).

The fundamental component of achieving successful relationship marketing is the infrastructure of the organization – the culture, leaderships, skills, resources, synergy, co-ordination and co-operation of the employees within the organization. Without these key factors being addressed by the organization, success in the external market is likely to be limited. The basis of these areas was included within your studies in Unit 3 'Marketing planning, implementation and control'.

The overall aim of internal marketing, therefore, is to ensure that everybody within the organization contributes towards developing a marketing-oriented, customer-focused culture in order to improve levels of services to customers.

It is necessary that an integrated approach towards achieving customer satisfaction is taken by the whole of the organization to optimize the skills, talents and abilities that employees have on offer to meet the needs of the external market.

In Unit 3, 'Marketing planning, implementation and control', we looked at the importance of internal marketing as part of the implementation process, and saw that indeed, internal components and infrastructure needed to be in place in order for the corporate goals and marketing objectives to be achieved.

Therefore, the key to managing internal relationships is having a rational understanding of the key factors listed below, in order to establish a basis for the relationship between employees to be built in the context of trust, co-operation and commitment.

The same benefits operate in the internal context of marketing also, with perhaps the difference being that employee relationship termination may well result in the employee switching to competing organizations. Should an employee move to a competitor, they take with them a lot of inside knowledge of their previous employer, which ultimately will influence them within their new role. This should obviously be avoided.

## Internal stakeholders

Internal stakeholders are people who are likely to be involved in internal marketing and those who operate within the boundary of the organization and who have an effect on the organization's overall performance. The stakeholders are likely to include shareholders, directors, management and the workforce.

As stakeholders, they expect to receive some reward for their efforts, through either payment or share options.

The way in which staff are paid can often have a significant bearing upon their overall performance and often the provision of a stake in the organization is a good incentive and motivational factor.

## Internal relationship marketing techniques

In the main, most organizations now recognize the pivotal importance of internal marketing in respect of achieving robust customer relationships with their external customers. However, organizations do need to address a number of key issues in relation to successful implementation, all of which have been covered within Unit 3 'Marketing planning, implementation and control'. As a reminder, these are the key components of internal marketing success:

- Create an internal awareness of the corporate aims, objectives and overall mission
- Determine the expectations of the internal customer
- Communicate to internal customers
- Provide appropriate human and financial resources to underpin the implementation of the marketing strategy
- Provide training in order that employees have the appropriate skills and competences to undertake the task at hand
- Implement a change in tasks and activities appropriate to the objectives of the organization
- Provide a structure whereby cross-functional integrated teams across business units can work together, in order to aid communication of business activity relating to the achievement of corporate goals
- Provide the systems and processes that enable successful delivery of services and products, enabling employees to successfully implement them and achieve organizational success
- Maximize the opportunity for customer interaction through effective management of service levels, e.g. response times, reply processes
- Institute internal monitoring and control.

For internal marketing to be successfully implemented, a planned approach is essential to allow evaluation and measurement of the successful execution of the plan.

The plan could be designed with the following headings:

- Internal vision
- Aims and objectives
- Internal marketing strategy
- Segmentation, targeting and positioning
- Marketing programme (to include all elements of the marketing mix)
- Implementation
- Monitoring and control of the success or failure of execution.

## Question 8.2

Why is it important to have highly motivated personnel in order to successfully implement a relationship marketing programme within the organization?

Importantly, in terms of managing customer relationships, internal marketing forms the basis of the 'relationship management chain' (Figure 8.5).

```
                MANAGING INTERNAL MARKETS
                • Market planning – internal
                • Culture, climate and employee retention
```

| Define the value proposition | Segmentations targeting and positioning | Operations and delivery systems | Measurement and feedback |
| --- | --- | --- | --- |
| Understand the customer value | Identify the preferences | Mass customization | Service process monitoring |
| Where can we add value? | Segment profitability analysis | Partnering | Customer satisfaction studies |
| Competitive benchmarking | Configure the value package | Process re-engineering | Employee satisfaction studies |

```
                MANAGING INTERNAL MARKETS
                • Market planning – external
                • Customer relationship management
```

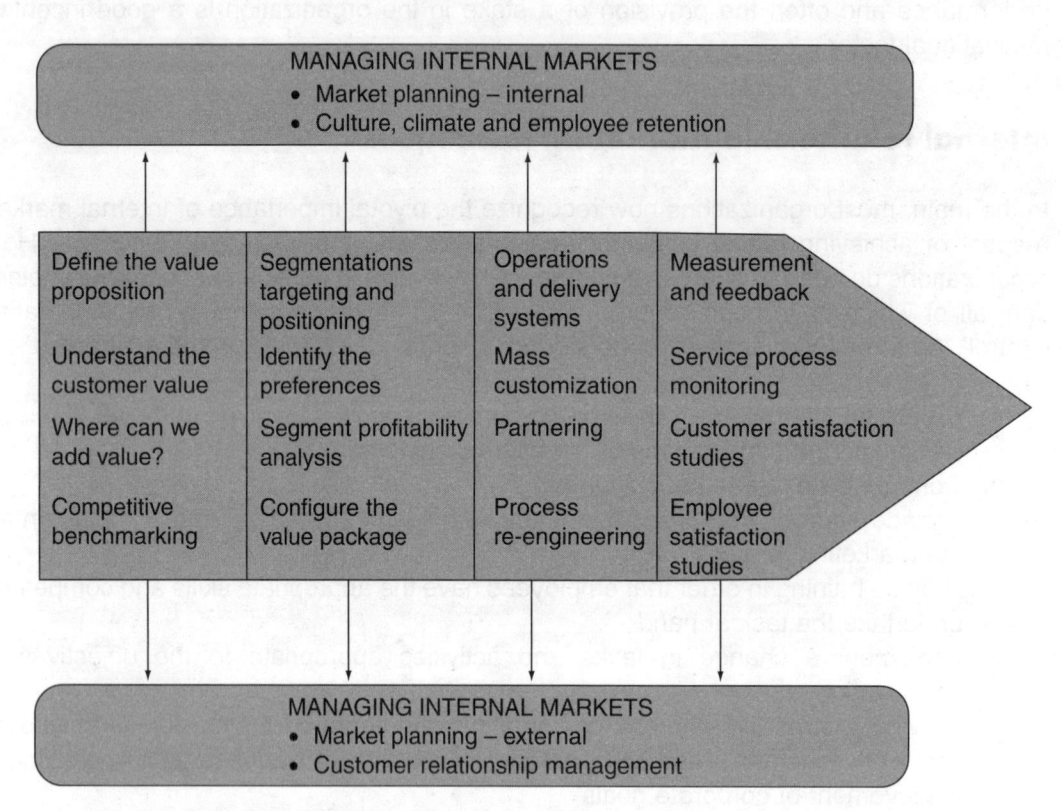

*Figure 8.5* The relationship management chain
*Source*: Adapted from Payne, Christopher, Clarke and Peck (1998)

Essentially, to establish a really effective relationship chain within the organization will require a focus upon a number of critical issues – to which we made reference earlier:

o  Defining the value proposition
o  Identifying appropriate customer value segments
o  Designing value systems
o  Managing and maintaining delivered satisfaction.

# The relationship marketing plan

It is essential that an organization manage the scope and range of relationships within the marketing environment, in order to achieve all-round success.

As the management of relationships in each of the markets we have defined is critical to the achievement of the overall customer retention objectives, there must be crystal-clear linkages that bridge the objects and the markets (see Figure 8.6).

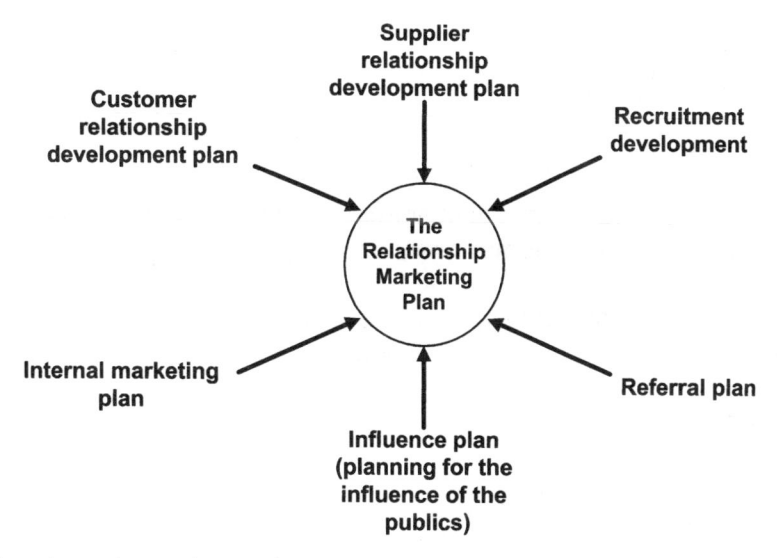

*Figure 8.6* The relationship marketing plan
*Source*: Adapted from Payne, Christopher, Clarke and Peck (1998)

In order to achieve a meaningful relationship marketing plan, you have to consider the needs of each of the individual markets in order for it to be successfully implemented. The linkages between each audience should be clear, and they should all be directed towards the same overall purpose. The successful implementation of such a plan will most likely impact upon the achievement of retention goals.

## Summary

The move from transaction marketing to relationship marketing has meant that the marketing planning process has now taken on a new set of dynamics. It is no longer purely based around developing a marketing mix to meet organizational goals, it is much broader in perspective, and the task much bigger.

Essentially, organizations who are truly committed to developing a relationship marketing approach will need to be supported by a structure, culture and overall organizational climate that will enable each of the functional business units within the organization to align and co-ordinate themselves to develop an integrated approach to the achievement of the overall marketing objectives of every market.

Principally, the role of the relationship marketing plan is to ensure that there is a synergy, consistency, coherence and cohesiveness, and a 'pan-company' approach, to the implementation of the marketing plan.

> **Study tip**
>
> Question 4 in the December 2003 examination paper was based upon relationship marketing in the context of a not-for-profit organization, examining closely the role of developing stakeholder relationships and how to develop relationships to achieve a successful increase in donations. These types of questions require an in-depth understanding of relationship market, which can be applied in any given context.

## Extending knowledge

### Recommended reading

There are some useful articles that appear from time to time in *Marketing Business* in respect of relationship marketing and customer retention.

Other reading comes from *Relationship Marketing for Competitive Advantage* by Payne, Christopher, Clarke and Peck (1998) – Chapters 1, 4 and 8.

### Bibliography

Gronroos, C. (1994) 'From marketing mix to relationship marketing: Towards a paradigm shift in marketing', *Management Decision*, **32**(2), pp. 4–20.

Kotler, P., Armstrong, G., Saunders, J. and Wong, V. (1998) *Principles of Marketing*, FT Prentice Hall.

Morgan, R.M. and Hunt, J.D. (1994) 'The commitment-trust theory of relationship marketing', *Journal of Marketing*, **58** (July), 43–48.

Payne, A., Christopher, M., Clarke, M. and Peck, H. (1998) *Relationship Marketing for Competitive Advantage*, Butterworth-Heinemann.

> Sample exam questions and answers for the Marketing Planning module as a whole can be found in Appendix 4 and past examination papers can be found in Appendix 5. You should undertake Question 4 from the December 2003 examination paper.

# unit 9 international marketing

## Learning objectives

With the ongoing evolution of global markets, it is of primary importance that the function and practice of marketing in an international context is considered.

The underpinning indicative content, i.e. the syllabus areas to be covered, include:

o Explain how marketing plans and activities vary in organizations that operate in an international context and develop an appropriate marketing mix.

Syllabus element: 4.1

## Introduction

In order to survive in the marketing environment in the 21st century, alternative methods of growth, expansion, diversification and differentiation are playing an increasing role in everyday business. Expansion into international markets is one of the more common ways of fulfilling growth and market development objectives.

Around the world managers are realizing the increasing necessity for their organizations to develop skills, awareness and knowledge to enable them to manage the international market development process. That knowledge and understanding includes an insight into the expectation of international customers, their cultures and their existing levels of awareness of products and services that you might offer.

As an international marketing manager the demands on you will present an interesting challenge as you strive to understand the cultural diversity of doing business in other countries.

One of the many misunderstandings in the business environment is that international marketing is exclusively for large organizations. This is a great misconception, as the whole world is a marketplace, presenting many profitable marketing opportunities for all. Every country and every region offers new and exciting challenges, and a different range of marketing opportunities, which in essence will arise from its own particular needs. Understanding these needs as a marketer is of pivotal importance. Marketing after all is the process of identifying, anticipating and satisfying customer requirements profitably.

Unit 9 International marketing

## Why go international?

For many organizations going 'international' will ultimately be to fill a gap that will affect the organization's ability to expand in the long term. These gaps in organizational performance will be due to a number of reasons:

- *Intensity of the competition* – An organization may expand, first, because there may be less intensity of competition overseas, or second, because some organizations are finding the intensity of competition so virulent in their own country, that they are unable to survive without an alternative strategy.
- *Saturated domestic market* – As competition continues to intensify it is likely that businesses can no longer sustain the level of competitive advantage and market share, therefore the alternative is to look for market growth and market development opportunities elsewhere.
- *Product life cycle differences* – As a product moves through its life cycle it is subject to many levels of change, in functionality, style and quality. However, in order to avoid deletion from the product range, international markets provide new opportunities for the same product, perhaps for a different use, or alternatively there is a cultural and time lag in the country. For example, the Hillman Minx has long been obsolete in the UK but is a common sight on the roads of Tehran, Iran. So while the product has expired in most of the Western world, there has been life thereafter.
- *Excess capacity* – Where an organization is operating successfully in the domestic market, but operating below optimal capacity, then there is excess capacity available to produce more products for different markets. Particularly important here would be issues relating to marginal costing. If economies of scale were appropriate, marginal costing could reduce the price significantly in order to overcome the barriers of entry into new markets.
- *Comparative advantage* – Organizations may establish, as a result of their research, that they actually have comparable advantage over their international rivals, perhaps in their own domestic market. The advantage might be skills based, technology based, access to raw materials, etc.
- *Financial reasons* – There are a number of financial reasons why an organization may decide to take the international route. These might include investment incentives, availability of venture capital and grants from local authorities.
- *Organizational issues* – On many occasions early entries into international markets can almost happen by default. Organizations involved in mergers or acquisitions may find that their partners in the product have international operations, of which they then become a part.
- *Geographical diversification* – This will likely happen as a result of some of the other factors covered. To avoid competitive intensity, saturated markets, etc., the organization will expand geographically into new areas.

## Levels of international marketing

The decision to exploit international marketing opportunities will be a strategic one; it will be linked to corporate and financial goals and will involve considerable financial risk. Therefore the decision must be an informed one. Strategic evaluations will be considered and the exploitation of any opportunities will have to be justified, with the provision of a high level of substantiating information.

The key to making the right decision will be gaining understanding of the different levels of international development available backed by market research into the chosen countries in order to ascertain the strategic fit between the hosting nation and your own organization..

The various levels for international marketing are as follows:

- *Domestic/regional marketing* – which involves the company manipulating a series of controllable variables such as price, advertising, distribution and the product in a largely uncontrollable external environment that is made up of different economic structures, competitors, cultural values and legal infrastructure within specific political or geographic boundaries. For the United Kingdom, this is a challenging issue, particularly with the very close links relating to our relationship with continental Europe through the European Union. While in normal domestic or regional settings there is only one common language to deal with, for example within the United States of America, Europe has the situation where in some respects there is no one dominant language and while English is widely spoken, it most certainly is not a prerequisite for joining the EU. This immediately erects cultural barriers.
- *International marketing* – which involves operating across a number of foreign country markets in which not only do the uncontrollable variables differ significantly between one market and another, but the controllable factors in the form of cost and price structures, opportunities for advertising and distributive infrastructure are also likely to differ.
- *Global marketing management* – which is a larger and more complex international operation. Here a company co-ordinates, integrates and controls a whole series of marketing programmes into a substantial global effort. Here the main objective of the company is to achieve a degree of synergy in the overall operation so that by taking advantage of different exchange rates, tax rates, labour rates, skill levels and market opportunities, the organization as a whole will be greater than the sum of its parts.
- *Export marketing* – is where the organization trades its goods and services across all national and political boundaries. There are two types of exporting, direct and indirect.
- *Direct exporting* – is where an organization sells their goods and services directly to a host country. This will mean that they will need to invest much resource, time and effort in establishing business links within international markets. This may mean establishing a physical presence in the marketplace.
- *Indirect exporting* – is where an organization with limited resources trades internationally through the most simple and low-cost method available. Quite often their profile will be raised through a number of market entry methods, for example the use of an agent, or an export house.

To clarify this a little more, let us look at the differences in domestic and international marketing, as shown in Table 9.1.

*Table 9.1* Domestic versus international marketing

| Domestic marketing | International marketing |
|---|---|
| Main language | Many languages |
| Dominant culture | Multi-culture |
| Research straightforward | Research complex |
| Relatively stable environment | Often unstable environment |
| Single currency | Exchange rate problems |
| Business conventions understood | Conventions diverse and unclear |

# The international marketing environment

International marketing carries with it a high element of financial risk, as there are many uncertainties, some of which are significant and often many times greater than those facing a company operating in just one marketplace. Therefore, it is of primary importance that before entering any overseas marketplace, the organization has a thorough understanding of the nature and characteristics of the marketplace. This is effectively undertaking a marketing audit, but in an international context.

Earlier in this book within Unit 2, 'The marketing audit', there was some discussion about the nature and extent of the external marketing environment. The environmental influences that should be considered in the context of international marketing are still the same, namely SLEPT, but let us look at how it balances out for international considerations.

Figure 9.1 illustrates some of the considerations of international marketing.

**Technological**
Satellite communications
ISDN
Internet websites
Superhighway

**Economic**
Developed economies
Emerging economies
Lesser developed countries
Currency

**Political**
Operating restrictions
Discriminatory restrictions
Physical actions

**Environmental influences on international marketing**

**Social/cultural**
Language
Religion
Aesthetics
Values & attributes
Social organization
Material culture

**Legal**
Local domestic laws
International law
Home domestic laws

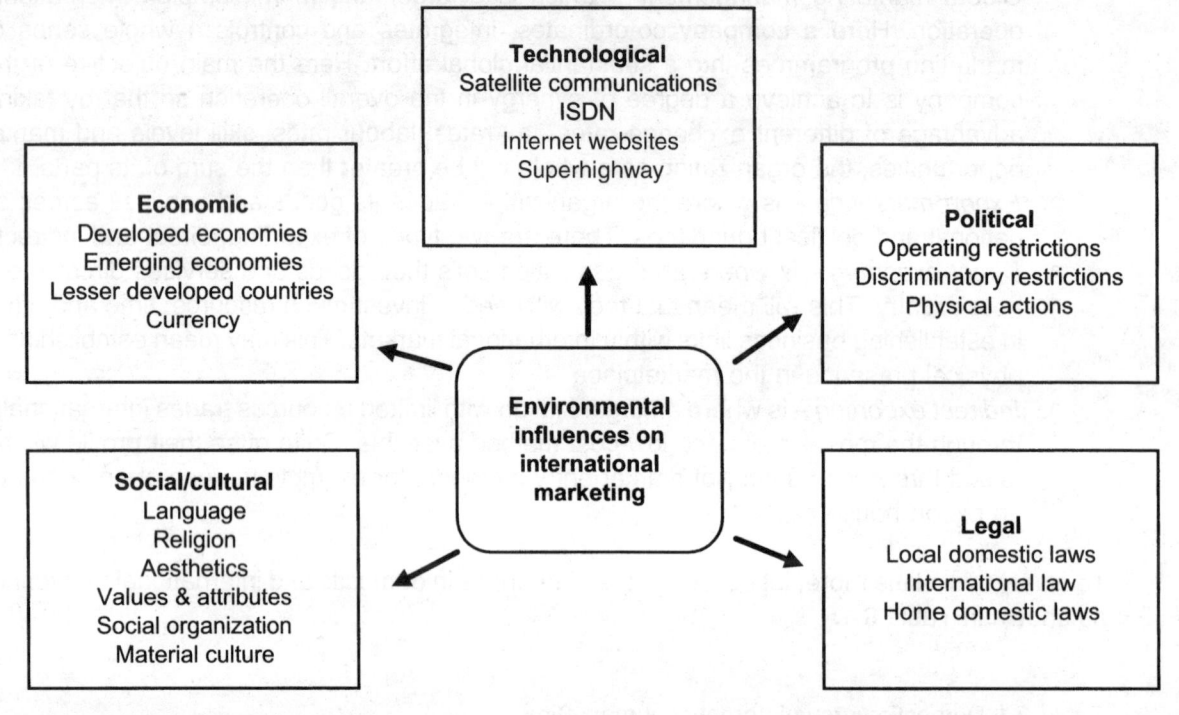

*Figure 9.1* Cultural framework

## Social/cultural factors

Cultural differences are apparent from one end of the UK to the other, or one end of China to the other, but between different countries it would appear that in some instances they are enormous. You will find a range of different social interests and a variety of different customer behaviour patterns. Failure to understand them on the part of the organization could end in disaster, as it did several years ago when McDonald's moved into Iran. That country was less than delighted at Western intervention and it resulted in Iranians doing significant damage to the buildings.

Cultural differences are very significant, with considerations of religion, languages, education, symbols – these differences are often termed as cultural gaps. Clearly these will cause operational problems with the marketing mix and the ability to develop global brands. For example, Pepsi-cola had to change its 'Come Alive with Pepsi' campaign theme as in Germany it was translated as 'Pepsi Out of the Grave'!

These factors present many challenges for marketers, in terms of their ability to meet such a broad range of customer needs under the social and cultural banners. While product specifications – the tangible element of the mix – might be almost identical, the services mix – the level of customer services and technical support required – may be very diverse, dependent upon the infrastructure and expectations of the host country.

The challenges will be across the whole range of the marketing mix, not just the traditional elements of pricing, distribution and advertising, but also the 3Ps of the services mix, which will present significant challenges for the marketer.

Religious cultures present a very interesting challenge, particularly in Middle Eastern countries, where the role of women is different to the Western world. Marketers must be very sensitive to the varying levels of cultural diversity if they wish to be successful in international marketing terms.

## Question 9.1

Identify two countries that you are familiar with and draw up a list of potential social/cultural differences. You should do this by identifying four cultural characteristics and then compare and contrast them across both countries.

### Legal environment

Legal systems will invariably be different, both in context, content and meaning. You may have to think of law as being the 'rules of the game' for international trading.

There are four key considerations for international law:

1. *Domestic laws in the home country* – At the same time as working within international law requirements, you also have to consider your own country's legal requirements.
2. *Local domestic laws* – These are all different. The only way to survive through the legal systems abroad is to employ external agents, experts in the country, to manage the legal side of the business for you.
3. *International laws* – There are many international laws that affect the marketing of products and services overseas. For example international conventions and agreements, trade embargoes, International Monetary Fund (IMF) and WTO regulations, treaties, patents, trademarks, etc.
4. *Laws and international marketing activity* – These laws will affect each element of the marketing mix in different ways; it could be product patents or advertising restrictions, many of which exist in the Middle East.

There have been many interesting legal cases relating to international marketing and also cases of major organizations giving up on trying to achieve new market entry strategies because the red tape has been too difficult to get through. For example, Mercedes and

Kellogg's both were interested in pursuing entry into India, but it was just too difficult to broker their way through the endless bureaucracy and red tape.

## Economic environment

There are fairly wide extremes in relation to the economics of varying countries. For example, Ethiopia, where average earnings are considerably less than $100 per annum, through to North America, where the average *monthly* earnings are in excess of $2000. The differences between Southern American economies and those of the Asia Pacific Rim are considerable. A further example of differences in economies is that in Tokyo you have to work for less than 25 minutes to buy a Big Mac from McDonald's, whereas in Mexico City you have to work for 80 minutes to buy exactly the same product.

## Three categories of the economic environment

1. *Developed countries* – The majority of the Western world would be classified as developed, e.g. Japan, Europe and the USA. The NAFTA (North America Free Trade Area) countries, the European Union and Japan account for over 80 per cent of trade in the Triad economies, the Triad being a global triangle within which trade exists – three different groups of cultures and economies coming together.
2. *Emerging economies* – Countries such as India, China, South America (in particular Brazil) are defined as emerging because of the successful change in direction of their internal economic policy which has in turn produced a growing demand for every type of Western product, e.g. mobile phones, cars, computers etc.
   All of these present significant marketing opportunities, but also significant marketing mix challenges, as the marketer deals with the wide range of international trade issues.
3. *Less developed countries* – Typically this means that the per capita income is extremely low, which in turn inhibits the amount of disposable income for regeneration in the economy. Common characteristics of such countries are poor communications networks, poor transportation system, high levels of poverty, low levels of education and health care.

### Currency/interest rate risks

World economic instability and currency variations are potentially very damaging to organizations. A rapid drop in one particular currency can wipe away almost immediately the benefit of doing business abroad, in fact it can be the difference between organizations managing to sink or swim. This is something that has been very much in the forefront of everyone's mind since September 11, 2001 and also the war on Iraq that commenced in the spring of 2003 and which, whilst now formally over, still continues internally and quite violently.

Rises or falls in interest rates can also have significant effects, as we have seen in the UK in the past, where high interest rates make international trading difficult, as UK products and services are expensive.

Then you have the issue of the single European currency, monetary union within Europe, with the objective of bringing stability to the European economy.

## Political

In Unit 2 of this text, we explored the volatile nature of politics in respect of the external environment. As we watch world events unfold it is only too clear to see that international markets can be significantly erratic and volatile politically. For example, in the wake of the sad and prominent events of September 11, we saw the USA forging very close ties with countries from within the European Union. However, in March 2002, there was a political eruption over the exporting of steel into the USA, as they seek to enforce tariffs on the importation of European steel. This has created a significant backlash. In addition to this there is complete disruption at one of the critical political domains, the United Nations, where in essence critical countries such as France, Germany and Russia have taken a stand against many other European countries in relation to the War on Iraq in 2003, creating significant tensions in the European political environment.

## Technological environment

The biggest single influence of recent times on international trade has to be the Internet and the technological revolution. Principally, the effect of the Internet has manifested itself by reducing the world to a global village, with trade, communication and information being easily and readily available.

With the evolution of satellite and digital and mobile/video phone technologies, the marketplace has become much more accessible, without there necessarily being a physical presence. The continuing levels of innovation may go some way in the future to easing some of the burdens on international trade, as there may be a sharp decrease in trade barriers as a result of the Internet. As we saw in the case of Lufthansa, it will see a sharp reduction in marketing costs.

## Question 9.2

List five ways in which the Internet will aid international trade.

# Know your markets

Marketing research is critical in all markets, but when trading overseas, and effectively operating in a vacuum, the need for comprehensive information is essential. There are two components to marketing research:

1. The need to understand customers and their buying behaviour
2. The need to understand the marketing and operating environment.

International research is complex and difficult to manage. It is very costly and time-consuming and the outcome is not always very meaningful. The consequences of collecting incorrect or inappropriate information could be immeasurable.

Organizations failing to carry out effective marketing research could find themselves missing significant market opportunities, or alternatively finding that the supposed opportunities identified do not exist. Either way, without the right information on the proposed market, the organization could lose out.

The role of the international researcher for the organization will be to produce a clear overview of the current state of the marketplace. This should include examining issues such as the SLEPT factors, demand for products, ability to pay, levels of competitor activity, ability to meet the political and legal requirements of the host country and, of course, the technological ability of the country concerned.

There are three key functions an international market researcher should undertake:

1. *Scanning international markets to identify and analyse the opportunities* – This will include looking at accessibility, profitability and market size of existing markets, latent markets and potential markets.
2. *Building marketing information systems to monitor international environment trends and patterns of trade* – This includes the collection of primary and secondary data and ongoing external audits to monitor the pace of change or the stability of the host economy.
3. *Carrying out primary research for specific reasons* – This would include potentially carrying out test marketing and measuring the feasibility and viability of trading in the host country as well as the impact that this trade would have on the marketing mix and the implications of changing the mix to meet a range of different customer needs.

The key to successful market entry is to ensure that markets are scanned and analysed, and comprehensive market profiles are built up and detailed country studies undertaken.

## Understanding the external marketplace

We have already looked at the intricacies of analysing the external environment, through the use of PESTEL or SLEPT. However, there are some specific market performance indicators in relation to key economic indicators that you might need to ascertain the position of. They include:

- Population size and growth
- Population density and concentration
- Population age and distribution
- Disposable income and income distribution
- *Economic activity* – where is the concentration of economic/financial generation?

These indicators will highlight to you the economic position of the country and its status in relation to its level of development, e.g. emerging economies or less developed economies, such as India or Ethiopia.

Other indicators include areas such as:

- Natural resources
- Topography
- Climate
- Energy and communication
- Urbanization
- Differential inflation levels.

Clearly, understanding these indicators will give you a broad brush picture of the state of the host nation you are considering, which provides a sound basis on which to judge the level of perceived risk in market entry.

## Understanding consumer and business buying behaviour

Business buyer behaviour is something you will cover in Unit 10, 'Industrial/business-to-business, FMCGs and services marketing', but in an international context it is essential that you understand the key principles and structures behind business-to-business buying.

From a domestic perspective, the typical focus would be:

- The structure and composition of the DMU (decision-making unit)
- Organizational influences upon purchasing
- The role of technology
- The business/industrial buyer process
- The personal characteristics of the buyers.

These factors, combined with an understanding of the marketing environment, would provide you with a robust management information system that would serve to underpin any decisions that might be made in respect of international expansion.

Ultimately, before a market entry strategy can be considered you need to be aware of the market potential:

- Market size
- Competition
- Resource
- Customer demands and the ability to purchase
- Accessibility
- Barriers to entry.

## International research

The research process, as seen in Unit 3, while needing to be formal, must have key objectives to be achieved. In the instance of international marketing research, the key questions and objectives, as recommended by Fifield, Lewis and Carter (2001), are:

- Where to go?
- How to get there?
- What shall we market?
- How do we persuade them to buy it?

## Developing an international marketing information system

With every information system there need to be criteria for essential information to be collated in order that an informed decision might be made. To assist with this, refer to the 12Cs analysis model for creating an information system:

1. **Country**

    (a) General country information
    (b) Basic SLEPT data
    (c) Impact on environmental dimensions.

2. **Choices**

    (a) Analysis of supply
    (b) International and external competition
    (c) Characteristics of competitors
    (d) Import analysis
    (e) Competitive strengths and weaknesses.

3. **Concentration**

    (a) Structure of the market segments
    (b) Geographical spread.

4. **Culture/consumer behaviour**

    (a) Characteristics of the country
    (b) Diversity of cultural grouping
    (c) Nature of decision-making
    (d) Major influence on buyer behaviour.

5. **Consumptions**

    (a) Demand and end-use analysis of economic sectors that use the product
    (b) Market share by demand sector
    (c) Growth patterns of sectors
    (d) Evaluation of threat of substitute products.

6. **Capacity to pay**

    (a) Pricing
    (b) Extrapolation of pricing to examine trends
    (c) Culture of pricing
    (d) Conditions of payment
    (e) Insurance terms.

7. **Currency**

    (a) Stability
    (b) Restrictions
    (c) Exchange controls.

8. **Channels**

    (a) Purchasing behaviour
    (b) Capabilities of intermediaries
    (c) Coverage of distribution costs
    (d) Physical distribution infrastructure.

9. **Commitment**

    (a) Access to market
    (b) Trade incentives and barriers
    (c) Custom tariffs
    (d) Government regulations
    (e) Regulations on market entry.

10. **Communication**

    (a) Promotion
    (b) Media infrastructure and availability
    (c) Which marketing approaches are effective
    (d) Common selling practices
    (e) Media information.

11. **Contractual obligations**

    (a) Business practices
    (b) Insurance and legal obligations.

12. **Caveats**

    (a) Factors to be aware of.

## Acquiring secondary data

Typical sources of secondary data might include:

- Specialist trade press
- Quality press, journals and magazines
- Trade associations
- *Directories* – Kompass and Euromonitor
- Major universities and business schools
- Public libraries
- Local chambers of commerce
- Bankers
- International consultancies
- Electronic media
- Published research
- Competitors' published research
- Export houses and freight forwarders
- Embassies, both domestic and that of the host country.

In the past, marketing research into international markets has been difficult and at times completely unreliable. When a local national agency carried out research projects on behalf of potential international marketing organizations, quite often the information collected and then presented could give the organization a very biased view of the state of the nation.

The biggest inhibitors of international research are language and culture. Both these characteristics can be interpreted very differently depending upon the country of origin.

Lack of appropriate marketing information on any geographical area is dangerous, but to commence trading overseas without a thorough investigation of the opportunities and threats is completely negligent of the organization.

Unit 9 International marketing

With the use of modern technologies, the standard and availability of market research information is much improved. There are databases and CD-ROMs, in addition to the banks of information stored on the WWW. Due to the ongoing emergence of a significant range of international trading organizations, both commercial and political, more reliable information is starting to emerge, some of which has been collected through worldwide research initiatives.

However, while the situation is improving considerably, researching international markets is an enormous task.

## Acquiring primary research

Primary research in international markets can be a very difficult process. Obvious difficulties include:

- Costs associated with primary data are traditionally high
- Language and cultural differences
- *Sampling* – geographical diversity
- Non-response
- Social organization
- Terminology.

Of course primary research can be undertaken through the traditional routes of questionnaires, focus groups, experimental and observation research.

Once the data have been accessed and analysed, the organization is then in a position to start making decisions in relation to entering the market and how to enter the market, i.e. what international channel options are open to them.

### Question 9.3

What are the implications of collecting primary data from less developed countries?

### Market entry strategies

Market entry strategies are based around a strategic decision taken to trade internationally. Ultimately it will form part of the overall corporate and marketing strategy. However, it is useful to understand the basis of the different entry strategies.

Having established the following facts, the organization should be able to choose the most appropriate method of international expansion:

- The company objectives in relation to the size and value of the market
- The financial resources required to commence trading
- The existing marketplace
- The level of competition that exists
- The nature and characteristics of the market
- Pricing issues
- The nature of the product/service
- Timings.

Answering these questions should enable the organization to decide on the most appropriate method of trading internationally.

- *Licensing* – The positive side to licensing is that it requires relatively low levels of investment. Licensing is usually based around a contract that enables a second party, the licensee, to produce products or services, have technological know-how, research and development information and trade marks that belong to another organization, namely the licenser. Both parties sign an agreement that then outlines terms and conditions for the use of the above.
  The advantages include a low level of commitment, reduced market entry costs and the ability to enter smaller markets in a more cost-effective way.
  Disadvantages could include being tied into a long-term relationship, particularly if conflict evolves, and competition from the licenser.
- *Agents* – Agents are effectively overseas sales personnel, who operate in a range of markets on behalf of different organizations. Agents will usually work on a retainer basis with commission or on a commission basis. Their role is to create an awareness of your organization and the products and services it has to offer, ultimately with the view to securing a sale.
  Agents are often very successful as they will operate in their local marketplace which then reduces some of the barriers to entry that organizations often face when trying to gain entry into new markets.
  Agents should be selected for their financial strength, their contacts within the host country, the nature and extent of their relationships with organizations and their skills, abilities and resources.
- *Franchising* – Franchising was covered in Unit 4 'Theories of communication', under Distribution, which you should read again to refresh your mind. Franchising is a very common way of operating overseas. Think about how many outlets McDonald's, KFC and Pizza Hut, etc. have around the world. You can probably see from those very examples the success of franchising on a global scale.
- *Company acquisition* – This actually refers to gaining market entry by buying an existing company in the country where you wish to trade. The advantage of this is that you are buying an existing going concern and therefore the infrastructure is in place, but the financial risk involved is considerable.
- *Wholly owned subsidiary* – Probably one of the most expensive methods of international business is setting up a wholly owned subsidiary, which means that the organization will effectively set up a fully fledged business overseas. This will include very significant overheads and is therefore a very costly option.
- *Joint venture* – Is really a variation of the above, but instead of a total investment into another country, your organization may choose to buy into another country, through a joint venture, potentially buying up to half of a compatible business. This is a very common practice. There are many advantages of this process, as organizations share market research, product development, marketing planning and implementation, capital and resources both human and financial. You will often find that organizations join forces for competitive reasons, or even for technological know-how.

There are also many disadvantages, such as trust with the other partner, differences in aims and objectives and strategies. One partner may hold a greater stake than the other; that in itself can cause much conflict.

Unit 9 International marketing

> **Question 9.4**
>
> Explain the differences between international and export marketing.

## Case history

### Cathay Pacific seeks closer ties with Chinese Airlines

Hong Kong's flag carrier Cathay Pacific Airlines Ltd wants closer ties with China's largest airlines so it can cash in on the country's rapid industrial growth.

A director of Cathay Pacific, Raymond Yuen, was cited by *South China Morning Post* as saying 'that such an alliance would help the regional airlines become more competitive with links in outbound traffic'.

Yuen said that the huge demand in China's aviation industry had prompted the need for more co-operation with mainland companies. He said closer co-operation could take the form of code sharing and joint selling of air tickets, partnership cargo operations, pilot training and other back-up services.

From now until the year 2006, China will need a total of 1600 Boeings and Airbuses, an average of 4.5 pilots are needed for each plane.

*Source*: Lexis-Nexis.

## Potential barriers to entry

While these are potential market entry strategies, there are a number of barriers to entry that organizations must consider how they will overcome.

Barker and Kaynak (1992) list the following important areas:

- Too much red tape
- Trade barriers
- Transportation difficulties
- Lack of trained personnel
- Lack of export incentives
- Lack of co-ordinated assistance
- Unfavourable conditions overseas
- Slow payment by buyers
- Lack of competitive products
- Payment defaults
- Language barriers.

By selecting the right market entry channel, many of these barriers may possibly be overcome; therefore careful consideration of the most appropriate entry method for the most successful outcome is crucial. The more informed the organization, the clearer the country profile, the easier it will be to identify the best method for the organization.

# The implications on marketing plans

Again, from your earlier studies you should be very familiar with marketing plans and the marketing mix. What you need to consider now, looking at them in an international context, is how in some instances organizations may need to amend their plans and mix to meet the needs of the particular market.

One thing you must be clear on is that it does not matter where in the world you operate, or have a physical presence, the concepts of marketing and customer orientation are exactly the same.

When trading internationally, organizations will clearly need to break their markets down into a number of different segments, which in turn become target markets.

While the organization may have one set of corporate objectives, which include international marketing, it is highly likely that they will have a number of varying plans and strategies to reflect the local demands of each country. In turn this means that the marketing mix could also be different.

The organization produces products or services for the benefits their customers want to gain. Therefore, it is critical to ensure that the organization's product offering fits the requirements of the host country. For example, almost every country in the world uses irons or hairdryers. While the main functions, characteristics and mechanisms are the same, the power supplies and sockets are different. Therefore, an organization must reflect on this element and amend their products accordingly. Should they do this, it would flag up a change to the product element of the marketing mix.

The key question the organization must then ask is should their product offering be standardized or differentiated?

Product life cycles and product positioning will also vary according to the country of operation. This will be due to issues such as market demand, market growth, the pace of change and competitive activity.

Under 'product' the issue of branding will also have to be considered. Organizations will need to consider the benefits of branding and whether or not their brand is meaningful in the country in which they operate.

## Product

New products for international markets will effectively need to go through the same new product development process as within the domestic country setting. Product opportunities should be referenced against aspects relating to its development such as:

- *Manufacturing requirements* – home and abroad
- Marketing research
- Ability to purchase the product
- Customer needs, wants and expectations in relation to the product
- Fit with existing product portfolio
- Trademark and patenting agreements for overseas
- Local and international safety standards
- Technology demands
- Technical support
- After-sales support
- Whether or not it should be standardized or adapted for local use.

## Pricing

Clearly pricing will be an issue where there could be significant variances. This could be because of currency exchange rates, international or local legislation, distribution and storage costs, as well as the cost of manufacturing the products.

In many instances organizations could be subject to varying taxes and tariffs, which will affect their pricing policy. Obviously the method of payment and speed of payment will also be a critical issue.

The influences on price will be very similar to the ones highlighted in the 'Price operations' unit of this text, but careful consideration must be given to the economic situation and economic indicators within the host country.

Being able to control the pricing strategy in international markets will depend upon the degree of regulation employed on a local basis. However, controlling prices will be an essential activity in order to sustain market share, competitive positioning and a degree of continuity within the chain.

Issues of price sensitivity will vary from country to country, but cultural diversity will have an influence on the perceived value proposition.

## Place

The big factor in this area will be accessibility and the cost of accessibility. There are many logistical challenges with distribution, including warehousing, storage, transportation network, etc. The selection of the appropriate market entry strategy will influence the way in which distribution can effectively be managed.

Clearly, with the growing impetus of the Internet, the dynamics of distribution are sure to change in the coming years, and while there is some instability, currently organizations such as Amazon have proved it can work.

Management of channel members will require serious consideration and could prove to be a logistical nightmare. However, the following points should be taken into account:

- Set-up costs of the channel and members
- Level of investment required
- Level of incentive required
- Synergy with the local/domestic channels
- Management and control of the overall process.

## Promotional mix

This area is possibly the most interesting and the most complex to deal with, because of the nature of social/cultural differences from country to country. There are many challenges to be faced under this banner. These include:

- Language
- Image
- Relationships
- Corporate identity
- Product image

- o Company image
- o Methods of advertising
- o Tolerance of advertising
- o Marketing ethics
- o Available media
- o Adult literacy levels
- o Accessibility of information
- o Agencies.

As a result of so many different facets of culture within so many different countries it is highly likely that the organization will need to develop a range of different marketing and promotional mixes to match the host country's market.

Again the importance of defining a good country profile is highlighted. This should be based around a wide range of issues critical to the successful development of a marketing strategy. This then ensures that the organization achieves a true marketing and customer-oriented focus, producing products they want, where they want, when they want, at a price they want to pay and responding to promotions that are meaningful.

## Question 9.5

Choosing a country of your choice, discuss how you perceive the effects of economic and environmental trends on international product development.

# Globalization

In the final part of this unit, we consider the advantages and disadvantages of global marketing, and discuss whether plans and mixes should be global and whether we should be thinking global and acting local.

For a long period of time we have heard terms such as the global village, the borderless world. This was an idealism of the 1990s but the surge towards standardization has been considerable as organizations see the potential for cost saving through economies of scale. Organizations constantly struggle to find the balance of just how far they should go, how much they should standardize, how much should they adapt to meet the needs of the global market.

So far there has only been limited success in developing a standardized global marketing strategy. It has been suggested that the only likely place for this type of strategy to really succeed is on the Internet, where the world is a global village. The same product, price, distribution channel and promotional campaign are used across the globe.

Often people associate organizations such as McDonald's or Coca-Cola with being truly global. While their brand is global, they do have variations on a theme to meet the customer expectations of the market they operate within. While they are global in market coverage, they localize in both tastes and language; they are global, but local.

Globalization is often characterized by the standardization of the marketing mix, and while this in essence would seem the most cost-effective and efficient way to move forward, it may not be the most competitive.

## Standardization versus adaptation

### Standardization

An organization seeking to globalize would have to consider standardizing almost all of the following elements:

- Market access
- Industry standards
- Technology
- Products
- Services
- Promotion
- Distribution
- Customer requirements
- Competition
- Communication.

The implications of standardizing the organization's approach present the marketer with a significant challenge, as moving towards a standardized marketing mix has no guarantee of success in all markets.

### Adaptation

In many respects standardization may seem the easiest approach, i.e. one product and one approach for all; however, in the real world this is not always possible and therefore adaptation has to be considered.

Adaptation can mean that the whole or part of the marketing mix has to be changed to meet the changing needs of different nations.

Adaptation of the *product* involves many companies in changing their products to meet local needs and conditions. For example, Nokia is known to have customized some of its phones to meet the needs of every major market.

As for *promotions* some organizations will again either adapt the promotional strategies for each of their companies or change. There are known and obvious difficulties with not adapting promotions, as culturally there are many areas that are taboo. One of the greatest causes of conflict in promotional activities can be something as simple as the use of colour. For example black is thought to be unlucky in China, whilst white is a mourning colour for Japan and green is associated with jungle sickness in Malaysia.

Furthermore the names of products can also cause conflict and misunderstanding. One of the biggest product name changes was the change in the name of a Snickers bar from Marathon, to actually 'standardize' the name of the chocolate bar product.

*Pricing* creates many a tension in international markets as many companies find it difficult to set international prices. One of the main problems for those companies trading internationally is that of the cost of distribution. If the company is to be profitable in its dealings then the cost of distribution should be passed on to the customer. However, if the company wishes to be extremely competitive, then this becomes a slightly more challenging issue.

In recent times it is evident that economic and technological forces have had a significant impact upon global pricing. Closer to home, we have seen the introduction of the Euro over the last couple of years reduce the differentiation in prices across Europe and the price and indeed value is now more transparent and measurable.

Added to all of this, the opportunity and ability to shop online means that prices are now more evident and that as such 'price transparency' is now required.

We have already alluded to the fact that there are issues with *distribution*. For many companies the challenges of distribution and the cost of distribution can often make international trade more prohibitive and difficult to achieve successfully and competitively. Channels of communications vary so much from country to country, however, that there is often no choice but to tailor and adapt distribution requirements to meet channel needs for both the consumer and the B2B customer.

Clearly, the ultimate decision whether or not to standardize or adapt products can only be based upon knowledge and a wide range of information about each foreign market, its channels, features, cultures and characteristics.

## Benefits of globalization

There are number of advantages and disadvantages associated with globalization. The advantages are that globalization is more straightforward, in that it seeks to use one set of tools to meet one global set of customers. This provides economies of scale, supposed fairness and equity and potentially greater accessibility, and could potentially lead to the organization being very competitive on a cost basis. But you may ask yourself: do we want one product for all?

Clearly, there are a number of disadvantages associated with standardizing the mix, as it could prove to be a very inhibitive practice that could cause immense difficulty when trying to meet the needs of so many different facets and such extreme target markets.

The key success factor in achieving any marketing strategy, including globalization, is to ensure that the organization keeps a constant watch on the global marketing environment.

Organizations should monitor change, identify strengths and weaknesses, opportunities and threats and then aim to build a strategy based around customer satisfaction, increasing profitability, head marketing share and achieving global competitiveness.

As the world becomes a smaller place through the power of ICT then true globalization and complete standardization may one day be achieved. In the meantime, thinking global and acting local is the most a customer- and marketing-oriented organization can achieve.

## Summary

The issues relating to international marketing and globalization are considerable. But the key to its success is to remember the purpose of marketing. It is critical to the organization not to see international markets as a special project or view them in isolation.

Critical to any decision in relation to international marketing is sufficient information on which to base a decision. Organizations should never underestimate the power of market research in giving them a snapshot of the bigger picture. That picture will show the many different facets of the target country, which is when the organization identifies whether to globalize or localize.

Because marketing is dynamic and ever-changing and because of the growing participation of the Internet in the marketing environment today, globalization will continue to be an objective for which many organizations should strive.

To remain competitive the organization will need to make a number of major decisions based on who their market is, where their market is, the status of the economy of their markets and the opportunities they present.

Staying ahead of the competition will be critical and therefore for many years to come organizations will increasingly need to develop and use a range of marketing information, market entry strategies and overall marketing strategies to keep the balance between globalization and localization, and customer satisfaction.

## Study tip

As a result of the growth in international marketing, clearly it is playing a more prominent role in our everyday lives. The examination of Marketing Planning is no exception. One of the key tips to consider is that whenever the situation permits you to, include reference to internationalization, globalization, as being key market driving forces in the economy. Virtually every exam paper has an international marketing question on it, and this should be a good indicator to you to highlight its importance.

## Extending knowledge

### Recommended reading

In addition to reading this text, and your recommended text, you may find it helpful to read some of *International Marketing Strategy* by Isobel Doole and Robin Lowe (2004), in particular Chapters 3, 4, 9, 10 and 11. This book is the recommended text for International Marketing Strategy and the Postgraduate Diploma level.

You will see in the exam question below that you are asked to provide an example of excellence in respect of continuous assessment. It is therefore advisable that you actually follow the press – *Marketing*, *The Economist*, among others to observe the nature of international marketing and also the successful implementation of international marketing strategy across the world.

## Bibliography

Barker, T. and Kaynak, E. (1992) 'An empirical investigation of the differences between initiating and continuing exporters', *European Journal of Marketing*, **26**(3), 27–35.

Dibb, S., Simkin, L., Pride, W. and Ferrell, O. (2001) *Marketing: Concepts and Strategies*, 4th European edition, Houghton Mifflin.

Doole, I. and Lowe, R. (2004) *International Marketing Strategy*, Thomson Learning.

Fifield, P., Lewis, K. and Carter, S. (2001) *International Marketing*, Butterworth-Heinemann.

Kotler, P., Armstrong, G., Saunders, J. and Wong, V. (1998) *Principles of Marketing*, FT Prentice Hall.

---

Sample exam questions and answers for the Marketing Planning module as a whole can be found in Appendix 4 and past examination papers can be found in Appendix 5. Both appendices can be found at the back of the book.

# unit 10
## industrial/business-to-business, FMCGs and services marketing (including the services mix)

### Learning objectives

This unit is one of three units looking at the application of marketing in a number of given contexts, to help you understand the broad diversity of marketing, given different situations, different markets and different customers.

The indicative content of the syllabus is as follows:

- Develop a marketing plan and select an appropriate marketing mix for an organization operating in any such context as B2B and services

- Describe how a plan is developed for the human element of the service encounter, including staff at different levels of the organization

- Explain how the physical evidence element of the integrated marketing mix is developed

- Explain how a plan covering the process or the systems of delivery for a service is developed

- Determine an effective extended marketing mix in relation to the design and delivery of service encounters (SERVQAL).

Syllabus elements: 4.2, 4.4, 3.12, 3.13, 3.14

# Business-to-business marketing

## Introduction

There are varying terms to describe the B2B markets, however, one of the more commonly used ones is 'organizational markets'. Principally, this is where the buyers within the organizations buy on behalf of them. This could include a range of different products from computer equipment, forgings, welding, stationery, various plant and equipment that might be needed in order to get the job done.

Organizational markets include organizations such as manufacturers, hotels, hospitals, conference centres, wholesalers and sometimes retailers, local authorities, government bodies to name but a few.

There are many implications of organizational markets, but in short they include:

- *Geographical diversity* – they can be spread very far and wide
- Size of the decision-making unit
- The issue of 'preferred supplier status'
- Size of purchase
- Frequency of purchase
- Negotiation of contracts
- Lead time between order and delivery.

One of the most important factors that you must identify with, particularly from a forecasting position, is that industrial demand in B2B markets is derived from consumer demand. This may be difficult to follow at first, but if you think of any consumer product you should be able to work out that the need for the production factory, the raw material supply and the transportation services all depend on the demand for the product. They would disappear if the consumer demand for the product actually declined.

An obvious example of this would be cars. Although you may not be overly familiar with the level of manufacturing, components and raw materials that go into the building and production of cars, you must have some concept of the size of the enterprises that make cars and deliver them to their customers throughout the world. A further example of this was the potential demise of the Rover factory. There was massive concern about the impact of factory closure in the West Midlands if another buyer was not found for the Rover plant. The impact of the demise of the Rover car would have been a loss of almost 100 000 jobs in the UK motor parts industry.

The same applies to every industrial product, although it is often difficult to visualize the extent of supply chains, with the different manufacturers and their network of suppliers and distributors.

## Characteristics of business/industrial buying behaviour

There are many characteristics of organizational markets, which will ultimately distinguish their buying behaviour and DMU in comparison to consumers and service-based decisions. They include:

- *Organizational size* – This will be a vitally important factor as organizational buyers will often be placing high volume or high price orders. The size, order capacity and nature of the organization will reflect the buying potential.
- *Nature of products purchased* – Essentially, many organizational buyers have to buy items which the consumer would not have any use for.

- *Buyer behaviour* – Affects the organization not the individual's motivation.
- *Size and influence of the decision-making unit* – This can be considerable and involve many individuals or groups of individuals.
- *Customer relationships* – Tend to be closer and more involved than in a typical business-to-consumer relationship. The level of involvement will most likely be high.
- *Power of buyers (Porter's Five Forces)* – The buying capacity and employment opportunities provided by organizations are often of major importance in a community, so the organization has some local, and maybe national, power, which can influence politicians.

## Organizational buying

Organizational buying behaviour, like that of a consumer, will be very much influenced by a range of different factors:

- The amount of money available
- The size/volume of purchase
- The level of risk involved
- The timeframe for decisions
- The buying situation
- The purpose of the purchase
- Competitive offers
- Credit terms and conditions of purchase
- Delivery lead times
- Packaging
- Environmental factors
- Supply and demand
- Inelastic demand
- Fluctuation in demand
- SLEPT influences
- Organizational objectives
- Individual and interpersonal.

As a marketing manager, it is essential that you understand the different degrees to which you could find yourself involved, within organizational markets. You will find that in many organizational markets many products are bought on a repeat purchase basis, possibly the same order sizes, qualities and quantities. There is little difference between these transactions and the consumer buying, and the selling situation will be based upon 'order taking' perhaps rather than order making.

However, for some rebuys, in particular modified rebuys, the process will often be more involved and perhaps require more technical advice, sales support and negotiations. Past experience will have a big effect on the decision and the DMU will be strongly affected by technical matters.

It is in the 'new buy' or 'new task', which involves perhaps the buying organization embarking upon a new project or a new job, that marketing must be used to its full effect, so we shall look closely at the information required, the time and resource involvement the contract might require, and the level of technical support. Essentially, as a marketer you will need to identify the level of involvement the contract will entail.

While it is vitally important to understand all of these influences, it is also essential that you are aware that one of the key influences in the buying process is the actual buyer themselves.

## Understanding the nature of business-to-business buyers

Quite clearly the role of an industrial buyer in an organizational market is going to be at the opposite pole from that of a typical consumer. Their objectives and motivations are going to be entirely different, as they are based around the organization, its function and its customers. Generally they are better informed, more demanding, more technically minded, and they also manifest more rational behaviour than consumer buyers.

However, while their focus might be the organization, as a marketing manager you should be aware that sometimes their own personal goals and hidden agendas might actually influence the purchasing decision. While the motivation is supposed to be organizationally focused, some buyers do gain psychological satisfaction from the purchase process. Essentially, they are human and their human and personal feelings will on occasions influence the decision.

The organizational/industrial buyer will be very interested in the overall value proposition; they have a duty and responsibility to the organization and stakeholder alike, to execute the best deals for their business. For a typical buyer, the key considerations in relation to the value proposition will include quality, delivery, service and price. The range of products available and the level of innovation an organization demonstrates will also play a role in influencing their thinking.

For large and more specialized products, you should expect a buyer to require significant amounts of data, market information, performance specifications, technical specifications, and it is also likely they will require a great deal of consultancy-style support in order that they have the complete picture andeco make a fully informed decision.

Because of the nature of their role, they will also involve themselves with competitor organizations and therefore will be fully aware of different options and alternatives available. As a marketing manager, you will therefore need to understand clearly the nature, scope and threat the competition will provide.

When all is said and done, organizational buyers are probably far more rational than individual buyers, they are less likely to be compulsive buyers, but what they will be is informed, demanding and focused upon achieving the best deal for the organization.

To give you a somewhat clearer picture of the high level of involvement in the organizational marketing context the Howard Sheth model of industrial buying might be helpful (Figure 10.1).

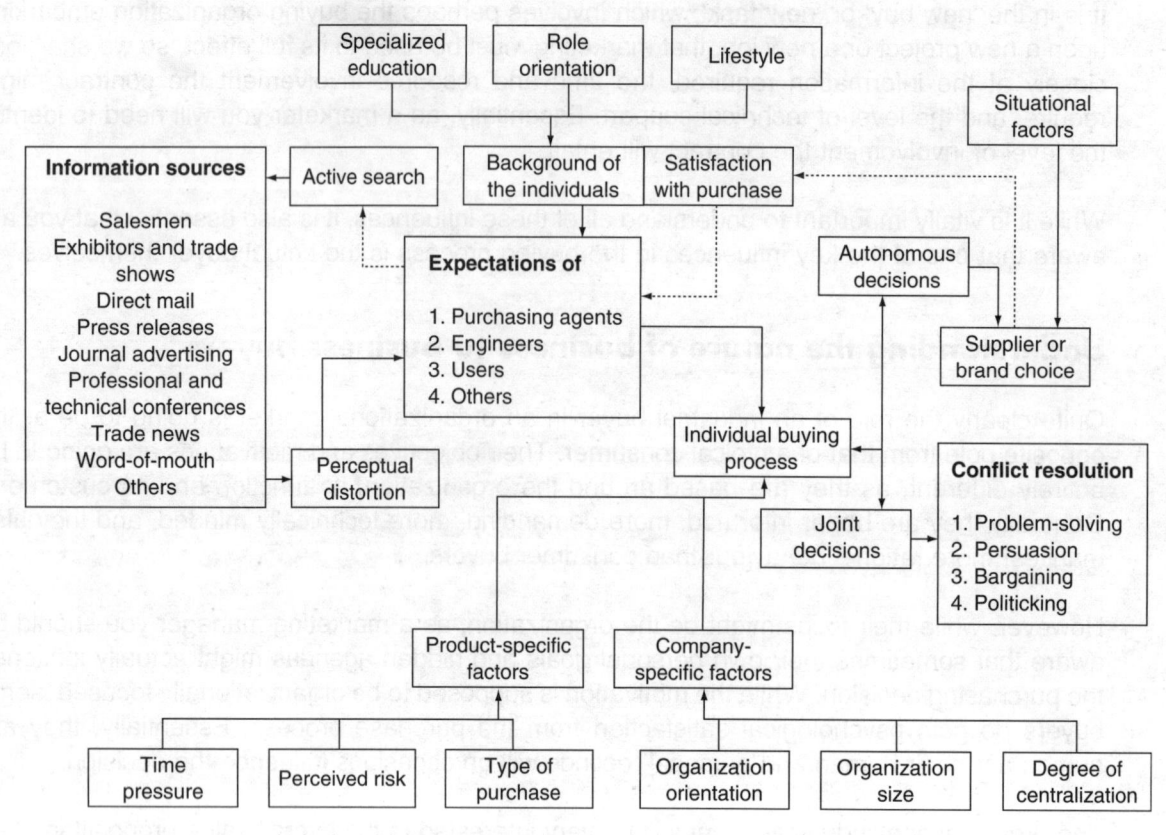

*Figure 10.1* Howard Sheth model of industrial buying behaviour

## Question 10.1

With your knowledge of the selling process gained in Unit 4, 'Promotional operations', of this book, outline the nature of the sales relationship that would be developed in the purchase of a motorway maintenance contract, which would be managed and co-ordinated by a large civil engineering consultancy.

### Market segmentation for organizational marketing

As many companies supply to a wide range of industries it is wise to segment the market so as to serve a specific market segment more thoroughly. It is equally essential to specifically target your products at special groups in organizational markets as it is in consumer-based markets.

Segmentation criteria may include:

- *Type of industry* – It may be possible to specialize, but even if this is not possible there may be common characteristics in some industries. For instance, aircraft manufacturers need specific certificates, which can only be supplied by approved companies; other industries have their own special needs.
- *Size of company* – The 'size' of a company may be measured by turnover, number of employees, output or capital employed. Many large companies have professional buyers, so they tend to evaluate their suppliers differently.
- *Type of product* or *service required.*

- *Type of buyer* – Some big companies allow their branch factories to buy, others do not. Some companies put limits on the value to which the branch factory buyer can go without asking for higher authority.
- *Geographical location* – There may be some parts of the country which have specialist needs, in which case you can segment them on that basis.

For gaining a clearer insight into both geographic factors and demographic factors, a look at the following additional criteria might be of assistance:

- SICs
- Census of the population (most recently in April 2001).

To understand the nature of the organizational requirements you will need to know:

- The nature of the benefits sought
- The degree of formality of the buying organization
- The people involved in the buying process.

Segmentation, however, is not perhaps as commonly used in organizational markets, and while it is an ideal, often the markets are limited in size, which makes it perhaps a little less appropriate.

## The buying and decision-making process in organizational markets

It is here that the most important difference between industrial and consumer buying becomes almost self-evident. Traditional consumer-based markets aim directly at the customer or consumer, i.e. the end-user, and therefore understanding customer satisfaction levels is essential. However, in organizational markets the motivations are different. The key to customer satisfaction is on-time delivery, quality of the products, arriving undamaged in order to meet production deadlines. It involves heavy-duty distribution requirements, stock handling, serious packaging and, of course, tightly negotiated deals.

The sales lead is likely to originate from a requirement within the company that emerges as a result of either the buying organization tendering for work (and therefore needing technical specifications and prices) or orders that have been placed by customers, and the buyer may have to buy raw materials, components, services, machines and even, perhaps, some design work.

There are a number of problems relating to organizational decision-making that perhaps put some of the above into focus:

- *Precipitation* – Why is the decision being made, what is it supposed to achieve, what are the benefits, what are the cost cuttings available?
- *Product specification* – Quality, quantity, characteristics, attributes, service levels, pricing.
- *Preferred supplier* – It is likely that supplier selection will be based upon a short list of known suppliers, creating a major barrier to entry for new suppliers. They will almost definitely have some key criteria that they will work on based upon past experience of their supplier base.
- *Commitment* – Will the chosen supplier be committed to the process, deliver on time, understand the nature of the problem?

Within the buying process there are a number of roles that might emerge based upon the level of technical specification being presented. Therefore, in a highly technical specification sale the following roles might be very significant:

- Supplier relationship management
- Supplier sourcing
- Evaluating tenders
- Negotiation
- Financing
- Order placing
- Performance evaluation
- Purchasing.

From the internal perspective of a supplying organization, i.e. a supplier to the organization market, you will additionally be involved in liaison with production and engineering divisions:

- Research and development processes and findings
- Assessing return on financial investment, managing methods of financing, costing and any borrowing in relation to the purchase
- Marketing of the products.

The process of the supplier/buyer relationship is quite a complex web and does in the main require a level of mutual understanding and co-operation and support on both sides.

## The decision-making process

You will be familiar with the consumer decision-making process, as explained in Unit 5, 'Product Operations', therefore Figure 10.2 will need little explanation. However, what it does do is explain which elements are relevant to new tasks, modified rebuys and straight rebuys (repeat purchases).

|  | Buy classes | | |
| --- | --- | --- | --- |
|  | New task | Modified rebuy | Straight rebuy |
| 1. Problem recognition | Yes | Maybe | No |
| 2. General need description | Yes | Maybe | No |
| 3. Product specification | Yes | Yes | Yes |
| 4. Suppliers' search | Yes | Maybe | No |
| 5. Proposal solicitation | Yes | Maybe | No |
| 6. Supplier selection | Yes | Maybe | No |
| 7. Order-routine specification | Yes | Maybe | No |
| 8. Performance review | Yes | Yes | Yes |

Figure 10.2 Buy grid
Source: Adapted from Worsam (2000)

## The buying centre – the decision-making unit

Like consumer markets, organizational markets have a decision-making unit, or a buying centre. However, the dynamics and scope of the task are considerably higher.

The roles of a typical decision-making unit for an organizational market are as follows:

- *User* – The machine operator – the person who actually uses the product.
- *Influencer* – Typical influencers will be users, suppliers, research and development staff, accountants, buyers, sales representatives, external consultancy representatives, etc.
- *Decider* – On this occasion it is more likely to be 'deciders'. These might include a management team, a tendering committee, an individual buyer, shareholders – this really will vary depending upon the extent and financial involvement of the decision.
- *Buyer* – The person who will handle the internal supplier sourcing, information seeking, handle negotiations with the suppliers.
- *The gatekeeper* – This is likely to be a member of the secretarial or administrative staff, handling the flow of information inbound and outbound through the organization.

## Question 10.2

What are the distinctive differences between a consumer decision-making unit and an industrial decision-making unit? (Refer to your studies in 'Theories of communication' for information about the consumer DMU).

## Relationship marketing in organizational markets

A poor purchasing decision from an organizational buying perspective could be fairly catastrophic and therefore every opportunity has to be taken to ensure that the risk inherent in the decision, and therefore in the relationship, is reduced.

The history and previous experience of the organization will be an imperative to the final choice of supplier that an industrial buyer will make, amid other key factors. However, gaining preferred supplier status gives a positive stance, so that when the tendering process has a close outcome, the strength of the preferred supplier relationship secures the deal.

There are three key components linked to the relationship marketing stance:

1. The *durability of the relationship* – The length of time over which a supplier/buyer relationship will continue (in some industries a purchase can take 12 months and above to secure).
2. *Economics* – The investment of time and money in the relationship actually enhances relationships and preferred supplier status opportunities.
3. *Social dimensions* – Because of the duration of the relationship it is likely that it might take on some form of social dimensions. While this is inevitable, mixing business with pleasure can sometimes cause conflict. Having said this, some supplier/buyer relationships, according to research, extend beyond 20 years.

Essentially there are likely to be two approaches to managing the supplier: adversarial and collaborative.

*Adversarial* – the characteristics pertinent to this approach include:

- Regular price quotes
- Little co-operation
- Quality and delivery thresholds meet lowest denominator
- Emphasis on lowest unit price
- Multiple suppliers.

*Collaborative* – the characteristics of this approach will include:

- Few suppliers
- Long-term and long-standing relationships
- Partnerships
- Frequent planned communications
- Integrated approach to operations
- Quality and timescales designed in and met
- Emphasis on the value proposition but the key being value for money – i.e. the lowest cost for the highest quality.

## Question 10.3

Why is it important for a supplier to establish a strong relationship with the buyer, and what are the benefits overall?

### The marketing mix for organizational marketing

As with any consumer products, there is a need to tell the organizational buyer that your product exists, just as in any other type of marketing, and the specific nature of most organizations makes it fairly easy to segment the total market. However, telling the customer that your products exist is a different matter when dealing with these buyers; they are usually professional people, probably having or aiming to have a qualification as good as yours, and they are just as ambitious as you are.

Some advertisements will be useful 'to put the company on the map', but the organizational buyers will be more interested in brochures/catalogues or complete information packages explaining the company's portfolio of products and services, and price lists for standard products.

#### Product

The product may range from tiny components through to massive projects such as a ship or aircraft. Obviously, there is quite a difference between marketing small screws, in packs of several hundred each, and the marketing activities that go into a large construction of a car park or motorway.

For a product that has been designed for a specific customer, all the features required are already there, and the marketing manager can concentrate on other things. There are also products that are built to agreed international standards so that they can be interchangeable, at least in theory, because the standards usually specify the dimensions and minimum performance ratings.

## Place

The demand for a distributor can be very challenging, particularly with very large products, or indeed very heavy products. There is likely to be a wide distribution network, which will be similar in many ways to the wholesaler/retailer system used in consumer marketing. Therefore, some of the key areas of managing a distribution channel covered in Unit 8, 'Place promotions', will be comparable in this situation.

In addition, some manufacturers will make their products so that they exceed the minimum performances shown in the standards. This added value does distinguish the product from the rest, and can be a valuable selling point if your distributors are trained to use it.

## Price

Pricing will take on a different dimension, and will be based around a variety of different methods, from negotiation through to tendering. It is often quite complex and highly competitive. You will find that there is less likelihood, however, of organizational markets switching due to price, as reliability is equally important.

In respect of available budget, this will of course vary from B2B, but it is likely that the scope of the budget will be limited and not as significant as in some consumer-based markets.

## Promotion

The promotional mix itself is shown in Figure 10.3 and its major uses in Figure 10.4.

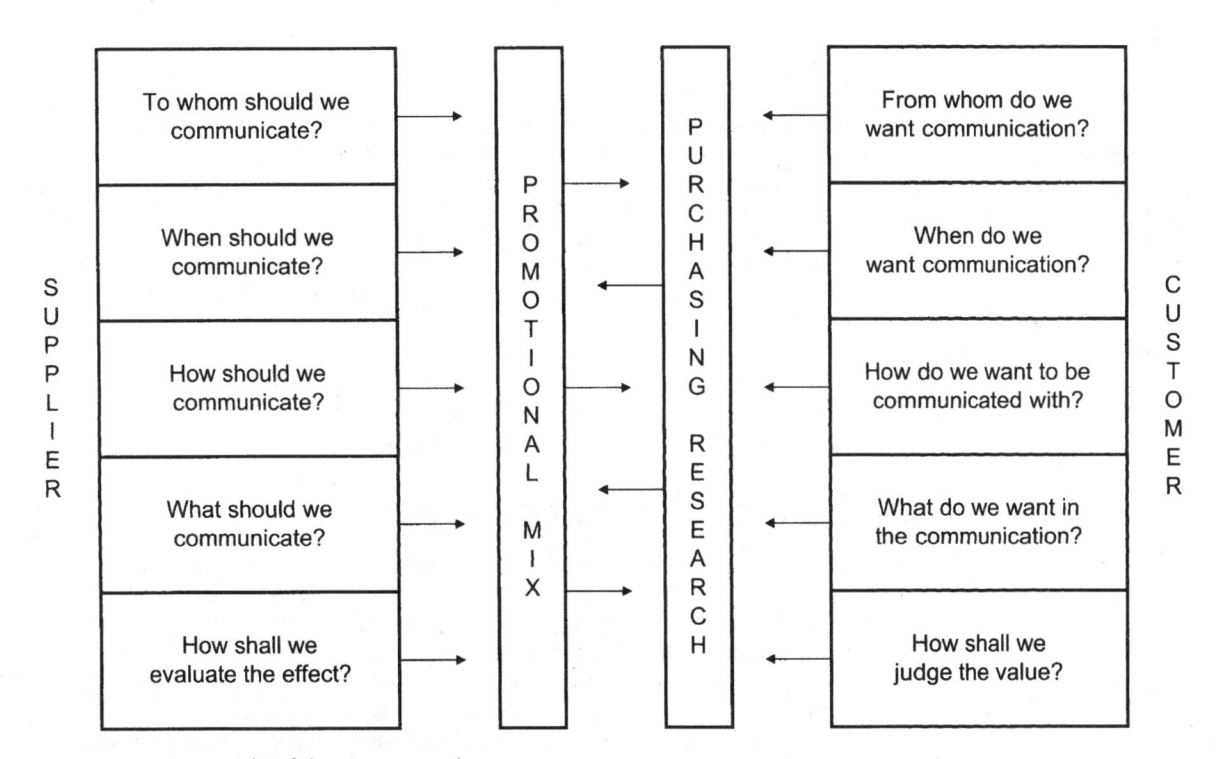

| SUPPLIER | | PROMOTIONAL MIX | PURCHASING RESEARCH | | CUSTOMER |
|---|---|---|---|---|---|
| | To whom should we communicate? | → | ← | From whom do we want communication? | |
| | When should we communicate? | → ← | ← | When do we want communication? | |
| | How should we communicate? | → | ← | How do we want to be communicated with? | |
| | What should we communicate? | → ← | ← | What do we want in the communication? | |
| | How shall we evaluate the effect? | → | ← | How shall we judge the value? | |

*Figure 10.3* Role of the promotional mix
*Source*: Adapted from Hill and Hillier (1977)

| Types | Use |
|---|---|
| Public relations | As in all forms of marketing, to secure favourable mention and restrict and/or counter unfavourable. With trade press and industry-specific features in the major newspapers there is ample opportunity to create PR opportunities. |
| Press advertising | National press is broadband and not often cost-effective, with the obvious exceptions of those organizations who operate in the customer markets and thus allow the industrial marketer to ride along if brand extension has been achieved. |
| Trade press | Highly targeted. Most effective for awareness and to stimulate a first response perhaps via a reader's enquiry service. Major opportunity for linked advertising and PR. Quality of trade journals varies widely. |
| Direct marketing | Mainly direct mail because many lists exist. Need to be careful to select with care and shorten where possible. Can be very important to develop one's own list and protect it rigorously. |
| Directories | Very valuable for services in paricular. *Yellow pages* and *Talking pages* are extremely effective for certain businesses. Beware not to subscribe to an unknown directory and never pay for space without having ordered it first. |
| Exhibitions | Most valuable in many areas. An opportunity to display product, to meet with existing customers, to develop and qualify leads and to sell (many forget that they can sell from a stand!). Also a valuable opportunity for competitive contact and research. Should be used positively, never simply to 'show the flag'. |
| Brochures, sales literature | Educational and informative, they should supplement, not be expected to carry the whole message. A range of mix and match, targeted literature will be needed in most areas. |
| Audio-visual | Can be simply educational and ephemeral but can also be used to positive effect if designed to achieve something that is otherwise difficult, such as a visit to a remote location. Can be mounted in the buyer's office using easily portable equipment as part of a sales pitch. |
| Computer | Few salespeople are today properly equipped without the ability to interrogate a database whilst with the buyer. Quotations can be printed on the spot, as can contracts, Via a modem a link to a senior manager can be established and a deal struck. Computers will support audio-visual presentations that can easily be tailored to need ahead of each visit. |
| Sales promotion | It is possible in some markets to add a 'temporary inducement at point-of-sale'. Not to be confused with discounts, however, unless SP gifts are of low value they may be perceived as bribes. It is better to target them on benefits to the organization or the department, not on the buyer. |
| Give-aways | Can be useful as reminders of phone numbers, etc. They also provide an opportunity to make contact. Probably the best are the long-lasting ones such as desk pads and diaries – but these benefit from tailoring to need rather than simply being bought off the sheff with the buyer's initials added (i.e it is better to invest quite heavily and do a proper job because the give-away says a lot about you and your organization). |

*Figure 10.4* Major uses of the promotional mix

There are many sources of support and things that can be done to help the sales representatives and these usually involve the provision of quality catalogues, where they are appropriate, or such items as films to show your products in use. Such films and brochures can give clients a better idea of how to use the products and some of them will be flattered if you can feature their products along with your own.

The role of the salesforce could be quite intensive and involved, from actually establishing the lead through until the order placement. This might involve qualifying leads, sorting and evaluating them against an established criterion.

Quite often the promotion consists simply of the knowledge of the salesperson, and he or she must be able to help designers or get someone in who can.

For the large construction projects, which take months or years to complete, the marketing team must match the DMU in terms of rank and status, in the early stages at least.

In the organizational marketing sector, marketing takes on a totally different meaning. Many organizations still do not embrace marketing in the same way and do not necessarily have organized or structured marketing activity. This often means that marketing can be random and ad hoc in nature.

Industrial organizations will need to develop a competitive advantage, indeed a competitive edge. Therefore, in many sectors a serious cultural change may need to be initiated in order for those sectors to impact seriously upon the competitors and maintain their stake within the marketplace.

## Developing a marketing strategy for FMCGs

Clearly, when any FMCG company is developing a brand in today's market it is likely to be sold far afield. In the UK, this will include across Europe and many other parts of the world. Therefore, when considering the development of new products and brand strategies, we should not be insular in our approach, but more global in our vision.

To do this, significant investment is required. A key writer, Lynch (as noted by Brassington and Pettitt, in *Principles of Marketing*, 2000) declared the following criteria to be essential for building that brand, both at home and on a European basis:

1. *Resources* – It is estimated that a marketing communications budget of not less than $60 million is needed for 3 years to establish a brand.
2. *Quality* – The need for consistent quality in both the product and the brand name is critical. Logistical and administrative procedures supporting the product should not be underestimated and are vitally important.
3. *Timing* – According to Lynch, it will take at least 5 years to establish a Euro-brand, as opposed to a shorter term on a national basis.

When you consider these three criteria very closely, this puts Euro-branding out of reach of many organizations. Additionally, many organizations may find it difficult to deal with cultural and language differences across Europe and the rest of the world. Just consider this statistic for a moment: only 40 per cent of all adults in Europe understand the English language, yet it is the most widespread language.

The net impact of this, which is also critical, is that packaged goods must take on a multilingual stance, or a non-verbal approach, or substantial amounts of expenditure will become necessary on packaging for the same products in a number of different languages.

The FMCG market is particularly competitive. Take, for example, the number of Coca-Cola-like drinks that there are available, or the number of different brands and types of toothpaste available, or washing liquids and powders, or even petrol. This, in itself, is an indication of how serious it is for any organization to develop an appropriate product and brand strategy.

Further considerations for FMCPG (fast-moving consumer packaged goods) organizations are the use of brand names and product names, and whether they should be used independently or combined: for example, Cadbury's Crème Eggs, or Cadbury's Flake; or Heinz Baked Beans, Walkers Crisps. Each of these organizations uses the brand and product name simultaneously. The brand name and the product are then closely associated. This means that the brand and the product develop an integrated approach and a message that associates the two. Often the message will be related to quality of the product, assists the organization in developing a competitive position, or even takes away the price-sensitive nature of the market. For example, many people will buy Kellogg's cereals over and above supermarket brands, yet Kellogg's are more expensive.

When Cadbury brings out new products, consumers associate the product and the brand. For example, there is Cadbury's Caramel Bar, now there is also Cadbury's Nuts about Caramel. It is therefore potentially easier to introduce new products or extend product lines, based upon the success of existing product and brand associations.

On the other hand, there are also many benefits attached to existing as two separate entities, as practised by Lever Bros, Smith and Nephew, Johnson and Johnson to name but a few.

- The benefits of independent branding and product association include preventing the downfall of a company from damage to a particular product. The damage is limited to the product rather than the brand.
- It can also allow greater activity with packaging and promotions generally, when organizations are not restricted to using the same company corporate image on every element of their activities.
- It allows for the product name to become a generic term. A good example here is that in the UK, we call paper hankies 'tissues'. In Iran, all tissues are known as Kleenex. It doesn't matter what the brand is; the brand has become the product. This is an interesting concept when considering marketing brands and products internationally.
- When an organization is test marketing a new product, through the NPD process, it will not be damaged in the same way should the product fail the test-market process.

The list of advantages and disadvantages is endless.

Earlier on in your studies, we considered a broad range of factors associated with the marketing mix, such as the PLC and the new product development process. Interestingly, many FMCG products have an extremely long life cycle. For example, look at Kellogg's Cornflakes, Heinz Beans, Heinz Ketchup, Mars, Persil, etc. All of these brands have products that have gone on for years and years, both in Europe and indeed broader international markets. By the same token, there are products under these brands that have had face-lifts, modifications, new and more innovative versions introduced, but all based around the original concept.

Therefore, new product development plays a critical role in ensuring that new and interesting products are always being developed, but the financial support and infrastructure to do that come from the significant success of existing products. Many of the products within the FMCG market would fall into the 'cash cow' category, generating significant income, with the initial investment long gone.

Of course, the success of any product is not singularly based around just the product and branding element of the marketing mix; it is based around the success of a well-developed and integrated marketing mix. Therefore, we should also consider the other elements of the marketing mix and how they impact upon FMCPGs.

## Place

When developing a new brand, it is imperative to consider the nature of the product and then its distribution requirements. Many of these factors will be based upon the characteristics of the product.

Firstly, an organization must consider whether its strategy will be intensive, selective or exclusive. In the case of most FMCPGs, the distribution strategy will be intensive. This means that the majority of FMCPGs appear in many outlets. For example, chocolate bars appear in just about every food shop, petrol station, leisure outlet, newsagent, supermarket, corner shop, chemist, and even in places such as Petsmart. Chocolate is therefore subject to intensive distribution.

The advantage of this distribution method to every customer is the fact that the product is accessible anywhere, in an instant. A new slant on this, of course, is that in fact you can do your shopping for FMCPGs from your home, through the Internet. This puts a completely new dimension on the consideration of distribution strategies for any significant FMCPG organization.

When using this type of distribution strategy, the organization will, of course, be clear that market coverage is far more important than the type of store selling the product, hence the number of non-vehicle-related products within petrol stations.

Whilst an intensive strategy is the way forward and has been for decades, one critical element that must be considered is quality. This is not particularly a problem for tinned packaged goods, but with more perishable items or frozen goods, manufacturer quality standards must be considered. Poor handling of such products can be costly to the organization, not only in terms of mistakes made, but also in respect of damaged reputation.

A further element of intensive distribution relates to the channel choice. Often with FMCPGs it is extensive and involves a lot of intermediaries. The most typical channel is:

Manufacturer ⟶ Wholesaler ⟶ Retailer ⟶ Consumer

*Figure 10.5*

Having said this, where large supermarkets are involved, the situation may be slightly different, and could cut out the middlemen, making the channel more cost-effective.

Intensive distribution is probably the most efficient way of making the product as widely available as possible, but total distribution costs may be high, especially where small retailers are concerned and unit orders are low.

## The marketing mix for FMCGs

### Price

For a marketer in an FMCG sector, pricing will be an extremely difficult component to manage. You will be aware that the FMCG sector is intensely competitive, with many like organizations striving for market share. Concepts such as price skimming are less likely to be relevant in this particular market, and it is more likely to see loss leader, penetration marketing or even promotional pricing activities being undertaken in relation to FMCGs. Competitive pricing is also an issue. You see this regularly, with one coffee producer offering extra reward points in association with the supermarket, whilst another producer will give you 20 per cent extra free, or indeed reduce the recommended retail price accordingly.

Pricing is a volatile area. FMCG organizations will need to be highly responsive to consumer needs and market demands. In many respects, FMCGs can be subject to supply and demand elements, particularly based on raw material values, which makes the competitive demand harder to manage.

### Promotion

One of the most common forms of communication in the FMCPGs area is advertising and sales promotion. As you have already seen, a considerable amount of money is invested in this sector every year.

For example, when Kellog's launched its new cereal brands in the UK, it spent £8.6 million, including £3.3 million on outdoor media and £3.9 million on television advertising. Later on at the turn of the century, over £750 million was spent by the top 10 UK advertisers. This included advertisers such as Coca-Cola, Nescafè, Persil, etc. Seventy per cent of that advertising spend went on television. So you can see what a live and exciting area this is.

Consumer-oriented appeals are probably the most challenging that an agency may face, as the level of competition is so massive in the marketplace, with every organization wanting to differentiate from the direct competitors. The main purpose of this approach is to get consumer attention by association, for example, Gary Lineker and Walkers Crisps.

A further issue is that of sales promotions. We are constantly bombarded with various sales promotion offers, not only directly from the manufacturer, but also in association with large supermarkets and indeed petrol stations.

The introduction of awards schemes has been one of the key factors in the development of sales promotions. For example, Sainsbury's and Boots both encourage you to go to booths within the stores to swipe your card, to get the best incentive bargains of the day.

Common sights are 'Buy one, get one free', 'Gain 500 extra reward points', 'Get 2p per litre off petrol' – and so the promotional battle goes on.

In the FMCG market, the main elements of sales promotions are:

- Display materials
- Packaging
- Merchandising
- Direct mail (coupons, competitions, premiums).

# Marketing of services

*Delivering services is people's business: only great customers and great employees can guarantee great service quality.* (Hans Kasper)

There are a number of problems and challenges associated with the management and implementation of service organization, relating to a wide range of factors such as the gap between expectations and what is delivered, evidence on the service proposal being limited and different perspectives on what constitutes quality service.

In order that an organization can deliver any form of service, they will need to recognize what that actually means in practice.

The purpose of this part of the unit is to address the particular issues associated with service delivery and how the process of continuous improvement is essential to the successful implementation of service offerings.

## Services defined

Dibb, Simkin, Pride and Ferrell (2001) define a service as:

*An intangible product involving a deed, a performance or an effort that cannot be physically possessed.*

You may recall that when examining the 'product' element of the marketing mix, we briefly looked at the intangible element of the product and noted that the product itself was normally tangible, i.e. had a physical dimension to it.

Services are usually divided into two main sectors, consumer services and business services.

1. *Consumer services* – Include marketing in non-profit-making organizations such as education, health, charities and government. Profit-making sectors include financial services, personal and professional services, leisure, entertainment and tourism.
2. *Business services* – Include repairs and maintenance, consultancy, leasing/contract hire, transportation, recruitment, advertising, marketing research, financial services, to name but a few.

## The structure of the services sector

A good benchmark of the significance of services marketing both home and abroad is the number of people employed in various service jobs.

The service sector is growing and evolving rapidly. For example, in the UK, over 64 per cent of the workforce are employed in a services related industry and in Europe as a whole over 61 per cent of the workforce are in the services industry.

One of the main reasons for the significant growth in the services sector is related to lifestyle. It would appear that while a potential economic slowdown might be looming, the services sector will possibly suffer a little less than areas such as manufacturing, as services are now a core part of everyday existence.

In the main, people are spending more of their income on insurance packages, financial services packages, convenience services, travel and leisure and many organizations provide employees with private health packages. People now buy time. In 1999 there was an article in the *Observer* relating to families' 'purchasing time'. To enable time-starved families to spend quality time together many more people were buying services such as laundry, cleaning, gardening, take-aways, etc.

## Service characteristics

### The difference between product and services
There is a distinct difference between the marketing of goods and services. The one common factor is that customers purchase goods and services for one reason only – they want the benefits a product can provide. Having said that, it is critical that you understand the difference between the two.

Services have four main characteristics:

1. Intangibility
2. Inseparability of production and consumption
3. Perishability
4. Heterogeneity.

Let us look briefly at each characteristic in turn.

### Intangibility
Services are intangible, because there is no physical product, nothing to be touched, tasted, smelled or heard before being purchased. The difficulty being, therefore, that the customer will be unable to perceive, imagine, or fully understand the nature of what they are to receive.

The challenge for the service provider, therefore, is to ensure that they determine the extent of intangibility and how, if necessary, tangible elements could be included to aid the understanding and expectation on the part of the customer.

A key characteristic of intangibility is that once that service performance has taken place, it cannot be used again. The performance was for that occasion only. For example, the training that you have undertaken cannot ever be delivered in exactly the same way again, it will never be repeated word for word in the same way, because effectively you have consumed the service. If the quality was poor or the standard of the course director was poor, nothing can be done about that particular performance. It could be improved for the next time, but the service would then be a different service.

### Inseparability
There is a definite distinction between products that are bought and used over and over again by the same customer, and that of services which are essentially consumed as they are purchased. A simplistic example of this might be having your hair cut or staying in a hotel. Should you decide to have your hair cut by one particular stylist, then it is not possible for another client to have the same hair cut at the same time, because you have purchased it and consumed it. Another example of this would be the use of a hotel room. If you use the hotel room on the night of 1st June then nobody else can use it that night; you have consumed the service the hotel provided on the occasion.

The implication for this particular component is that the involvement of the customer in the production and delivery of the service means that the service provider must take care in what is actually being produced.

## Perishability

Because services are produced and consumed at the same time, they are perishable, i.e. they cannot be stored for later sales or later usage. If the service is not used then, it cannot be used again. Again a hotel is a good example of that. If you did not use that room on the night of the 1st June and nobody else booked in the room, it could not be used again on that night, because that night has now gone. If the hair appointment isn't filled, and the time passes by, then effectively that appointment has perished, gone forever.

The implications of this relate to fluctuations in demand. Those which are unexpected pose a serious threat to the organization, in that they actually lose potential income, as a result of the time of use of the service passing by.

This is quite a serious problem for the service sector. Should the appointment not be booked, the bed not slept in, the car not hired or the flight seat remain empty, each of the providers of that service have seen the service perish and therefore they cannot gain any income from time not used. This is why you can purchase last minute flights or holiday deals, as organizations would rather take less income for the provision of the service than no income at all.

## Heterogeneity

Heterogeneity, or variability, effectively means difference. Going back to the example of a training course, there could be two training courses running on the same day, the same materials are being used and the rooms being used are exactly the same. The difference comes in the delivery. Each of the course directors will be different. They will have different appearances, different personal characteristics and different styles. It is unlikely that you would ever receive exactly the same service twice.

From a business perspective, the implication is that marketing services then becomes a difficult task, as each time you sell a service, there is no real guarantee that the service will be as good as you may say it is, as it is often down to human behaviour, or unfortunately and all too often true, human error. It is difficult to determine the quality and level of service provided as the service is not a product that can be quality assured before dispatch; it is produced as it is consumed. This also makes pricing the service very difficult.

The main difference between products and services is the tangible versus the intangible. Tangibility does to a degree give you guarantees of performance, of quality and of value for money. Therefore, marketing a tangible product enables you to balance the marketing mix more successfully and you are then able to deliver a key set of standards to the customer.

## The uncertainties of service

As we have established, delivering service quality presents a tremendous challenge to the marketer on a day-to-day basis. From a customer's perspective, it can be very difficult to qualify what you expect from a quality service because your personal expectations will quite often differ from others. However, from a marketing point of view, it is you and your perspective as a customer that will define how the service quality expectations are defined and delivered.

It is therefore necessary to stop for a moment and consider the interface between the service and the customer.

The main characteristics of this process can be identified thus:

- The customer is physically present, i.e. the place where the service is delivered
- The service and delivery process are interdependent (simultaneous production and consumption).

Within this interface it becomes clear that a potential 'uncertainty' arises between what the customer actually wants and what the customer is actually going to be provided with.

According to Mudie and Cottam (1999), this uncertainty arises for a number of reasons, but mostly because service deliverers fail to understand, for example, the following key customer inputs:

- Physical state of body (e.g. for a fitness clinic)
- Mental state of mind (e.g. for an education service)
- State and complexity (e.g. of a car for detecting faults during a service)
- Capacity (e.g. of clothing and carpet fabrics to withstand chemical treatment)
- Amount and nature of customer information (e.g. for medical diagnosis).

Essentially what happens is that in the above situations it becomes clear that the service provider is unsure about the customer's state of mind, which in turn, can affect their preparedness for creating and delivering an effective service.

During the service delivery, the customer can actually be portrayed as posing problems for an organization by being disruptive, rude, ignorant or even arrogant and essentially fail to comply with the service demands. Principally this is due to the lack of understanding in the interface situation and potentially the wrong fit being delivered – i.e. the wrong service to the right customers.

## Question 10.4

Explain your understanding of 'customer uncertainty'.

It is very rare that organizations ever supply either a pure product or a pure service, it is more often a combination of the two. For example, if you buy a new car or TV, you rarely just buy the product. It is normal for products to have warranties and customer services support as part of the value-added element of the product. This essentially means that there are two components to consider, the core service and the peripheral service.

The *core service* relates to the core technical feature of the service; for example, if you are travelling by train, the service will be to get you to your destination in a safe and reliable manner. By the same token you are taking the CIM Advanced Certificate in Marketing Course, and the service is to provide you with a learning package that provides career enhancement, self-achievement and actualization. Essentially, therefore, the core service is what is at the heart of the package, and every effort should be made to communicate this to your customers.

The *peripheral service*, however, is almost like the distribution channel, it is the way in which the service is supported or implemented, i.e. the check-in desk at the airport, the ticket office at the railway station. Therefore, the peripheral service relates to the facilitation of and support of the core service.

## Meeting customer expectations

Understanding customer expectations is the same as understanding customer buying behaviour. However, on this occasion understanding the behaviour and perceptions before and after the event is essential, in order to understand whether the service either exceeds expectations, meets expectations or indeed fails to meet expectations.

According to Mudie and Cottam (1999), service organizations need to understand and recognize the importance of the first law of services, which states:

*Satisfaction = perception – expectation*

However, as you can imagine, this is likely to be quite a subjective measure, as everybody's interpretation is probably different.

Measuring consumer perceptions in the service industry is essential in order that continuous improvement can be adopted, and that the appropriate market mix is designed. Essentially, the role of the organization will be to determine the views of the customers, against the perception of the organization.

## The service mix – physical evidence, people and process

The marketer has a full tool bag when it comes to marketing services; there are the traditional 4Ps: product, price, place and promotion. In addition there are the physical environment, the people and processes – the other 3Ps that ultimately give the opportunity to establish a high-quality service provision on behalf of the organization.

### The physical environment – physical evidence

The physical element of the marketing mix relates to the physical environment, the place from where the services are prepared and delivered. For example, the restaurant where you go to have a meal out is the physical environment. The restaurant is where the service is delivered and consumed.

From a marketing perspective it does help support the marketing of services as the physical element of the service brings some consistency and guarantee of quality and does enable the basis for a brand to be established and built upon. There are many examples of this, for example with chain restaurants such as Pizza Hut, BeefEaters, Brewers Fayre, etc. They are all well-known brands where the physical environment has played a significant role in relation to service delivery. Increasingly in the hospitality industry there is a growing emphasis on the image created by the physical environment and it plays a significant role in the USP of the organization.

The physical environment can be represented in quite simple ways, through staff wearing uniforms, similar interior design and often the same menus, special offers and promotions. This is reassuring for the customer, to know that the brand is meaningful and familiar.

Therefore, when establishing a marketing mix for services, the physical environment plays a significant role in stabilizing the quality perception of the organization, similar to the way in which a product can.

You should be aware that services can be administered both mechanically, e.g. on the Internet, or through automated voice handling mechanisms, but also through a physical human contribution.

### The importance of people to the marketing mix

The people element of the mix is quite complex in that the one big inconsistency in planning for the marketing mix is human nature. The role of customer-facing personnel is very difficult and demanding and at times extremely frustrating. Therefore, it is difficult not to let that frustration show and affect the level of customer service then being delivered.

The people element of the marketing mix in today's marketing environment is critical, as customer service is seen to be one other major value-added component of the customer's overall purchasing experience.

Managing the people aspect of the marketing mix requires a high degree of interpersonal skills and a strong internal marketing programme, whereby the internal members of staff, 'people', have their roles and responsibilities and overall contribution to the purchasing process communicated to them. For them to be effective and for the organization to go some way towards guaranteeing quality, the people aspect of the mix must include:

- *Investing in staff and training* – Product and organizational training
- *Empowerment of staff* – Encouraging staff to be involved to make a contribution
- *Internal marketing* – Communicating to them and motivating them to achieve
- *Decision-making capacity* – To enable staff, within their empowerment factor, to make decisions relating to the delivery of the service.

Sadly, one of the most significant impacts upon the service industry, the Internet, is reducing the number of people involved in customer service delivery and is effectively very process-oriented.

### Process

The process element of the marketing mix will always need to be managed with the customer in mind. What are their expectations, their needs and wants in relation to the service experience?

Process is about developing processes for the delivery of service that will add value to the customer experience. For example, when staying in a hotel, you would expect the booking in and out process to be concise, fast and efficient. To add value to the customer experience when staying in hotels, many of them put your bill under the door for your information, overnight, which makes checking out faster and efficient.

The process of booking a holiday or flight should be the same. The customer requires the whole service to be a positive experience; therefore, processes are critical to that value-added aspect of the product or service.

It is important that organizations develop systems that allow the service provider to ensure a seamless transition throughout the customer service experience and should develop an approach that allows inputs and outputs from the customers to be handled effectively. Processes should in essence be 'invisible' not evident, but essential to the customer experience.

Well-designed processes are needed as the service is delivered to ensure that the customer gets through with minimum fuss and delay and that all elements of the service are properly delivered.

This will, as mentioned in the hospitality context, take into account the use and collection of information, payment procedures, queuing systems and task allocation.

This is of major importance to the financial services industry where much effort has gone into ensuring that services are more accessible to customers, via telephone and Internet service provision. The way in which security systems and processes have been designed to enable customer security and also providing 24/7 access for customers in their own home and whenever and wherever they want it, has been ingenious and is now one of the biggest online success stories of all time.

As a result of the success banks are aiming to create further flexibility and offer incentives to encourage customers to use Internet banking, including such things as reduced interest charges.

### The impact of the Internet upon process

One of the reasons that many organizations are being drawn to the Internet is for the advancement and continuous improvement in customer services, but also to ensure that customer service is more cost-effective to deliver.

Currently, on the process side of the marketing mix, the Internet is still causing many aggravations and frustrations. You have probably heard of or experienced the process of filling your shopping basket online, only for the server to go down and 30 minutes shopping input to be lost. While this is a technological problem it is also a service process problem, which means that organizations need to understand the technology requirements, time-out settings, etc. on personal computers and give more guidance and advice on purchasing a service through this mechanism.

A further example of process is automated voice handling. Many financial services organizations have developed a process for enabling customers to ring through, giving them a number of options to choose from. This then means that they can go through to the right department and not waste time working their way around the organization trying to find the correct person to speak to. Clearly there are disadvantages with this process, for example waiting for long periods to get answers, but the process is now becoming common practice.

E-mail looks like an exchange of letters. In reality it is a form of speech – it is conversation. But it is speech without gestures. No smiles to take the edge off tough statements or nods.

## Question 10.5

Explain with examples the importance of the 3Ps of the services mix.

## The marketing mix in the context of services

The marketing mix does play a role, as has been suggested now on a number of occasions, but the lack of tangibility poses a serious problem to its design and implementation.

### Product

You have to convert this to think in terms of benefits, but there are often products also associated with services and the products may have a big influence. The 'product' of dry cleaning is the cleaner clothing, or the benefit of clean curtains that would not fit in your electric washing machine. The benefit may also be psychological rather than physical.

### Price

Price reflects quality levels, whether we like it or not. The basic idea of charging as much as customers will pay may be reasonable for products where customers have a choice of whether or not to buy the product, but would that be reasonable for essential services, such as business consultancy, secretarial services, medical and dental treatment? This is actually like asking a question 'How long is a piece of string?' The price charged for a service will be based around the service value proposition, the levels of tangibility that might offset concerns about levels of intangibility. Therefore, when the delivery of a service provides a tangible benefit, pricing becomes more objective. Of course other factors such as demand and market forces will play a significant role.

Evaluating value in terms of price is always highly subjective; however, the price of a service can create demand and entice customers.

In a more traditional manner, travel companies do charge according to demand – if you travel by rail at peak periods you pay a lot more than you would if you went later in the day. The same applies to electricity – there are much lower 'off-peak' charges in the night because the demand is lower then but the generators still have to run.

### Place

One of the key characteristics of services is that the actual service provider may deliver them directly to you. However, there are a lot of services that do not involve the customer being present. You can transfer money via the Internet or telephone banking, you can order flowers, all of which are away from the place of service delivery. However, physical evidence can play an important part in this, for example within a bank, hotel or restaurant, when the role of the place becomes quite important.

### Promotion

We have already given several examples of the promotion of services, such as those offered by Egg, Lufthansa and easyJet. Promoting services is more difficult the higher the level of intangibility, and there is a likelihood of customer uncertainty being aroused.

We are all subject, on a daily basis, to a surge of advertisements, promotions and direct mail in relation to financial services, pensions, holidays, flights, rail travel – the list is endless. There is probably a close correlation between the level of advertising for services and that for products. The justification of the core service has to be at the heart of the message for customers to listen, retain and respond.

Service positioning will be a big issue in establishing the core values of the service and therefore this will need careful consideration in the context of any promotional activity.

Principally, whatever the promotion, 'don't promise what you can't deliver'.

## The key components of designing a services mix

While we have looked at the importance of the 7Ps in relation to the marketing mix, we also need to consider the eleven design elements that run in parallel with the 7Ps. Mudie and Cottam (1999) suggest that the following design principles are considered:

- *Customer contact* – What is the level of contact between the organization and the customer during the delivery of the service?
- *Service mix* – How many service offerings will there be, how effective will they be, what will the services portfolio consist of?

- *Location* – Should the service go to the customer, or the customer be drawn to the service?
- *Design* – Practical design extends from basic logos and letterheads through to uniforms, physical structures and therefore is a component of the 7Ps.
- *Technology* – What technology will be required for the delivery of the service – will it be reliable, what are the customer expectations and what will the impact be?
- *Employees* – Success will hinge on the organizational culture, the level of support, the strength of internal marketing, the appropriate and adequate resource base to support them in their work.
- *Structure* – The structure will go a long way towards determining the organizational culture and establishing lines of command.
- *Information* – Good MIS systems will be useful in ensuring appropriate levels of information are available to support the service delivery and understand customer expectations.
- *Demand* – The level of demand for a service will affect the standards of delivery.
- *Procedures* – As in process – it is essential to understand the nature of the processes required for successful execution of the service.
- *Control* – The only way in which continuous improvement can be understood and quality standards measured is through a range of monitoring and control processes.

## The importance of service quality

People, physical evidence, process – these three elements of the marketing mix are critical to the delivery of exceptional service quality. They are responsible for reducing waiting times, long check-in lines at the airport, getting quick answers on financial services packages, to name but a few.

It will always be difficult for a service-related organization to deliver 100 per cent quality, but with the complete marketing mix at its disposal, service should be improving all the time.

When it comes to marketing a service versus a product the considerations are the same for delivering service quality (see Figure 10.6). Service-related organizations should always consider:

- What the customers expect
- Service specifications (in the same way as there are product specifications)
- *Employee performance* – quality of their delivery, training needs
- Managing customer service expectations – making sure quality is achieved.

```
┌──────────────┐  ┌──────────────┐  ┌──────────────┐  ┌──────────────┐
│ Understand   │  │              │  │              │  │ Managing     │
│ customer     │  │ Service      │  │ Employees    │  │ service      │
│ expectations │  │ specifications│ │ (people)     │  │ expectations │
└──────┬───────┘  └──────┬───────┘  └──────┬───────┘  └──────┬───────┘
       │                 │                 │                 │
       └─────────────────┴────────┬────────┴─────────────────┘
                                  ▼
                    ┌─────────────────────────────┐
                    │      Service Quality        │
                    │        Reliability          │
                    │       Responsiveness        │
                    │         Assurance           │
                    │          Empathy            │
                    │ Tangible/intangible dimensions │
                    └─────────────────────────────┘
```

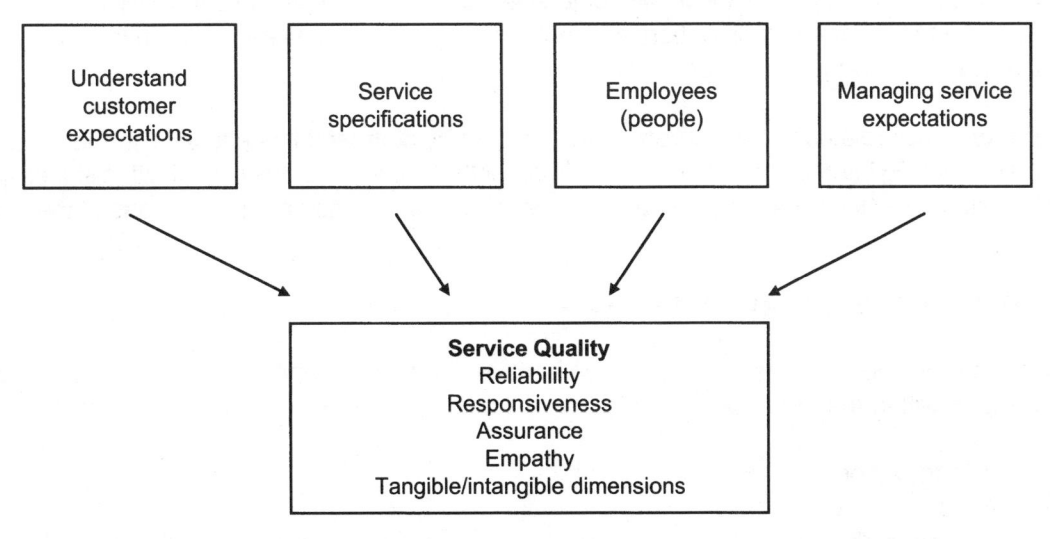

*Figure 10.6* The dynamics of service quality – SERVQUAL

SERVQUAL aids the measurement of service delivery and seeks to measure quality within the service sector. It looks closely at five factors as listed below and shown in Figure 10.6:

1. *Reliability* – Ability to perform the promised service dependably and accurately
2. *Responsiveness* – Willingness to help customers and provide a prompt service
3. *Assurance* – Knowledge and courtesy of employees and their ability to inspire trust and confidence
4. *Empathy* – Caring, individual attention the organization provides its customers
5. *Tangibles* – Physical facilities, equipment, appearance of personnel.

SERVQUAL measures the gap between customer and management perceptions of the quality issue.

The gaps, highlighted by B. G. Dale in *Managing Quality* (1994), are as follows:

- *Gap 1* – Consumer expectations – managers' perceptions of consumers' expectations
- *Gap 2* – Managers' perceptions of consumers' expectations – service quality specifications actually set
- *Gap 3* – Service quality specifications – actual service delivery
- *Gap 4* – Actual service delivery – external communications about the service
- *Gap 5* – Resources.

Quality and reliability are often used synonymously. Part of the appeal and acceptability of a product or service will depend on its ability to function satisfactorily over a period of time, and also a measure of reliability.

Principally, quality can be used as a tool for competitive advantage, and can be a powerful strategic weapon within the organization.

Managing the differing levels of quality in services is, as we have established, more difficult than for goods overall, as a result of issues relating to levels of tangibility and intangibility.

Quality management has to be based around the three key elements of the services marketing mix: the people, the physical evidence and the process. Analysis of performance in each of these areas would help the organization ascertain their position both from a customer perspective and a competitive perspective. High scores or ratings in each of these is likely to be a positive factor. If it is the reverse, there are some severe financial penalties to face.

Quality measurements and quality objectives are highly important and will be the basis in establishing customer perception and achieving customer satisfaction. Principally, promises that are made should be kept.

Performance relates to the delivery of the product by staff, and it is essential in that respect that there is strong internal marketing support in order that the ethos of the organization shines through, that staffs are highly motivated and influence the basis of consumer perceptions of the service.

## Implementing a quality culture

Quality can be used as a tool for competitive advantage, and can be a powerful strategic weapon within the organization. This would include addressing the following elements:

- Innovation
- Status
- Leadership

- o Rewards
- o Values
- o Developments of a learning organization
- o Empowerment to achieve challenging goals.

The successful measurement of a quality culture may manifest itself in the following ways:

- o People see for themselves the need for quality management tools
- o Motivators and champions start to emerge
- o People talk of processes and not of functions
- o People volunteer to take on tasks, which previously have involved considerable management intervention.

The quality guru Claus Moller suggested that there are 12 golden rules to aid quality implementation and improvement, all of which are particularly pertinent to the delivery of good quality service:

- o Set personal and corporate quality goals
- o Establish personal accountability
- o Check how satisfied customers are with your efforts
- o Regard the next link as a valued customer
- o Avoid error
- o Perform tasks more effectively
- o Utilize resources well
- o Be committed
- o Learn to finish what you have started
- o Control stress
- o Be ethical
- o Demand quality.

Moller emphasized the need for administrative procedures to improve rather than an improvement in the delivery process, as it is often the one that lets the other down. He further emphasized the need to use checklists, personal performance standards, ideal performance levels and actual performance levels (Moller, 1988).

Essentially, quality is the key to success, and in the context of services people are the key to achievement.

## Monitoring and evaluating service

There are a number of key issues that impact upon quality measurement:

- o The difference in perception between employees and customers
- o The inseparability of production and consumption
- o The individuality of employees' performance and customers' perceptions.

There is a proposed formula for measuring these components:

- o *Customer expectations* – Service organizations' perceptions of customer expectations
- o *Customer experience* – Service organizations' perceptions of customer experience.

This is based on the different expectations of 20 customers receiving the same service, and is probably very subjective as each of them will feel differently and therefore the analysis could be rather inconclusive. However, while the feedback might be diverse, it is likely that some useful information might manifest itself in order that future improvements might be made.

To be able to continuously improve the level of service offered, to understand the gaps, the confusion, the customer uncertainties, the following monitoring and evaluation processes could be implemented:

- *Marketing research* – To gather information about services, and delivery of them
- *Data collection* – Frequent reviews
- *Observing respondents* – as they receive the service
- *Interviewing respondents* – To understand their perceptions and expectations versus their experience
- *Customer satisfaction surveys* – Questionnaires to monitor customer satisfaction
- *Mystery consumer experience* – Include a mystery person in the delivery of the service
- *Evaluating dissatisfaction* – Examine the main causes of customer dissatisfaction
- *Monitoring image* – How is the image of the service perceived
- *Performance appraisals* – of staff involved in the delivery of the service
- *Employee group discussions* – Internal marketing practice.

## Question 10.6

Why is it important to evaluate the delivery of services?

## Summary

Marketing to organizations and industries is different in practice from consumer marketing, but uses the same principles. The demand is managed differently and the buying process has to be accepted as it is. Quite often the delivery in the time promised is more important than price alone.

The range of marketing opportunities is very wide and the range of products can be bewildering. The buyers are professionals, and their motives for buying are quite different from those of consumers. Instead of looking at their own individual needs they will be accountable to the organization for making the right purchase decision in order for the supply chain to function satisfactorily.

The 4Ps can still apply to marketing to organizations but with a different emphasis. Distribution of some products is similar to that for consumer goods, but there are also some quite big differences.

There is a stronger need to maintain a competitive edge, because of the professionalism of the buyers and the competitors.

The importance of services in the modern economy is shown by the fact that Britain, and most other developed countries, are now service economies, with more than 50 per cent of gross spending being on services and 64 per cent of the workforce employed in services.

Services have to be marketed but there are more differences than similarities with the marketing of products. The problems arise from the features of services – their intangibility, inseparability from the provider, perishability and the impossibility of stocking up for future sale. There is also the potential variation of quality due to the fact that people, who vary in performance day by day, provide the services.

The marketing mix for services includes the 4Ps of product marketing, with the addition of people, physical evidence and the process or methods of providing the service. However, the importance of the eleven elements of design should not be underestimated.

Ultimately, as with all marketing strategies, plans and implementation of various marketing mixes, the quality of the product and service provision should be a matter of 'excellence'.

## Study tip

Because of the growing importance and influence of services in the economy, it is natural that this should be reflected in the syllabus and the examination. Therefore a total grasp of the subject will be vital.

By the same token, business-to-business applications play a major role and are frequently the source of exam questions.

The test will be of your ability to apply marketing in a variety of different contexts, this means organizational marketing, services marketing, international marketing and not-for-profit-marketing. In doing this you will develop very versatile marketing skills that will make your transition from one industry to another a little smoother than perhaps it might be.

## Extending knowledge

### Recommended reading

In addition to reading your recommended text, you will find it useful to gain a more in-depth understanding of some of the services issues by reading the following chapters from *The Management of Marketing Services* by Peter Mudie and Angela Cottam (1999) – Chapters 1, 3, 5, 10, 11 and 12.

## Bibliography

Brassington, F. and Pettitt, S. (2000) *Principles of Marketing*, Thomson Higher Education.

Dale, B.G. (1994) *Managing Quality*, Prentice Hall.

Dibb, S., Simkin, L., Pride, W. and Ferrell, O. (2001) *Marketing: Concepts and Strategies*, 4th European edition, Houghton Mifflin.

Hill, R.W. and Hillier, T.J. (1977) *Organizational Buying Behaviour*, Palgrave Macmillan.

Moller, C. (1988) *Personal Quality*, Time Management International.

Mudie, P. and Cottam, A. (1999) *The Management of Marketing Services*, Butterworth-Heinemann.

Worsam, M. (2000) *Marketing Operations*, Butterworth-Heinemann.

---

Sample exam questions and answers for the Marketing Planning module as a whole can be found in Appendix 4 and past examination papers can be found in Appendix 5. You should undertake Question 1 (a) which is part of the case study, from the June 2004 Examination Paper.

# unit 11
# not-for-profit, SMEs and virtual marketing

## Learning objectives

This unit looks at the role of marketing within not-for-profit organizations, SMEs and virtual markets. The profile of all three has gained in prominence in the past 10 years.

The indicative content in relation to this unit includes:

- Develop a marketing plan and select an appropriate marketing mix for an organization operating in any context such as voluntary, not for profit and SMEs.

- Explain how marketing plans and activities vary in organizations that operate in a virtual marketing place and develop an appropriate marketing mix.

Syllabus reference: 4.2, 4.3

## Charities – not-for-profit marketing

One of the certainties in life is that we need money to survive, as few things in this world can be either acquired or achieved without money. The key role of any charity therefore, has to be to generate income in order to achieve the aims and objectives defined by the board and management of the charity. Increasingly, charities are recognizing the value of marketing, and there has been a distinct change, as more and more charities emerge into the arena of different forms of retailing, sponsorship and event organizations. However, their approach to retailing takes on very different dynamics to that of a traditional retailer.

Charities as retailers work very much on a non-business-marketing basis. The shops are stocked with goods that mainly have been donated, and therefore the necessity to purchase stock does not exist at the same level. In addition to this, charity shops are manned by volunteer workers, therefore payroll costs are a minimum in comparison to mainstream retailers.

Many of the bigger charities involve themselves in 'high-profile charitable events', for example Children in Need, Red Nose Day and the London Marathon, or various 'party in the park' type events, or major rock/pop festivals, probably the most significant event of this type being 'Live Aid' run by Bob Geldof. In hosting and managing these events the benefits include considerable publicity, both in terms of TV and press coverage, and usually fairly significant donations.

Unit 11 Not-for-profit, SMEs and virtual marketing

One of the major differences between profit-making and non-profit-making businesses is that their perspective on life provides for an interesting range of dynamics. As profit-making business are very focused on making money, charities are focused and dedicated to changing people's lives and really making a difference in the most horrendous situations.

## Case history

### Ronald McDonald House Charities

**Ronald McDonald Care Mobile Programme**

To help address the growing need for access to health care for millions of children worldwide, Ronald McDonald House Charities announce the launch of a fleet of Ronald McDonald Care Mobiles, mobile paediatric healthcare units that deliver free medical and dental care directly to underserved children in their own neighbourhoods. Plans call for 12 mobile healthcare programmes in operation by the end of 2001 and a projected 40 by the end of 2005, making this one of the most extensive mobile healthcare programmes ever undertaken.

Ronald McDonald House Charities will launch the first Ronald McDonald House Care Mobile outside the US later this month in Buenos Aires, Argentina. Through the Ronald McDonald Care Mobile Programme, McDonald's see that they can be part of the solution to the serious healthcare access problem facing children today.

The Ronald McDonald Care Mobile helps reduce reliance on expensive and inappropriate health resources, such as hospital emergency departments. The programme also provides continuity of care by providing follow-up services and referrals to primary care physician, dentist or paediatric sub-specialists and helping eligible families enrol in a government assisted health insurance programme such as 'Insure Kids Now'.

**Background of Ronald McDonald Charities**

Ronald McDonald House Charities in 33 countries around the world, 240 Ronald McDonald houses in 25 countries and a legion of more than 25 000 volunteers. Ronald McDonald House has helped millions of children and their families in local communities around the world.

Ronald McDonald House Charities, a not-for-profit organization, creates, funds and supports programmes that directly improve the health and well-being of children. The charity makes grants to not-for-profit organizations and provides support for all Ronald McDonald Houses and Mobiles. To date they have contributed some $300 million to children's programmes. www.rmhc.org

*Source*: Lexis-Nexis.

Typically the board for a charity will comprise of a number of professionals who will be ultimately responsible for the effectiveness of the organization in supporting appropriate causes. They will be responsible for allocation of funds, utilization of resources and a number of specialist activities that the charity might be planning to embark upon.

The source of funds for not-for-profit organizations will come from a range of government bodies, lottery funds, trust funds and in some instances corporate funds from large organizations that support the specific work of the not-for-profit organizations, particularly if there is vested interest in their work.

That covers all the services we mentioned above, but it could also cover a lot of the most visible charities, such as the Red Wings Horse and Donkey Sanctuary, which runs a thriving mail order business. Profits from the mail order business are reinvested directly back into the business for future care and development work.

## Marketing planning for charities

### Setting objectives

You will have noticed by now that all marketing activities start with some measurable objectives, and so it is with charities and non-profit-making organizations, although the measurement of achievement is not always so straightforward.

The prime objective of charities will reflect their desire to enhance the quality of lives. For example, a typical objective might be 'To serve the needs and wants of the "users" through the financial contributions, time and support of the public donor.'

The objectives in general terms tend to be used as an umbrella for several more specific objectives, which deal with problems that occur from time to time. This makes the measurement of achievement of the objectives, in the marketing sense, difficult. Marketers are used to dealing in money terms, or units sold, but that is not possible for the work of, say, helping to save sea birds from polluted seas, or of saving an old building so that future generations can enjoy the view from the balcony.

Essentially, the most likely objectives that charitable organizations will seek to achieve is to gain surplus funds through donations and sales of merchandized products, so that they can use the income generated to achieve their objectives. Therefore, the role of the Charitable Trust Board and its members will be to ensure that the income is properly and appropriately managed.

The objectives set will very much be formed on the basis of the nature and purpose of the marketing audit undertaken. This auditing activity will be essential in determining the scale of the charitable needs in the 'users marketplace' to gain a full understanding of the level of donations required and how they might be appropriated in the future. This essentially allows organizations to clearly define their 'marketing opportunities'.

Typical auditing will obviously be upon a SLEPT basis, but with a particular focus on some of the following areas:

- Other similar charitable activities (competitive charities)
- Research into focused areas of needs
- Breadth and depth of the situation
- Economic situation of area of country involved
- Taxation benefits for charitable giving
- Facts and figures in relation to the number of potential users in one market
- Resources available
- Scale of user needs
- Levels of charitable giving in these areas previously
- Level of publicity in relation to user problems
- Political influence and involvement in particular area of need and available funding
- Social responsiveness to charitable giving
- Legal loopholes for charities
- Trends on the most popular forms of attracting donations.

These are just a few examples of information that might be needed to underpin the objective-setting and strategy development of the charitable organization.

## Marketing segmentation and targeting for charities

The market segmentation process for charities consists of closely targeting individuals who are able to support the charity through donations of money, equipment and time in order to assist them in meeting the objectives of the charity and meeting the needs of their users.

The key targets for charities will include:

- *Donors* – Those who give funds and equipment
- *Volunteers* – Those who will give their time and effort to support the charitable cause
- *Clients* – Users of the charitable trusts, funds and services.

Obviously in mainstream marketing of profit-making organizations the segmentation process is very scientific, and focuses on the whole range of marketing mix activities, such as targeting customers for different variations of the marketing mix.

Charity marketing has to offer some benefit, and that is not always easy to visualize. The flag days have the answer – you put some money in the box, and in return get a flag to stick on your clothing to show that you have paid up. Because the feeling of well-being that comes from donating some of your hard-earned money soon wears off, it is essential for the charity to provide a tangible indicator of your generosity, usually in the form of a flag or sticker, which serves as a tangible reminder of your willingness to support the charity concerned.

That is one aspect of the marketing activities of charities, but there is a further vast 'target market' in companies. If some of the profits made by companies can be donated to charities, the improvement in funding might be quite dramatic. This is rather different from appealing to the individual – the company has no conscience and cannot get the benefit of 'feeling good' because of having donated some money.

## Marketing planning and control

Planning is as vital to charitable organizations as it is to any commercial venture, as it is necessary to take a structured approach to implementation in order to achieve the objectives defined by the charitable board.

However, planning takes on two dimensions:

- To generate high levels of income from donations
- To allocate and apportion funds to particular products efficiently and effectively.

It is essential that considerable control be implemented over the planning process, in order that levels of accountability can always be achieved. Therefore, monitoring and control processes should be implemented in order that evidence of fund management can be provided. Objectives will be SMART in the same way as commercial objectives are.

While there has been a focus on voluntary workers earlier on, there are paid staff who deal with corporate fund-raising and therefore have played a different role, because they have to show the public and charitable stakeholders that they are above reproach in the way in which they manage charitable funds. However, there are also donors who like to gain high profile coverage of their donations, and who like to see that there is a measurable commercial benefit in giving money, or lending facilities to a charity.

It is likely that many of the significant donors will want ultimate recognition for their contributions, as this is a way of reaping commercial benefits. Therefore, publicity of this nature has to be jointly managed by the charity and the organization for mutual benefit and gain. Charitable managers must therefore ensure that the credibility of the donor is satisfactory in order that there is no backlash of public support, due to the dubious nature of donors.

However, the approach taken to marketing planning is slightly different in nature, while the marketing mix does have similar characteristics. Therefore, it is essential at this time to look at the nature of not-for-profit organizations and compare and contrast them with profit-making organizations, before looking at the combined approach to the marketing mix. In respect of control, there will be a number of key areas that the charities should involve themselves in the measurement of:

- The environment in which they operate
- Consistency and quality in the level of service offered
- Customer satisfaction
- Competence of staff and ability to manage and implement programmes effectively
- Effects of internal and external communications.

## Question 11.1

Explain three key methods of acquiring donations for charities.

## Question 11.2

Who are the three important audiences a charity needs to target and why are they so important?

## What is a non-profit-making organization?

While there are a number of definitions for non-profit-making organizations they are not universally agreed.

### Definition

**Non-profit-making organization** – An organization whose prime goal is non-economic. However, in pursuit of that goal it may undertake profit-making activities.

### Definition

**Alternative non-profit-business marketing** – Activities conducted by individuals and organizations to achieve some goal other than ordinary business goals of profit, market share or return on investment (Dibb, Simkin, Pride and Ferrell, 2001).

Charity is not the only form of 'not-for-profit-making' organization. There are many other types of organizations. Bodies such as the armed forces, police, probation service, ambulance service and a number of support societies are also not-for-profit organizations.

The determination of non-profit-making realistically relates to the focus and objectives of the business. The whole ethos of not-for-profit organizations relates to the use of funds for particular reasons; they are accountable for the specific allocations of funds against objectives. Accountability in not-for-profit organizations is a serious business.

## Not-for-profit marketing versus profit marketing

A not-for-profit marketing organization typically faces a very different range of challenges in terms of both managing and marketing their business. In the absence of a product or service to sell in the same way as profit-making organizations, its marketing focus is primarily to provide a range of products and essential support services for little or indeed no charge to the user. It will usually have multiple objectives and multiple publics, to whom it offers multiple services, but the funder of the service is different from the receiver.

Principally, profit-making organizations focus their attention on a number of profitable markets that have very tightly defined profitable targets. This purpose of the profit-making will not only be to cover their overhead costs from the income generated from the sales of products and services, but to provide a dividend for shareholders and to generate funds for investment in growth and diversification opportunities. Profit-making organizations such as business-to-business, consumer, industrial or services-related industries, have in the main been the focus of marketing in the context of this book.

While the focus of profit-making organizations' customer base is customers and consumers, the focus of a charity will be on the receivers, the people who benefit from their services, who indeed then effectively become the 'user'.

For not-for-profit organizations, marketing is now playing a pivotal role in raising considerable funds that will not only serve the 'receivers' end of the service, but also fund the management and resourcing of the charity. There has, however, been a lot of controversy about mismanagement and misuse of funds within charities.

Therefore the focus of marketing for non-profit-making organizations will principally be on attracting substantial donations, equipment and voluntary support in order that they can achieve the defined objectives of the organizations.

Many non-profit-making organizations have very scarce resources and often struggle to achieve their corporate objectives, but the challenges they face are very demanding and very different, as the stakeholder audience is often extensive.

## The motivational factors influencing not-for-profit marketing and profitable organizations

All organizations, both profit and not-for-profit, will benefit from having a clearly defined understanding of the customer base, i.e. consumers or users. Therefore, in that respect, there are many similarities in the motivation of both profit-making and non-profit-making organizations, in that they both need income to survive.

The profit-making organization needs income to enable it to survive, to aid continuous improvement, and to meet profit objectives and shareholder objectives. The non-profit-making organization also needs income to survive, and to continue to provide a considerable service to needy and worthy causes, but the income is channelled in different directions.

The main difference in respect of motivation is the use of the word 'profit'. Both organizations are committed to generating as much money as possible, but effectively the use of that money is very different.

The non-profit-making organization does not make a profit in the same sense that perhaps a profit-making organization does. Whatever the source of income, it will be directly invested back into the organization whereby all money will go into supporting the work of the business.

Therefore, while motivational factors may be similar to a degree, the word 'profit' creates different dynamics for the diverse nature of the organizations. So while profit motivates profit-making organizations, the focus of delivering a range of invaluable services is the main motivation of not-for-profit organizations.

## Marketing planning for not-for-profit marketing

### Setting objectives

The nature and dynamics of objectives for this particular sector differ again. For example, the objectives of a church might be to 'inform the public about the doctrine of the church and encourage a growth in church membership'. This is particularly relevant as recent statistics have shown a drastic reduction in church membership in the last 10 years.

The most likely source of funds in the case of not-for-profit organizations may be from government sources, lottery funds, and local authorities or industrial support for the purpose of the project. In addition to this, income might be generated by membership subscriptions and charitable donations. In the Church of England, for example, the money will come from church offerings, donations and tax benefits, among others.

Setting objectives and controlling them may prove difficult for the marketer working in not-for-profit organizations. A marketing manager employed by a charity may have the same type of ambitions as his or her opposite number in a profit-making organization, and he or she may not think that the objectives which are aimed at by the charity will provide the career advancement opportunities that he or she wants, and so perhaps may think they should be changed.

### Marketing planning and control

It is essential that in order to control the achievement of objectives, through the implementation of the marketing plan, not-for-profit managers use the range of information that they should have collected through undertaking some form of marketing audit, to define objectives and implement a range of controls.

Controls will be based around the product/services mix, in order that quality is maintained and standards delivered. In addition to this, financial controls must be in place to ensure that funds are pulled in, in order to achieve the objectives defined by the organization.

While the principles are the same, sometimes, because of the nature of the organization and the number of volunteers involved, the waters become a little muddied, and the overall objectives of the organization fail to be achieved.

Unit 11 Not-for-profit, SMEs and virtual marketing

Objectives, while SMART, can be difficult to measure. While objectives might be related to creating awareness, it will be difficult to determine the level of awareness as perhaps advertising is not measured in the same mechanical way as it is with commercial organizations.

However, in organizations such as universities, a very business-like approach is now taken to planning and control, with an increasing emphasis on accountability, quality and service levels. They have had no choice but to change the way they operate to be much more business-oriented and focused.

## Question 11.3

In what ways do not-for-profit organizations differ from mainstream commercial organizations?

### Managing the marketing mix – charities and not-for-profit organizations

Charities and not-for-profit organizations are more similar to services than to manufacturers, and it may put their marketing into perspective if we try to see how the 7Ps of service marketing fit in with their activities. However, one thing that should be considered in developing and optimizing the effect of the marketing mix is the ability for each charity to retain some form of competitive advantage, in terms of gaining preference for charity giving to their own organization.

- *Product* – Is equivalent to the benefit that charities provide to donors; the feeling of well-being, either for an individual or the staff and management of a commercial enterprise.
- *Place* – You may think that 'place' is not important to the collectors of money for charities, because all money is of equal value wherever it comes from. However, in some instances it is vitally important, for example, with the need for charity shops to play a significant role in income generation. For Oxfam in particular this is a vital source of income, therefore distribution of stores on as intensive a basis as possible is desirable.
- *Promotion* – Is very relevant, as has been seen earlier in the text, with sponsorship, publicity and PR playing a major role in the marketing activities. There is a heavy involvement in direct marketing and specifically targeting home-owners to donate to charities on a regular basis.

Promotion of non-profit-making organizations is increasing and becoming much more high profile in order that they may gain support, membership and potentially donations to further enhance the work they undertake. This may be more focused in terms of specialist journals relevant to the organizations, and direct mailing base.

- *Price* – As a concept price will vary between both charities and non-profit-making organizations. For charities, price will hold two interests, the amount of money generated and the cost of programme implementation.

However, the not-for-profit-making local authority assesses the amount of money they will need for the next year, then works out the amount to be charged to each household.

- *People* – People certainly matter in charities and in non-profit-making organizations: the charities depend on non-paid-for help from volunteers, and the work that they do, in marketing terms, is very much 'people-oriented'. The various non-profit-making organizations are people-oriented too. There are people involved in the interface with the public, naturally, and the characteristics of these people can make the marketing activities more, or less, effective depending on how well they relate to other people.

- *Physical evidence* – Is needed – if you know what a charity will achieve with your donation you may feel disposed to give more money, and when you have to pay for the services of the local authority, without much choice, you do expect to see some physical evidence of the use of the money.
- *Process* – In charity and non-profit-making organization terms process is about making it easy to donate money. The charities collect money in the street, or on the doorstep, and they all show donors how to make their contribution more effectively. The days of the street collection may be numbered, as people complain that there are too many of them.

The non-profit-making organizations seldom have to ask the public to be donors, because their funds come directly or indirectly from some form of public source, but their dealings with the public must still be smooth and efficient. The public are often in the position of customers and owners, although the ownership is indirect.

## Case history

### The largest virtual call centre ever – Red Nose Day

Since Comic Relief began we've raised, through the Red Nose Day, over £337 million and have given to over 7000 projects. This money has helped poor and disadvantaged people in the UK and Africa turn their lives around. 60 per cent of this money is spent in Africa and 40 per cent within the UK.

Comic Relief support a range of activities. In Africa the six key areas of focus include:

1. People affected by *conflict and wars*
2. *Women and Girls*
3. People living in *towns and cities*
4. *Disabled People*
5. *Pastoralists* – people who traditionally make a living from raising cattle, goats and sheep – and hunter-gatherers
6. People living with and affected by *HIV and AIDS*.

In the UK the key areas of focus include:

- *Young people* who are struggling with various crises in their lives such as being homeless, sexually exploited or coping with mental health problems
- Women and children experiencing *domestic violence*
- *Refugees and asylum seekers* who have fled their countries because of persecution. They arrive in the UK with nothing and need to rebuild their lives
- *Older people* who are treated without dignity and respect, whose rights are ignored and who are, in some circumstances, experiencing abuse
- People living in *local communities* who are working together to tackle poverty and disadvantage to make their area a better place to.

Red Nose Day in 2003 saw more than 163 call centre sites join together in what is thought to be the biggest ever virtual call centre in the history of the telephone.

Around 20 000 volunteers staffed 12 000 lines to field donation calls and as if that wasn't enough many of the centres were raising money themselves!

Go to www.rednoseday.com for more information.

*Unit 11 Not-for-profit, SMEs and virtual marketing*

It is appropriate to mention the changing nature of some of the non-profit-making organizations. I have mentioned the way in which some charities have taken up marketing activities, with good effect, and it is evident that since the 1990s there has been a growing move to make the non-profit-making organizations more accountable for the money they spend.

### Different marketing adoption in not-for-profit organizations

In Table 11.1 you can see the variety of ways in which the adoption of marketing has been implemented in a range of different not-for-profit organizations.

*Table 11.1* Marketing's adoption

| | | |
|---|---|---|
| Colleges and universities | 1. | The product range is under constant review, the physical environment is of concern and more efficient methods of teaching are being devised. |
| | 2. | Promotion has sharpened and the importance of internal marketing is being recognized. |
| | 3. | Staff needs, both teaching and support, are identified using HRM techniques; recruitment ads are more professionally produced and placed; selection is more concerned with effectiveness than qualifications. Training is budgeted and encouraged. |
| | 4. | Funding sources are targeted and marketing plans developed to maximize the probability of achievement. Trans-EU funding requires a long-term commitment. Commercial sponsorship needs activities targeted to meet the sponsor's needs. |
| Hospitals | 1. | Excess demand and budgetary constraints are causing hospitals to allocate their resources very carefully. |
| | 2. | Sponsorship and the aid of voluntary groups such as 'Friends of the Hospital' has to be solicited and the benefits be seen to be valued. |
| Doctors | 1. | Excess demand and budgetary constraints are causing doctors to consider which patients they can afford to accept on to their lists. |
| | 2. | There is a growing resentment in the population because the tradition of open access is now restricted. This presents a serious need for doctors to use marketing to show that they are not responsible for Government actions. |
| Charities | 1. | Funds must be solicited from a variety of sources. |
| | 2. | Beneficiaries of the charity must be located and encouraged to apply and/or accept support. |
| | 3. | Internal marketing must co-ordinate and motivate the individuals who work for the charity either in an employed or voluntary capacity. |
| Social organizations | 1. | Many long-standing organizations such as the YMCA, the Scouts and the Churches are losing members and suffering from lack of income. Marketers face the twin problems of redefining mission and corporate policies to provide what people require today and securing the necessary funds to generate an upturn in membership. |

## Question 11.4

You are a marketing manager for a well-known charitable organization. You have been asked to justify to the Board the reasons why the charity should not employ an advertising agency to undertake promotional work on their behalf.

Unit 11 Not-for-profit, SMEs and virtual marketing

> **Study tip**
>
> Question 4 in the December 2003 Marketing Planning paper was set in the context of not-for-profit organizations and explored the concepts of relationship marketing as a mechanism for increasing donations. Therefore it is important from an examination perspective to understand the relative importance of other business contexts and be prepared to respond in an applied way to examination questions in relation to them.

## Marketing for SMEs

For many SMEs marketing is a wide-ranging term which covers the process of identifying potential buyers and gaining their purchasing commitment in order to facilitate and generate sales; whilst ensuring such sales are profitable. In many respects this approach is no different from much larger corporations, and at times the approaches taken to developing marketing strategy and plans can also be similar but obviously on a much smaller scale.

Offering products or services that have a real demand is central to the operation of an effective marketing strategy. It is important to identify the market for a product or service in order to be able to correctly satisfy their needs.

Developing unique selling points which differentiate a product or service or even a company from its competitors is essential – whilst creating corporate image that is clearly recognizable. Success in marketing can be measured by increases in sales, turnover and profits.

Frequently small businesses in particular misjudge their markets and do not achieve expected sales targets. This often leads to insufficient cash flow and poor profits. An effective marketing strategy and a real understanding of the marketplace is imperative in order to grow and develop a successful business.

### Marketing strategy and planning for SMEs

SMEs, like large FMCG companies or not-for-profit companies, need to be specific about each objective and consider how they will reach each objective, how often they will review it, what it will cost and the results expected from these actions.

The benefits of a marketing plan are that they highlight the things that the company was not aware of, thus preventing making costly errors. It sets out clear marketing objectives and allows the company to look back and find out what had gone wrong and enables them to put things right.

It is imperative to know the strengths and weaknesses of the business. The best way to assess them is to use SWOT (Strengths, Weaknesses, Opportunities, Threats, etc.) analysis. Strengths include having a large customer base, viable range of products, skilled staff, low-cost base, a good information technology system, a strong balance sheet, etc. Weaknesses are generally the opposite of your strengths.

Opportunities may be weak competition, a growing market, availability of new grants and lower interest rates. These are external market forces. Threats are generally the opposite of what you see as opportunities. SWOT analysis will provide lots of answers which SMEs are often not aware of.

Identify the factors critical for success. This may mean reviewing how new products are developed, improving quality, reducing costs, or better customer care. Set your objectives, look at the options, consider the practicalities and check that your plan is achievable.

The marketing plan is an integral component of all business plans and it is something that many SMEs, particularly very small companies, often overlook. The marketing plan is of importance in documenting and setting targets and objectives for the business whilst acknowledging potential competitive issues. It is advisable to refer to the marketing plan and indeed the business plan from time to time to establish whether the targets and objectives are being met. A marketing plan is a prerequisite when applying for a loan or a grant and is often the one time when small companies seem to get remotely near to any form of planning activities.

## Outline marketing plan for SMEs

Many smaller organizations find it difficult to understand the importance of planning and even more so the types of information and activities involved in creating a marketing plan. Below is a list of activities SMEs should undertake when preparing a plan.

1. Collect data and review the plan as a whole
2. Decide on the content
3. Plan the design and layout
4. Write it up clearly and simply
5. Assemble all the finalized information for your marketing plan
6. Include a competitor's comparison table
7. Prepare a SWOT analysis
8. Include objectives
9. Include sales forecasts
10. State the marketing strategy
11. Provide a detailed plan of action
12. Include a timetable for implementation
13. Put in some key controls in order to monitor the plan
14. Keep the plan to between 10 and 20 pages.

## The marketing mix for SMEs

### Product

All products have a pattern of demand. Initial demand may be limited, although effective marketing efforts should ensure growth in demand. However, this demand will eventually peak and decline. This usually results in the product being discontinued. This process is termed the 'product life cycle'. In every market, as new products are introduced, older ones become obsolete. New products usually replace older ones, although in some cases changes in purchasing patterns can result in markets disappearing altogether.

Effective advertising and sales promotion can help to increase demand for SMEs and extend the life of older products. This is a commonly used approach by much larger corporations and has been successful; there is therefore no reason why it cannot be equally so for small businesses. However, please note that this is not always affordable, so SMEs do have to be creative with their promotional budgets.

The best way to protect SMEs against all products declining at the same time is to have a portfolio of products which peak their life cycles at different phases. This helps to spread the marketing and development workload more evenly whilst ensuring a more constant flow of income. Again this is the strategy followed by a larger organization, but some SMEs do have a broad portfolio of products and it is therefore important to spread development costs where possible as it becomes a drain on very valuable resources.

### Place
Many companies use wholesalers and retailers rather than sell direct to customers. The reason for this is that they do not have the resources to sell direct to large numbers of customers.

Most small to medium sized manufacturing businesses prefer to invest in the production side of their business instead of the distribution side and are unable to afford their own distribution networks and are reliant on outsourcing to others. In distribution there may be several layers of intermediaries. Once they have selected their distributors, they will need to work hard to motivate them so that they will promote and sell your products. This really relates to the issue of volume and profit for the intermediaries, in order to make it worth their while.

It may be necessary to evaluate these distributors in terms of sales quota attainments, promotion of your products and services offered to customers.

### Price
When trying to establish prices consideration should be given to whether high or low volume sales would be achievable. High volumes usually require lower pricing in order to sustain sales. It may be useful to draw a break-even chart to illustrate the relationship between the cost of production and profits. Markets are often sensitive to price changes.

Price wars are often deemed as something that only happens with larger organizations, but this is not so. Even the local hair salons, small family furniture stores, and many other smaller business, often involve themselves in small scale price wars on a local level, some of them even trying to take on the larger organizations to gain local market share. These types of price wars can prove to be costly whilst forcing down the long-term willingness of customers to pay the true value of a product or service. For example local furniture stores taking on bigger furniture chains will struggle to achieve the economies of awarded to large organizations for buying bulk stock. It can therefore be financially stretching and could cause severe financial damage to the organization. When discounting products or perhaps offering discounts on a regular basis, setting a higher selling price can help to maintain margins. Also, selling certain products or services at a loss may encourage sales of other products whilst gaining market share and brand awareness. The following factors are key to determining effective pricing:

- Sales targets
- Maintaining price stability
- Increasing market share and product sales
- Meeting or beating competitor pricing
- Maximizing profits and margins.

### Promotion
Communication with existing and potential customers is an important aspect of marketing. Advertising, sales promotion, public relations, publicity and personal selling may be used to communicate with customers.

Sales promotion covers a range of activities to get the message across to the market. Promotional activity involves providing various short term incentives to stimulate sales of a product or service. It may involve advertising on radio, TV, in newspapers, on the Internet and in magazines. Classified directories such as Yellow Pages and posters may also be used. Alternatively direct mail, which may include letters, electronic mail messages, newsletters, brochures and coupons, may be used. However, many organizations might struggle to be able to afford TV advertising at a local level, although many channels are aiming to making TV advertising more financially viable for all not just the larger corporation. You may have seen the recent range of TV advertisements using the cast of *The Bill*, the UK television drama series focused on a London borough police station. The cast have been used to highlight to smaller companies the misconceptions about the cost of advertising in an attempt to draw them to TV advertising where relevant.

Sales promotion for SMEs in particular involves generating awareness of the company and its products or services whilst providing customers with reasons to make purchasing commitments. The aim of sales promotion is to attract new customers or gain repeat purchases whilst persuading purchasers of rival products to switch supplier. This is a concept familiar to much larger organizations, and it is increasingly something that SMEs are grasping with some speed.

### Implications of implementing the marketing mix for SMEs

Whilst the above are ideas for implementing the marketing mix for SMEs, life is never that straightforward. It is important to understand that SMEs in particular experience a diverse range of difficulties and barriers to implementation not necessarily experienced by large companies, partly because their planning activities are more structured, detailed, monitored and controlled. These difficulties can include:

- Lack of resources
- Lack of money
- Poor cash flow
- Lack of formal budgeting
- Lack of experience
- Short-term planning
- Entrepreneurial but not contained
- Growth unplanned and often unmanageable.

Key websites for advice on marketing for SMEs include:

- www.cim.co.uk – Small Business Solutions
- www.businesslink.org
- www.scottish-enterprise.com
- www.businessconnect.org
- www.idbni.co.uk

## The virtual marketing environment

The evolution of Internet marketing and digital technologies has moved at a rapid pace. Key underlying trends behind the move towards Internet marketing are:

- Consumer time poverty
- Consumers looking to take control
- Convergence of technologies
- Shift from physical to digital technologies
- Shift from assets to knowledge.

## Key virtual trends

There has been a massive growth in online households over the past 4 years, and between 1998 and 2002 there is a forecasted growth of an average of 40 per cent in ownership of PCs with online access within Europe. According to recent quarterly government Internet reports (www.statistics.gov.uk) 51 per cent of UK consumers have accessed the Internet. In the age group of 16–24 the figure is much higher, at 88 per cent.

The average age of Internet shoppers is suggested to be around 34, with some 39 per cent of 15–25-year-olds involved in online shopping, 34 per cent of 25–34-year-olds and 29 per cent of 35–44-year-olds shopping online and being continually exposed to Internet marketing.

However, *Marketing in Business* (CIM's membership magazine) suggests that when considering all Internet-users, it is apparent that a relatively low proportion of them are actually making online purchases. These figures are lower than e-commerce hype suggested and reinforce the view that the Internet is primarily used for product search, evaluation and selection rather than the actual purchase.

Because there is great innovation and rapid change, it is difficult to forecast the future impact on technology of promotions and comprehend what is to come, however there is considerable information to be found in many different domains that shows trends in how ICT is going to emerge in the future. Clearly the growth in e-commerce is going to provide many promotional opportunities for all of the ICT modes of communication, but with the major growth anticipated through Internet, interactive and digital communications.

In a recent article published on the official UK Statistics website (www.statistics.gov.uk) titled 'Towards a Measurement Framework for International e-commerce' it is clear that governments all over the world are concerned to be prepared for the evolution in terms of technology and skills, so that their countries have the potential to grow and enter new markets in a new and different way. The basis of this paper is to consider e-commerce readiness, usage and impact across global markets. The project is working on benchmarking activities across nine major economies, including the UK.

e-Commerce is likely to have a huge impact on the way we do business in the future and has led to dramatic growth in trade, increased markets, improved efficiency and effectiveness and has transformed business processes. This benchmarking exercise is realistically trying to ascertain what standards other nations are operating at, and identify gaps in the way in which e-commerce is used to bring the UK up to a global standard.

One particular strand of the survey into UK business has actually asked businesses about their use of e-commerce and other communication technologies to aid their business.

Whilst the outcome of the survey is very long and complex, the basis of it is to measure and predict e-commerce requirements for the future. We know that currently, less than 10 per cent of the world population actually has Internet access and that by the end of 2005 the global access figure is expected to grow to 1 billion from 445 million users.

No other medium has grown in the same way and had the impact that the Internet has appeared to achieve. It is the only medium that has actually taken away slight market share from other media.

It is clear that many businesses, large and small, are consistently increasing their budget expenditure on e-commerce, which illustrates that Internet marketing is very much alive and kicking.

Significant increase in the number of consumers accessing the Internet continues, and they use it both to inform their purchase decision and for purchases. Two key examples and success stories in relation to Internet activities are easyJet and Cisco Systems. Both businesses generate over 90 per cent of their revenue via the Internet.

### Mobile Internet trends

It is anticipated that should some of the problems associated with WAP technology be resolved that the mobile Internet business could be worth in excess of £15 billion by 2004, and that the end-users of mobile Internet technology are likely to spend $200 billion (£150 million) in 2005.

It is known that mobile Internet providers such as Ericsson are planning the next generation improvements for mobile technology and plan to realize a much improved service by 2011.

### Interactive TV trends

Whilst the focus of this has been on e-commerce and potentially the growth of the Internet, CIM's website www.connectedinmarketing.com provides some interesting predictions about growth in terms of interactive TV. Fletcher Research predicts that by 2003 more than half of UK homes will have interactive TV.

What this means is that by 2004 interactive TV may overtake the PC for online access from home. Current estimates predict that PC penetration will level at 53 per cent but government figures suggest that interactive TV will reach approximately 95 per cent penetration within 10 years.

It is clearly evident that the Internet may have changed the preconceived ideas about the way in which companies do business and deal with their customers, but interactive TV could take this forward and exploit the new relationships to full potential.

### Digital TV trends

It is likely, as we know, that digital TV will overtake the PC market by some way by 2004, as the number of personal PCs within the home reaches saturation point. It has already been reported that HSBC claims to have registered some 1.3 million hits and is enjoying a high level of repeat users. Obviously digital solutions are the way forward.

It is hoped that whilst the scope of ICT is broadening and the range of communication opportunities is growing that organizations do not lose sight of the purpose of various technologies and that they are defined and developed in order to improve and build the scope of customer services and customer care.

It is clear that the shape of advertising, direct and interactive marketing, sales promotions and many more tools will change over the next decade quite considerably. As competition increases due to market saturation organizations will be looking for new and innovative methods of promotional activities and promotional communications in an integrated way, with increasing emphasis on the integrated. The integrated marketing communications mix in the future is likely to change to accommodate this and more and more organizations are expected to make more of their budgets available to mobile, digital and interactive communications.

After grasping some of these facts and figures you will no doubt realize that the Internet and digital technologies are a vital ingredient of the promotional mix, but also a vital component within the realms of direct marketing.

The whole basis of Internet marketing is that it will facilitate an interactive customer relationship online. It will enable frequent, customized and targeted messages to specific customers or customer groups.

## What are the business business benefits of virtual marketing?

The virtual marketing environment provides a number of significant business benefits to organizations and they can be broken down to four key areas as follows:

1. *Market penetration* – Because of the nature of the Internet and its global communications ability, organizations can now sell more products to more markets, which were not necessarily accessible previously because of cost. The Internet can also be used to create a more broad awareness of the organization, its products and services and give an overall profile of the organization to potential customers.
2. *Market development* – In this situation, the Internet can be used to sell products into completely new markets, taking advantage of low-cost advertising internationally without the necessity of supporting sales physically, in the customer's country.
3. *Product development* – The Internet is excellent for supporting the development of new products and services and testing them out in the electronic world.
4. *Diversification* – In this sector new products are developed which are sold into new markets. Good examples of this are Dell and Hewlett-Packard, who extended their market considerably. Dell suggests that the Internet supports $6 million worth of sales every day.

The Internet can be used in many ways to support marketing activities:

- *Sales* – Achieved through increasing awareness of brands and products, supporting buying decisions and enabling online purchase.
- *Marketing communications* – The use of the website for marketing communications is very powerful, particularly as surfing the Net is an increasing activity.
- *Customer service* – Supplementing telephone operators with online information. First Direct Bank and Egg are examples of organizations moving in this direction.
- *Public relations* – The Internet can be used as a new channel for public relations and provides the opportunity to publish the latest news on products. For example when you log on to AOL.com, a news page and a number of advertisements and banners appear.
- *Marketing research* – Earlier in this section we discussed how the research collected from websites in addition to the databases available enabled organizations to acquire a very clearly defined profile of their customers and their customer characteristics.

## The advantages of Internet marketing

So far a picture is evolving of a dynamic electronic world that has increased access on a global basis, that is fast-moving, effective and informative. In terms of marketing the key benefits of an Internet presence can be summarized as follows:

- *Cost reduction* – Achieved through the need for less resources, less need for actual physical presence, less paper-based activity, particularly relevant to promotional activities and day-to-day business trading.
- *Competitive advantage* – Who wants to be a dinosaur? Organizations need to stay ahead of the Internet game and aim to add value through the Internet and introduce new initiatives that will add overall competitive advantage.
- *Capability* – The Internet provides new opportunities for the development of new products and services.

- *Communication improvements* – The Internet is a powerful communications tool, with global coverage, and can improve communications for both external and internal marketing.
- *Control* – The Internet may provide better quality of market research information through a range of Internet tracking devices.
- *Customer service improvements* – The Internet contains a number of interactive databases that can provide varying levels of information, at speed, improving customer response times. For the Internet banks, banking can take place 24 hours a day, every day.

## The disadvantages of Internet marketing

- *The Internet replaces people* – As we have seen in the financial services sector over the last 2 to 3 years, there has been a vast reduction in the number of personnel required as a result of the automation of online banking.
- *The possible demise of High Street shops* – It has been suggested that within 30 years retail outlets will be a novelty and will be completely taken over by the Internet. However, this is still to be proven.
- *The loss of the personal touch* – There is the issue of de-personalizing business activity. The electronic world now works on a virtual rather than physical basis. Organizations must ask themselves about the loss of physical control. Is physical control an added value element of the business, or are speed and efficiency more important?
- *Security and privacy* – There are still issues of security and privacy, in addition to general regulation and control of information on the Internet. Under general regulation, there will of course be the issue of data protection. How do organizations ensure that this can be managed satisfactorily? This presents a significant challenge. Currently many organizations are seeking to ensure that they are not caught out with the various data protection laws currently in place.
- *Accessibility* – Another issue relating to the Internet is that of accessibility by the majority. While there is a significant increase in the number of homes having a personal computer and growing Internet access across different parts of the world, and it is still anticipated that it will grow significantly, will it continue to grow to meet the expectations of industry?
- *Technological defects* – It has been suggested that there is still a long way to go to iron out some of the technical difficulties to overcome customer dissatisfaction with the process.
- *Information overload* – Massive amounts of information make the Internet difficult to work around and hence people spend significantly longer online searching for their information needs. Therefore, the Internet could be perceived as being expensive and time-consuming.

It is suggested that in the future only the most reluctant electronic shopper may still be concerned with these technicalities, but the majority will actually want the new forms of service on offer to them.

From the organization perspective the initial financial investment must be considered. However, many organizations will surmise that they have to invest early on to get long-term profitability and competitive advantage in the future.

## The product

The development of product concepts, packaging concepts and associated services will also change as a result of emerging technologies.

Some of the key effects technology has had on the 'product' are as follows:

1. The speed of new product development has changed dramatically; taking a product from concept to reality is more dynamic. With CAD systems, production technology and shorter distribution systems, the product can at times go to market at a rapid speed. This can make us far more competitive in the marketplace.
2. The nature of packaging could change ultimately. As distribution options vary, packaging will no longer have to be designed for the retail outlet, but be designed for a delivery process that takes it to the customer's door. Therefore, more fragile items will have to have increasingly secure packaging. Foodstuffs might have to have more solid and secure packaging to deal with various delivery methods.
3. The method of delivery will revolve around postage and couriers as delivery comes to you directly, not via a retail outlet.
4. Warranties and guarantees might have to be rewritten to cope with the range of different delivery techniques involved in the process.

## Price

One of the significant problems still associated with the Internet and shopping is often the lack of transparency in pricing structure. One of the key elements of the Internet is transparent pricing, ensuring that customers understand and have clearly explained to them the structure of their purchase, the way it is priced, and the associated delivery and warranty costs.

Price is a central consideration, and as the infrastructure of the world changes shape, so will the economics associated with it, and ultimately so will the way products and services are priced in the future.

Where previously companies would have had to include the cost of the middleman, and the share of the retail outlet, they now have to consider the cost of the Internet server, the customer service infrastructure and the potential change in shape of the distribution costs.

As a marketing manager, you will have to find the balance between increased delivery costs on a more direct one-to-one basis, and the reduction in distribution channel costs. Added to all of this will be packaging costs, and the changing nature of advertising.

## Promotion

One of the difficulties that many marketers are currently facing is the greater fragmentation of their existing market. Tesco, when they commenced their online shopping project, had large Tesco stores across the country, and then provided an add-on service through 'Internet shopping', effectively allowing time-starved people to shop from the comfort of their own homes, whilst at the same time meeting the demands of the other part of the target audience, who still like to go to the supermarket to undertake their weekly shop. This has of course been followed by all major supermarket chains, including Sainsbury's and Waitrose.

Whichever way you look at it, there are now two alternative modes of shopping, which require two alternative modes of distribution, pricing to allow for additional delivery costs, and of course, promotions, to deal with the different media that shoppers are now using.

Advertising as an element of promotion is undergoing a significant change, with the vast amount of small one-line advertisements ever-increasing on a daily basis. You hear of innovations such as 'interruption advertising'; for example, when you put your computer on, an advertisement suddenly pops up on your screen.

## Dynamic marketing

The whole point of this section on virtual marketing has been primarily to enlighten you, focus you on the necessity not to think about marketing as a straightforward, theoretical process, but to think of marketing as a dynamic, fast-moving, ever-changing activity. The one thing that is definite about marketing is that it is subject to constant change and nowhere more so than in this expanding new field of virtual marketing.

Therefore, if we were to summarize some of the impacts of the Internet and digital technologies upon the marketing mix and marketing in general, they would be as follows:

- Increased market penetration
- *Market development* – taking existing products to new markets
- Product development
- Diversification.

## Summary

Planning and controlling go together, and in this respect there is no basic difference between the activities of FMCGs, B2B, B2C or virtual environments and those of non-profit-making organizations.

However, the big difference for charities is their dependence on the unpaid work of volunteers; you cannot make the same demands on volunteers that you can on employees. Also, you do not have the power to threaten them with dismissal – many employees tolerate the job because they need the money, either now or in the future, so they cannot walk out. It is almost impossible to estimate the value of volunteer workers, and controlling them is a matter of good organization and the appropriate expressions of gratitude for their help. There is more need for charities to be seen to be using their money wisely than there is for commercial companies, as a donor who thinks that money is being wasted may not feel like giving money next time round. Donations to such television marathons as Children in Need improved when some of their successful projects were shown in the course of the programme.

The marketing philosophy is now becoming a permanent feature of not-for-profit organizations. It has been necessary to introduce marketing gradually, so as to highlight a 'customer-centred' focus, which had not previously been noticeable.

For SMEs it is also important to increase the emphasis on planning and the customer-centred focus; often the mere fight for survival (particularly very small businesses) finds them struggling with these concepts. However, SMEs need to ensure that they follow the same basic principles as those larger organizations but on a scale appropriate to their business. There are some key fundamental issues that should be addressed.

Ultimately the virtual environment is changing the way that all sectors do business and the rapidly changing market is presenting many new challenges and opportunities to extend business both locally and globally and increasingly in a more transparent way.

It is clear to see that with the increasing emphasis on digital and Internet technologies, virtual activities will continue to grow and expand to incorporate a range of new and innovative marketing ideas.

> **Study tip**
>
> The importance of not-for-profit-marketing has grown in significance over the past years within the marketplace, and a reflection of this might emerge in the exam paper. In recent years, this particular topic has been the centre of the mini-case study, therefore it is essential to understand the concepts and context of charities and not-for-profit and how they have emerged and become much more marketing-focused.

## Extending knowledge

To learn more about the evolving power of ICT and potential trends you can look up some of the following websites:

www.connectedinmarketing.com
www.wnim.com
www.statistics.gov.uk
www.cyberatlas.com
www.nua.ie
www.isi.gov.uk

> **Bibliography**
>
> Brassington, F. and Pettitt, S. (2000) *Principles of Marketing*, Thomson Higher Education.
>
> Chaffey, D., Mayer, R., Johnston, K. and Ellis-Chadwick, F.E. (2000) *Internet Marketing*, Prentice Hall.
>
> Dibb, S., Simkin, L., Pride, W. and Ferrell, O. (2001) *Marketing: Concepts and Strategies*, 4th European edition, Houghton Mifflin.
>
> **Useful websites include:**
>
> www.cim.co.uk
> www.wnim.com

> Sample exam questions and answers for the Marketing Planning module as a whole can be found in Appendix 4 and past examination papers can be found in Appendix 5. Both appendices can be found at the back of the book.

# appendix 1
# guidance on examination preparation

## Preparing for your examination

You are now nearing the final phase of your studies and it is time to start the hard work of exam preparation.

During your period of study you will have become used to absorbing large amounts of information. You will have tried to understand and apply aspects of knowledge that may have been very new to you, while some of the information provided may have been more familiar. You may even have undertaken many of the activities that are positioned frequently throughout your Coursebook, which will have enabled you to apply your learning in practical situations. But whatever the state of your knowledge and understanding, do not allow yourself to fall into the trap of thinking that you know enough, you understand enough, or even worse, that you can just take it as it comes on the day.

Never underestimate the pressure of the CIM examination.

The whole point of preparing this text for you is to ensure that you never take the examination for granted, and that you do not go into the exam unprepared for what might come your way for 3 hours at a time.

One thing's for sure: there is no quick fix, no easy route, no waving a magic wand and finding you know it all.

Whether you have studied alone, in a CIM study centre, or through distance learning, you now need to ensure that this final phase of your learning process is tightly managed, highly structured and objective.

As a candidate in the examination, your role will be to convince the Senior Examiner for this subject that you have credibility. You need to demonstrate to the examiner that you can be trusted to undertake a range of challenges in the context of marketing, that you are able to capitalize on opportunities and manage your way through threats.

You should prove to the Senior Examiner that you are able to apply knowledge, make decisions, respond to situations and solve problems.

Very shortly we are going to look at a range of revision and exam preparation techniques, and at time management issues, and encourage you towards developing and implementing your own revision plan, but before that, let's look at the role of the Senior Examiner.

# A bit about the Senior Examiners!

You might be quite shocked to read this, but while it might appear that the examiners are 'relentless question masters' they actually want you to be able to answer the questions and pass the exams! In fact, they would derive no satisfaction or benefits from failing candidates; quite the contrary, they develop the syllabus and exam papers in order that you can learn and then apply that learning effectively so as to pass your examinations. Many of the examiners have said in the past that it is indeed psychologically more difficult to fail students than pass them.

Many of the hints and tips you find within this Appendix have been suggested by the Senior Examiners and authors of the Coursebook series. Therefore you should consider them carefully and resolve to undertake as many of the elements suggested as possible.

The Chartered Institute of Marketing has a range of processes and systems in place within the Examinations Division to ensure that fairness and consistency prevail across the team of examiners, and that the academic and vocational standards that are set and defined are indeed maintained. In doing this, CIM ensures that those who gain the CIM Certificate (Stage 1), Professional Diploma, formerly known as Advanced Certificate (Stage 2) and Professional Postgraduate Diploma (Stage 3), are worthy of the qualification and perceived as such in the view of employers, actual and potential.

Part of what you will need to do within the examination is be 'examiner friendly' – that means you have to make sure they get what they ask for. This will make life easier for you and for them.

Hints and tips for 'examiner friendly' actions are as follows:

- Show them that you understand the basis of the question, by answering *precisely* the question asked, and not including just about everything you can remember about the subject area.
- *Read their needs* – how many points is the question asking you to address?
- Respond to the question appropriately. Is the question asking you to take on a role? If so, take on the role and answer the question in respect of the role. For example, you could be positioned as follows:

    'You are working as a Marketing Assistant at Nike UK' or 'You are a Marketing Manager for an Engineering Company' or 'As Marketing Manager write a report to the Managing Partner'.

These examples of role-playing requirements are taken from questions in past papers.

- Deliver the answer in the format requested. If the examiner asks for a memo, then provide a memo; likewise, if the examiner asks for a report, then write a report. If you do not do this, in some instances you will fail to gain the necessary marks required to pass.
- Take a business-like approach to your answers. This enhances your credibility. Badly ordered work, untidy work, lack of structure, headings and subheadings can be off-putting. This would be unacceptable in the work situation, likewise it will be unacceptable in the eyes of the Senior Examiners and their marking teams.
- Ensure the examiner has something to mark: give them substance, relevance, definitions, illustration and demonstration of your knowledge and understanding of the subject area.
- See the examiner as your potential employer, or ultimate consumer/customer. The whole purpose and culture of marketing is about meeting customers' needs. Try this approach – it works wonders.

*Appendix 1 Guidance on examination preparation*

- ○ Provide a strong sense of enthusiasm and professionalism in your answers; support it with relevant up-to-date examples and apply them where appropriate.
- ○ Try to do something that will make your exam paper a little bit different – make it stand out in the crowd.

All of these points might seem quite logical to you, but often in the panic of the examination they 'go out of the window'. Therefore it is beneficial to remind ourselves of the importance of the examiner. He/she is the 'ultimate customer' – and we all know customers hate to be disappointed.

As we move on, some of these points will be revisited and developed further.

## About the examination

In all examinations, with the exception of Marketing Management in Practice at Advanced Certificate (Stage 2) level, the paper is divided into two parts.

1. Part A – Mini-case study = 50 per cent of marks
2. Part B – Option choice questions (choice of two questions from four) = 50 per cent of the marks (each question attracting 25 per cent).

For the Marketing Management in Practice paper, the same approach is taken, however, all of the questions are directly related to the case study and in this instance the case material is more extensive.

Let's look at the basis of each element.

### Part A – The mini-case study

This is based on a mini-case or scenario with one question, possibly subdivided into between two and four points, but totalling 50 per cent of marks overall.

In essence, you, the candidate, are placed in a problem-solving role through the medium of a short scenario. On occasions, the scenario may consist of an article from a journal in relation to a well-known organization.

Alternatively, it will be based upon a fictional company, and the examiner will have prepared it in order that the right balance of knowledge, understanding, application and skills is used.

### Approaches to the mini-case study

When undertaking the mini-case study there are a number of key areas you should consider.

#### Structure/content
The mini-case that you will be presented with will vary slightly from paper to paper, and of course from one examination to the next. Normally the scenario presented will be 400–500 words long and will centre on a particular organization and its problems or may even relate to a specific industry. However, please note that for Marketing Management in Practice, the case study is more significant as all the questions are based upon the case materials.

The length of the mini-case study means that usually only a brief outline is provided of the situation, the organization and its marketing problems, and you must therefore learn to cope with analysing information and preparing your answer on the basis of a very limited amount of detail.

## Time management

There are many differing views on time management and the approaches you can take to managing your time within the examination. You must find an approach to suit your way of working, but always remember, whatever you do, you must ensure that you allow enough time to complete the examination. Unfinished exams mean lost marks.

A typical example of managing time is as follows:

Your paper is designed to assess you over a 3-hour period. With 50 per cent of the marks being allocated to the mini-case, it means that you should dedicate somewhere around 100 minutes of your time to both read and write up the answer on this mini-case, leaving a further 80 minutes for the remaining questions. Some students, however, will prefer to allocate nearer half of their time (90 minutes) on the mini-case, so that they can read and fully absorb the case and answer the questions in the context of it. This is also acceptable as long as you ensure that you work extremely 'SMART' for the remaining time in order to finish the examination.

Do not forget that while there is only one question within the mini-case, it can have a number of components. You must answer all the components in that question, which is where the balance of times comes into play.

## Knowledge/skills tested

Throughout all the CIM papers, your knowledge, skills and ability to apply those skills will be tested. However, the mini-cases are used particularly to test application, i.e. your ability to take your knowledge and apply it in a structured way to a given scenario. The examiners will be looking at your decision-making ability, your analytical and communication skills and, depending on the level, your ability as a manager to solve particular marketing problems.

When the examiner is marking your paper, he/she will be looking to see how you differentiate yourself, looking at your own individual 'unique selling points'. The examiner will also want to see if you can personally apply the knowledge or whether you are only able to repeat the textbook materials.

## Format of answers

On many occasions, and within all examinations, you will most likely be given a particular communication method to use. If this is the case, you must ensure that you adhere to the requirements of the examiner. This is all part of meeting customer needs.

The likely communication tools you will be expected to use are as follows:

- Memorandum
- Memorandum/report
- Report
- Briefing notes
- Presentation
- Press release
- Advertisement
- Plan.

Make sure that you familiarize yourself with these particular communication tools and practise using them to ensure that, on the day, you will be able to respond confidently to the communication requests of the examiner. Look back at the Customer Communications text at Certificate level to familiarize yourself with the potential requirements of these methods.

By the same token, while communication methods are important, so is meeting the specific requirements of the question. This means you must understand what is meant by the precise instruction given. *Note the following terms carefully*:

- *Identify* – Select key issues, point out key learning points, establish clearly what the examiner expects you to identify.
- *Illustrate* – The examiner expects you to provide examples, scenarios and key concepts that illustrate your learning.
- *Compare and contrast* – Look at the range of similarities between the two situations, contexts or even organizations. Then compare them, i.e. ascertain and list how activities, features, etc. agree or disagree. Contrasting means highlighting the differences between the two.
- *Discuss* – Questions that have 'discuss' in them offer a tremendous opportunity for you to debate, argue, justify your approach or understanding of the subject area – *caution*: it is not an opportunity to waffle.
- *Briefly explain* – This means being succinct, structured and concise in your explanation, within the answer. Make your points clear, transparent and relevant.
- *State* – Present in a clear, brief format.
- *Interpret* – Expound the meaning of, make clear and explicit what it is you see and understand within the data provided.
- *Outline* – Provide the examiner with the main concepts and features being asked for and avoid minor technical details. Structure will be critical here, or else you could find it difficult to contain your answer.
- *Relate* – Show how different aspects of the syllabus connect together.
- *Evaluate* – Review and reflect upon an area of the syllabus, a particular practice, an article, etc., and consider its overall worth in respect of its use as a tool or a model and its overall effectiveness in the role it plays.

*Source*: Worsam, *How to Pass Marketing* (Croner, 1989).

## Your approach to mini-cases

There is no one right way to approach and tackle a mini-case study, indeed it will be down to each individual to use their own creativity in tackling the tasks presented. You will have to use your initiative and discretion about how best to approach the mini-case. Having said this, however, there are some basic steps you can take.

- Ensure that you read through the case study at least twice before making any judgements, starting to analyse the information provided, or indeed writing the answers.
- On the third occasion read through the mini-case and, using a highlighter, start marking the essential and relevant information critical to the content and context. Then turn your attention to the question again, this time reading slowly and carefully to assess what it is you are expected to do. Note any instructions that the examiner gives you, and then start to plan how you might answer the question. Whatever the question, ensure the answer has a structure: a beginning, a structured central part of the answer and, finally, always a conclusion.
- Keep the context of the question continually in mind: that is, the specifics of the case and the role which you might be performing.

*Appendix 1 Guidance on examination preparation*

- Because there is limited material available, you will sometimes need to make assumptions. Don't be afraid to do this, it will show initiative on your part. Assumptions are an important part of dealing with case studies and can help you to be quite creative with your answer. However, do explain the basis of your assumptions within your answer so that the examiner understands the nature of them, and why you have arrived at your particular outcome. *Always ensure that your assumptions are realistic.*
- Only now are you approaching the stage where it is time to start writing your answer to the question, tackling the problems, making decisions and recommendations on the case scenario set before you. As mentioned previously, your points will often be best set out in a report or memo type format, particularly if the examiner does not specify a communication method.
- Ensure that your writing is succinct, avoids waffle and responds directly to the questions asked.

## Part B – Option choice questions

Each Part B is comprised of four traditional questions, each worth 25 per cent. You will be expected to choose two of those questions, to make up the remaining 50 per cent of available marks. (Again please note that the structure is the same for Marketing Management in Practice, but that all questions are applied to the case study.)

Realistically, the same principles apply for these questions as in the case study. Communication formats, reading through the questions, structure, role-play, context, etc. – everything is the same.

Part B will cover a number of broader issues from within the syllabus and will be taken from any element of it. The examiner makes the choice, and no prior direction is given to students or tutors on what that might be.

As regards time management in this area, if you used about 100 minutes for the mini-case you should have around 80 minutes left. This provides you with around 40 minutes to plan and write a question, to write, review and revise your answers. Keep practising – use a cooker timer, alarm clock or mobile phone alarm as your timer and work hard at answering questions within the timeframe given.

## Specimen examination papers and answers

To help you prepare and understand the nature of the paper, go to www.cim.co.uk/learningzone or to access Specimen Answers and Senior Examiner's advice for these exam questions. During your study, the author of your Coursebook may have on occasions asked you to refer to these papers and answer the questions. You should undertake these exercises and utilize every opportunity to practise meeting examination requirements.

Each of the Professional Diploma, formerly known as Advanced Certificate (Stage 2) coursebooks have at the end of them some examination questions and guidance provided by the authors and Senior Examiners, where appropriate, to provide you with some insight into the types of questions asked.

The specimen answers are vital learning tools. They are not always perfect, as they are answers written by students and annotated by the Senior Examiners, but they will give you a good indication of the approaches you could take, and the examiners' annotations suggest how these answers might be improved. Please use them.

*Appendix 1 Guidance on examination preparation*

The CIM learning zone website provides you which links to many useful case studies which will help you to put your learning into context when you are revising.

## Key elements of preparation

One Senior Examiner suggests the three elements involved in preparing for your examination can be summarized thus:

1. Learning
2. Memory
3. Revision.

Let's look at each point in turn.

### Learning

Quite often students find it difficult to learn properly. You can passively read books, look at some of the materials, perhaps revise a little, and regurgitate it all in the examination. In the main, however, this is rather an unsatisfactory method of learning. It is meaningless, shallow and ultimately of little use in practice.

For learning to be truly effective it must be active and applied. You must involve yourself in the learning process by thinking about what you have read, testing it against your experience by reflecting on how you use particular aspects of marketing, and how you could perhaps improve your own performance by implementing particular aspects of your learning into your everyday life. You should adopt the old adage of 'learning by doing'. If you do, you will find that passive learning has no place in your study life.

Below are some suggestions that have been prepared to assist you with the learning pathway throughout your revision.

- Always make your own notes, in words you understand, and ensure that you combine all the sources of information and activities within them
- Always try to relate your learning back to your own organization
- Make sure you define key terms concisely, wherever possible
- Do not try to memorize your ideas, but work on the basis of understanding and, most important, applying them
- Think about the relevant and topical questions that might be set – use the questions and answers in your Coursebooks to identify typical questions that might be asked in the future
- Attempt all of the questions within each of your Coursebooks since these are vital tests of your active learning and understanding.

### Memory

If you are prepared to undertake an active learning programme then your knowledge will be considerably enhanced, as understanding and application of knowledge does tend to stay in your 'long-term' memory. It is likely that passive learning will only stay in your 'short-term' memory.

Do not try to memorize parrot fashion; it is not helpful and, even more important, examiners are experienced in identifying various memorizing techniques and therefore will spot them as such.

*Appendix 1 Guidance on examination preparation*

Having said this, it is quite useful to memorize various acronyms such as SWOT, PEST, PESTEL, STEEPLE, or indeed various models such as Ansoff, BCG, GE Matrix, Shell Directional Policy Matrix, etc., as in some of the questions you may be required to use illustrations of these to assist your answer.

## Revision

The third and final stage to consider is 'revision', which is what we will concentrate on in detail below. Here just a few key tips are offered.

Revision should be an ongoing process rather than a panic measure that you decide to undertake just before the examination. You should be preparing notes *throughout* your course, with the view to using them as part of your revision process. Therefore ensure that your notes are sufficiently comprehensive that you can reuse them successfully.

For each concept you learn about, you should identify, through your reading and your own personal experience, at least two or three examples that you could use; this then gives you some scope to broaden your perspective during the examination. It will, of course, help you gain some points for initiative with the examiners.

Knowledge is not something you will gain overnight – as we saw earlier, it is not a quick fix; it involves a process of learning that enables you to lay solid foundations upon which to build your long-term understanding and application. This will benefit you significantly in the future, not just in the examination.

In essence, you should ensure that you do the following in the period before the real intensive revision process begins.

- Keep your study file well organized, updated and full of newspaper and journal cuttings that may help you formulate examples in your mind for use during the examination
- Practise defining key terms and acronyms from memory
- Prepare topic outlines and essay answer plans
- When you start your intensive revision, ensure it is planned and structured in the way described below. And then finally, read your concentrated notes the night before the examination.

## Revision planning

You are now on a critical path – although hopefully not too critical at this time – with somewhere in the region of between 4 and 6 weeks to go to the examination. The following hints and tips will help you plan out your revision study.

- You will, as already explained, need to be very organized. Therefore, before doing anything else, put your files, examples, reading material, etc. in good order, so that you are able to work with them in the future and, of course, make sense of them.
- Ensure that you have a quiet area within which to work. It is very easy to get distracted when preparing for an examination.
- Take out your file along with your syllabus and make a list of key topic areas that you have studied and which you now need to revise. You could use the basis of this book to do that, by taking each unit a step at a time.

*Appendix 1 Guidance on examination preparation*

- Plan the use of your time carefully. Ideally you should start your revision at least 6 weeks prior to the exam, so therefore work out how many spare hours you could give to the revision process and then start to allocate time in your diary, and do not double-book with anything else.
- Give up your social life for a short period of time. As the saying goes 'no pain – no gain'.
- Looking at each of the subject areas in turn, identify which are your strengths and which are your weaknesses. Which areas have you grasped and understood, and which are the areas that you have really struggled with? Split your page in two and make a list on each side. For example:

| Planning and control | |
|---|---|
| **Strengths** | **Weaknesses** |
| Audit – PEST, SWOT, Models | Ratio analysis |
| Portfolio analysis | Market sensing |
| | Productivity analysis |
| | Trend extrapolation |
| | Forecasting |

- Break down your list again and divide the points of weakness, giving priority in the first instance to your weakest areas and even prioritizing them by giving them a number. This will enable you to master the more difficult areas. Up to 60 per cent of your remaining revision time should be given over to that, as you may find you have to undertake a range of additional reading and also perhaps seeking tutor support, if you are studying at a CIM Accredited Study Centre.
- The rest of the time should be spent reinforcing your knowledge and understanding of the stronger areas, spending time testing yourself on how much you really know.
- Should you be taking two examinations or more at any one time, then the breakdown and managing of your time will be critical.
- Taking a subject at a time, work through your notes and start breaking them down into subsections of learning, and ultimately into key learning points, items that you can refer to time and time again, that are meaningful and that your mind will absorb. You yourself will know how you best remember key points. Some people try to develop acronyms, or flowcharts or matrices, mind maps, fishbone diagrams, etc., or various connection diagrams that help them recall certain aspects of models. You could also develop processes that enable you to remember approaches to various options. (But do remember what we said earlier about regurgitating stuff, parrot fashion.)

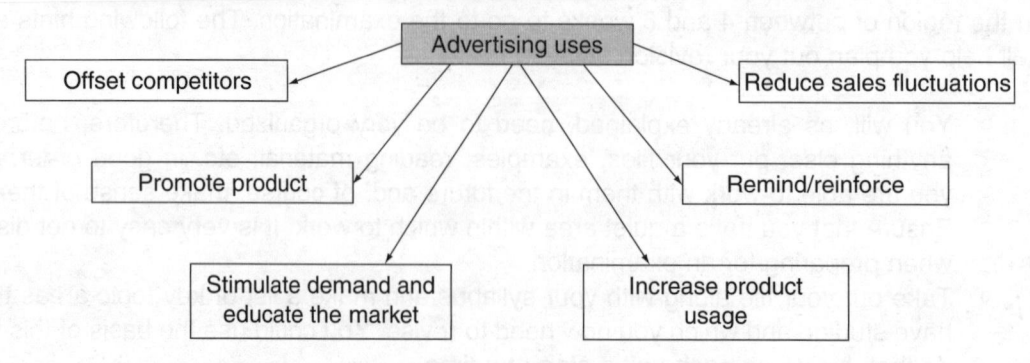

*Figure A1.1* Use of a diagram to summarize key components of a concept
*Source*: Adapted from Dibb, Simkin, Pride and Ferrell, *Marketing Concepts and Strategies*, 4th European edition (Houghton Mifflin, 2001)

*Appendix 1 Guidance on examination preparation*

Figure A1.1 is just a brief example of how you could use a 'bomb-burst' diagram (which, in this case, highlights the uses of advertising) as a very helpful approach to memorizing key elements of learning.

- Eventually you should reduce your key learning to bullet points. For example: imagine you were looking at the concept of Time Management – you could eventually reduce your key learning to a bullet list containing the following points in relation to 'Effective Prioritization':

    – Organize
    – Take time
    – Delegate
    – Review.

- Each of these headings would then remind you of the elements you need to discuss associated with the subject area.
- Avoid getting involved in reading too many textbooks at this stage, as you may start to find that you are getting confused overall.
- Look at examination questions on previous papers, and start to observe closely the various roles and tasks they expect you to undertake, and importantly, the context in which they are set.
- *Use the specimen exam papers and specimen answers* to support your learning and see how you could actually improve upon them.
- Without exception, find an associated examination question for the areas that you have studied and revised, and undertake it (more than once if necessary).
- Without referring to notes or books, try to draft an answer plan with the key concepts, knowledge, models and information that are needed to successfully complete the answer. Then refer to the specimen answer to see how close you are to the actual outline presented. Planning your answer, and ensuring that key components are included, and that the question has a meaningful structure, is one of the most beneficial activities that you can undertake.
- Now write the answer out in full, time-constrained and written by hand, not with the use of IT. (At this stage, you are still expected to be the scribe for the examination and present handwritten work. Many of us find this increasingly difficult as we spend more and more time using our computers to present information. Do your best to be neat. Spidery handwriting is often off-putting to the examiner.)

When writing answers as part of your revision process, also be sure to practise the following essential examinations techniques:

1. Identify and use the communication method requested by the examiner.
2. *Always have three key parts to the answer* – an introduction, middle section that develops your answer in full, and a conclusion. Where appropriate, ensure that you have an introduction, main section, summary/conclusion and, if requested or helpful, recommendations.
3. Always answer the question in the context or role set.
4. Always comply with the nature and terms of the question.
5. Leave white space. Do not overcrowd your page; leave space between paragraphs, and make sure your sentences do not merge into one blur. (Don't worry – there is always plenty of paper available to use in the examination.)
6. Count how many actions the question asks you to undertake and double-check at the end that you have met the full range of demands of the question.
7. *Use examples* – to demonstrate your knowledge and understanding of the particular syllabus area. These can be from journals, the Internet, the press, or your own experience.

*Appendix 1 Guidance on examination preparation*

8. Display your vigour and enthusiasm for marketing. Remember to think of the Senior Examiner as your Customer, or future employer, and do your best to deliver what is wanted to satisfy their needs. Impress them and show them how you are a 'cut above the rest'.
9. Review all your practice answers critically, with the above points in mind.

## Practical actions

The critical path is becoming even more critical now as the examination looms. The following are vital points.

- Have you registered with CIM?
- Do you know where you are taking your examination? CIM should let you know approximately 1 month in advance.
- Do you know where your examination centre is? If not, find out, take a drive, time it – whatever you do don't be late!
- Make sure you have all the tools of the examination ready. A dictionary, calculator, pens, pencils, ruler, etc. Try not to use multiple shades of pens, but at the same time make your work look professional. *Avoid using red and green as these are the colours that will be used for marking.*

## Summary

Above all you must remember that you personally have invested a tremendous amount of time, effort and money in studying for this programme and it is therefore imperative that you consider the suggestions given here as they will help to maximize your return on your investment.

Many of the hints and tips offered here are generic and will work across most of the CIM courses. We have tried to select those that will help you most in taking a sensible, planned approach to your study and revision.

The key to your success is being prepared to put in the time and effort required, planning your revision, and equally important, planning and answering your questions in a way that will ensure that you pass your examination on the day.

The advice offered here aims to guide you from a practical perspective. Guidance on syllabus content and developments associated with your learning will become clear to you as you work through this Coursebook. The authors of each Coursebook have given subject-specific guidance on the approach to the examination and on how to ensure that you meet the content requirements of the kind of question you will face. These considerations are in addition to the structuring issues we have been discussing throughout this Appendix.

Each of the authors and Senior Examiners will guide you on their preferred approach to questions and answers as they go. Therefore where you are presented with an opportunity to be involved in some activity or undertake an examination question either during or at the end of your study units, do take it. It not only prepares you for the examination, but helps you learn in the applied way we discussed above.

*Appendix 1 Guidance on examination preparation*

Here, then, is a last reminder:

- Ensure you make the most of your learning process throughout.
- Keep structured and orderly notes from which to revise.
- Plan your revision – don't let it just happen.
- Provide examples to enhance your answers.
- Practise your writing skills in order that you present your work well and your writing is readable.
- Take as many opportunities to test your knowledge and measure your progress as possible.
- Plan and structure your answers.
- Always do as the question asks you, especially with regard to context and communication method.
- *Do not leave it until the last minute!*

The writers would like to take this opportunity to wish you every success in your endeavours to study, to revise and to pass your examinations.

Karen Beamish
*Academic Development Advisor*

# appendix 2
# assignment-based assessment

## Introduction – the basis to the assignments and the integrative project

Within the CIM qualifications at Professional Certificate and Professional Diploma level there are several assessment options available. These are detailed in the outline of modules below. The purpose of an assignment is to provide another format to complete each module for students who want to apply the syllabus concepts from a module to their own or a selected organization. For either qualification there are three modules providing assessment via an assignment and one module assessed via an integrative work-based project. The module assessed via the integrative project is the summative module for each qualification.

|  | Entry modules | Research & analysis | Planning | Implementation | Management of Marketing |
|---|---|---|---|---|---|
| **Professional Postgraduate Diploma** | Entry module– Professional Postgraduate Diploma | Analysis & Evaluation | Strategic Marketing Decisions | Managing Marketing Performance | Strategic Marketing in Practice |
| **Professional Diploma** | Entry module– Professional Diploma | Marketing Research & Information | Marketing Planning | Marketing Communications | Marketing Management in Practice |
| **Professional Certificate** |  | Marketing Environment | Marketing Fundamentals | Customer Communications | Marketing in Practice |
| **Introductory Certificate** |  | Supporting marketing processes (research & analysis, planning & implementation) ||||

Outline of CIM 'standard' syllabus Syllabus-Stage 3 Issue 1 (2 Sept 03).doc © The Chartered Institute of Marketing September 2003

The use of assignments does not mean that this route is easier than an examination. Both formats are carefully evaluated to ensure that a Grade B in the assessment/integrative project route is the same as a Grade B in an examination. However, the use of assignments does allow a student to complete the assessment for a module over a longer period of time than a 3-hour examination. This will inevitably mean work being undertaken over the time-span of a module. For those used to cramming for exams writing an assignment over several weeks which comprises a total of four separate questions will be a very different approach.

Each module within the qualification contains a different assignment written specifically for the module. These are designed to test understanding and provide the opportunity for you to demonstrate your abilities through the application of theory to practice. The format and structure of each module's assignment is identical, although the questions asked will differ and the exact type of assignment varies. The questions within an assignment will relate directly to the syllabus for that particular module, thereby giving the opportunity to demonstrate understanding and application.

# The assignment structure

The assignment for each module is broken down into a range of questions. These consist of a core question, and a selection of optional questions. The core question will always relate to the main aspects of each module's syllabus. Coupled with this is a range of four optional questions which will each draw from a different part of the syllabus. Students are requested to select two optional questions from the four available. In addition, a reflective statement requires a student to evaluate their learning from the module. When put together these form the assessment for the entire module. The overall pass mark for the module is the same as through an examination route, which is set at 50 per cent. In addition, the grade band structure is also identical to that of an examination.

## Core question

This is the longest and therefore most important section of your assignment. Covering the major components of the syllabus, the core question is designed to provide a challenging assignment which tests the theoretical element, yet also permits application to a selected organization or situation. The rubric on the front of the assignment will give you clear guidance in respect of word limits, therefore pay close attention to them and the overall requirements of CIM in relation to the use of appendices. However, it is clear that the appendices should be kept to a minimum. Advice here is that they should be no longer than five pages of additional pertinent information.

## Optional questions

There are a total of four questions provided for Professional Certificate and Professional Diploma of the syllabus from which a student is asked to select two. Each answer is expected to provide a challenge although the actual task required varies. The rubric on the front of the assignment will give you clear guidance in respect of world limits, therefore pay close attention to them and the overall requirements of CIM in relation to the use of appendices. These are designed to test areas of the syllabus not covered by the core question. As such it is possible to base all of your questions on the same organization although there is significant benefit in using more than one organization as a basis for your assignment. Some of the questions specifically require a different organization to be selected from the one used for the core question. This only occurs where the questions are requiring similar areas to be investigated and will be specified clearly on the question itself.

*Appendix 2 Assignment-based assessment*

Within the assignment there are several types of questions that may be asked, including:

- *A report* – The question requires a formal report to be completed, detailing an answer to the specific question set. This will often be reporting on a specific issue to an individual.
- *A briefing paper or notes* – Preparing a briefing paper or a series of notes which may be used for a presentation.
- *A presentation* – You may be required to either prepare the presentation only or deliver the presentation in addition to its preparation. The audience for the presentation should be considered carefully and ICT used where possible.
- *A discussion paper* – The question requires an academic discussion paper to be prepared. You should show a range of sources and concepts within the paper. You may also be required to present the discussion paper as part of a question.
- *A project plan or action plan* – Some questions ask for planning techniques to be demonstrated. As such, the plan must be for the timescale given and costs shown where applicable. The use of ICT is recommended here in order to create the plan diagrammatically.
- *Planning a research project* – Whilst market research may be required, questions have often asked for simply a research plan in a given situation. This would normally include timescales, the type(s) of research to be gathered, sampling, planned data collection and analysis.
- *Conducting research* – Following on from a research plan, a question can require the student(s) to undertake a research gathering exercise. A research question can be either an individual or a group activity depending upon the question. This will usually result in a report of the findings of the exercise plus any recommendations arising from your findings.
- *Gathering of information and reporting* – Within many questions, information will need gathering. The request for information can form part or all of a question. This may be a background to the organization, the activities contained in the question or external market and environmental information. It is advisable to detail the types of information utilized, their sources and report on any findings. Such a question will often ask for recommendations for the organization – these should be drawn from the data and not simply personal opinion.
- *An advisory document* – A question here will require students to evaluate a situation and present advice and recommendations drawn from findings and theory. Again, any advice should be backed up with evidence and not a personal perspective only.
- *An exercise, either planning and/or delivering the exercise* – At both Professional Certificate and Professional Diploma, exercises are offered as optional questions. These provide students with the opportunity to devise an exercise and may also require the delivery of this exercise. Such an activity should be evidenced where possible.
- *A role-play with associated documentation* – Several questions have asked students to undertake role-plays in exercises such as team-building. These are usually videoed and documentation demonstrating the objectives of the exercise provided.

Each of these questions related directly towards specific issues to be investigated, evaluated and answered. In addition, some of the questions asked present situations to be considered. These provide opportunities for specific answers relating directly to the question asked.

In order to aid students completing the assignment, each question is provided with an outline of marking guidance. This relates to the different categories by which each question is marked. The marker of your assignment will be provided with a detailed marking scheme constructed around the same marking guidance provided to students.

For both the core and optional questions it is important to use referencing where sources have been utilized. This has been a weakness in the past and continues to be an issue. There have been cases of plagiarism identified during marking and moderation, together with a distinct lack of references and bibliography. It is highly recommended that a bibliography be included with each question and sources are cited within the text itself. The type of referencing method used is not important, only that sources are referred to.

## Guidance for completion of assignments

The latest assignment briefing documents include 'Assessment Criteria', which should indicate to you the type of information and format that CIM are seeking.

These 'Assessment Criteria' should not replace any assignment briefing that is usually undertaken by your module tutor. It is most important that, when assignments are issued, discussions take place between your group and tutor to clarify your understanding of the assignment brief and what is required. Remember that your tutor will receive Tutor Guidance Notes from CIM for each assignment briefing and therefore, they will be able to clarify points of concern for you.

Please note that the Marking Criteria are NOT included with the student brief, but that it is acceptable for your tutor to communicate, in very general terms, where the majority of the marks can be gained.

Once marked, you are usually allowed to have your assignments returned together with a Feedback Sheet, completed by the marker(s), that identifies the strengths and weaknesses of your work. However, no marks will be communicated to you by your tutors before the CIM Moderation process has taken place. Final grades will be sent to you from the CIM by the usual process in February or August, depending on when assignments were submitted for moderation.

Although you will not be penalized for exceeding the recommended word-count, CIM expect you to be presenting work in a professional format and manner, which includes being concise. Therefore the appropriate length of the assignment set will be considered under the last section of each marking scheme which allows approximately 8–10 per cent for presentation.

## General issues to consider when completing the assignments

### Question focus
It is very noticeable that a number of students do not focus fully on what the assignment requires. You need to ensure that you consider the assessment criteria and ensure that you have addressed each point. It is very surprising that many pieces of coursework do not include certain sections required and thus lose marks because of this. Although you will not be given the weighting for each assessment criterion, you can ask your tutor to suggest the level of importance for each (as they will have the actual weighting from CIM which cannot formally be communicated to students).

### Academic referencing
You need to remember at this level you are required to justify your thoughts and the theory which you apply. You need to illustrate your work with fully referenced but appropriate models or frameworks. Higher grade work tends to display an excellent understanding of the theory, by illustrating models and then applying them to the question.

It is expected that you have read quite widely at this level, therefore you need to demonstrate this. Therefore, you must ensure that you reference fully and appropriately within all coursework as you would for coursework within a University degree. It is very disappointing to see good work which is either not referenced fully or referenced incorrectly. Remember that you are applying theory in most cases, which you have gleaned from your textbooks, the theory has not come out of your head, so you must reference appropriately. This means that you must include a bibliography also. It is best to use the Harvard style of referencing, i.e. within the text you would write:

Beamish and Ashford (2004)

If you use a direct quotation in the body of your work you would need to add the appropriate page number to your reference such as

(Beamish and Ashford, 2004, p. 235)

You would then include this in the bibliography at the end as follows:

Beamish, K. and Ashford, R. (2004). *Marketing Planning: CIM Coursebook*, Oxford: Butterworth-Heinemann.

### Report style or layout

Most of the coursework will require you to write in a report format, so you need to ensure that you use a professional format. Therefore you will need to include a title page, contents page, use numbered headings which are underlined and include the bibliography and appendices as appropriate. It is very surprising that many pieces of work suffer from poor and inconsistent layout. You need to ensure that you are referencing appropriately as discussed above. You need to ensure that you are writing in the third person rather than the first (i.e. 'The report will cover ...' rather than 'I will cover ...').

### Use of appropriate examples and application to the case researched

Good work clearly demonstrates knowledge and understanding by referring to appropriate examples to back up your answers. There are usually a high proportion of marks which are available for application of the theory to the organizations researched, therefore you need to ensure that your work is not just theoretical but does relate to the company.

### Study skills in terms of in-depth understanding of the syllabus

It is evident that a number of pieces of coursework are lacking in a number of areas. In some cases, the work seemed to reproduce lecture material rather than answering the question specifically or applying the theory to an example. You should ensure that you are aware of the content of the syllabus. Each piece of coursework details the element of the syllabus which is being tested, so you need to check the syllabus to ensure that you are aware of the area being tested to ensure that you respond accordingly.

### Tutor feedback

Even though you will not be issued with your coursework mark by your tutor (until it has been processed by CIM), you are entitled to feedback from your tutor. You may need to press your tutor for this, but ideally you should receive feedback which will help you to approach your next piece of work with this in mind.

Remember, your tutor marks your work and then it is sent to CIM for moderation at the end of the process in one batch, so your tutor will not know during the programme the exact mark that CIM will issue you to you as CIM may change some of the marks during the moderation process.

### Future coursework approaches

It should be remembered that on many occasions you will be required not only to investigate an organization for the coursework, but you may be required to undertake further research in secondary sources such as market reports (e.g. Mintel, Keynote, etc). Therefore, you should be used to trawling your local or study centre's library (where appropriate) for appropriate sources. The better marks will be awarded for work which illustrates such research (as long as it is appropriate).

You are often required to undertake a micro- and/or macro-environmental analysis. Here, it is expected that you reference your findings relating to the elements of the environment (e.g. reference to political issues from *The Economist*, changes in social trends found in a Mintel report). This will ensure that you are justifying your comments appropriately and you are illustrating to the examiner that you have undertaken appropriate research. Remember you might find a wealth of information from internal reports from your organization. You must remember to reference them and if they are confidential, you must state this on the front of your assignment so that CIM are aware of this.

You will find that there is a range of coursework areas which will come up time and time again. They will be related to the major elements of the syllabus and often cover:

- Marketing planning process
- Budgeting and control issues
- External and internal environmental analysis
- Branding
- Application of the marketing mix
- PLC, NPD and product issues
- Pricing
- Distribution
- Promotions
- Services marketing mix and service quality
- International marketing issues
- Customer relationships.

Much of the coursework will require you to identify the role of marketing planning and/or the concept being tested. Again, you need to ensure that you cover these areas appropriately and include appropriate references.

It is strongly recommended that you should ensure that you read the CIM Senior Examiner's report. There are a high number of candidates who are making some very simple mistakes and it seems clear that they are not aware (or are not taking any notice) of the guidance offered by CIM. Indeed, this section of the book has been written by the CIM Senior Examiner and was written after the first moderation process had taken place for the Marketing Planning coursework.

There is some clear evidence that a number of candidates are relying on the CIM Coursebook as their only source of reading, although this practice, clearly, does not offer enough reading for candidates to pass the coursework. Candidates should consult the CIM reading list and read from the *core texts and trade publications* as well as the Coursebooks.

You should try to develop deep learning rather than a surface learning approach, i.e. do not just learn facts but ensure that you are able to apply them or offer valid examples. This will allow you to analyse the coursework question fully, identify the focus and apply your knowledge to the specific context given.

## Personal development

Completing the coursework may seem to be more time-inefficient than studying for the examinations. This is usually because you will need to physically undertake research, write longer reports than just revising for an examination. However, you should take the opportunity to relate your work to your organization or a company which interests you.

*Appendix 2 Assignment-based assessment*

However, once you have completed this coursework, obviously it is yours to keep, therefore, you could use it to illustrate your studies and development at your performance review or any forthcoming job interviews. Therefore, you may find that although you have put a major amount of effort into the Marketing Planning coursework, there may be more benefits for you than just completing an examination in the subject.

# Professional Diploma assignments – Marketing Planning

Divided into four different elements, the Marketing Planning module covers all the major aspects of marketing. As such, questions can be drawn from a number of different areas. For each of the four elements, a sample question is given together with an evaluation of the type of answer that would be expected at this level.

### An overview of the approach to the Marketing Planning Assignments by the senior assessor – Dr Ruth Ashord

CIM Briefs and Student Work

This section commences with the instructions for the Marketing Planning Assignments, which are issued by CIM, to a CIM centre and then despatched to the candidates wishing to undertake the assessment via coursework. After each question, there is a critique of what is required and a discussion of strengths and weaknesses found in the work from candidates who undertook these assignments.

### Marketing Planning Assignments

There are **THREE** separate elements to the complete assignment, as detailed below:

1. The **Core Section** is compulsory and worth 50 per cent of your total mark.
2. The **Elective Section** has four options from which you must complete **TWO**. EACH of these options is worth 25 per cent of your total mark
3. The rubric will provide clear guidance on the word limits as explained earlier.

*Please Note*: As these assignments have been designed to test the application of knowledge, it will be insufficient to rely on theory alone for your answers. All work should be professionally produced, with arguments presented that are compelling and well reasoned. Any sources of information, definitions, methodologies and applications should be stated.

It is suggested that the answers for all the sections should be based on an organization of your choice, preferably your own, and that you should use the same organization throughout. This will present a more holistic account and involve you in less research.

If you are not in a position to use your own organization, you may use an alternative organization with which you are familiar, but your choice should be made following discussion with your tutor to ensure the best use of your study time.

You should submit your assignment by securing pages in the top left hand corner with a treasury tag – do not use staples as these can come apart. No folders or wallets will be accepted.

The above word-counts are guides only and you will not be penalized if you do exceed this recommendation. However the professionalism of the presentation of your assignment, which includes producing concise and appropriate work, will be taken into consideration.

## Core Section – Using the marketing mix in the public sector – 50 per cent weighting

### Question 1

You have been approached to prepare a report on the use of the extended marketing mix within a public-sector organization. In order to achieve this, you will need to prepare a comparison between for-profit and not-for-profit organizations:

1. Demonstrating the role of marketing, a marketing orientation and
2. Use of the marketing mix. This should be illustrated through examples of how the selected organization can move towards a greater marketing orientation.

*Note*: This is an individual answer; as such the report must be completed individually and not as part of a group.

### Syllabus References
1.1, 1.2, 1.4, 1.5, 3.2, 3.3, 3.5, 3.7, 3.8, 3.9, 3.10, 3.11, 3.12, 3.13, 3.14, 4.1, 4.2

| Assessment Criteria | Marks Available |
|---|---|
| o Selection of appropriate public-sector organization | 4 |
| o Background to marketing and a marketing orientation | 12 |
| o Coverage of the extended marketing mix | 16 |
| o Application to selected organizations | 16 |
| o Presentation, format and tone of report | 2 |
| Total | 50 |

### Question 1

This required candidates to write a formal report based on a number of areas. Therefore, candidates should have included title page and contents pages, covering the areas required. There should have been summary as well as a conclusion and an appropriate academic bibliography and appendices (which are not included in the word count).

The context for this assignment was the public sector however, the assignment called for a comparison between for-profit and not-for-profit. Therefore, candidates should have been able to use their own work experience be it from either of these sectors.

The first section should have been an academic review of the role of marketing and marketing orientation in both sectors. Therefore, the work should have commenced with an introduction of not-for-profit organizations contrasted with profit organizations. Then there could have been specific information about an organization, which had been researched. There were four marks available for the selection of the appropriate public-sector organization.

An academic review of the role of marketing in these sectors should have been offered. Here, academic references should have been used, not only from the recommended textbook, but also from others and marketing journal articles if possible (i.e. *Journal of Marketing Management*) to illustrate reading. This should have been quite analytical, relating the role of marketing in both sectors and critiquing this.

Appendix 2 Assignment-based assessment

The next section should have related to marketing orientation. Here, a brief history could have been included, relating to product and sales orientation. This should also have been applied to the public-sector organization chosen by the candidate, to illustrate understanding. These sections together were worth 12 marks.

The next section required a discussion of the use of the marketing mix for the public-sector organization. Here, an analysis of the extended marketing mix as applied to such an organization was required. Indeed, the question called for examples illustrating how an adaptation of the marketing mix could move the organization towards a greater marketing orientation. The treatment of the distribution element would have been quite important for a public-sector organization. There were 16 marks for the coverage of the extended marketing mix and 16 marks for the application of the marketing mix to the organization.

A solid conclusion should have been included, which summarized the points made and highlighted the main differences between profit and not-for-profit sectors. There were two marks for presentation, format and tone of the report.

## Question 1
### Strengths of candidates' work

Good answers illustrated the adaptation of the marketing mix to examples and illustrated this, i.e. downloading website addresses illustrating the communications messages, etc.
Better answers considered the 7Ps of the extended marketing mix
Good academic referencing illustrating reading in journals
Good structure of the report and diagrams illustrating points made
Good answers illustrated an analysis and comparison between both sectors for each element of the report.

### Weaknesses of candidates' work

Used only one book as a reference throughout
No bibliography included
Did not include any consideration of the concept of marketing orientation
Did not contrast both sectors
Wrote academically only and did not apply the answer
Poor structure and presentation.

## Elective Section – 25 per cent weighting for each of TWO options

You are required to complete TWO of the four options within this section. As previously stated, it will be most beneficial in terms of research etc. if the organization chosen for the Core Section is also used in this section.

## Option – The role and purpose of Marketing Planning – 25 per cent weighting

### Question 2
Your CIM class has been approached to prepare a 20-minute presentation on marketing planning to a local college. They intend to introduce marketing planning into the management of the college, an activity which has not been covered previously.

From the class, you have been selected to prepare this presentation which should include the purpose of marketing planning, its purpose and the need to consider wider changes in the marketing environment.

*Note*: This is an individual question; as such this assignment must be completed individually and not as part of a group. You are NOT required actually to carry out the presentation.

Recommended word count 1,500 words excluding relevant appendices.

## Syllabus References
1.1, 1.2, 1.3, 1.4, 1.5, 2.1, 2.2, 2.3, 2.4, 2.5, 2.6, 2.7, 2.10, 4.1, 4.2

| Assessment Criteria | Marks Available |
| --- | --- |
| o The background to marketing planning and its role within other aspects of planning | 4 |
| o The role and purpose of marketing planning | 10 |
| o The need for clear analysis of the internal and external marketing environment | 10 |
| o Quality and standard of presentation and notes | 1 |
| Total | 25 |

## Question 2

This is the first of the elective assignments. This is an interesting one, as it required candidates to prepare a 20-minute presentation on marketing planning for presentation to a local college.

Here, candidates were really expected to prepare Powerpoint slides which would be appropriate for this presentation. However, more than just the slides was required. Many candidates included the Powerpoint slides and the notes page where they explained what would have been orally presented with the slide.

The actual content of the presentation should have allowed the discussion of the value of marketing planning within a college setting. The answer should have considered the source and benefits of planning, together with an integrated approach to the planning process.

There should have been an introduction or background to marketing planning and its role within other aspects of planning for the college selected. There were four marks available for this.

The next section of the presentation should have considered the role and purpose of marketing planning. This was worth 10 marks.

The presentation should have included the need for clear analysis of the internal and external marketing environment. This was worth 10 marks.

All sections should have been fully justified with academic references and academic models or frameworks.

*Appendix 2 Assignment-based assessment*

**Strengths of candidates' work**

Excellent and well-designed slides with comprehensive additional notes
Good justification for the content of the presentation – i.e. use of academic references or frameworks to underpin issues presented
Good contextualization to a college situation, citing good examples throughout.

**Weaknesses of candidates' work**

Slides only submitted, with no discussion
No academic referencing
Poor layout – i.e. no slides just poor notes submitted
No application to the college scenario.

## Elective Section: OPTION – Briefing on Budgets and Planning Control – 25 per cent weighting

### Question 3

Your Manager has asked you to prepare a set of briefing notes about budgets and their role in marketing planning for use within a range of areas in your organization or an organization of your choice. A range of organizational planning initiatives has been introduced in recent years; however, the effectiveness of these has been limited due to poor budgeting and control.

These should act as a guide to anyone involved in the planning process. In particular, the notes should cover the following aspects:

- The importance of the marketing environment
- The role of budgets and
- The purpose and implementation of control processes.

*Note*: This is an individual question; as such the briefing notes must be completed individually and not as part of a group. Recommended word count 1500 words excluding relevant appendices.

### Syllabus References
1.1, 1.2, 1.3, 1.4, 1.5, 2.1, 2.2, 2.3, 2.4, 2.5, 2.9, 2.10

| Assessment Criteria | Marks Available |
| --- | --- |
| Selection of organization and situation | 2 |
| Coverage of the marketing planning process and application | 4 |
| Analysis of the internal and external marketing environment | 4 |
| Budgeting | 7 |
| Implementation/control aspects | 7 |
| Format and layout of briefing notes | 1 |
| Total | 25 |

## Question 3

This was not a popular question and those who did answer it did not score many marks as most answers were very weak.

The question required the candidate to prepare a set of notes about budgets and the role of budgets in marketing planning for use within a range of areas within their organization. There were two marks for the selection and explanation of the company used in the answer. The question did not state marketing planners and therefore a candidate should not have presumed this.

Broken down, the assignment should have covered the importance of marketing environment and there were four marks available for this. This was quite an easy section.

The second section should have discussed the marketing planning process and the application for the company being discussed. Again, this was just a background piece and was only worth four marks.

The majority of the marks were available for the role of budgeting (seven marks). Here, a discussion of the types of budgets, methods of securing budgets, the reasons for budgeting, etc. should have been discussed and justified using academic references.

The next section should have included the purpose and implementation of control processes within the marketing plan, which should have been linked back to the marketing planning process. Again, academic references should have been used here and this was worth seven marks also.

In essence, this assignment was about role of budgets and control mechanisms within the marketing planning process, however, this was not how it was answered in general.

**Strengths of candidates' work**

> Good format presented
> Academic references underpinning issues raised.

**Weaknesses of candidates' work**

> The majority of the assignments were very poor because the area of budgeting was confined to one or two paragraphs, limited to just stating different methods of budgeting. Some did not even cover or address budgets in any way
> Some answers were not academically justified or contextualized.

## Elective Section: OPTION – Advice on Marketing – 25 per cent weighting

### Question 4

Your section of the company has volunteered to take part in the 'business advice week' for a number of local business start-ups.

As part of your role, you have been asked to advise a new business, dealing in bespoke furniture manufacture, on how they can use customer relationships and other human elements within marketing planning. The organization has developed a marketing plan for use in obtaining a business load; however, few of the proposed actions in the plan have occurred.

*Appendix 2 Assignment-based assessment*

Prior to your advice session you have been asked to prepare a short report to use as a basis for your recommendation. This should identify the need for marketing planning, together with outlining your recommendations for the use of customer relationships and other human elements of the marketing mix. It also needs to be relevant to the situation the organization finds itself in, i.e. that of a new start-up.

*Note*: This is an individual question; as such the report must be completed individually and not as part of a group. Recommended word-count 1500 words excluding relevant appendices.

### Syllabus References
1.1, 1.2, 1.4, 3.11, 3.12, 4.2

### Assessment Criteria                                         Marks Available

- Setting the scene for the advice session                              3
- The role of marketing planning and its use in a range of settings     3
- The role of the marketing mix in marketing planning                   3
- Use of customer relationships within the marketing mix                5
- Use of human elements of marketing mix                                5
- Inclusion of context within report and recommendations                5
- Detail, format and tone of report                                     1

Total                                                                  25

## Question 4

This question was mainly about marketing planning and customer relationships within the marketing mix. There were many sections to this question and, as such, candidates should have ensured that they covered them all. Here, the context was given, i.e. bespoke furniture manufacturer.

The answer should have been brought into the context of a report. In addition this should have identified the role and purpose of customer relationships – drawing them into recommendations.

The answer should have commenced with a discussion or introduction to the advice session which was worth three marks. The next section should have related to the role of marketing planning, especially in this sector. Again, academic references should have been used here to justify the advice offered. This was worth three marks also.

The concept of customer relationships and relationship marketing should have been discussed. Academic frameworks and references here would have helped this section. Some consideration of the real types of customers which this manufacturer would have experiences should have been included. This was worth five marks. This section should have gone on to consider the role of the marketing mix in marketing planning 7Ps should have been discussed (as the people element was specifically requested). This should have been linked to the concept of customer relationships.

A section of the 'people' element of the extended marketing mix was required. Here, the textbooks are rather weak, so further reading and justification was required, along with actual recommendations for the company.

There were five marks available for the inclusion of the context of the furniture manufacturer within the report, therefore, the report should have finished with a section on recommendations for this company.

### Strengths of candidates' work

Some works were very well presented as a well applied report
Good academic references were included, using frameworks from a range of texts and journal articles on relationship marketing
A good section on applied recommendations was included.

### Weaknesses of candidates' work

Poor definition or discussion of the concept of customer relationships
Poor consideration of the people element within the marketing mix
Work not contextualized to the manufacturing organization given in the question.

## Elective Section: OPTION – Re-branding – 25 per cent weighting

### Question 5
You have been given the role of re-branding a product/service of your choice. The brand has been poorly positioned for several years and the re-branding exercise is designed to meet the needs of a new segment of customers. Using both branding and the extended marketing mix, develop and justify your recommendations for this product/service.

*Note*: This is a question answer; as such the question must be completed individually and not as part of a group. Recommended word-count 1500 words excluding relevant appendices.

### Syllabus References
1.5, 3.1, 3.3, 3.4, 3.5, 3.8, 3.9, 3.10, 3.11, 3.12, 3.13, 3.14

| Assessment Criteria | Marks Available |
| --- | --- |
| o   Selection of suitable product and organization | 5 |
| o   Identification and explanation of the role of branding within marketing | 7 |
| o   Brand repositioning | 7 |
| o   The use of the marketing mix within the repositioning process | 5 |
| o   Presentation and format of the answer | 1 |
| Total | 25 |

### Question 5
This question relates to the area of branding and, is a new area of the old Marketing Operations syllabus. As such, it becomes even more important for candidates to understand the concept of branding in greater detail. This question offered the candidate the opportunity to re-think brands which they may have always wanted to change but have never had the chance.

Thus the candidate may select any brand, explaining the current position of the brand. This would form the introduction to the report. The selection of a suitable product and organization was worth five marks and thus a quite important section.

An academic discussion of the role of branding within marketing should have been included. Here, academic references should have been included as there is a vast wealth of literature in this area for both corporate and product brands. This part was worth seven marks.

Appendix 2 Assignment-based assessment

A justification and discussion of the repositioning of the brand identified was required. Here, perception maps should have been discussed to develop the argument. Some candidates may have wished to consider segmentation and targeting recommendations prior to this if a new segment was being considered. This was worth seven marks.

The explanation of the marketing mix to achieve the new brand positioning was required. Certain elements of the marketing mix would have been discussed more fully such as the promotions element, to communicate the new positioning. Again, justification and examples should have been offered in relation to the selected brand. This section was worth five marks.

The question specifically required justification and at this level, it is very important that candidates adhere to this instruction.

**Strengths of candidates' work**

Excellent explanation and illustration of the current brand positioning and good justification for the reposition brand strategy
Good use of academic references to explain the role of branding (at all levels)
Good use of perceptual maps related to the target market requirements were included.

**Weaknesses of candidates' work**

The work was not presented well and illogical in format
Lack of justification throughout
Purely academic piece of work with no real application.

## Conclusion

The clues are in the CIM briefing schedules. When undertaking the assignment, look at the assessment criteria and ensure that you cover all elements! It is disappointing to see the lack of academic references, or perhaps the use of just one or two books in the assignment work. This does not indicate good reading in the area.

Tutors will be able to provide you with suggestions of further reading where required, so take advantage of this.

Remember, these assignments are not just marked by the tutor, but they are sent to CIM and they are moderated, so ensure that if your work is confidential, this is marked clearly and boldly on the front.

This sort of assignment work is a very good method of ensuring that deep learning has taken place and this has to be illustrated within the work. These assignments are not marked as exam papers as they have not been prepared in such a restrictive environment, therefore, assessors are looking for different work as indicated in this section.

# Submission of assignments/integrative project

The following information will aid both yourself, your tutor who marks your work and also the CIM assessor who will be moderating your work and moderating the integrative project. In addition the flow diagram represents the process of an assignment/integrative project from start to final mark.

*Appendix 2 Assignment-based assessment*

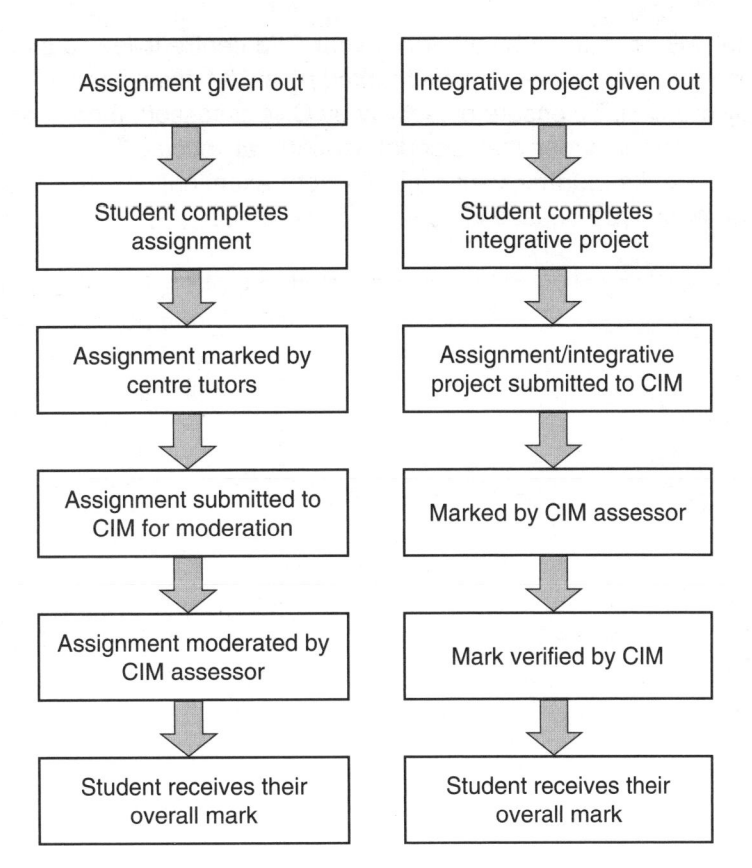

```
Assignment given out              Integrative project given out
          ↓                                   ↓
  Student completes                   Student completes
     assignment                      integrative project
          ↓                                   ↓
  Assignment marked by              Assignment/integrative
     centre tutors                  project submitted to CIM
          ↓                                   ↓
  Assignment submitted to             Marked by CIM assessor
    CIM for moderation
          ↓                                   ↓
  Assignment moderated by             Mark verified by CIM
      CIM assessor
          ↓                                   ↓
   Student receives their            Student receives their
      overall mark                       overall mark
```

*Figure A2.1* The assignment/integrative project process

When completing and submitting assignments or the integrative project, refer to the following for guidance:

- Read through each question before starting out. Particularly with the core question there will be a considerable amount of work to undertake. Choose your optional questions wisely.
- Answer the question set and use the mark guidance given regarding the marking scheme.
- Reference each question within the assignment and use a bibliography.
- Complete all documentation thoroughly. This is designed to aid both the CIM and yourself.
- Ensure that the assignment is bound as per instructions given. Currently assignments are requested not to be submitted in plastic wallets or folders as work can become detached or lost. Following the submission instructions provided aids both CIM administrators and the CIM assessor who will be marking (integrative project) or moderating (assignments) your work.
- Complete the candidate declaration sheet showing that you have undertaken this work yourself. *Please note that if you wish the information contained in your assignment to remain confidential you must state this on the front of the assignment.* Whilst CIM assessors will not use any information pertaining to your or another organization, CIM may wish to use the answer to a question as an example.

*Appendix 2 Assignment-based assessment*

An assignment will be marked by a tutor at your CIM centre followed by moderation by a CIM assessor. The integrative project will be marked by a CIM assessor as per an examination with moderation by the CIM. To ensure objectivity by CIM assessors there exists a mark-in meeting prior to any marking in order that standardization can occur. The senior assessor for each subject also undertakes further verification of both examinations and assessments to ensure parity between each type of assessment.

*Dr Ruth Ashord – Senior Examiner, February 2004*
*Based on the appendix written by David Lane,*
*Former Senior Moderator (Advanced Certificate),*
*February 2003*

# appendix 3
# answers and debriefings

## Unit 1

### Debriefing Question 1.1

Marketing would have been required to define the level of service Egg would be required to offer. They would have been involved in the service development stage, taking Egg as a brand from conception to reality. In order to do this the marketing function would have had to consider the 'people, process and physical' elements of the marketing mix process. This would have been developed in association with the human resources function.

Human resources would have been responsible for considering resource implications, developing appropriate recruitment and selection strategies, enabling training and skills development and assigning the correct personnel to the job in order to achieve high performance levels.

The two functions would need to understand the concepts, the resources, the processes and the physical environment requirements. This could not be achieved while working in isolation or in a vacuum.

Egg's success is clearly as a result of an integrative strategy worked through from the top of the strategy and planning hierarchy down to the bottom. The success for marketing was the rapid rate at which brand recognition grew and the significant number of hits on the websites within a short period of time. Ultimately corporate planning provides focus and direction for the whole organization. It is from here that the infrastructure of the organization to support the corporate requirements is shaped, formed, structured and organized in a way that will ensure ultimate customer satisfaction and high performance and profitability for the organization.

### Debriefing Question 1.2

Specific barriers might include:

- General resistance to restructuring
- Lack of co-operation due to scarce resources
- Breakdown in communication
- Obstructive behaviour
- Political barriers
- Cultural barriers

*Appendix 3 Answers and debriefings*

- Functional barriers – lack of co-operation and agreement among business units
- Employee relations issues
- High turnover of staff
- Political infighting
- Management not prepared to change.

Barriers might be created as a result of:

- Lack of communication (one of the biggest single factors in creating barriers to change)
- Lack of consultation
- Autocratic management style
- Failure to address the resourcing issue, which can force complete lack of co-operation
- Inappropriately skilled staff
- Fear of the unknown
- Unrealistic targets
- Lack of top-down commitment to the planning process.

## Debriefing Activity 1.1

Typical changes might include:

- New information systems
- Restructuring/reorganization
- New management
- New products/service offerings
- *Diversification* – change in direction
- Mergers/acquisitions
- Downsizing.

These are just a few of the modes of change organizations frequently encounter.

Drivers for change might include:

- Efficiency drivers
- Stakeholders
- Competitive forces
- Evolution of information communication technology (ICT)
- External drivers of change
- Political or economic forces.

# Unit 2

## Debriefing Question 2.1

The long-term effect on Exxon of consumer pressure and demonstrations by stakeholder audiences could go two ways:

They will respond to consumer pressure and adhere to the requirements of the Kyoto summit, but they will effectively reduce their bottom line and overall profitability quite significantly. This will bring pressure from shareholders, and will ultimately mean that they will fail to fulfil their long-term profit objectives.

If they fail to respond to consumer pressure, it is likely that consumer pressure will grow, that competitors will take the opportunity to attack Exxon in its moment of weakness and that the results could potentially be catastrophic.

It is likely that whichever way Exxon go, this particular demonstration will do them untold damage in the short to medium term and that a range of marketing and PR activities will be required to start to undertake damage limitation.

## Debriefing Question 2.2

Potential opportunities might include:

- Anti-ageing products
- Provision of nutrients and vitamin supplements
- Provision of food supplements
- Opportunities to provide medical bandages, stockings
- Incontinence pads, etc.

The key to this is that while the example is a healthcare products company, there are so many opportunities available as the demographic trend is that the 'grey market' is living for longer. There are opportunities to provide products that both enhance that life cycle and support it practically.

## Debriefing Question 2.3

A SWOT analysis of your own organization or one you will know well should present many of the components listed within the SWOT analysis grid (Figure 2.4). Clearly recommendations to overcome weakness should highlight a transferring of a weakness into a strength, which would potentially see a change in internal marketing objectives to remedy some of the situations your weaknesses currently present.

For example:

Lack of resources should be converted into a strength, by taking a planned approach to increasing the current resource base, through organizational growth and investment.

Aged technology – this could become a strength again, through planned investment.

Weak supplier relationships can also be converted into a strength, by changing the basis of their agreement, incentivizing them, managing them closely and effectively. Be aware of opposing competitive forces, and divert their attention into alternative areas.

*Appendix 3 Answers and debriefings*

# Unit 3

## Debriefing Question 3.1

SWOT effectively identifies the key components in relation to the internal and external environment.

It draws a substantial amount of the marketing audit together and provides the basis of the decision-making process by giving a clear insight into the dynamics of the marketing environment.

| | |
|---|---|
| Strengths of the organization | What the organization does well |
| Weaknesses of the organization | What the organization could improve |
| Opportunities for exploitation by the organization | Where the organization can go to |
| Threats that face them | The inhibiting factors of growth |

It provides the basis of strategy development and acts as an indicator when establishing market entry strategies, growth strategies, marketing penetration strategies, new product development, etc.

## Debriefing Question 3.2

Some of the key benefits of a gap analysis might include:

- It provides an insight into how much there is to achieve between where the organization is now and where it is going
- It provides an insight into exactly how much marketing activity the organization may need to undertake in order to meet the corporate goals
- It provides the basis for strategy development such as market growth, or market development strategies that might fill the gap
- It will provide the basis on which to consider the resources required in order to fill the gap
- It forces the organization to consider carefully the realism of the objectives it has set, versus what is realistically achievable
- It identifies the potential for competitive activity and being prepared to be proactive in order that the competitor does not fill the gap in place of the organization.

In essence it gives the basis on which to formulate a strategy and develop a planned approach.

## Debriefing Question 3.3

Differentiation is a highly significant way of establishing a long-term competitive advantage, in order to retain market share. Therefore it is essential that the business looks for a number of ways to add value to the product/service offering in a way that makes its offering more attractive than that of its competitors. The value, however, has to be perceived as such by its customers.

Differentiation therefore provides the foundation on which to compete on price, promotions, product benefits and distribution options.

## Debriefing Question 3.4

Benefits of being a market follower are:

- Less perceived risk
- Allowing the leader to make the mistakes
- The organization works on a follower basis, therefore strategies are generally reactive
- Wherever the leader goes you can follow – therefore entry strategies, etc. are usually already defined and the groundwork is done for the follower.

## Debriefing Question 3.5

- Segmentation and targeting are crucial to the success of any organization. It is a necessary process that enables the organization to understand who its customers are, how they buy, what they buy, their lifestyle and their expectations.
- It is important to know where they are, their characteristics, their beliefs and values, in order that you can specifically target their needs and expectations directly through your marketing offering.
- *The benefits are significant.*
- Failure to undertake this activity could be catastrophic as you could lose market share, competitors will move in and attack your inability to target the market specifically and ultimately will erode your competitive advantage in the marketplace.
- Failure to undertake segmentation and targeting will mean that the organization is planning in a vacuum, targeting and positioning to an audience who do not necessarily exist.
- Therefore it is essential that the organization fully researches the market and understands it in order that it can respond to its needs.

## Debriefing Question 3.6

Positioning statements should reflect issues relating to:

- Quality
- Service
- Price
- Accessibility
- Brand image
- Benefits/characteristics.

Think of the perceptual map and how you would explain the positioning of British Airways against Virgin Express – links to quality, price, service, delivery, etc., spring to mind.

## Debriefing Question 3.7

Communications is the vital component of internal marketing. It is the bridge between the organization and its employees. It is the very channel that will not only inform and communicate change, but also the channel that will indicate to the organization the employees' willingness and commitment to change.

Furthermore, communication is a vital component to all members of the organization in order that they understand the vision and mission, and what their responsibility and contribution is towards achieving the corporate goals.

*Appendix 3 Answers and debriefings*

Good internal marketing will erode some of the barriers to the implementation of the marketing plan, in order that effectiveness and efficiency can be achieved.

Communications can act as a motivator to the organization, it can act as a tool that conveys inspiration, encouragement and commitment and leadership.

The list of benefits of communicating internally is endless, but ultimately to achieve organizational success, you need to take the 'internal customer' with you. Therefore communicating values, commitment, vision, empowerment and the mission, effectively and efficiently, proactively, not reactively, might enable a smoother transition to new working practices and processes.

Internal marketing should be targeted and planned in order to gain the most success.

# Unit 4

## Debriefing Question 4.1

Brand loyalty and customer retention are significant priorities of organizations today. It is a known fact that retaining customers is more cost-effective than gaining new ones.

The basis of brand loyalty, therefore, is through market research, aligning and associating your brand, its values and mission, with your customers.

One of the benefits of brand values is that customers will associate them with inbred and inherent values of their own lives and those of the organization. In a business sense these values should be exploited in order to achieve brand loyalty and ultimately develop a brand preference.

Therefore the brand, all that it stands for, image, association, values, assets, should be highly targeted and customer characteristics closely matched.

## Debriefing Question 4.2

Objectives provide definition and direction for the advertising campaign, but they also put into context the marketing strategy and plan in respect of implementation.

Setting of objectives ensures that there is value to the advertising programme, that is measurable, achievable, realistic and timebound.

It is essential that the objectives also relate to other elements of the promotional mix, so that the advertising is relevant and complementary to the promotional mix strategy.

## Debriefing Question 4.3

Advertising acts as a support mechanism for the remainder of the promotional mix, in order to create the awareness, interest, desire. Other elements of the marketing mix might then create the incentive to act, or inducement to adopt, indeed take the decision to purchase.

With more emphasis on direct response advertising, there is perhaps less of a necessity for some other promotional mix activities, but in the main it is helpful to optimize as many tools as possible for reinforcement of the message.

*Appendix 3 Answers and debriefings*

## Debriefing Question 4.4

Typical sales promotional activities from manufacturer to consumer include elements relating to a pull strategy, pulling the products up through the supply chain for adoption and purchase:

- *Encouraging trial* – samples, gifts, trial drives of vehicles – allow customers to decide for themselves.
- *Disseminating information* – information packs on a door-to-door basis, perhaps closely linked with a direct marketing campaign (again utilizing the integrated marketing communications approach).
- *Trading up* – encouraging customers to trade up from their existing models – a typical activity of car manufacturers and white goods manufacturers.

## Debriefing Question 4.5

Typically sales promotion adds value to advertising by providing the incentive to purchase and the response mechanism, to trial, gain more information, increase sales, encourage repeat purchase and for competitive responses to competitive activities.

Advertising therefore creates the awareness; promotion is the means by which customers have the incentive to respond.

## Debriefing Question 4.6

PR complements the promotional mix in a number of ways – these are just some ways to point you in the right direction:

- Creates a broader awareness of the brand and the organization
- Increases coverage to principal events and draws further attention to the corporate brand and profile
- It represents the organization fully in both a negative and positive response to events
- It provides the basis for securing greater awareness of product developments and products launched
- It is a form of advertising
- As a function it might run sales promotion campaigns
- It covers a broader potential audience than perhaps advertising and therefore creates awareness in new markets.

## Debriefing Question 4.7

The promotional mix should take an integrated approach to ensuring successful achievements of the marketing objectives and implementation of the strategy. Therefore, advertising, sales promotions and direct marketing present the opportunity for an awareness-raising, incentive-boosting, informative communications campaign.

As previously suggested, advertising creates the awareness, sales promotion creates the incentive and the direct mail (direct marketing) provides the channel for communication in relation to the promotion, possibly including a voucher.

These three promotional mix mechanisms are very compatible promotional tools.

# Unit 5

## Debriefing Question 5.1

The core of the BMW business is the base-line car for the purpose of this question. To take the product from the core to the augmented product will include the development of a range of added value extra components, such as stereos, car alarms, superior finish, computerized traffic systems, etc.

Augmenting the product provides the manufacturer with an opportunity to differentiate their products, target different groups of customers with the same core model, but with specification differences, to meet the needs of all customers within the appropriate market segments.

## Debriefing Question 5.2

The contents of the briefing should focus on cars, in particular:

- *Vehicle modifications* – including quality, functionality and style
- Differentiation activities, brand and product differentiation
- Potential repositioning or re-branding
- *Increase in promotional activities* – advertising, sales promotions, direct mail
- A range of different pricing strategies, very specifically targeted for maximum effect
- *Increase in competitive activity* – therefore prepared attacks required.

## Debriefing Question 5.3

The BCG matrix is a highly useful tool in ascertaining both the position of products and their competitive positioning in relation to market share, and potential growth opportunities.

In terms of its overall use, it is an extremely useful planning tool, whereby plotting the position of products on the matrix provides you with information to underpin the planning process. Some of the information provided will be:

- Competitive position
- Stage in the PLC
- Potential for growth
- Necessity for deletion
- Level of investment required to sustain market share
- The need for repositioning
- Market development opportunities
- Market penetration strategies.

Level of expected profitability from products.

Appendix 3 Answers and debriefings

All of the above information, in addition to many more elements, will be fed into the marketing audit process, which ultimately feeds into the marketing strategy. At this stage the contribution that the product will make, proposed changes, new product development strategies, modification programmes, etc. will be decided. Therefore BCG is a planning tool to support both strategic level decision-making and future product planning opportunities.

# Unit 6

## Debriefing Question 6.1

The following are some of the key points to be discussed:

- Seasonal variation
- Business market rates
- *Services issues of intangibility* – if the room is not filled on a particular night the income from that room is lost for ever – should a lower price be charged in order that the room might be filled?
- Time influences
- Regional variances
- *Income* – state of economy – boom or bust
- Disposable income levels
- Customer perception
- Competitive activity.

## Debriefing Question 6.2

Justifying the value proposition will be quite a challenge and therefore the following marketing activities could be undertaken – these are only some of the activities you could undertake:

- *Product positioning* – perceptual mapping
- *Brand development* – brand association – establishing brand preference
- *Advertising* – promoting benefits and functionality of the products – creating high levels of awareness
- Market testing
- Trial programmes
- Product differentiation
- Defining tightly targeted groups through the segmentation process
- Establishing quality measures with quality being perceived as a visible component of the purchase
- *Price skimming* – sometimes pricing might justify quality (however this can be precarious overall)
- Competitive positioning
- *Distribution strategies* – availability of product, exclusivity of outlets, etc.

*Appendix 3 Answers and debriefings*

### Debriefing Question 6.3

The overall impact of competitive pricing in the 21st century is:

- Intense rivalry
- Competitor warfare
- Profit margins narrowing
- Price reductions unsustainable in the long term
- Industry infrastructure suffering
- A route to mass unemployment
- Saturated markets
- High levels of innovation to overcome competitiveness
- *Shorter life cycles* – less opportunity for maturity and profit
- High quality/low price.

### Debriefing Question 6.4

It is essential that pricing objectives reflect marketing objectives, in order that the marketing plan can be successfully implemented.

If marketing objectives are based on growth, then pricing objectives have to reflect the ability to achieve growth through appropriate pricing strategies. Similarly, if market penetration is the focus of the marketing strategy, then market penetration activities should be undertaken.

Price will be a key influence in meeting profitability goals (ROI goals) and therefore key influences, costs, and external drivers, combined with the marketing strategy, should shape closely pricing objectives in order for successful execution and implementation of the marketing plan.

## Unit 7

### Debriefing Question 7.1

Changes in lifestyle have impacted upon distribution in some of the following ways:

- Less time/time-starved individuals
- The need for more convenience products
- The necessity to shop out of hours
- More choice and selection in retail outlets
- Shopping is a highly significant leisure activity
- Direct marketing becoming increasingly desirable
- The strength and power of the customer and consumer pull the product to market
- Increasing customer demands
- Customers more clued into value propositions
- Increasing debt
- More flexible payment systems.

## Debriefing Question 7.2

The producer can achieve cost-effectiveness through introducing intermediaries into the channel in the following way. They should be encouraged to facilitate, undertake logistical management and provide transactional management.

Incentivizing organizations to undertake this level of activity, i.e. through promotional support, merchandising support, profit share, etc., can cost significantly less than resourcing and managing the following functions:

| | |
|---|---|
| Marketing information | Analyse information such as sales data. Carry out research studies |
| Marketing management | Establish objectives, plan activities and manage, co-ordinate financing, risk-taking. Evaluate channel activities |
| Facilitating exchange | Choose and stock products that match buyers' needs |
| Promotion | Set promotional objectives, co-ordinate advertising, personal selling, promotions, etc. |
| Price | Establish pricing policies, terms and sales |
| Physical distribution | Manage transport, warehousing, materials handling, stock control and communication |
| Customer service | Provide channels for advice, technical support, after-sales service and warranties |
| Relationships | Facilitate communication, products, parts, credit control, etc. Maintain relationships between manufacturer and retail outlets, and customer/consumer |

## Debriefing Question 7.3

The basis of your decision and justification should include the following points:

It is likely that this will be the basis of selective distribution in the medium term. While palm-tops are highly popular, the diffusion process is relatively slow with the overall prices still being moderately expensive. Therefore, costs of associated valued-added components are also relatively high at this stage.

The concept of palm-tops and portable keyboards is excellent, but again diffusion will be slow.

Currently this product is not widely available and while it is not sufficiently exclusive to fall under 'exclusive distribution', it is nowhere near a mass market, low price product.

In terms of market segmentation and targeting, the likely contenders for the use of this product will be Bs and C1, middle, junior and supervisory managers.

Essentially the uses of these products and the associated technicalities of using palm-tops will require some level of technical support and know-how, which would not typically match against the requirements of an intensive distribution strategy.

## Debriefing Question 7.4

Disintermediation refers to the process of selling directly between the organization and the customer, without the assistance of traditional intermediaries and more in line with the association of cybermediaries.

*Appendix 3 Answers and debriefings*

The benefits of this method of selling, as in the case of companies such as mytravelLite.com, are that the cost of physical and human resources are considerably reduced and the need for significant building of bricks and mortar is less likely.

It speeds up the process of transaction considerably, it closes a sale more effectively, and it provides growth opportunities and cost reductions.

The cost of marketing activities is reduced and the necessity for marketing support to intermediaries will cease to exist.

The process of disintermediation may bring the producer/supplier much closer to their customers. In doing this, with the electronic footprint method of collecting information on an underpinning database, the organization can potentially get much closer to targeting specific customer needs and expectation.

# Unit 8

## Debriefing Question 8.1

You will very likely be surprised at the extent of relationships that you are currently involved in within the workplace, however the challenge will be to manage them successfully in the true context of relationship marketing.

## Debriefing Question 8.2

Highly motivated personnel are an essential ingredient and should be developed by the organization in order that their skills and abilities are optimized, particularly as they are the frontline people with whom customers actually interact.

Their ability to help, support, guide and service will hopefully turn them from customer into client, client into advocate and advocate into partner, and will be crucial to the achievement of customer loyalty and customer retention within the organization.

# Unit 9

## Debriefing Question 9.1

As this question is based upon a country of your choice you should identify key differences such as

- Religion
- Education
- Place of women in society
- Work ethics
- Social behaviour

- Leisure persuits
- Language barriers
- Values
- Political affinity.

Look at the cultural framework in Figure 9.1 and identify at least two possible options of cultural diversity and discuss them.

## Debriefing Question 9.2

The Internet will aid trade in some of the following ways:

- Opening up more markets
- Reducing barriers to entry on a country-by-country basis
- Make companies more competitive
- Cost-effective
- Reduces the need for high investment in marketing
- Creates opportunities to establish a more direct relationship with the customer
- Potentially a less risky venture, depending upon the distribution channel
- Reduces the implications of channel management
- Price-competitive and price-sensitive
- Enables fast response times to transactions
- No time barriers.

The list could go on – see how many more you can get.

## Debriefing Question 9.3

The implications for collecting primary data from lesser developed countries:

- Very expensive
- Not easily accessible
- Language barriers
- Terminology
- Geographic diversity within the host country
- Cultural differences
- Reliability and bias in the data collection
- Lack of response (non-response).

## Debriefing Question 9.4

International marketing is an overall strategy that initiates international trade from a strategic level. The process of international marketing then devises appropriate marketing strategies based upon robust market research.

Export marketing is a distribution option available to the organization, i.e. as opposed to actually having bricks and mortar in a country, exporting is an alternative channel option.

*Appendix 3 Answers and debriefings*

### Debriefing Question 9.5

*Economic* indicators would include the ability to afford the product being produced

- The exchange rate
- Cost of development in international markets
- *Technology* – costs of implementing appropriate levels of economy
- Market share
- Disposable income
- Per capita income
- Cost of raw materials
- Availability of raw materials
- *Environmental* – Kyoto Agreement and other similar agreements in relation to the use and disposal of materials and chemicals
- Packaging
- Transportation restrictions
- Positioning of plant in respect of environmentally friendly zones.

These are just an example of some of the possible answers you might come up with.

# Unit 10

### Debriefing Question 10.1

The following activities are likely:

- Once the original interest had been registered by the buyer, it is likely that the consultancy would spend some time understanding the nature and complexity of the project – highlighting that this will likely be a high involvement sale.

The process might include some of the following as an illustration of high-level involvement:

- The consultancy would then spend some time drawing up provisional specifications in consultation with the buyer, prior to entering the formal tendering process.
- This would involve further meetings, references and information being provided by both organizations, in order to gain a mutual understanding of the situation.
- The consultancy is likely to be one of many involved within the tendering process, therefore it will be essential that they understand the full details of the requirements before proceeding to tender.
- It is likely that the tenderer will work on partnership arrangements with contractors in order to actually be able to fully price the work, estimate lead times, and draw up resource specifications that will deliver the technical support.

### Debriefing Question 10.2

Typical differences will include:

- The consumer process could be more impulsive
- Individual decisions can be made without reference to others
- Complexity of the purchase is less

- Number of decision-makers may be one or even a family of four – but not a huge team of decision-makers
- Purchaser is the person who pays for the product
- The user is probably the same person, or passes it on as a gift to the end-user or consumer
- *The influencer* – this will vary, but will relate to cultural, social and personal influences rather than organizational.

## Debriefing Question 10.3

Establishing sound and robust relationships with buyers is essential in order to achieve some of the following:

- Gain preferred supplier status
- Gain trust
- Collaborate and establish partnership agreements that are mutually beneficial
- Flexibility
- Respect, honesty
- A stronger likelihood of quality and delivery.

## Debriefing Question 10.4

Customer uncertainty relates to the gap between understanding the customer and their expectation and what the service deliverer actually provides.

The gap, so to speak, can cause a range of different behaviours in the customer as a result of the gap in delivery and their expectation, and thus highlight 'customer uncertainty' in respect of what they have received, as opposed to what they expected.

## Debriefing Question 10.5

The additional 3Ps of the marketing mix are an imperative in order to enable the successful execution of the services marketing campaign. The original 4Ps of the marketing mix fail to take into account the service deliverables, i.e. the people, the processes and, where appropriate, the physical evidence. As services are very people-oriented, these mix elements need to be introduced.

They are vital to enabling service delivery, service success, and give a basis on which to develop a service-based strategy.

However, the 4Ps do have a function, indeed the elements are complementary to the 3Ps in order that the mix may be priced, promoted and delivered.

## Debriefing Question 10.6

The basis of evaluation of services delivery could be along the lines of the following points. These are some suggestions that you might find consolidate your learning:

- To ensure that quality delivery is taking place
- To identify the gaps in delivery performance and delivery goals
- To identify the gap in expectations between the consumer and the delivery
- To be able to implement a programme of continuous improvement

*Appendix 3 Answers and debriefings*

- To ensure that quality prevails as a core denominator in the programme
- To ensure that customer uncertainties do not continue to arise and that the perception gap is filled
- To be a learning organization
- To understand customer dissatisfaction
- To ascertain levels of satisfaction
- To ensure that the design criteria were successful
- To measure the effectiveness of administrative and peripheral elements of the services mix.

# Unit 11

## Debriefing Question 11.1

Three methods of gaining funds for charitable donations might include some of the following:

- Charitable event organization
- Door-to-door collections
- Selling of merchandise
- Internet
- *Major appeals* – Red Nose – Children in Need
- Sponsorship of participants in major events (London Marathon)
- Corporate sponsorship
- Corporate donations
- Bequests from wills.

## Debriefing Question 11.2

Targeting for Charities

- *Target donors* – This is in order to continually remind them of the need for their donations; they are in the main the backbone of the financial support needed in order that the charitable objectives can be achieved.
- *Target volunteers* – In order that fund allocations can be maximized, charitable work is therefore carried out by volunteers. The more volunteers, the less funds are committed to the running costs of the charities.
- *Clients/users* – They are targeted in order that the organization can carry out their works to a target audience who need their services, their support and their financial contributions. Therefore clients might be homeless, disabled, suffer from MS, starving, blind, to name but a few. They need to be aware that there are resources available to make their life easier.

## Debriefing Question 11.3

Not-for-profit organizations differ from commercial organizations in the following ways:

- Not-for-profit, means profit is not the focus of their business, however income generation is
- Objectives will be based around making people's lives better, rather than making money to benefit shareholders and the board
- Highly accountable to their members and donors

- Less resources available to do the job well
- Target market very broadly based (geographically diverse and culturally diverse nations)
- Measurement and control less easy to implement and monitor
- The nature of the marketing audit will focus on very specific areas
- Heavy reliance on stakeholders
- Donors give money for nothing in return, rather than receive anything for their contribution.

## Debriefing Question 11.4

You should be thinking along the following lines.

An advertising agency would be inappropriate for the following reasons:

- Too costly, this might be an inappropriate use of funds – agency costs historically high
- Work can be done by professional volunteers without a fee attached
- Agencies would need to understand the nature and culture of charities, this could be time-consuming and possibly not achievable
- Charity work is capable of achieving its own publicity, and can be managed in-house more satisfactorily overall.

# appendix 4
# sample exam questions and answers

## ELEMENT 1 (15 per cent of syllabus)

### The marketing plan in its organizational and wider marketing context

**Questions/Tasks**
1. Explain the other business functions other than marketing which contribute towards satisfying customer needs and wants.
2. Evaluate the role of the marketing plan in relation to an organization's business definition.
3. Explain the synergistic planning process, which the organization will need to consider when developing the marketing plan for new products.
4. Explain the components of the marketing plan.
5. Consider an organization of your choice, explain how this organization demonstrates its corporate and social responsibility.
6. Explain the potential impact of wider macro-environmental forces on the business, such as ethical and social responsibility issues.
7. Evaluate the role of the marketing plan in relation to the company's business definition.
8. Discuss the strategic elements of the marketing plan and explain how this impacts on the marketing mix at an operational level.

## ELEMENT 1 (15 per cent of syllabus)

### The marketing plan in its organizational and wider marketing context

**Answers**
1. **Explain the other business functions other than marketing which contribute towards satisfying customer needs and wants.**

This question requires you to consider the different business functions and consider their contribution to the marketing function. Therefore you will need to consider: finance, purchasing, production, research and human resources or personnel.

*Finance* – sets budgets, considers requirements for the organization from a financial perspective and objectives. In terms of credit (where customers come into contact with the finance function) this needs to be considered from a customer's perspective and the integration with the marketing objectives.

*Appendix 4 Sample exam questions and answers*

*Purchasing and logistics* – this focuses on economic purchase quantities, standardization and the price of materials and considers the organization's objectives in terms of purchasing as infrequently as possible which can reduce flexibility and responsiveness. Therefore the marketing philosophy needs to be considered and the relationship marketing approach has a major impact on purchasing in terms of working more closely with the marketing function to offer good levels of service, etc.

*Production* – the objectives for this function are usually to operate long and large production runs with few variations. However, this may be in conflict with the marketing requirements where particularly for b2b customers, further customization is required to meet needs.

*Research and development* – here, usually long lead times are required to allow further development and testing. However, marketing usually wants to be the first to market and cut back the development time required. Also in some cases the R&D becomes very product orientated instead of customer-orientated and this is a constant consideration of the marketing function.

*Human resource management* – again, especially for service organizations the human element of the service delivery from a marketing perspective is essential. However, the objectives of the HR function may be to reduce man-hours and increase automation, which could have a detrimental impact on the service provision. Thus, again there is often a conflict between these functions, where marketing identifies the requirements for a quality service provision but the HR budget will not be adequate to provide the resources required by the marketing function.

2. **Evaluate the role of the marketing plan in relation to an organization's business definition.**

This question requires an answer which considers an understanding of marketing philosophy. Thus the answer would need to consider the aim of marketing planning linked to customer focus to achieve marketing orientation or philosophy. Some emphasis on the contrast with product and sales orientation and focus. The implications for marketers would need to be debated such as anticipating and satisfying current and future customer needs and wants. The consideration of service quality should also be debated as customers often are selling on to final consumers (b2b).

3. **Explain the synergistic planning process, which the organization will need to consider when developing the marketing plan for new products.**

This question requires some discussion and explanation of marketing planning in terms of analysis, planning, implementation and control. A discussion of the synergistic approach to marketing planning should identify the feedback and links to the continuous planning cycle and the importance of this.

The synergistic approach could be considered by addressing the following. The elements of analysis including the macro- and micro-environmental scanning and the internal marketing audit, results in the development of the SWOT analysis. This informs the marketing objectives in relation to the current capabilities and the current situation. Thus, the marketing objectives inform the strategy to be adopted within the marketing plan, including segmentation, targeting and positioning. The corporate plan will have informed some of the strategic decisions which the organization will have decided upon, such as product development or market leader approach in terms of the organization's strategic intent. The marketing decisions in relation to the operationalizing of the strategy will involve a consideration of the organization's capabilities and corporate objectives. The control and evaluation of the marketing plan will be an important activity and should be ongoing. This should lead to feedback into the planning process and allow the plan to be adapted if necessary.

*Appendix 4 Sample exam questions and answers*

The following framework illustrates the links between the marketing plan and the corporate plan, illustrating the synergistic approach.

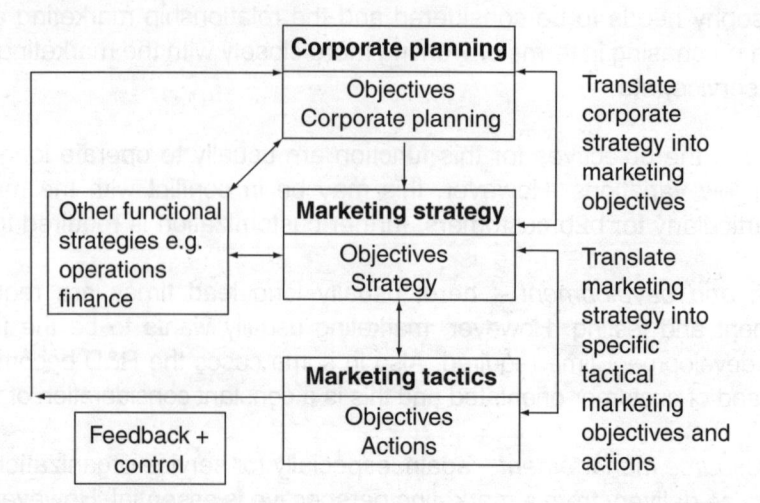

*Figure A4.1 Marketing planning*
*Source*: Drummond, G. and Ensor, J. and Ashford, R., 2003

### 4. Explain the components of the marketing plan.

This requires a good understanding of each of the components of the marketing plan and should also consider the steps involved in developing such a plan.

Marketing plan components:

- *Corporate objectives/business mission* – These come from the corporate plan and inform the direction and focus of the marketing plan. These could be linked to market leadership and financial objectives for the organization.
- *Marketing audit* – External macro and micro analysis and the internal analysis. Here the analysis tools are used such as PESTEL, Porter's Five Force analysis, gap analysis, BCG matrix, GE matrix etc. An understanding of the internal and external environment which is required to inform the marketing plan.
- *SWOT analysis* – This is prioritized to illustrate the summary of the marketing audit and indicate the key issues which need then to be considered further.
- *Business objectives* – these are taken from the business plan
- *Marketing objectives* – The marketing objectives are likely to be linked to market share or sales targets. Long, medium and short-term objectives should be identified and some of which should be SMART.
- *Marketing strategies* – should be identified here. Again, analysis tools could be used to help decide on objectives such as BCG matrix illustrating current and desired positions. The Ansoff growth matrix will offer guidance for the consideration of strategic options such as market penetration, product development etc. Porter's generic strategies are likely to have been considered at the corporate level but could be considered here also.
- *Segmentation* – targeting and positioning – the key area in the strategic section of the marketing plan will consider these issues. The corporate plan may indicate the markets in which the company will operate, but the marketing plan will consider the segmentation strategy, targeting and resulting positioning strategy. This will be linked to the branding decisions.
- *Marketing mix decisions* – The strategy will inform the decisions in relation to pricing, product, place and extended Ps – people, process and physical evidence. Here, the marketing communications plan will be developed.

- *Budget decisions* – will need to be taken throughout the strategic and operational areas of the plan. The methods of determining the marketing plan will be considered.
- *Monitoring and control* – The plan will need to identify the methods of monitoring and evaluating the plan. These methods will need then to be applied and the evaluation will lead into the next planning phase.

**5. Consider an organization of your choice, explain how this organization demonstrates its corporate and social responsibility.**

This question would require an answer which addresses the concept of corporate and social responsibility and apply it to an organization. Thus the answer would consider that there are a number of issues which marketers must understand when considering their role. Marketers are much more aware of their responsibility towards society in terms of moral and ethical responsibilities of business. The recognition of the social and environmental impact of marketing must be appreciated, such as economic, legal and, importantly, ethical concerns.

Society has become more concerned about factors such as the environment and safety issues, which have grown out of consumerism and green marketing issues. Consumers are demanding and getting healthier and safer products from marketers. Many organizations today are considering the corporate and social responsibility (CSR) programmes, which are often linked to the corporate reputation. Thus, in reality, CSR programmes are often managed by the corporate communications or public relations function within an organization.

**6. Explain the potential impact of wider macro-environmental forces on the business, such as ethical and social responsibility issues.**

This question requires an answer which is a little fuller than the previous one. The answer would consider other issues such as culture and ethics. Ethics should be considered from business ethics and personal ethics.

Business ethics should consider issues related to global sourcing issues (such as chosen suppliers, labour prices, etc.), international marketing issues (chosen markets and ethical behaviour) and market research issues (in gathering and using data for marketing purposes). Personal ethics include issues connected to bribery and participation in unethical practices such as working conditions etc.

Further issues such as corporate responsibility in relation to animal welfare, health and safety and environmental issues such as product content and disposal would also need to be debated.

**7. Evaluate the role of the marketing plan in relation to the company's business definition.**

The answer here should consider the aim of marketing planning linked to customer focus to achieve marketing orientation or philosophy. This should be contrasted with product and sales orientation and focus. Further implications for marketers should be considered such as anticipating and satisfying current and future customer needs and wants. Some thought about the consideration of service quality as customers often are selling on to further consumers in a business-to-business context.

**8. Discuss the strategic elements of the marketing plan and explain how this impacts on the marketing mix at an operational level.**

The strategic elements of the marketing plan will consider the segmentation, targeting and positioning decisions. This will be very much linked to the branding decisions and thus, in turn, to the product, pricing, promotional and distribution decisions in order to communicate a distinctive and differentiated positioning for the product/service.

The consideration of growth strategies will also have an impact on the marketing mix decisions. For example, the decision to concentrate on a market penetration strategy will mean that there will be an emphasis on trying to build further relationships with current customers to entice them to purchase more frequently or in larger quantities. Thus loyalty programmes will need to be devised and promotions considered achieving this objective. There will also be a focus on trying to entice competitor's customers to purchase the organization's products or services. Thus again, this will have major ramifications for the promotional/communications plan where messages will need to concentrate on certain benefits derived from the product and promotions to encourage trial will need to be devised.

## ELEMENT 2 (20 per cent of syllabus)

### Marketing planning and budgeting

#### Questions/Tasks

1. Explain environmental scanning and discuss why it is important for marketing planners to undertake such an audit.
2. Explain the potential problems of undertaking an environmental audit.
3. Identify why the BCG matrix is often used in portfolio planning.
4. Why might the BCG matrix be criticized as a marketing management tool?
5. Identify the elements of a PESTEL and SWOT analysis and explain their importance for marketing planning purposes.
6. Explain the concept of 'gap analysis' as used in marketing planning.
7. With reference to appropriate theory, recommend how such a 'gap' could be filled by an organization.
8. Explain and evaluate the different approaches for setting the marketing budget for the mix decisions included in the marketing plan.
9. Recommend methods for evaluating and controlling the marketing plan for an FMCG brand.
10. An organization has indicated that it intends to identify more domestic and international segments to target when planning its market development strategy. Evaluate the concept of segmentation and targeting, including the benefits of segmentation.
11. Recommend how the following variables for segmentation could be used for a product of your choice:
    lifestyle
    benefits sought

## ELEMENT 2 (20 per cent of syllabus)

### Marketing planning and budgeting

#### Answers

1. **Explain environmental scanning and discuss why it is important for marketing planners to undertake such an audit.**

The question requires an answer which illustrates a good understanding of the element of the macro and micro environment and importance of undertaking continuous research to identify the implications from the analysis. The macro environment considers the uncontrollable PESTEL players in the environment. The micro environment comprises customers/buyers, suppliers and competitors (Porter's Five Forces analysis could be undertaken here).

Environmental scanning, which is the systematic collection and evaluation of information from the wider marketing environment which might affect the organization and its strategic marketing activities, is undertaken by marketing planners. Of course, it is also very important for public relations and reputation management, where environmental scanning is considered more from a media perspective and it is undertaken on a daily basis.

The approach to scanning can vary from being very well organized and purposeful to being informal and random. However, it is very important, albeit difficult, as marketers need to be aware of changes in the environment which could have an impact on either their markets, customers, suppliers and competitors. Although the players in the environment are out of the control of the organization, understanding what is happening in the environment offers the organization opportunity to respond appropriately. If this sort of analysis is not being undertaken on a regular basis, the organization will be very slow to react to changes in the environment as they will not be aware of them until it has a major impact on the organization's commercial activities.

### 2. Explain the potential problems of undertaking an environmental audit.

The question requires an answer which illustrates good understanding in the area, illustrating critical thought and analysis. The key problems of undertaking an environmental audit are:

- *Access/difficulty of gathering up-to-date data* – this is often difficult in certain countries where information may be thin on the ground or unreliable.
- *Currency of data* – some published data may not be as current as required in a particular situation.
- *Ability to analyse the data meaningfully* – again, often it is difficult to undertaken good analysis from data gathered from many sources. Sometimes an overload of data makes the task impossible.
- *Data not being specific enough for the business* – often the data gathered are not related specifically to the requirements of the organization and thus poor information may lead to poor decisions being made.
- *Expense* – it is costly to undertake research on a regular basis and thus some organizations suffer from a lack of research and analysis of the environment because they feel it is too expensive to undertake.
- *Frequency of data collection* – this is a difficult area for most organizations in determining how often to undertake such scanning and meaningfully analyse it.

### 3. Identify why the BCG matrix is often used in portfolio planning.

This question requires an understanding of how the BCG (or Boston) matrix can be used as an analysis tool. The BCG matrix classifies products or strategic business units on the basis of their market share relative to that of their competitors and according to the rate of growth in the market as a whole. The matrix is divided into four sections with 'Cash Cows' having high market share but in low growth markets, 'Stars' which are products enjoying high market share in a high growth market, 'Question Marks' being products with low market share but in a growing market and 'Dog' products which have low market share in low growth markets. The split on the horizontal axis is based on a market share identical to that of the firm's nearest competitor.

Products are positioned in the matrix as circles with a diameter proportional to their sales revenue. Forecast sales figures are also plotted for each product, which will indicate the potential movement of the product on the matrix. It is then possible to see clearly, in a diagrammatic form, the portfolio

*Appendix 4 Sample exam questions and answers*

of products or businesses and make strategic decisions about them. Each company looks for a balanced portfolio of products, which can easily be recognizable using a Boston matrix, rather than a sheet of pure figures – thus this tool is often used within organizations. However, there are a number of problems using this type of analysis tool as it only concentrates on two elements (market growth and share) – which may not be important in a particular situation.

**4. Why might the BCG matrix be criticized as a marketing management tool?**

This question really follows on from the previous one. A good start would be to explain the Boston matrix, but as this is explained above, this answer will concentrate on just the points relating to the criticisms of the tool. The main criticisms of this concept are as follows:

1. This matrix oversimplifies product analysis and relies on two variables only – market share and market growth
2. Often it is difficult to identify the actual 'market' in which the rate of growth is measured
3. There is an assumption about profitability and market share which may not be the case for all industries
4. The exact information about the nearest competitor may not be accessible.

**5. Identify the elements of a PESTEL and SWOT analysis and explain their importance for marketing planning purposes.**

This question requires an answer which illustrates good understanding of these two analysis tools and thus they need to be explained.

It is important that marketing managers are able to understand the environment in which they are operating. This means that a systematic PESTEL analysis will need to be undertaken on a regular basis. The PESTEL analysis includes:

- Political factors such as changes in government and the ramifications of their strategies such as tax levels, pollution policies, education issues, etc.
- Economic factors such as the impact of the trade cycle, disposable income, inflation, etc.
- Social/cultural issues such as the ageing consumer, increases in one-parent families, changing values, attitudes and beliefs – to smoking for example.
- Technological factors such as the increased rate of computer capability, production methods, etc.
- *Environmental issues* – such as attitudes towards pollution, energy use, etc.
- *Legal issues* – such as changes in advertising legislation for tobacco, regulations and codes of practice for promotions, etc.

The environmental scanning or PESTEL analysis should help to identify the opportunities and strengths of an organization and its products/services. It is also important that a SWOT analysis is undertaken to help plan the marketing mix, which includes:

- Strengths of the product/service/organization
- Weaknesses of the organization
- Opportunities available to the organization (external factors)
- Threats which may come from the competition or other external factors.

This analysis helps the marketer understand the environment in which the organization is operating and thus the marketing plan can be devised taking account of the issues identified.

### 6. Explain the concept of 'gap analysis' as used in marketing planning.

Malcolm McDonald in *Marketing Plans That Work* (Butterworth-Heinemann, 1997) states the following: 'Gap analysis states that if the corporate sales and financial objectives are greater than the current long-range forecasts, there is a gap which has to be filled' (p. 89). Therefore, this indicates that gap analysis is something which marketing managers need to monitor and consider in terms of filling the gap should one occur.

A gap is where corporate sales and financial objectives are greater than the current long-range forecasts in marketing planning. Gaps can be either operational gaps or new strategies gaps.

### 7. With reference to appropriate theory, recommend how such a 'gap' could be filled by an organization.

In general the methods for filling the gap relates to considering more appropriate objectives, productivity or growth strategies.

The operations gap can be reduced or filled in two main ways:

1. *Operations Gap*

This can be filled by improving an organization's productivity. This could be by reducing costs, consideration of an improved sales mix, or by increasing prices if the product or market will bear this. If improved productivity is one method by which the expansion gap is to be filled, care must be taken not to take measures such as to reduce marketing costs by 20 per cent overall. The portfolio analysis undertaken during the marketing audit stage will indicate that this would be totally inappropriate to some product/market areas, for which increased marketing expenditure may be needed, while for others 20 per cent reduction in marketing costs may not be sufficient.

Another most effective method is by introducing market penetration via stimulating increased usage and increasing market share. Market penetration should always be a company's first option, as it is less risky. This could be done quite quickly by concentrating on loyalty schemes for existing customers of dried food, encouraging customer retention and increasing communications such as sales promotion for large orders. It makes more sense in many cases to move along the horizontal axis for further growth before attempting to find new markets. The reason for this is that it normally takes many years for a company to get to know its customers/markets, and build up a reputation.

2. *New Strategies Gap*

This can be filled by reducing the marketing objectives. This is quite radical, but realistic. A further method is by undertaking market extension or market development – e.g. find new user groups, enter new segments, geographical expansion, i.e. rather than concentrating on dried fruit for baking purposes, the company could consider dried fruit for handy snacks such as lunch pack boxes of raisins or speciality goods. Other strategies are considering product development and/or diversification – e.g. selling new product to new markets. For example here, enter the dried food markets for animal food rather than human food.

The marketing audit should ensure that the method chosen to fill the gap is consistent with the company's capabilities and builds on its strengths. For example, it would normally prove far less profitable for a dry goods grocery manufacturer to introduce frozen foods than to add another dry foods product. Likewise, if a product could be sold to existing channels using the existing sales force, this is far less risky than introducing a new product that requires new channels and new selling skills.

*Appendix 4 Sample exam questions and answers*

8. **Explain and evaluate the different approaches for setting the marketing budget for the mix decisions included in the marketing plan.**

   This question requires an answer which considers a range of different approaches towards budgeting. Critical review of each method would be required.

   One of the easiest approaches to setting the budget is by considering the precedent, historic and incrementalism methods.

   Calculation models for setting the marketing budget include rule of thumb; affordability; maintaining a share of industry spend; maintaining parity with the competition; objective and task approach or output budgeting.

   Further thoughts on budget setting include the experiential approach, i.e. 'suck it and see'.

   However, in reality, most budgets are not really calculated, they tend to be set by negotiation. Organizations must consider either the bottom-up budgeting approach – initiative lies at the product management level and resource demands are pushed up through the organization – or the top-down budgeting approach which involves greater control by top management.

9. **Recommend methods for evaluating and controlling the marketing plan for a brand.**

   This question calls for an understanding of the methods used for evaluating marketing plans. This is often a neglected area of the syllabus and not fully covered in many text books. Thus further reading should be considered.

   There are four main areas where control mechanisms should be considered within the marketing plan, i.e. management control, financial control, efficiency control and strategic control.

   - *Management control* – This includes areas such as performance appraisal for staff and the workforce, benchmarking procedures, etc. against other organizations.
   - *Financial control* – This includes financial controls which most companies are adept at calculating. It could include trend analysis, comparison, liquidity ratios, debt ratios, activity ratios, etc.
   - *Efficiency control* – Here, this area considers the optimum value from marketing assets.
   - *Strategic control* – The easiest method of control is to measure marketing activities against market performance or objectives set.

10. **An organization has indicated that it intends to identify more domestic and international segments to target when planning its market development strategy. Evaluate the concept of segmentation and targeting, including the benefits of segmentation.**

    This question demands a range of knowledge relating to a number of concepts and thus all elements of the question: i.e. segmentation, targeting and positioning and benefits of segmentation, need to be answered.

    Segmentation is a way of sub-dividing a market into homogenous sub-groups that can be targeted with a specific marketing mix and in order to be able to target customers more specifically and understand their needs and motivations.

Philip Kotler (*Marketing Management*, Prentice Hall, 1997) identified the following stages, which also illustrate the importance of segmentation to the positioning of the product:

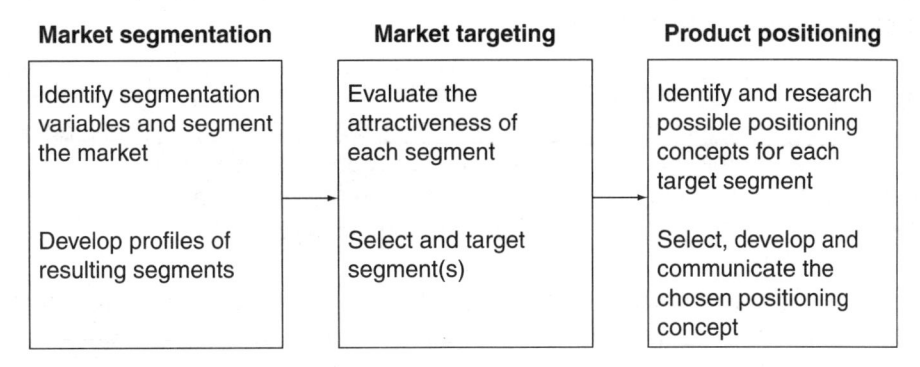

| Market segmentation | Market targeting | Product positioning |
|---|---|---|
| Identify segmentation variables and segment the market | Evaluate the attractiveness of each segment | Identify and research possible positioning concepts for each target segment |
| Develop profiles of resulting segments | Select and target segment(s) | Select, develop and communicate the chosen positioning concept |

*Figure A4.2* Segmentation, targeting and positioning

## Explanation of segmentation, targeting and links to positioning

There are a number of methods which can be used to segment consumers or buyers; demographics, geographics, psychographics and through behaviour segments.

- *Demographic segmentation* – This method would enable the company to see the population characteristics of their buyers. This method uses age and gender as the main indicators. The company would be able to use this information to determine how old their buyers were and if certain drinks appealed more to male or female buyers.
- *Geographic segmentation* – This would help the company to determine where the major retailers were based geographically, i.e. north/south domestic market, and the international market. This is important as certain countries may require different formulas because of different taste requirements.
- *Psychographic segmentation* – This type of segmentation gives a picture of the social class, standing, characteristics, income and education levels of buyers. It will help to build a profile of what they are likely to be interested in, know about and care about and link to their lifestyle. This is one of the most useful forms of segmentation as it uses a range of information.

However for a market segmentation strategy to succeed the market needs to be measurable, accessible and substantial enough to make the desired profits and be a distinct group with their own attitudes, beliefs and behaviours.

## Targeting

There are three main concepts involving the adaptation of the marketing mix (price, product, place and promotion) when targeting each segment. They are:

- *Undifferentiated targeting* – Using one marketing mix to target all segments of the market. This is not a very customer-orientated method.
- *Differentiated targeting* – Use a few different marketing mixes for a couple of main segments of the market.
- *Concentrated targeting* – Use one specific marketing mix for each segment of the market – e.g. specific marketing mix for the health drinks market.

## Positioning

Although the question has not specifically requested comments about positioning, it is important to discuss positioning briefly.

Having identified an appropriate target market for the drinks range, the company will need to develop a marketing mix to fit a given place in our customer or consumer's mind. Using marketing research, the position of competitor's products should be identified for the segment which is to be targeted, and this will indicate gaps in the market and help to determine how to position the new drinks range in the most favourable way.

A range of perceptual maps are used to map customer's perceptions (using variables which are important to the target market) of the competitor's products and thus determine the positioning of the new drinks range.

## Benefits of segmentation

The growth of specialized segments in a market has resulted in firms producing goods and services that are more closely related to the requirements of particular kinds of customers. Instead of treating customers as the same, companies have identified sub-groups of customers whose precise needs can be more effectively met with a targeted approach.

The marketing mix can be tuned more precisely and thus the pricing, distribution, product and communications policies should relate to the target customer more specifically.

Segmentation can help the company achieve a better understanding of itself and the environment. The company has to ensure that they analyse their competitors' offerings and understand the gaps in the market to be able to fill them effectively.

11. **Recommend how the following variables for segmentation could be used for a product of your choice.**

    Lifestyle
    Benefits sought

This question requires an answer which is related to a specific product or range.

## Segmentation variables for the drinks market

The following variables could be used for the drinks market:

- *Lifestyle* – This involves intangible variables such as the beliefs, attitudes and opinions of the potential customer. It has evolved in answer to some of the shortcomings of other methods of segmenting the market. This type of segmentation is a means of getting further under the skin of the customer as a thinking being. In defining the lifestyle of the consumer, this allows the market to sell the product not on superficial, functional features, but on benefit that can be seen to enhance that lifestyle on a much more emotional level.
- In this instance, drinks could be related to activities, interests, opinions – such as an aspirational sports drink which is targeted at 18–30 year old males who are very much sports orientated.
- *Benefits sought* – This variable can have more a psychological slant than just end usage and can link in very closely with both demographic and psychographic segments. This

type of variable could lead the company to look at a range of healthy drinks related to the benefits of health, i.e. sugar reduced, vitamin enriched, low alcohol, etc. Another benefit sought could be convenience, i.e. a sports drink which offers a shot of energy, lunch box drinks, premixed cocktails, etc.

# ELEMENT 3 (50 per cent of syllabus)

## The extended marketing mix and related tools

### Questions/Tasks

1. Critically evaluate the different strategic models, which you could consider for the development of market share and growth.
2. Explain the relevance of the Ansoff matrix in achieving the sales growth target.
3. Explain how an organization with an objective to increase market penetration would adapt the marketing mix to achieve this objective.
4. Explain and critically appraise the role of branding at both the product and corporate level.
5. Explain the use of the marketing communications mix elements in developing a new product branding strategy.
6. Critically evaluate reactive and proactive approaches to new product development.
7. Explain the following terms and offer examples for cosmetic products:

    (a) replacement products
    (b) re-launched products
    (c) imitative products.

8. Critically evaluate the following approaches which this organization will need to consider when setting its pricing strategy:

    (a) marginal analysis
    (b) break-even analysis.

9. Identify the main external factors from the macro and micro environment affecting this organization's pricing strategy.
10. Explain what is meant by the augmented product.
11. Critically discuss the key issues which a marketing manager will need to take into account when considering alternative or new distribution channels.
12. Explain the key benefits of an effective management programme for the physical distribution of products.
13. Explain how the integration of the marketing communications mix can achieve a product or brand repositioning.
14. Explain how technological advances can be used specifically within the promotional elements of the communications mix.
15. Explain how the Internet could be used as an important promotional tool.
16. Considering the advances in direct marketing communications, what are the key implications for marketing communicators for the future?
17. Explain the importance of developing and maintaining relationships with your stakeholders.
18. Recommend an appropriate extended marketing mix for your organization to ensure that relationships with the salient stakeholders are developed and managed.
19. Discuss the role of internal marketing and explain why it is important for services marketing.
20. Explain the concept of service quality and recommend an effective extended marketing mix in relation to the service delivery and service encounters for the consumers for a service of your choice.

*Appendix 4 Sample exam questions and answers*

# ELEMENT 3 (50 per cent of syllabus)

## The extended marketing mix and related tools

### Answers

1. **Critically evaluate the different strategic models, which you could consider for the development of market share and growth.**

This question demands a good knowledge of the Ansoff matrix and at least one other concept. The answer should offer a critical discussion of key strategic marketing development models:

*Ansoff growth matrix* – critical explanation of each strategy: product development, market development, market penetration and diversification. Brief explanation of how these are achieved.

*Porter's Generic Strategies* – critical explanation of focus, cost leadership and diversification strategies and briefly explain how these could be achieved. Some candidates may discuss competitive positions such as market challenger, leader, follower and nicher.

Some answers could consider the BCG matrix in terms of helping to identify the mix for the portfolio. This would be acceptable.

2. **Explain the relevance of the Ansoff matrix in achieving the sales growth target.**

Ansoff has proposed a useful framework for detecting new intensive growth opportunities called a product/market expansion grid. The company first considers whether it could gain more market share with its current products in their current markets – known as market penetration strategy. The next consideration is the development of new markets for current products – known as market development strategy. Then the company considers if it can develop new products to its current markets – product development strategy, and finally a diversification strategy may be considered where it might develop new products for new markets.

|  | Current products | New products |
|---|---|---|
| **Current markets** | Market penetration strategy<br>• gain customers from competitors<br>• retain loyal customers<br>• ensure customers buy more frequently | Product development strategy<br>• develop new products<br>• adapt existing products |
| **New markets** | Market development strategy<br>• enter new countries<br>• enter new niche markets<br>• different segments | Diversification strategy<br>• usually achieved by mergers and acquisitions<br>• most risky option |

*Figure A4.3* Product/market expansion grid

3. **Explain how an organization with an objective to increase market penetration would adapt the marketing mix to achieve this objective.**

The question demands that the answer is quite applied and illustrates an understanding of the operationalistion of strategic decisions in relation to the Ansoff matrix.

An organization whose objective is to increase market penetration is intending to increase its market share by continuing to market its existing products into existing markets. However, there will be an emphasis on trying to:

- Gain customers from competitors
- Retain loyal customers
- Ensure customers buy more frequently or in larger quantities.

Thus the following strategies will need to be adapted:

- *Product* – it is likely that larger pack sizes will be developed to encourage more product being purchased.
- *Price* – promotional pricing may be used in the short term to entice buyers who would normally purchase a competitor's product.
- *Distribution* – an emphasis on intensive distribution will be developed to ensure that the product is fully available.
- *Promotion/communications* – this is one of the main elements which will need to be used to communicate messages to competitor's customers. Advertising will concentrate on 'adding value'; sales promotions will be used in terms of pricing or banded packs or bonuses, cross promotions may be used with a CSR theme etc.; direct marketing and a loyalty programme would be developed to retain customers and build trust and loyalty; public relations would be used to communicate the offers and the CSR/cross promotions angle.

4. **Explain and critically appraise the role of branding at both the product and corporate level.**

This question really has two parts – corporate and product branding. Thus the answer needs to consider both elements here.

- *Role of corporate branding* – the corporate brand is inextricably linked to corporate reputation – the company is the brand name. Thus the corporate identity and image help to communicate the reputation and must be managed appropriately. Umbrella branding is where the company name and product name identifies the product and thus the corporate brand is important to link a product line. The link with corporate identity, corporate image and reputation needs to be emphasized. The management of the corporate brand is also important for wider stakeholders' perceptions of the company, for example it can have a major impact on the company stock. The corporate brand also includes the internal communications. In essence, the corporate brand is usually managed by corporate communications or public relations functions and may not be the remit of the marketing function. This can be very problematic in terms of ensuring constant messages to stakeholders.
- *Role of product branding* – need to consider the benefits of branding in terms of differentiating the product from competitors' products and to communicate the positioning strategy, offers an emotional link to customer, the reduction of risk for intermediaries, defends against competition, allows premium pricing, helps targeting, increases power over retailers etc. The use of brand extension strategies is available for strong product brands – licensing and gentle stretching. Branding offers a brand a personality and emotional 'added value'. There are different approaches to branding such as linked branding, range branding, product brand and generic branding. Indeed, brands have become a major point of strategic focus in companies and the concept of the brand has been widely applied: brands have a balance sheet and income value and have become recognized as tradable assets with a market value.

*Appendix 4 Sample exam questions and answers*

5. **Explain the use of the marketing communications mix elements in developing a new product branding strategy.**

For all new brands, the key objective is to generate awareness and for consumer products, purchase or trial. Targeting issues should be considered. Thus the communications mix needs to achieve such objectives. Major investment in advertising (to generate rapid awareness) and usually sales promotion (for trial) is required. The use of publicity for a new brand is crucial as it is more credible than advertising. The use of new technology in terms of communications is important.

6. **Critically evaluate reactive and proactive approaches to new product development.**

This question again is a two part question and requires an answer which considers both approaches to NPD.

- *Reactive approach* – this is where the company is happy to respond to competitors rather than seeking to outmanoeuvre them. This strategy allows other companies to take the risk of breaking new ground. This approach ensures that the organization avoids launch errors. The emphasis for the organization is on application and design engineering rather than developing a new to market product. Many organizations take this approach as it is less costly and less risky for them.
- *Proactive approach* – this is where the organization sets out to find new ideas before the competition. There is specific commitment to research and development. Much resource is expended on consumer research and market awareness. The company is willing to take major risks and the company culture encourages enterprise. NPD using this approach is expensive and time-consuming with no guarantee of success. However, success can lead to the company being the first in the market, allowing them to employ skimming pricing policies and being known as the leader.

7. **Explain the following terms and offer examples for cosmetic products:**

    (a) Replacement products
    (b) Re-launched products
    (c) Imitative products.

The question demands an understanding of NPD and the following section discusses the terms in relation to NPD.

- *Replacement products* – these are new to consumers, but replace existing products for a company. This type of product is more common nowadays because research teams tend to be commissioned to work upon product refinements rather than upon new innovations. An example here would be a new shampoo specifically for the grey market with vitamins for older hair care. This may replace a product which was losing sales.
- *Re-launched products* – these are products which require some rejuvenation. Generally, they are products which are in the decline stage of the product life cycle and a decision has to be made about whether to delete this product or re-launch it. An example here could be by changing the emphasis of a product's benefits for specific needs for the grey market – i.e. anti-wrinkle face cream, which was previously a moisturising cream.
- *Imitative products* – these are sometimes termed 'me too' products as the company follows a successful competitor's products. This approach reduces the costs of development and offers more chance of success for the product. An example here could be a 2 in 1 shampoo specifically for the grey market, building on the success of the 2 in 1 shampoos.

*Appendix 4 Sample exam questions and answers*

**8. Critically evaluate the following approaches which this organization will need to consider when setting its pricing strategy:**

   (a) Marginal analysis
   (b) Break-even analysis.

This question demands an understanding of pricing strategies. There are a range of approaches to pricing strategies considering cost, volume and profit. This is the accountant's costing perspective.

There is a range of different types of costs in regard to a product or service:

- *Fixed cost* – a cost that does not change according to the increase in the number of units produced, i.e. rent and rates for the premises.
- *Variable costs* – a cost that changes according to the number of units produced, such as raw materials.
- *Total costs* – a sum of fixed and variable cost times the quantity produced.
- *Average cost* – this is the total cost divided by the number of units produced.
- *Marginal analysis* – this is concerned with the additional cost incurred by the production of one more unit, where the marginal revenue is the extra income derived from selling one extra unit. The point where marginal revenue is equal to marginal cost, where each additional unit sale generates more revenue than costs but is considered uneconomic to produce extra units. This approach considers relationship between profit and price, total revenue and total cost.

At the heart of marginal analysis lies the search for the point where marginal revenue is equal to marginal cost. Up to that point, each additional unit sale generates more revenue than it incurs cost, and therefore it is worth producing and selling that unit. Beyond that point, however, the situation is different. Each additional unit begins to incur more cost than it can earn in revenue. Thus it becomes increasingly uneconomic to carry on producing extra units.

- *Break-even analysis* – shows the relationship between total revenue and total cost in order to determine the profitability at different pricing levels. The break-even point is the point at which total revenue and total cost are equal. Producing beyond this point generates increasing levels of profit.
- Knowing how many units at any given price would have to be sold in order to break-even is important and it also shows the impact on contribution to fixed costs and profit of alternative price levels.

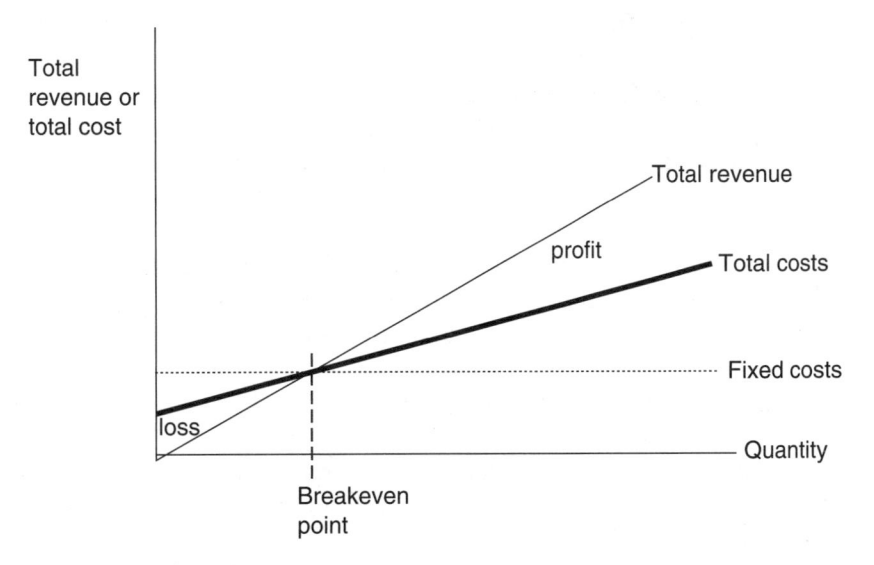

*Figure A4.4* Illustration of break-even point

9. **Identify the main external factors from the macro and micro environment affecting this organization's pricing strategy.**

This is a demanding question and to give a good answer it would be best to apply it to a particular example. Here the low-cost airline industry is considered.

There are four key factors that affect pricing decisions, also known as the 4Cs:

- *Cost* – related to the actual costs involved
- *Consumer/customer* – related to the price the consumer will pay
- *Competition* – related to competitors' prices for substitute or complimentary products
- *Company* – related to the company's financial objectives.

These elements will now be considered from an environmental analysis.

## Main external factors affecting the pricing strategy for the low-cost airline industry

When considering the macro environment, the following issues impact on this industry:

- Impact of the terrorist attacks on the World Trade Centre on September 11, 2001 in relation to levels of confidence nationally and internationally
- Customer concerns over safety of air travel and terrorism
- World wide decline in economic conditions and consequently disposable income
- Decrease in international travel industry for holidays and business travel
- Changing trends for holiday destinations (more emphasis on local),
- Aviation fuel costs (international fuel prices and potential conflict in oil states)
- Internet and technological advances in teleconferencing, i.e. the increased use of webcams and video conferencing thus reducing need for business travel.

The micro environment illustrates a further range of issues for this industry:

- Competitors' reaction to macro environment, i.e. major airlines reduction in pricing strategies
- The growth of new and existing low-cost air travel competitors
- B2B industry decline in travel
- The company's financial situation (i.e. objectives ROI, profit maximization, survival); market share and growth requirements, positioning, volume, etc.
- Customer reaction to international problems has meant that the customer is far more price sensitive and therefore, more potential demand for low-cost airlines
- Customer's expectations of service quality are increasing – even for low-cost air travel.

All of these issues have an impact on an organization in the difficult market of air travel and thus some of the major international players are facing major problems and are adapting their own pricing policies to encroach on the low-cost air market.

10. **Explain what is meant by the augmented product.**

In planning the product portfolio, the marketer needs to think through different levels of the product as each level adds more customer value and the total of all the levels constitute a customer value hierarchy. The fundamental level is the core benefit such as 'knowledge' when buying a book, the second level is the basic product – i.e. the pages, cover, etc. The third level is the expected product, a set of attributes that the buyer normally expects and agrees to when they purchase the product. The fourth level is this *augmented product*. This is where the product must meet and exceed the customers' desires beyond their expectations. For example a book manufacturer can augment the product by adding enhancements via the Internet for only those who have purchased the book.

Today's competition mainly takes place at the product augmentation level. Product augmentation leads the marketer to look at the buyer's total consumption system. However, the marketer has to realize that the product-augmentation strategy will cost money and the benefits can soon become expected benefits by the customer.

Kotler adds the fifth level at the potential product, which encompasses all the augmentations and transformations that the product might ultimately undergo in the future.

**11. Critically discuss the key issues which a marketing manager will need to take into account when considering alternative or new distribution channels.**

The key issues which a marketing manager will need to take into account when considering alternative or new distribution channels are as follows:

- Organization's objectives and resources
- Customers' characteristics, requirements and levels of service
- Product characteristics such as the size, weight and durability
- After sale service
- Competitors' channels
- Channel characteristics, such as availability, etc.
- Risk, control, costs involved related to the organization
- Logistics management issues such as inventory levels, handling issues, warehousing and transportation
- Impact on other marketing mix elements.

**12. Explain the key benefits of an effective management programme for the physical distribution of products.**

The main objective of physical distribution is to decrease costs while increasing service to the customer. The manager will need to consider the order processing, materials handling, warehousing, inventory management and transportation issues. Managers strive for a good balance of service, costs and resources. Therefore, effective planning is paramount to ensure that this happens by determining what level of customer service is acceptable yet realistic in terms of costs. As physical distribution affects every element of the marketing mix, it is important that the customers' needs are at the top of the list.

- *Customer satisfaction* – the key benefit of an effective physical distribution programme should be the offer of a high quality service, which should lead to a significant impact on customer satisfaction. Indeed, companies can differentiate their offerings by considering their physical distribution in relation to their competitors' and ensuring a good service level. For example some companies offer guaranteed 'next day' delivery. If managed effectively, it could be possible to position the company's offerings on the basis of the levels of service, which could lead to achieving a sustainable competitive advantage.
- *Company efficiencies* – if the programme is managed effectively, there should be opportunities to ensure reductions in the inventory costs, whilst maintaining a supply of goods adequate for the customers' needs. This should lead to increased profitability.

*Appendix 4 Sample exam questions and answers*

13. **Explain how the integration of the marketing communications mix can achieve a product or brand repositioning.**

The answer will identify the proposed new positioning for the product or brand, which may be in the decline stage of the PLC and indicate a perception map for the old positioning. The new positioning strategy will be identified and justified. The new target segments will be identified/ justified and this will be congruent with the explanation of the repositioning strategy.

Marketing communications mix adaptation – the communications objectives will be identified – i.e. to communicate the new brand values etc. and raise awareness of new positioning. The marketing communications mix will be identified and justified for this consumer product – advertising – specifying most appropriate media, publicity to be generated, sales promotion for switching behaviour, etc. All elements of the communications mix should be considered in relation to the media consumption and profile of the targeted segment.

14. **Explain how technological advances can be used specifically within the promotional elements of the communications mix.**

The advances in technology have had a major impact on the promotional mix which an organization will be using.

- *Advertising* – DRTV direct response advertising has allowed advertising to achieve more than just awareness – data can be captured and responses can lead to converts. The introduction of satellite television and digital technology has allowed for more sophisticated targeting and interactivity via traditional advertising. The use of the Internet site as an advertising window or banner advertising on other linked sites has been evident in the last 5 years. The use of CD-ROMs as a vehicle for advertising has been apparent.
- *Sales promotions* – the sophistication of databases and the direct mailing of sales promotions has been very powerful for some organizations. The use of the website and the 'free downloadable program or screen saver' has allowed the marketer to become more creative.
- *Personal selling* – the role of personal selling has now declined due to the use of automated customer-handling technology. This has been seen to cut costs whilst not eroding the service to the customer, however, in reality this has not always been effective and many customers are becoming disillusioned.
- *Public relations* – the use of the website as a relationship building tool has been effective for some organizations. For both internal (staff) and external audiences (customers, journalists, community, etc.) it has been easier to communicate using the Internet and mobile technology. For example, internal newsletters can be communicated on the intranet, press releases to journalists can be e-mailed instantly with digital pictures using satellite technology (which has cut time by days when considering international communications or reporting). The web can be used as an important communication tool in times of crisis management such as disasters or accidents when accurate and instantly changing information to the public will be crucial.

15. **Explain how the Internet could be used as an important promotional tool.**

The Internet and the production of an effective website can be an important promotional tool for most organizations, although in many organizations it is still not fully developed to its maximum potential. The communications objectives for the site must be set for each target audience – this could include raising awareness only, encouraging online sales, educating the market, launching a new product, gathering information for a direct mail campaign, etc.

*Customer relations* – as a practical exercise, look at a number of websites for major consumer products and evaluate them from the following checklist:

- How easy was it to find the website?
- How long did you stay on it and why?
- What information did you gain?
- Was the site selling products or just offering information?
- What was your overall impression as a consumer (rather than a CIM student)?
- How recently was the site updated?
- Did the website link effectively to the other promotional tools used by the organization (e.g. was there evidence of an integrated campaign?)
- Would you go back to the site again? Did you bookmark it?

A good website should offer the visitor a rich experience and it should 'fit' with the overall current communication strategy – e.g. there should be a consistency of message. There should also be a good design and flow of information, access to secure ordering systems (if appropriate), added value (perhaps in the form of 'free downloadables' or links to mailed sales promotions).

*Media relations* – the website can also be dedicated to developing media relations. This can be one of the most potent public relations tools as reporters can access information which they may need, at any time of the day or night and if prepared carefully, in a format that is ready to use.

*Investor relations* – as the financial community is used to using the Internet, a corporate website can also be important for investors accessing information. This would include the annual reports being posted on the site.

*Community relations* – the website can also be used for developing community relations. This site could include information relating to the promotion of local joint projects, contributions to arts and culture, invitations to open days and educational pages.

As can be identified from the above, the strategic design and use of the website is growing in importance in today's marketplace and this must be considered as part of an integrated communications strategy.

16. **Considering the advances in direct marketing communications, what are the key implications for marketing communicators for the future?**

When considering information technology and direct marketing communications, the following key implications are of growing importance to marketers:

- It is getting easier for all levels to communicate to customers and stakeholders and therefore the development of relationship marketing techniques should be more effective
- The level of customer interactivity is becoming very powerful
- Communications are becoming faster and more economical
- Organizations are becoming more global and subject to more competition
- The Internet is getting more secure and accessible to many segments of the market
- The need to ensure consistent messages with other communications tools is of paramount importance
- It is easier to obtain customer and competitor information
- Customers are becoming more sophisticated in using technology
- Therefore, there are increases in changes of lifestyles, individualism, behaviour and home shopping habits

*Appendix 4 Sample exam questions and answers*

- There needs to be more research into the new IT-literate consumer behaviour
- EPOS can offer the retailer better customer service and staff efficiencies
- Smart cards can be used as an effective tool, enabling the supplier to build up a much better picture of a customer
- The advancing power of the computer has allowed software to be developed and improved to analyse customer behaviour
- The fragmentation of the traditional media with more emphasis on two-way communications is now more apparent.

**17. Explain the importance of developing and maintaining relationships with your stakeholders.**

This question relates to relationship marketing and it also relates to salient stakeholders. Relationship marketing is applied in different sectors but emerged in the service sector due to the inseparable and often longitudinal nature of the exchange as could be found in the charity sector. The ladder of loyalty and customer retention (Christopher *et al.*) [see Unit 8 of this text, p. 204] illustrates the development of customer loyalty.

For any organization it is more efficient to keep customers rather than finding new ones, thus relationship marketing is important. A happy customer will come back for more. However, it has been proven that 68 per cent of people will go elsewhere if they received an indifferent service. This clearly indicates that there is room for improvement in this area for most companies.

- *Long-term* – organizations need to view any transaction as part of a long-term goal. If the customer is satisfied with the product/service they have received for the price they have paid they are more likely to return.
- A short-term outlook will consider a quick profit but not consider repeat purchases.
- *Trust* – if a customer trusts an organization, they have been treated well and they are more likely to return. Trust is a two-way process – if the business can trust its customer, they may offer a better deal. If the customer trusts the organization not to 'rip them off' then they are likely to return.
- *Win–win* – a better relationship will develop if both the organization and their customers gain by the transaction – both parties will seek its confirmation.
- *Loyalty* – loyal customers will spread the good news about a company and may even champion it. Loyalty is part of the long-term, win–win trusting relationship an organization should seek.

The key areas where a relationship opportunity exists in the case of a car dealership are as follows:

- Initial visit to the dealership by the potential customer
- Test drives
- Evaluation of alternative cars
- Purchase and transactions
- Delivery of the car
- *Direct mail* – this will help confirm a positive post-purchase analysis by the customer as well as building a rapport
- Servicing of the vehicle and breakdown.

18. **Recommend an appropriate extended marketing mix for your organization to ensure that relationships with the salient stakeholders are developed and managed.**

This question would need to be answered in relation to your organization. Therefore the following guide illustrates areas where this could be applied to your organization.

- *Product service system* – core service around which relationship can be established, service augmentation
- *Reinforcing promotions* – cross-selling business with linked companies
- *Post-purchase communication* – regular magazines or direct mail tailored to interests
- *Key account management* – for key stakeholders
- *Specialized distribution* – telephone/online, etc.
- *Relationship pricing* – multiple product purchase discounts
- *Customer service* – staff training, internal marketing, customer satisfaction
- Personalized processes.

19. **Discuss the role of internal marketing and explain why it is important for services marketing.**

Internal marketing involves selling marketing plans to key internal staff or employees. Piercy and Morgan's (1997) model of internal marketing indicates the implications for the marketing mix.

- *Product* – the product consists of market strategies and the marketing plan – therefore, the 'product' needs to be 'sold' in terms of values, attitudes and behaviour to employees so that they can buy into it.
- *Price* – this relates to the benefit to the employee of taking this marketing planning information on board. It relates to the personal psychological cost of adopting different key values, and changing the way jobs are done. Often it requires asking managers to step outside their comfort zones with new methods of operation.
- *Distribution* – this concerns the physical and socio-technical venues at which organizations will have to deliver the product and its communications – i.e. where should employees be targeted, e.g. Internet, staff canteens, etc.
- *Communication* – this is the most tangible aspect of internal marketing – communication media and the messages use to inform and persuade employees. There will be work on the attitudes of the key personnel in the internal marketplace and two-way methodology must be employed.

Importance of internal marketing for services – the service quality is very much influenced by the staff or employees, because of the inseparability of services production and consumption in relation to the provider, i.e. staff. Thus this requires that employees be totally on board for all service specifications etc. This means that good levels of communication, motivation and training are essential for service quality and this can only be influenced by internal marketing. Therefore, this is often managed by public relations personnel rather than human resource sections or departments.

20. **Explain the concept of service quality and recommend an effective extended marketing mix in relation to the service delivery and service encounters for the consumers for a service of your choice.**

This is a question which really includes two elements of the syllabus (3 and 4) and thus the answer needs to consider this.

Central to the delivery of any service is the service encounter between the provider and the customer, i.e. interactive marketing.

*Appendix 4 Sample exam questions and answers*

The answer will consider an explanation of the SERVQUAL model in relation to the chosen service – considers access, reliability, credibility, security, understanding the customer, responsiveness, courtesy, competence, communication and the tangibles.

The following model is an adaptation of the famous 'SERVQUAL' model, which was devised by Parasuraman, Zeithaml and Berry in 1985 (commonly known as PZB).

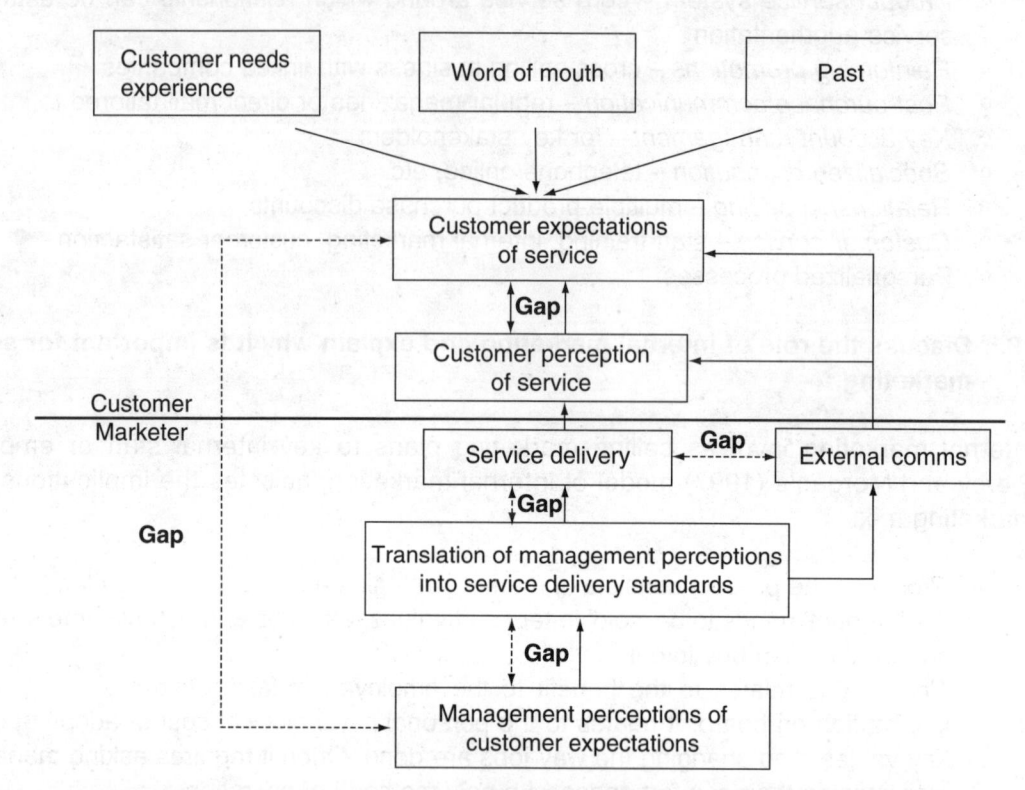

*Figure A4.5* A conceptual model of service quality and its implications
*Source*: Adapted from Parasuraman, A., Zeithaml, V.A. and Berry, L.L. *Journal of Marketing*, 1985, 49, 41–50

This model shows the problems that can occur in the delivery of a service as there are a number of gaps in terms of customer perceptions, expectations and management expectations and perceptions.

It is important that the gaps are identified.

- The gap between management perception and customer expectations will illustrate that the management may not appreciate the student/customers' needs
- The gap between service quality specifications and management perception – which means that the management does not set standards of performance
- The gap between service quality specification and the delivery of service – which means that operational personnel may be inadequately trained to meet the standards required
- The gap between service delivery and external communications – where the expectations from the promotional activity are not matched in practice
- The gap between perceived and expected service – where students/customers envisage a better service than the one that has been provided.

Consideration of the service quality gaps – customer expectations and perceptions of the service and the need for regular measurement and control. Problems of management misunderstanding customer wants, inadequate resources, inadequate delivery and exaggerated promises need to be considered further.

Extended marketing mix for services to improve the design and delivery of service encounter during the service chosen.

- *People element* – consideration of internal marketing for training and productivity purposes, staff training as many are volunteers, visible staff and staff productivity and motivation, employee/volunteer satisfaction and safety issues.
- *Process element* – effective systems and technology – design of the service process and the introduction of more advanced technology can help improve ticketing, queuing for specific games, to ensure good service levels. Improved customer interaction and moments of truth – service specifications. Links with external providers of transport, cleaning services, accommodation, etc. to integrate processes where possible.
- *Physical evidence element* – use of physical cues to symbolize the intangibles to the consumer/customer. Difference between essential evidence – logo, tickets, staff uniforms, all communications, etc. and peripheral evidence.

# ELEMENT 4 (15 per cent of syllabus)

## Marketing in different contexts

### Questions/Tasks

1. Justify how the marketing activities for an organization may vary in an international context.
2. Critically evaluate four different international market entry methods.
3. Discuss the factors which influence the choice of international market entry methods.
4. Contrast the different constraints which need to be considered for an FMCG company and a SME organization when developing the marketing plan.
5. Compare and contrast how marketing plans may vary for virtual and non-virtual companies.
6. Explain the criteria that affect a customer's perceptions of service quality.

# ELEMENT 4 (15 per cent of syllabus)

## Marketing in different contexts

### Answers
**1. Justify how the marketing activities for an organization may vary in an international context.**

This question requires an understanding of international perspectives and the marketing plan. The consideration of the international macro environment needs to be identified. This will include discussions about the sociocultural factors in particular international markets. Language, social structures, customs, religion, values, attitudes and morals will influence the decisions relating to the marketing mix.

However, the main debate is likely to be about the possibility of standardization versus adaptation and this may be discussed with the use of examples. There will be some consideration of culture, media and legal issues on the marketing mix.

*Appendix 4 Sample exam questions and answers*

**2. Critically evaluate four different international market entry methods.**

This question requires an answer which illustrates good understanding of a range of market entry strategies in international markets.

- *Direct export* – this means the production of products at home and then selling into an international market without the use of an intermediary. Thus responsibility for finding customers, negotiating with them and processing their orders and arranging shipment and after-sales service is left to the seller. This allows greater control by the organization and allows the development of experience in this market. However, this can be quite a slow entry process.
- *Indirect export* – this is where an organization produces goods at home and then sells them through an intermediary and therefore indirectly to a foreign buyer. The intermediary could be based in the seller's home country or in the foreign market and could be acting on behalf of the seller. An export agent is an example, where the agent acts on behalf of the seller, undertaking to sell on a commission basis into a particular market. In this case, there is more of an element of risk in terms of lack of control over the brand and the ultimate control of the product in the international market. The expertise in that market place is not built by the organization as the agent retains this. The agent could also be working for a competitor and this could be problematic.
- *Licensing* – this can be an attractive option for entering international markets. The licensor grants a licensee the rights to manufacture a product, use patents, use particular processes or exploit trademarks in a defined market in return for a royalty payment. This method is useful for markets that are very remote or not worth the costs of direct involvement. Control is retained and licensing helps to overcome high import tariffs, and also avoids the costs and commitment of direct investment. This is a particularly effective way of achieving technology transfer, that is, the movement of technological advances to new markets.
- *Master franchising* – this is where an organization in a country is given an exclusive right to develop a franchising system. This method is a very popular indirect method of entering international markets. The master franchisee can receive extensive training from the franchisor, not only in operating a unit, but also in franchisee recruitment, staff training and managing a franchised system. The franchisee is then responsible for using local knowledge and developing the network in a way that is satisfactory to the franchisor. The master franchisee earns a percentage of the fees or royalties paid by individual franchisees. This is a very effective method of quickly gaining market entry and building market share. The control is still maintained by the organization to a large extent.

**3. Discuss the factors which influence the choice of international market entry methods.**

This question could be answered from different approaches, but it does require the answer to consider strategic issues.

- *The length of the distribution channel* – how many intermediaries are there between the organization and the customer?
- Number of intermediaries, implications for exclusivity (limited number of outlets) and the company's objectives
- *Tasks and system for the distribution chain* – what would be the implications for logistics and physical distribution in international markets
- The risks involved in entering different international markets

- The human costs involved (including availability, skills required, work permits, labour law, union implications)
- The financial costs involved (including labour, transport, materials and manufacturing)
- The level of control in the market
- Impact for after-sales service
- Level of experience in the country and the ability to build experience
- The impact on the other marketing mix elements
- The level of flexibility
- *The legal implications* – controls and restrictions
- *Exchange control* – stability of local currency
- Taxation implications.

4. **Contrast the different constraints which need to be considered for an FMCG company and a SME organization when developing the marketing plan.**

This question is quite demanding as there is not much covered in the text books in relation to this area of the syllabus.

The consideration of different objectives will determine the marketing plan. A large FMCG company will often be interested in product development, market leadership, growth in market share. However, a small or medium sized organization may not be concerned with these objectives, and may concentrate more on the particular market place or niche market and they are likely to be a small fish in a large pond. Therefore, market share or leadership will not be a priority. More likely is the ability to grow the company and increase sales. Many SMEs tend to be less strategic in their approach and tend to operate on more of a tactical approach.

Often the availability of resources is very different between a large FMCG and an SME. Both financial and human resources will be limited in an SME, where staff may be required to be multi-tasked. There is likely to be a limited amount of financial resources for research and other areas such as expansion. This is possible in the FMCG but it is likely that such a company will have more long-term plans and be financially viable.

Budget sizes within SMEs are usually very small in comparison to larger companies. This is likely to have an impact on the marketing budgets, especially the communications budget. However, large FMCG organizations will often have the luxury of larger budgets for such communications in comparison to an SME. Indeed, often they will use communications agencies such as PR and/or advertising agencies, whereas SMEs view such services with scepticism.

5. **Compare and contrast how marketing plans may vary for virtual and non-virtual companies.**

This is an interesting question which again may not be covered fully in many text books. The question requires an answer which considers the elements of the marketing plan from both perspectives.

- *Market audit* – this element will not be very different for either type of organization as both will have to scan the environment to be aware of the macro and micro players which may impact on the organization.
- *Objectives* – the marketing objectives may be quite different or similar. For example, an online organization may have a marketing objective of achieving a particular market share or entering a particular market – such as Amazon.com.

*Appendix 4 Sample exam questions and answers*

- *Strategy* – brand requirements, segmentation, targeting and positioning may be different for such different organizations. With online companies the intangibility of the company means that trust and security in relationships with customers and suppliers has to be built via the corporate brand and the Web-based communications. Thus an emphasis on this area is very much required. Segmentation, targeting and positioning may also be different for an online organization as the segmentation strategy may be determined by access to a PC.
- *Marketing mix implications: packaging* – online organizations will need to consider packaging from more of a protective element rather than a communication tool.
- *Marketing mix implications: communications* – as previously stated for online organizations communications will be very important to build the brand and the products which cannot be felt or touched. Thus the website, direct marketing, publicity, etc. needs to be sophisticated to ensure a differentiation and to build security and trust in the minds of the buyers.
- *Marketing mix implications: price* – customers perceive virtual organizations to have less costs associated with their offerings, therefore, their expectations are that the products or services will be less expensive than similar goods purchased from a non-virtual company.
- *Service quality and encounter* – this is a very important element for online organizations as the customer will evaluate the organization more via the service which they receive.
- *Human resources* – different human skills may be required for online organizations.
- *Budgets* – again, this is an area where there may be some similarity between the two types of organizations, although logistic and order processing budgets for online companies may be larger.
- *Evaluation and control* – evaluation and control will be dictated by the differences highlighted above.

## 6. Explain the criteria that affect a customer's perceptions of service quality.

This question requires an answer which indicates a good understanding of services and in particular, service quality. There may be some discussion about the nature of services before the main body of the answer is given which relates to the criteria that affect a customer's perceptions of service quality.

Zeithaml, Parasuraman and Berry, in *Delivering Quality Service* (Free Press, 1990) cite 10 main criteria that between them cover the whole service experience from the customer's point of view. To contextualize these points, an example of a student evaluating a course at a university has been considered.

- *Access* – consideration of ease of access to the service for the student i.e. 24-hour access to computer lab or libraries
- *Reliability* – consideration of the service reliability in terms of the expected standard
- *Credibility* – is the service provider (lecturer or admin staff) trustworthy and believable?
- *Security* – the safety of the student on campus or at university is a major consideration for parents of the student
- *Understanding the customer* – does the university or service provider make an effort to understand and adapt to the student's needs and wants?
- *Responsiveness* – is the university quick to respond to the student and willing to help – i.e. if the student wants to see a lecturer with a piece of work, how easy is it to make an appointment?
- *Courtesy* – are the university staff polite, friendly and considerate towards the students, showing respect?

- *Competence* – are the university staff suitably trained to be able to deliver the level of education purchased?
- *Communication* – do the university staff listen to the students and take time to explain things to them, are they sympathetic to student problems and suggest appropriate solutions?
- *Tangibles* – are the tangible and visible aspects of the university suitably impressive or appropriate to the situation – i.e. the lecture theatres, student cafes, etc.?

In light of the above criteria, it is necessary for service providers to undertake regular measurement and evaluate the service provision on a continuous basis. However, it needs to be remembered that there are many problems which organizations face in this area, such as the potential misunderstanding of the student/customer's wants and the lack or inadequate levels of resources available within the university.

# appendix 5
# past examination papers and examiners' reports

**The Chartered Institute of Marketing**

## Advanced Certificate in Marketing – Stage 2

**Marketing Planning**

8.41: Marketing Planning

Time: 09.30-12.30

Date: 3rd December, 2003

3 Hours Duration

This examination is in two sections.

**PART A** – Is compulsory and worth 50% of total marks.

**PART B** – Has **FOUR** questions; select **TWO**. Each answer will be worth 25% of the total marks.

**DO NOT** repeat the question in your answer, but show clearly the number of the question attempted on the appropriate pages of the answer book.

Rough workings should be included in the answer book and ruled through after use.

© The Chartered Institute of Marketing

# Advanced Certificate in Marketing – Stage 2

## 8.41: Marketing Planning

## PART A

### The Coffee Shop Market – Starbucks

In some countries the coffee market has expanded more than threefold since 1995, with a range of coffee outlets, located on high streets in main towns, modelling themselves on successful American and Italian-style coffee shops. People can go into a coffee shop and buy one of a range of specialist coffee beverages and enjoy a very relaxing atmosphere to drink their coffee. Consequently, there has been an expansion in the market and a growth in high street coffee houses. In the UK alone there are a range of providers:

- **Costa Coffee** – Has 250 outlets and plans to have 500 by 2004/5. It also supplies coffee to low-cost airlines. The company is planning to launch a chain of sandwich style shops that also serve coffee.

- **Coffee Republic** – This is the largest independent operator in the UK. The company has almost doubled its number of outlets from 36 to 61 in 2000, increasing to 82 in 2001. It has recently hired marketing specialists to develop its brand identity and is seeking to develop its food offer to capture a growing lunchtime trade.

- **Coffee Nero** – This has 62 outlets in the UK and plans to expand to 250 outlets by 2004.

- **Madison's** – Has 48 coffee shops under the Madison brand and four under the name of its newly acquired chain Café Richoux. The company has developed an Anglicised format that incorporates American style and an Italian coffee offer. Its open bars and lounges are designed to appeal to female customers.

- **Starbucks** – Detailed below.

### Starbucks Coffee Shops

Starbucks coffee shops have been operating since 1971 and the company is US based. As a global company, the *Starbucks Experience* is about passion for a quality product, excellent customer service, and people. Starbucks has nearly 900 coffee houses in 22 markets outside North America.

Internationalisation began in 1996 for Starbucks, with the first coffee shop in Tokyo, "We have been amazed by the global acceptance and visibility of our brand in all our international markets," says Peter Maslen, President of Starbucks Coffee International.

Starbucks purchases and roasts high-quality whole bean coffees and sells them along with fresh, rich-brewed, Italian-style espresso beverages, a variety of pastries and cakes, and coffee-related accessories and equipment (primarily through its company-operated retail stores). In addition to sales through its company-operated retail stores, Starbucks sells primarily whole-bean coffees through a speciality sales group, a direct response business, supermarkets, and online at Starbucks.com. Additionally, Starbucks produces and sells bottled Frappuccino® coffee drink and a line of premium ice creams through its joint venture partnerships, and offers a line of innovative premium teas produced by its wholly-owned subsidiary, Tazo Tea Company.

The company's objective is to establish Starbucks as the most recognised and respected brand in the world. To achieve this goal, the company plans to continue to rapidly expand its retail operations, grow its speciality sales and other operations, and selectively exploit opportunities to strengthen the Starbucks brand.

**Coffee Shop Consumers**

During the last few years there has been an increasing trend towards the consumption of healthy food and drink products. This has lead to a decrease in coffee consumption, which is considered an unhealthy product, especially among those between 15 and 24 years old. Indeed, 13% of 15-24 year-olds do not drink coffee at all. Furthermore, club culture has also made bottled water and juice products more fashionable choices of drink.

Mintel research (2001) indicates that the use of coffee shops has become a habit among distinct sections of the public, notably the mobile, affluent professional. Women are particularly attracted to the non-threatening, singles-friendly environment that coffee shops offer.

The success of the coffee shop has been based on a youth friendly, aspirational clientele. However, long-term trends show that non-coffee drinking is on the increase among young people. Older consumers have not been specifically targeted, yet these adults are among the most likely to be consumers of specialised coffee products. High growth within the sector indicates that greater diversification is possible to meet as yet unsatisfied consumer demand among these groups.

The location of existing coffee shops has become a key factor which influences the way some people choose to visit branded coffee shops. Adults from socio-economic groups A and B are now four times more likely than C2 category adults to visit branded coffee shops, because they value highly a relaxed store design and ambience.

*Note:* *the above data has been based on a real-life organisation, but details have been changed for assessment purposes and do not reflect current management practices.*

## PART A

**Question 1.**

You have been appointed as a Consultant specialising in retail marketing to advise Starbucks on their brand.

a. Assess the main challenges in the marketing environment that are likely to impact on the Starbucks brand in the next two years, and explain the role of marketing information in conducting an external audit.

**(20 marks)**

b. With reference to appropriate theory, explain how Starbucks could expand their business in the next two years.

**(10 marks)**

c. Specifically considering the role of the brand, recommend the extended marketing mix decisions for your chosen growth strategies.

**(20 marks)**
**(50 marks in total)**

## PART B – Answer TWO Questions Only

**Question 2.**

You have been assigned to manage a Fast-Moving Consumer Good (FMCG) brand and are rather concerned about the current marketing budgets that have been set.

a. Explain what factors influence the marketing budget for such a brand.

**(9 marks)**

b. Explain and evaluate the different approaches for setting the marketing budget for the mix decisions included in the marketing plan.

**(8 marks)**

c. Recommend methods for evaluating and controlling the marketing plan for this FMCG brand.

**(8 marks)**
**(25 marks in total)**

**Question 3.**

Acting as an Advisor to the Marketing Director of a retail bank, write a report that:

a. Assesses the role of branding at both the product and corporate level.

**(8 marks)**

b. Recommends the use of the marketing communications mix in developing a new product branding strategy.

**(9 marks)**

c. Explains how pricing is developed as an integrated part of the extended marketing mix.

**(8 marks)**
**(25 marks in total)**

## Question 4.

You are the Marketing Manager for a not-for-profit service organisation of your choice.

a. Explain the importance of developing and maintaining relationships with your stakeholders.

**(10 marks)**

b. Recommend an appropriate extended marketing mix for your organisation to ensure that relationships are developed and managed.

**(10 marks)**

c. Explain how the marketing activities for this organisation may vary in an international context.

**(5 marks)**
**(25 marks in total)**

## Question 5.

Your organisation is planning to develop a new range of products to be targeted at an international market of your choice. Using examples:

a. Explain the role of innovation within organisations.

**(10 marks)**

b. Propose and justify an approach to new product development.

**(15 marks)**
**(25 marks in total)**

Appendix 5 Past examination papers and examiners' reports

# The Chartered Institute of Marketing

# Advanced Certificate In Marketing - Stage II

**Examiner's Report**

**41: Marketing Planning**
**Date: January 2004**

© The Chartered Institute of Marketing

# Advanced Certificate In Marketing -Stage II

**41: Marketing Planning – Examiner's Report**
**Date: January 2004**

## Introduction

This was the first examination session for the new subject at Advanced Certificate Stage II Marketing Planning. This examination paper conformed to the new format, i.e. Section A - Compulsory, was worth 50% and candidates had to answer two questions out of four, each question being worth 25%; therefore, there are no previous pass rates to which to compare. This report has been written after consultation with the Examining team and most of the points cited are common to many centres.

At this level (i.e. Stage II) examiners are looking for knowledge, understanding and application in all answers and thus candidates' papers were marked accordingly. The marking scheme indicates this approach and is available from CIM on the website.

The following section will consider the strengths and weaknesses of the candidates' answers.

## Strengths

(1) Use of appropriate examples or application to the case study given. Good candidates clearly demonstrated their knowledge and understanding by referring to appropriate examples to back up their answers - especially in the case study, where reference to the Starbucks brand was required.

(2) Good layout and presentation. Most good answers were presented well and were logical in format and structure. Report format should be used and the answer sectionalised, helping the flow of reading which gives the Examiner confidence in the candidate's work. There are no marks specifically available for layout at this stage of the CIM qualifications, however, candidates should still present their work well for all questions.

(3) Using appropriate models or frameworks. Higher grade answers tended to display an excellent understanding of the theory, by illustrating models and them applying them to the question set - such as the Ansoff matrix and full explanation in question 1b. These models or frameworks must be appropriately labelled and referenced correctly.

(4) Application of theory to the case or examples. The pass answers do not just cite the theory, they illustrate understanding by applying the theory to the case or to an example. This is always required in the compulsory question 1 but many candidates tended to just refer to the theory and not apply it. Many candidates just reiterate information given in the case study also - which does not demonstrate understanding or knowledge and should be avoided.

*Appendix 5 Past examination papers and examiners' reports*

(5) Good time management was evident in good examination papers from candidates. The pass answers illustrated that a good attempt was made and all sections of the question have been answered well.

## Weaknesses

(1) Misinterpretation of question requirements. The majority of candidates seemed to misinterpret question 1, which was very worrying as this was now worth 50% rather than 40% as on papers previously. This was most evident in the compulsory case study - Question 1a, 1b and 1c. Section 1a clearly required candidates to "explain the role of marketing information in conduction and external audit". However, many candidates did not address this at all, where as others wrote about secondary and primary research, which was not required. Within section 1b many candidates chose to write about the Boston matrix rather than the Ansoff matrix, which was not appropriate. The final section, 1c, required candidates to "consider the role of the brand" and again, many candidates did not address this for some reason. These areas will be discussed more fully further in the report.

(2) Understanding how to analyse a question. Some candidates in this session seemed to have particular problems in determining the following:

- The general subject area (e.g. question 2a - factors influencing the marketing budget)

- The focus or emphases required (e.g. 2c required candidates to recommend methods for evaluating and controlling the marketing plan, however, many wrote about the marketing planning process only.)

(3) Preparation and study skills in terms of in-depth understanding of the syllabus. It was evident that a number of candidates were lacking in a number of areas. In some cases candidates seemed to reproduce lecture material rather than answering the question specifically or applying the theory to an example or the case especially in question 3c which related to pricing as an integrated part of the extended marketing mix.

(4) Reluctance to comply with the question requirements. Many candidates chose to ignore exactly what was required in some questions and generally wrote about the key subject of the question - such as question 3b which required candidates to recommend an appropriate marketing communications mix in developing a new product branding strategy. Many candidates wrote about the marketing mix issues generally rather than the communications mix. In some cases, those who did address the marketing communications mix but did not consider the NEW product branding strategy wrote blandly about marketing communications, which was not appropriate for a new product or brand.

(5) Including everything about the subject, even if not related to the question requirements. This costs candidates precious time and often happens when they do not know what to include for the actual response. Also, this practice is very tedious for the Examining team, as they have to 'search' for the actual answer. Again, this was very evident in question 5b which required candidates to propose and justify an approach to new product development. Many candidates wrote in general about product life cycles and did not answer the question.

(6) Lack of practical examples. The best marks for questions are awarded to candidates who offer examples, which demonstrate the theory to which they are referring. This time, however, not many candidates managed to include a variety of examples within their answers. Candidates must demonstrate their knowledge, understanding and application of theory at this level. Therefore, including examples related to the area in question is required even if not specifically requested.

(7) Poor time management. This was a major problem for some candidates in some centres - many candidates seemed to not answer the final question on the paper. Tutors should try to ensure that their students have an opportunity to sit a mock examination prior to the actual examination. With the new format of the paper, candidates only need to answer the compulsory question and two others and so should apportion their time appropriately. If a candidate misses out a question or part of a question, because of the reduced number of questions now required on the paper, there is less chance of passing.

The next section of this report will consider each question on the examination paper and will firstly detail the approach required, indicating what the Examiner was looking for in the answer. Then a consideration of the strengths and weaknesses of the candidates' answers for each question will be discussed.

## Section A - Compulsory

### Question 1.

Approach Required

The case study was based on a live company and as such the issues in the questions were realistic. The first part of the question (1a) required candidates to assess the main challenges in the marketing environment which were likely to impact on the Starbucks brand in the next two years and also to explain the role of marketing information in conducting an external audit. This was worth 15 marks for the macro and mirco environment analysis and 5 marks for the role of information, and as such, candidates should have considered this in the timing of their answers. The answer should have included a PESTEL (macro) and 5 force (micro) analysis in relation to Starbucks case study. Candidates should have also written about the role of information in relation to the marketing audit. Therefore candidates should have illustrated their knowledge, understanding and application of the theory to the Starbucks case.

The second part of the question (1b) required candidates to consider appropriate theory and explain how Starbucks could expand their business within the next two years. The answers should have commenced with an explanation or discussion of the Ansoff matrix and then some discussion of the most appropriate strategy and justify this in relation to the Starbucks brand. Therefore, the answers should have discussed the theory and justified the recommended marketing strategies (such as product or market development), using the information in the case study, which was quite comprehensive. This was worth 10 marks.

The final part of this question (1c) required the candidate to recommend the extended marketing mix decisions for the chosen growth strategies, specifically considering the role of the Starbucks brand. Here candidates should have explained their chosen strategies and discussed the role of the brand in determining the marketing mix decisions for the chosen strategies. For example, candidates should have considered the potential of brand stretching with new products and targeting new markets if market development and product development strategies had been suggested. The answer should then have gone on to consider the marketing mix for each selected strategy. The answer relating to the role of branding was worth 8 marks and the marketing mix decisions were worth 12 marks.

### Strengths in candidates' answers

- Some candidates were able to offer a good PESTEL and 5 forces analysis which was related to the Starbucks case and utilised the information included.

- Many candidates were able to offer a good explanation of the role of information in terms of the market audit - therefore, their answers were well applied.

- Good answers discussed the Ansoff matrix and explained the most appropriate strategies in relation to the case study, offering good justification and support for the recommendations made.

- Better answers included a well annotated Ansoff matrix and then went on to explain each of the growth strategies, illustrating the application of each strategy such as market penetration and the use of loyalty schemes etc.

- Good answers discussed the role of branding and considered the potential brand stretching opportunities and limitations of the current Starbucks brand.

- Good answers for part 1c discussed not only the branding issues, but also the extended marketing mix for a range of appropriate growth strategies such as product or market development.

### Weaknesses in candidates' answers

- Many candidates only discussed a macro analysis and did not therefore consider the micro environment.

- Some candidates did not use any information from the case study and wrote theoretically about a PEST analysis, thus they did not pick up many marks.

*Appendix 5 Past examination papers and examiners' reports*

- Disappointingly, many candidates did not write about the role of information and missed this part of question 1a thus losing 5 marks immediately.

- Weak answers regurgitated information from the case study for section 1a.

- Many candidates did not fully discuss the Ansoff matrix, or got the diagram confused. Some discussed the Boston Matrix instead of the Ansoff matrix for question 1b!

- Weaker answers for 1c only considered the marketing mix in general rather than considering either the brand (thus 8 marks were immediately lost) or the case study information. Many answers were not applied to the case study.

- Some candidates did not write enough for the marks available and many missed out sections of the question; this could have been due to the miss management of time.

## Question 2

Approach

The first part of the question required the candidate to explain the factors which influence the marketing budget for a FMCG brand. Thus the answer should have been applied to an FMCG. This was worth 9 marks and the answer should have considered internal power, strategic contingencies, internal process controls, internal and external political influences, bargaining and corporate culture issues.

The second part of the question required candidates to explain and evaluate the different approaches for setting the marketing budget for the mix decisions included in the marketing plan. Thus the answers should have related to a range of budgeting approaches such as incrementalism, calculation models, experiential, negotiational, bottom-up and top-down methods. The answer should have included some EVALUATION of such methods also as requested in the question. This was worth 8 marks; however if the answer did not include any evaluation, the mark was limited to 4 marks only.

The final section of this question required candidates to recommend methods for evaluating and controlling the marketing plan for a FMGC brand. The answer should have included a discussion of areas such as management control (such as performance appraisal and benchmarking), financial controls (e.g. trend analysis, liquidity rations, debt ratios etc), efficiency controls such as optimum value from marketing assets, and strategic controls such as measuring marketing activities against market performances.

This was one of the newer areas on the syllabus and thus related to the second element of the syllabus. In general, this area has not been tested much on previous Marketing Operations papers and thus candidates did not do very well with this question. Indeed, many text books do not cover this well, so it is suggested that candidates consider much wider reading for this section of the syllabus (see: Drummond, Ensor and Ashford, 2003, Strategic Marketing, 2nd edition).

Appendix 5 Past examination papers and examiners' reports

**Strengths in candidates' answers**

- Good answers commenced and illustrated their work, with an explanation of the importance of marketing budgeting and control methods within the marketing planning process.

- Some candidates used some good FMCG examples when discussing the marketing budget.

- Good answers included a good evaluation grid, which evaluated each method of budgeting approaches.

- There were not many good answers for the second part or third part of the question, but some did include examples to illustrate the points made.

**Weaknesses in candidates' answers**

- Many candidates did not answer part 2a well and considered the marketing mix only.

- Many miss-timed their answers and wrote mainly about part 2a and 2b, offering only a couple of lines for part 2c.

- Some candidates missed out whole sections.

- Some candidates confused evaluation and control methods with the whole of the marketing planning process and clearly their answers lacked focus here.

- Many did not include references to an FMCG in their answers.

- The majority of candidates could not answer 2a or 2b well, and for either questionmade guesses about their answers which were not really sensible.

### Question 3

Approach

This question related to three areas of the syllabus, branding, marketing communications and pricing. The first part of the question required the candidate to assess the role of branding at both the product and corporate level. The answer required candidates to offer discussion about product and corporate branding and gives examples of each. This was worth 8 marks, 4 for each type of branding. Thus the candidate was required to illustrate their knowledge, understanding and application of theory.

The second part of the question required candidates to recommend the use of the marketing communications mix in developing a new product branding strategy. This was worth 9 marks. Candidates should have considered the appropriate marketing communications mix in relation to the launch of a new brand. Thus answers should have discussed investment for adverting to general rapid awareness and sales promotion for trials in the case of a consumer brand. If the answer was not applied to a new brand, the mark was limited to 4 marks only.

*Appendix 5 Past examination papers and examiners' reports*

The third part of the question required candidates to explain how pricing could be developed as an integrated part of the extended marketing mix. The answers should have considered pricing as it is linked to positioning and the segments targeted, with some consideration of the accountant or financial approach. This was worth 8 marks.

### Strengths of candidates' answers

- Good answers considered both product and corporate branding issues, considering corporate reputation, identity and image and product branding in terms of brand personality and added value etc.

- Good answers related to the marketing communications mix and requirements for NEW branding strategies. Thus advertising, sales promotion, public relations were considered and justified in light of the new brand discussed.

- The final section of the answer included an applied discussion of pricing strategies as an integrated element of the marketing mix.

- The answer included an introduction and a conclusion and illustrated knowledge, understanding and application.

### Weaknesses of candidates' answers

- Many candidates wrote in general about branding rather than corporate and product branding.

- A worrying number of candidates wrote about the marketing mix rather than the marketing communications mix.

- Some candidates wrote in general about the marketing communications mix rather than applying their answer to a new brand.

- Many candidates did not address the final part of the question well (3c) and thus wrote in general about pricing rather than answering the question.

- Many candidates did not include examples in their answers.

### Question 4

Approach

This question related to the implications of a relationship marketing approach for the marketing of a not-for profit organisation of the candidate's choice. The first part required candidates to explain the importance of developing and maintaining relationships with stakeholders. The answers should have discussed the concept of relationship marketing and why it is important for the not-for-profit organisation chosen. The answer should have identified the different stakeholders for this organisation. This was worth 10 marks.

*Appendix 5 Past examination papers and examiners' reports*

The second part of the question required candidates to recommend an appropriate extended marketing mix for the chosen organisation to ensure that relationships are developed and maintained. The answers should have related to the product service system, key account management, relationship pricing, customer services and implications for internal employees, specific communications with stakeholders, specialised distribution, personalised processes, specific physical evidence for stakeholders, etc. This section was also worth 10 marks, but if the answer was not applied to a not-for-profit organisation, this was limited to a maximum of 5 marks.

The final part of this question required candidates to justify how the marketing activities for the organisation chosen could vary in an international context. The answer should have included the implications of areas such as culture, media, and legal issues on the marketing mix. This was worth only 5 marks and so candidates should have not spent too long on this part.

**Strengths of candidates' answers**

- Not many candidates tackled this question and so there were only a few good answers which explained relationship marketing well and related it to a not-for-profit organisation.

- A few candidates explained well the stakeholder relationships and the marketing mix for each.

- Good answers covered a discussion on the international context in terms of culture, language and legal issues for the marketing mix.

**Weaknesses of candidates' answers**

- Those who did answer this question often only offered a very brief explanation of relationship marketing and stakeholders.

- Many candidates did not include an example of an origination and tended to answer the question purely from a theoretical perspective, thus losing marks.

- Many candidates did not include the implications for the extended marketing mix.

**Question 5**

Approach

This was a popular question. The first part required candidates to explain the role of innovation within organisations. Answers should have explained why organisations need to continuously innovate. The answer should have included the different types of innovation and the approach taken in terms of proactive or reactive. This was worth 10 marks.

*Appendix 5 Past examination papers and examiners' reports*

The second part of the question required candidates to propose and justify an approach to new product development. This was very straightforward and the answer should have considered the stages of NPD such as idea generation, screening, concept testing, business analysis, product development, test marketing, commercialisation and monitoring and evaluation. Each stage should have been explained and examples should have been used to apply the theory. This was worth 15 marks, however if the answer was not applied the mark was limited to a maximum of 7 marks only.

### Strengths of candidates' answers

- Most candidates discussed the role of NPD and could identify and fully discuss the stages of NPD.

- Good answers used an example to illustrate each stage.

- Good answers explained each stage of the NPD well and considered it in relation to a product.

- Better answers included examples throughout.

### Weaknesses of candidates' answers

- Candidates offered a list of NPD stages only.

- There was no real explanation of the role of NPD within organisations.

- Some candidates answered the two sections together but did not explain this to the examiner.

- The answers were often brief and not applied, and unfortunately were not better than answers found at Stage 1 of the CIM qualifications.

## Conclusions and the Future

It is strongly recommended to Course Directors that the communication of this Senior Examiner's Report to all Tutors and candidates involved with this subject, is extremely important. It seems clear that there are a high number of candidates who are making some very simple mistakes and it seems clear that they are not aware, (or are not taking any notice), of the guidance offered by this report and CIM.

There is some clear evidence that Tutors and candidates are relying on the CIM Workbook as their only source of reading, although this practice, clearly, does not offer enough reading for candidates to pass this examination. Candidates should consult the CIM reading list and read from the core texts and trade publications as well as the Workbooks.

There should be some emphasis on encouraging deep learning rather than a surface learning approach where candidates are just learning facts but unable to apply them or offer valid examples. This will allow candidates to analyse the question fully, identify the focus and apply their knowledge to the specific context given.

*Appendix 5 Past examination papers and examiners' reports*

Candidates should be taught to practice their time management in terms of the weighting for each part of the question as the format of the paper has changed from the previous Marketing Operations paper at this level. Candidates should get used to writing in an appropriate business format. Tutors should ensure that students are given an opportunity to sit a mock examination with feedback prior to the actual examination.

Tutors and candidates should remember that there are some areas of the syllabus which often appear on the examination paper and therefore, should ensure that they are familiar with the theory and practice in areas. It is recommended that candidates ensure that they are familiar with the theory in the areas of: marketing planning; budgeting; marketing communications, international contexts; corporate and product branding; the macro environment; service quality and internal marketing; gap analysis; NPD.

## The Chartered Institute of Marketing

# Professional Diploma in Marketing

## Marketing Planning

**41:** Marketing Planning

**Time:** 09.30-12.30

**Date:** 9th June, 2004

3 Hours Duration

This is a generic paper to cover the following qualifications: -

- Diploma in E-commerce and Marketing
- Diploma in Tourism

This examination is in two sections.

**PART A** – Is compulsory and worth 50% of total marks.

**PART B** – Has **FOUR** questions; select **TWO**. Each answer will be worth 25% of the total marks.

**DO NOT** repeat the question in your answer, but show clearly the number of the question attempted on the appropriate pages of the answer book.

Rough workings should be included in the answer book and ruled through after use.

© The Chartered Institute of Marketing

# Professional Diploma in Marketing

**41: Marketing Planning**

## PART A

### The 2008 Olympics in Beijing

In 2008, China will be hosting the Olympic Games. China is calling these games the "People's Olympics", and they are to be hosted in Beijing, which is ready to become a truly international city. Beijing is showing a new, vigorous image through its ongoing economic reforms.

By hosting the People's Olympics, there will be an emphasis on the value of human talent, ambition and achievement. Indeed, the organising Committee sees the Olympic Games as a catalyst for exchange and harmony between various cultures and people.

China aims to strengthen public awareness of environmental protection and promote the development and application of new technologies via the Olympics. The Chinese people love sports and the nation's athletic enthusiasm is evident in wide participation in sports activities among its 1.25 billion population with distinctive achievements of Chinese athletes at previous Olympic Games.

Celebrating the Games in Beijing in 2008 will offer a unique opportunity to inspire and educate a new generation of Chinese youth with the Olympic values, and to promote the Olympic spirit and the cause of sport in China and the world.

### The Olympic Organising Committee

The Beijing 2008 Olympic Games Bid Committee (BOBICO) is in charge of all matters related to Beijing's bid for the 2008 Olympic Games. BOBICO was founded on 6th September, 1999. The committee is made up of 10 departments. Its members include athletes, personnel from the education, science and culture circles and contributors from other social sections, as well as officials from the Beijing municipal government, the State General Administration of Sport and departments of the Central Government.

### Sponsorship

More than US$600 million is expected to be raised from the international sponsorship of the 2008 Games. A similar amount could be expected to be raised from domestic sponsorships within China from companies wanting to become anything from the official airline, bank, insurance company, telephone company, petrol company and travel agent, down to the official supplier of ice cream and waste management services. The committee aims to have the major corporate sponsors signed up before the 2004 Games in Greece, well ahead of the event.

Indeed the games are seen to be the biggest ever marketing opportunity for China and they are currently starting to develop the marketing plan. The plans for the marketing programme include a nation-wide contest in China to design a new logo for the 2008 Olympics to replace the well-known logo which was used for the Beijing bid. It aims to generate a new look with fresh marketing potential.

Preparation for the games in Beijing is everywhere in evidence, from signs in shop windows to pins on the lapels of shoppers. New roads, bridges, and stadiums are planned, a massive environmental protection programme is underway, and technological modernisation, from cell phones to Internet access, is expanding to every corner of the city.

"The Olympics have already speeded the pace of change in Beijing and across China," says Mr Liu Jing-min, Vice Mayor of Beijing and Executive Vice President of the Beijing 2008 Olympic Games Bid Committee. "The survey demonstrates that the people of Beijing embrace these changes, welcome the world to our city, and are prepared to host a great Olympics."

*The above data has been based on a real live organisation, but details may have been changed for assessment purposes and the case does not reflect the current management practices.*

*Source: Olympic Games web site*

## PART A

### Question 1.

You have been appointed as a Marketing Consultant to assist the Beijing Olympic Organising Committee. Write a report for the Committee that:

a. Assesses the potential impact of macro-environmental forces on the marketing plan for the Beijing Olympics, specifically considering the role of culture, ethical approaches, and social responsibility.

**(15 marks)**

b. Explains the role of the Beijing Olympic brand and explain the importance of the brand in attracting the targeted sponsorship required, critically identifying the methods, which could be used to develop the Beijing Olympic brand.

**(15 marks)**

c. Explains the concept of service quality and recommends an effective extended marketing mix in relation to the service delivery and service encounters for the consumers during the Olympic events.

**(20 marks)**
**(50 marks in total)**

## PART B – Answer TWO Questions Only

### Question 2.

You have been appointed as a Marketing Consultant to a small business to business company which is looking to gain financial funding.

a. Explain the components of a marketing plan which the company will need to write, discussing the synergistic planning process.

**(15 marks)**

b. Explain the role of the marketing plan in relation to the company's business objectives.

**(10 marks)**
**(25 marks in total)**

### Question 3.

You are a Marketing Management Consultant and have been asked to undertake a marketing audit for a double glazing and window frame company.

a. Explain the different processes and techniques used for auditing the marketing environment.

**(9 marks)**

b. Explain the potential impact of wider macro-environmental forces on the business, such as ethical and social responsibility issues.

**(6 marks)**

c. Explain the concept of segmentation, targeting and positioning which this company could consider.

**(10 marks)**
**(25 marks in total)**

### Question 4.

During a recession, an organisation of your choice has an objective to expand its market share by developing a market penetration strategy.

a. Explain how such a strategy could be achieved at an operational level and contrast this with a market development strategy.

**(15 marks)**

b. Explain how pricing decisions can help to achieve the organisation's objective.

**(10 marks)**
**(25 marks in total)**

## Question 5.

You are a Brand Manager for a consumer product of your choice, which appears to be in decline. You plan to revive and reposition this product in the market.

a.  Explain how you will reposition this product and justify which segments will be targeted.

**(10 marks)**

b.  Explain how you will integrate the marketing communications mix to achieve this new positioning.

**(10 marks)**

c.  Explain one method for evaluating your marketing plan.

**(5 marks)**
**(25 marks in total)**

*Appendix 5 Past examination papers and examiners' reports*

# The Chartered Institute of Marketing

# Professional Diploma in Marketing

## Marketing Planning

**41:     Marketing Planning**

**SENIOR EXAMINER'S REPORT FOR JUNE 2004 EXAMINATION PAPER**

© The Chartered Institute of Marketing

*Appendix 5 Past examination papers and examiners' reports*

# SENIOR EXAMINER'S REPORT FOR
# JUNE 2004 EXAMINATION PAPER

**MODULE NAME:** MARKETING PLANNING

**AWARD NAME:** PROFESSIONAL DIPLOMA

**DATE:** JUNE 2004

## Introduction

This was the second examination session for the new subject for the Professional Diploma, Marketing Planning. This examination paper conformed to the new format, i.e. Section A – Compulsory was worth 50% and candidates had to answer two questions out of four, each question was worth 25%. The figures indicate that this paper was handled slightly better than the December paper. This report has been written after consultation with the Examining team and most of the points cited are common to many centres.

At this level examiners are looking for knowledge, understanding, application and evaluation in all answers and thus candidates' papers were marked accordingly.

The following section will consider the strengths and weaknesses of the candidates' answers.

## General Strengths of Candidates

(1) Use of appropriate examples or application to the case study given. Good candidates clearly demonstrated their knowledge and understanding by referring to appropriate examples to back up their answers – especially in the case study, where reference to the Beijing Olympic brand was required.

(2) Good layout and presentation. Most good answers were presented well and were logical in format and structure. Report format is used and the answer is sectionalised, helping the flow of reading. This gives the Examiner confidence in the candidate's work. There are no marks specifically available for layout at this stage of the CIM qualifications, however, candidates should still present their work well for all questions.

(3) Using appropriate models or frameworks. Higher grade answers tended to display an excellent understanding of the theory, by illustrating models and them applying them to the question set – such as the SERVQUAL model and full explanation in question 1c. These models or frameworks must be appropriately labelled and referenced correctly also, there should be some EVALUATION of the theory at this level.

(4) Application of theory to the case or examples. The pass answers do not just cite the theory, they illustrate understanding by applying the theory to the case or to an example. This is always required in the compulsory question 1 but many candidates tend to just refer to the theory and not apply it. Many candidates just reiterate information given in the case study also – which does not demonstrate understanding or knowledge and should be avoided.

(5) Good time management is evident in good examination papers from candidates. The pass answers illustrate that a good attempt has been made and all sections of the question have been answered well.

**General Weaknesses of Candidates**

(1) Misinterpretation of question requirements. The majority of candidates seemed to misinterpret question 1, which was very worrying as this was now worth 50%. This was most evident in the compulsory case study – Question 1a, 1b and 1c. Section 1a clearly required candidates to "assess the potential impact of macro-environmental forces" However, many candidates did not address this at all, where as others only wrote about the cultural, ethical and social responsibilities. Within section 1b many candidates did not relate to theory and generally waffled about the brand, which was not appropriate at this level. The final section, 1c, required candidates to "explain the concept of service quality" and again, many candidates did not address this for some reason. These areas will be discussed more fully further in the report.

(2) Understanding how to analyse a question. Some candidates in this session seemed to have particular problems in determining the following:
- The general subject area (e.g. question 2a – discussing the synergistic planning process)
- The focus or emphases required (e.g. 5c required candidates to recommend methods for evaluating marketing plan, however, many wrote about the marketing planning process only.)

(3) Preparation and study skills in terms of in-depth understanding of the syllabus. It was evident that a number of candidates were lacking in a number of areas. In some cases candidates seemed to reproduce lecture material rather than answering the question specifically or applying the theory to an example or the case especially in question 5a which related to the explanation of a repositioning strategy.

(4) Including everything about the subject - even if not related to the question requirements. This costs candidates precious time and often happens when they do not know what to include for the actual response. Also, this practice is very tedious for the Examining team, as they have to 'search' for

*Appendix 5 Past examination papers and examiners' reports*

the actual answer. Again, this was very evident in question 2b, which required candidates to explain the role of the marketing plan in relation to objectives. Many candidates wrote in general about SMART objectives and did not answer the question.

(5) Lack of practical examples - the best marks for questions are awarded to candidates who offer examples, which demonstrate the theory to which they are referring. This time, however, not many candidates managed to include a variety of examples within their answers. Candidates must demonstrate their knowledge, understanding and application of theory at this level. Therefore, including examples related to the area in question is required even if not specifically requested.

(6) Poor time management – this was a major problem for some candidates in some centres - especially at certain international centres where many candidates seemed to not answer the final question on the paper. Tutors should try to ensure that their students have an opportunity to sit a mock examination prior to the actual examination. With the new format of the paper, candidates only need to answer the compulsory question and two others and so should apportion their time appropriately. If a candidate misses out a question or part of a question, because of the reduced number of questions now required on the paper, there is less chance of passing.

(7) Evaluation - many candidates write blandly about the subject matter but do not show the skills of evaluation. This is not specifically cited in a question usually, however at this level theory dumping is not acceptable, candidates should be able to evaluate the theory.

The next section of this report will consider each question on the examination paper and will firstly detail the approach required, indicating what the Examiner was looking for in the answer. Then a consideration of the strengths and weaknesses of the candidates' answers for each question will be discussed.

## SECTION A – COMPULSORY

### Question 1

Approach Required

This question contained three sections, the first related to the PESTEL/Macro/Micro analysis and should have included a good section on the role of culture, ethics and social responsibility – this was worth 15 marks. Candidates should have discussed all the elements of PESTEL and Porter's Five forces, specifically relating this to the case. There should have been sections evaluating the culture, ethics and social responsibility in this case. This was quite challenging as it was set in China and offered a wealth of opportunity to discuss these elements and the implications fully.

The second section required the candidate to explain the role of branding and the importance of branding and sponsorship (worth 10 marks), specifically suggesting methods to develop the Olympic brand which was worth 5 marks. Candidates should have discussed the theory of branding with referenced to services, using theory to back up their points. The methods of developing the Olympic brand should have been debated.

The third section required candidates to explain the concept of service quality (worth 10 marks) and then to recommend an extended marketing mix for this service (worth 10 marks). The answer required candidates to critically discuss SERVQUAL or another theoretical model (which is stated in the syllabus) in depth, then go on to recommend an extended marketing mix. Either 7Ps or the extended 3Ps were acceptable, however, they had to be applied to the case.

Strengths in candidates' answers

- Good candidates were aware of the Athens Olympics which are running in 2004 and used this information to help them answer the questions.
- Some very good answers discussed the ethical, cultural and social issues relating to the history of China and the current environmental issues.
- Good explanation of branding theory, relating to the importance of branding (emotional link, personality, added value etc) and the methods of branding were related to the Olympic brand and sponsorship (some related to the communication of the brand and the strategic nature of brand extension strategies). Many UK candidates cited the European 2004 football event, which ran in June 2004 as examples to back up their recommendations.
- Some good answers were able to present the SERVQUAL model accurately and discuss the nature of the model and its limitations.
- Some excellent recommendations for the 7Ps related to the case were observed.

Appendix 5 Past examination papers and examiners' reports

Weaknesses in candidates' answers

- Many answers only contained analysis relating to culture, ethical and social responsibility rather than the full analysis, which was required.
- Some candidates wrote generally about the analysis models rather than applying them to the case as required.
- Most answers for the branding section were very thin and did not include any theoretical underpinning, or not surprisingly any evaluation.
- Some did not include any methods for developing the Beijing Olympic brand.
- Most candidates wrote about the characteristics of services rather than service quality.
- Many candidates did not discuss the 7 or 3 extended Ps in relation to the case given.
- Many candidates missed out at least one section of the first compulsory question.

**Question 2**

Approach

The first part of this question required candidates to explain the components of a marketing plan the B2B company would need to write, also there should have been some discussion of the synergistic planning process. Here, candidates should have explained marketing planning and explained each section of the marketing plan for a B2B organisation, thus discussion of the theory used at each section was required. There should have been some application and evaluation at this level.

The second part of this question required candidates to explain the role of the marketing plan in relation to the company's business objectives. Here, candidates should have written about the link to customer focus and marketing orientation, some consideration of the implications for marketers should have also been discussed.

Strengths in candidates' answers

- Good candidates related their answer to the B2B SME
- A discussion of each phase of the marketing planning process, fully referenced and evaluated was the hallmark of an excellent answer.
- Some discussion about the synergistic planning process and the benefits of marketing planning was evident in good answers.
- A consideration of the marketing objectives in relation to the business objectives and the functional objectives was debated

Weaknesses in candidates' answers

- Some candidates just offered bullet points for each stage of the marketing planning process
- Some did not apply their answer to the B2B SME as required
- Poor answers offered a theory dump instead of evaluating the underpinning theory
- Most answers did not include a discussion of the synergistic planning process and thus lost 5 marks straight away
- Some just wrote about SMART objectives in general and did not answer the question for part 2B.

## Question 3

Approach

This question had three sections and the first part required the candidate to explain the different processes and techniques used for auditing the marketing environment. Here, candidates should have discussed, applied and evaluated a range of models such as PESTEL, Porters 5 Forces, SWOT, etc. The second part of the question required candidates to explain the potential impact of ethical and social responsibility issues. This should have been related to the situation given in the question i.e. double-glazing and window Frame Company. The final part of the question required candidates to explain the concept of segmentation, targeting and position, which the company should consider. Here, the answer should have indicated an application of the theory with some suggestions for the company.

Strengths in candidates' answers

- Good candidates seemed to excel with this question, offering a comprehensive understanding of the marketing planning process, taking models, applying and evaluating them.
- Good discussion about the ethical and social responsibility which impact on the window organisation such as use of environmentally friendly resources, sponsorship for charity, evaluation of selling methods.
- Excellent answers covered the theory of STP and then applied it to the window organisation, citing competitors and the issues required. Good use of bases for segmentation and perceptions maps was evident here.

Weaknesses in candidates' answers

- Weak candidates just put bullet points relating to the different section of the marketing planning process
- No discussion of theoretical models relating to audit tools, just a general discussion about marketing audit
- No application for each section – especially section 3b

- STP was very brief and not applied
- Some candidates only considered segmentation and positioning or just segmentation and targeting
- No conclusions

## Question 4

Approach

This question required candidates to explain how a marketing penetration strategy could be achieved at an operational level and contrast this with a market development strategy. Candidates should have explained the terms using the Ansoff matrix and then gone into depth about the operational issues such as loyalty retention, building and maintain customer relationships etc. This should have been contrasted by market development operational issues such as distribution channel consideration etc. The second part of the question required candidates to explain how pricing decisions could help the organisation's objectives. Answers should have considered promotional pricing and communications considerations.

Strengths in candidates' answers

- Good answers explained and evaluated the theory behind market penetration and market development strategies
- The answers then went into depth discussing the operational issues which could be used for both strategies, evaluating one against the other. Some candidates offered a table which illustrated this.
- Good answers for the second part, offered a gap analysis as an introduction and explained how this could be related to pricing as achieving the organisation's penetration objectives.
- Good discussion and evaluation of different but appropriate pricing for market penetration.

Weaknesses in candidates' answers

- Not able to discuss accurately marketing penetration or marketing development
- Confused Ansoff models offered
- Very brief theory dump with no application or evaluation
- Very poor answers relating to the pricing decisions – most wrote all they could about pricing rather than answering the question i.e. pricing to achieve market penetration.

## Question 5

Approach

This question had three parts to it. The first required candidates to explain how a consumer product in its decline phase could be repositioned, justifying the target segments. Candidates should have chosen a product and identified its current target market and positioning strategy, then they should have discussed the new segment and the repositioning strategy using a perceptual map to illustrate.

The second part of the question required candidates to integrate the marketing communications mix to achieve the new positioning strategy. Again, candidates should have refereed to their answer for part a and justified mixed/blended communications to ensure the successful repositioning of the chosen product/service. The final section required candidates to explain one method of evaluating the marketing plan. Answers should have included a discussion of sales analysis, marketing costs and profitability analysis for this company.

Strengths in candidates' answers

- Good discussion of a real product and its current position and target segment contrasted (with justification) with the proposed new positioning using a perceptual map
- Some good answers considered the theory of integrated marketing communications and offered good justification for their suggestions
- A good explanation of one evaluation method for the marketing plan, justifying why this is a good approach.

Weaknesses in candidates' answers

- General waffle about positioning with no perceptual maps or discussion of the old and proposed new target segments.
- Poor answers offered a list of communications tools with no explanation etc
- A range of marketing research tools was offered by a number of poor candidates, which did not answer the question.

### 3. Future Themes

It is strongly recommended, to Course Directors, that the communication of this Senior Examiner's Report to all Tutors and candidates involved with this subject, is extremely important. It seems clear that there are a high number of candidates who are making some very simple mistakes and it seems clear that they are not aware, (or are not taking any notice), of the guidance offered by this report and CIM.

There is some clear evidence that Tutors and candidates are relying on the CIM Workbook as their only source of reading, although this practice, clearly, does not offer enough reading for candidates to pass this examination. Candidates should consult the CIM reading list and read from the **core texts and trade publications** as well as the Workbooks.

There should be some emphasis on encouraging deep learning rather than a surface learning approach where candidates are just learning facts but unable to apply them or offer valid examples. This will allow candidates to analyse the question fully, identify the focus and apply their knowledge to the specific context given.

Candidates should be taught to practice their time management in terms of the weighting for each part of the question as the format of the paper has changed from the previous Marketing Operations paper at this level. Candidates should get used to writing in an appropriate business format. Tutors should ensure that students are given an opportunity to sit a mock examination with feedback prior to the actual examination.

Tutors and candidates should remember that there are some areas of the syllabus, which often appear on the examination paper and therefore, should ensure that they are familiar with the theory and practice in areas. It is recommended that candidates ensure that they are familiar with the theory in the areas of: marketing planning; budgeting; marketing communications, international contexts; corporate and product branding; the macro environment; service quality and internal marketing; gap analysis; SMES and implications for marketing strategy, evaluation of marketing plans.

# appendix 6
# curriculum information and reading list

## Aim

The Marketing Planning unit provides the essential knowledge and understanding for the Professional Diploma in the creation and use of operational marketing plans and the marketing process. It aims to provide students with an understanding of the differences in the internal organizational and external contexts within which operational marketing planning and marketing are carried out and the different models of marketing used to meet these contingencies. The unit aims in particular to ensure that the knowledge and understanding can be applied in the practical construction of appropriate and realistic marketing plans.

### CIM professional marketing standards

Bc.2    Create competitive operational marketing plans.
Cc.1    Create and build competitive brands.
Cc.2    Manage competitive brands.
Ec.1    Prepare a business case for a product/service and progress it to market.
Ec.2    Manage and maintain competitive products/services or portfolio.
Fc.1    Create competitive and sustainable pricing policies.
Fc.2    Manage the implementation and monitor the effectiveness of pricing policies.
Gc.1    Establish and develop effective support for channels to market.
Kc.1    Define measurements appropriate to the plan or business case and ensure they are undertaken.
Kc.2    Evaluate activities and identify improvements using measurement data.

## Learning outcomes

Students will be able to:

8.42.1  Explain the role of the marketing plan within the context of the organization's strategy and culture and the broader marketing environment (ethics, social responsibility, legal frameworks, sustainability).
8.42.2  Conduct a marketing audit considering appropriate internal and external factors.
8.42.3  Develop marketing objectives and plans at an operational level appropriate to the internal and external environment.

*Appendix 6 Curriculum information and reading list*

8.42.4 Develop the role of branding and positioning within the marketing plan.
8.42.5 Integrate marketing mix tools to achieve effective implementation of plans.
8.42.6 Select an appropriate co-ordinated marketing mix incorporating appropriate stakeholder relationships for a particular marketing context.
8.42.7 Set and justify budgets for marketing plans and mix decisions.
8.42.8 Define and use appropriate measurements to evaluate the effectiveness of marketing plans and activities.
8.42.9 Make recommendations for changes and innovations to marketing processes based on an understanding of the organizational context and an evaluation of past marketing activities.

## Knowledge and skill requirements

### Element 1: The marketing plan in its organizational and wider marketing context (15 per cent)

1.1 Describe the roles of marketing and the nature of relationships with other functions in organizations operating in a range of different industries and contexts.
1.2 Explain the synergistic planning process – analysis, planning, implementation and control.
1.3 List and describe the components of the marketing plan.
1.4 Evaluate the role of the marketing plan in relation to the organization's philosophy or business definition.
1.5 Assess the potential impact of wider macro-environmental forces relating to the role of culture, ethical approach, social responsibility, legal frameworks and sustainability.

### Element 2: Marketing planning and budgeting (20 per cent)

2.1 Explain the constituents of the macro environmental and micro environmental marketing audit.
2.2 Assess the external marketing environment for an organization through a PESTEL audit.
2.3 Assess the internal marketing environment for an organization through an internal audit.
2.4 Critically appraise processes and techniques used for auditing the marketing environments.
2.5 Explain the role of marketing information and research in conducting and analysing the marketing audit.
2.6 Evaluate the relationship between corporate objectives, business objectives and marketing objectives at an operational level.
2.7 Explain the concept of the planning gap and its impact on operational decisions.
2.8 Determine segmentation, targeting and positioning within the marketing plan.
2.9 Determine and evaluate marketing budgets for mix decisions included in the marketing plan.
2.10 Describe methods for evaluating and controlling the marketing plan.

## Element 3: The extended marketing mix and related tools (50 per cent)

3.1 Explain the role of strategy development in relation to developing market share and growth.
3.2 Explain how strategy formulation and decisions relating to the selection of markets impact at an operational level on the planning and implementation of an integrated marketing mix.
3.3 Explain the role of branding and its impact on the marketing mix decisions.
3.4 Describe methods for maintaining and managing the brand.
3.5 Explain how a product or service portfolio is developed to achieve marketing objectives.
3.6 Explain the new product development process (including innovative, replacement, re-launched and imitative products) and the role of innovation.
3.7 Explain pricing frameworks available to, and used by, organizations for decision-making.
3.8 Describe how pricing is developed as an integrated part of the marketing mix.
3.9 Determine the channels of distribution and logistics to be used by an organization and develop a plan for channel support.
3.10 Explain how the marketing communications mix is coordinated with the marketing mix as part of a marketing plan.
3.11 Explain the importance of customer relationships to the organization and how they can be developed and supported by the marketing mix.
3.12 Describe how a plan is developed for the human element of the service encounter, including staff at different levels of the organization.
3.13 Explain how the physical evidence element of the integrated marketing mix is developed.
3.14 Explain how a plan covering the process or the systems of delivery for a service is developed.

## Element 4: Marketing in different contexts (15 per cent)

4.1 Explain how marketing plans and activities vary in organizations that operate in an international context and develop an appropriate marketing mix.
4.2 Develop a marketing plan and select an appropriate marketing mix for an organization operating in any context such as FMCG, business-to-business (supply chain), large or capital project-based, services, voluntary and not-for-profit, sales support (e.g. SMEs).
4.3 Explain how marketing plans and activities vary in organizations that operate in a virtual marketplace and develop an appropriate marketing mix.
4.4 Determine an effective extended marketing mix in relation to design and delivery of service encounters (SERVQUAL).

*Appendix 6 Curriculum information and reading list*

# Related key skills

| Key skill | Relevance to unit knowledge and skills |
|---|---|
| Communication | Present and justify a marketing plan |
| Application of number | Conduct a marketing audit |
| | Use forecasting techniques |
| | Set objectives |
| | Set and justify a budget |
| | Measure marketing performance |
| Information technology | Use IT tools for forecasting, modelling options, budgetting and measuring performance for a marketing plan |
| Working with others | |
| Improving own learning and performance | Review current capabilities |
| | Identify opportunities and set realistic targets for development and learning |
| | Plan how these targets will be met (methods, timescales, resources) |
| | Use a variety of methods for learning |
| | Seek feedback, monitor performance and modify approach |
| | Assess effectiveness of learning and development approach |
| Problem solving | Formulate a marketing solution within defined constraints |
| | Select a marketing mix appropriate to a specific context |
| | Recommend changes to marketing processes |

# Assessment

CIM will normally offer two forms of assessment for this unit from which study centres may choose: written examination and an assignment. CIM may also recognise, or make joint awards for, units at an equivalent level undertaken with other professional marketing bodies and educational institutions.

# Recommended support materials

### Core texts

Dibb, S., Simkin, L., Pride, W. and Ferrell, O. (2005) *Marketing Concepts and Strategies*, 5th European edition, Boston: Houghton Mifflin.

Drummond, G., Ensor, J. and Ashford, R. (2003) *Strategic Marketing: Planning and Control*, 2nd edition, Oxford: Butterworth-Heinemann.

Lancaster, G., Massingham, L. and Ashford, R. (2002) *Essentials of Marketing*, 4th edition, Maidenhead: McGraw-Hill.

## Workbooks

BPP (2005) *Marketing Planning Study Text*, London: BPP Publishing.

Beamish, K. and Ashford, R. (2005) *Marketing Planning*, Oxford: BH/Elsevier.

## Supplementary readings

Adcock, D., Halborg, C. and Ross, C. (2004) *Marketing: Principles and Practice*, 4th edition, Harlow: Pearson.

Brassington, F. and Pettitt, S. (2002) *Principles of Marketing*, 3rd edition, Harlow: Prentice Hall.

Chaffey, D., Mayer, R., Johnston, K. and Ellis-Chadwick, F. (2002) *Internet Marketing: Strategy, Implementation and Practice*, 2nd edition, Harlow: Prentice Hall.

Doyle, P. (2001) *Marketing Management & Strategy*, 3rd edition, Harlow: Prentice Hall.

Hatton, A. (2000) *Definitive Guide to Marketing*, 2nd edition, Harlow: Prentice Hall.

Johnson, G. and Scholes, K. (2004) *Exploring Corporate Strategy*, 7th edition, Harlow: Prentice Hall.

Kotler, P. (2002) *Marketing Management*, 11th international edition, Harlow: Prentice Hall.

Kotler, P., Armstrong, G., Saunders, J. and Wong, V. (2005) *Principles of Marketing*, 4th European edition, Harlow: pearson.

McDonald, M. (2002) *Marketing Plans: How to Prepare Them, How to Use Them*, 5th edition, Oxford: Butterworth-Heinemann.

Palmer, A., Worthington, I. and Hartley, B. (2001) *The Business Environment*, 4th edition, Maidenhead: McGraw-Hill.

Payne, A., Christopher, M., Peck, H. and Clark, M. (1998) *Relationship Marketing for Competitive Advantage*, Oxford: Butterworth-Heinemann.

Piercy, N. (2001) *Market-led Strategic Change*, 3rd edition, Oxford: Butterworth-Heinemann.

BPP (2005) *Marketing Planning Practice and Revision Kit*, London: BPP Publishing.

BH (2005) *CIM Revision Cards: Marketing Planning*, Oxford: BH/Elsevier.

*Appendix 6 Curriculum information and reading list*

### Marketing journals

Students can keep abreast of developments in the academic field of marketing by reference to the main marketing journals, a selection of which are listed in the Appendix to this document.

### Press

Students will be expected to have access to current examples of marketing campaigns and so should be sure to keep up to date with the appropriate marketing and quality daily press. A selection of marketing press titles is given in the Appendix to this document.

### Websites

A list of websites that tutors and students may find useful is shown in the Appendix at the end of this document.

## Overview and rationale

### Approach

This unit has been developed to provide knowledge and skills required by operational marketing managers. It replaces the 'Marketing Operations' unit in the previous Advanced Certificate. This new unit has been based on statements of practice to ensure that it prepares students for practice at management level, concentrating on operational rather than strategic marketing decisions and the plan for the organization's or business unit's marketing activities. Students and tutors will notice that the unit is integrated both horizontally and vertically across the range of CIM qualifications.

It is anticipated that this unit will be exciting and more useful for today's and tomorrow's marketing managers. It will be more realistic in terms of knowledge and application of theory required for a professional qualification at this level. Students should find that they are able to apply the knowledge learned immediately within their employment and therefore add more value to this qualification.

### Vertical separation

- *Links from Professional Certificate* – This unit builds on Marketing Fundamentals at the previous level by developing a higher level of knowledge, understanding and skills for managing the operational marketing process. It also builds on the knowledge of the organization's environment developed in the Marketing Environment unit.
- *Links with Professional PG Diploma* – This unit underpins the units at Professional PG Diploma that relate to the global context, analysis and techniques for analysis, strategy formulation and techniques and the business strategy, as distinct from the operational marketing plan covered in this unit.

## Horizontal integration

As the backbone of Professional Diploma, this unit provides the key understanding and knowledge for this level. As such, it links across all the other units at this level.

- *Links with Marketing Research and Information* – The Marketing Research and Information unit emphasises the value of information and its importance for marketing planning decisions. Planning and managing the marketing information process, research methodologies and analysis techniques covered in Marketing Research and Information are an essential part of marketing audits (Element 2).
- *Links with Marketing Communications* – This unit links with the Marketing Communications unit as it is important that customers are identified and understood effectively before the marketing plan can be designed and implemented. Thus customer dynamics, including perceived risk and other consumer behaviour content, will be studied in Marketing Communications but should be considered when devising the marketing plan as per element 3.2. The communications and CRM applications will be considered in more detail in the Marketing Communications unit.
- *Links with Marketing Management in Practice* – There are clear links to the Marketing Management in Practice unit, which includes the development and implementation of a marketing plan at an operational level. Element 3.12 relates to the management of the people element of the marketing mix, which again links to the Marketing Management in Practice unit. The Marketing Management in Practice unit seeks to put into practice the knowledge and skills covered in this unit.

## Syllabus content

### Element 1: The marketing plan in its organizational and wider marketing context (15 per cent)

This part of the syllabus is weighted at 15 per cent of the total since it introduces the marketing planning process. It should form the basis of developing understanding from the Marketing Environment at Professional Certificate. This part of the syllabus ensures that the areas covered relate to the marketing planning process and how this relates to the organization's philosophy. The importance of marketers working closely with other business functions is also highlighted. Therefore, students and tutors should ensure that this is not taught or studied in a piecemeal fashion, but in relation to one or more organizations. The areas relating to culture, ethics, social responsibility, legal frameworks (such as data protection) and sustainability need to be emphasized and considered fully when exploring the marketing planning process for an organization.

### Element 2: Marketing planning and budgeting (20 per cent)

The unit ensures that the marketing planning process and budgeting is fully considered and this area is weighted at 20 per cent of the syllabus. Some of the content relating to certain elements will have been introduced in the Marketing Environment unit of the Professional Certificate. However, it should be emphasized that at this level more application of these areas is required, i.e. which are the most important economic factors impacting on the organization and what does this mean rather than just considering all the economic issues which could be listed in an audit.

Some of the more complex analysis tools are introduced in this element. It is important that these tools are not just learned but tutors and students must be able to apply these tools in practice as part of the marketing audit. For example, the construction of the BCG matrix for an organization for year one and year two will be more important than just an understanding of what the BCG can help to identify. Therefore, students and tutors are expected to use live or case study information to be able to complete an analysis.

*Appendix 6 Curriculum information and reading list*

The application of a SWOT analysis as part of a marketing audit in relation to either an organization, a product line or a brand will also be important. Students will also be expected to demonstrate their awareness of relevant legal and financial aspects covered by the Key Skills for Marketers. In other words, the tutors and students should not just be able to identify the strengths and weaknesses, opportunities and threats, but they must also be able to prioritise these for an organization. The SWOT should form the conclusion of the marketing audit and assist with the setting of marketing objectives. The setting of objectives should include an understanding of corporate objectives and strategic marketing objectives, but should concentrate on the operational objectives to achieve the marketing plan.

### Element 3: The extended marketing mix and related tools (50 per cent)

Students cannot come to this unit and specifically to this element without a basic understanding and knowledge of the marketing mix covered in Professional Certificate. Students coming directly into the Professional Diploma should complete the entry unit BEFORE starting this unit. The emphasis in this unit is on finding and applying solutions for different contexts using appropriate mixes.

This is the largest section of the syllabus and as such relates to the planning and implementation of the operational marketing mix. Therefore, students and tutors should ensure that they understand the impact of marketing strategy, i.e. they may need to consider the impact of concentrating on a marketing penetration strategy for the planning and implementation of the marketing mix. An understanding of segmentation strategy and the impact again on the targeting and positioning issues relating to the integration of the marketing mix tools will be required.

An understanding and application of the marketing mix relating to pricing, product, distribution, communications, processes, physical evidence and internal employees is required. Students and tutors should ensure that not only is the theory here understood in relation to the setting of operational objectives, but that the ability to make effective decisions about each element of the mix to ensure that the chosen strategy is achieved. Therefore, the syllabus requires not only understanding and knowledge, but also the ability to make recommendations about the effective mix decisions to ensure that strategies such as market development can be implemented for an organization with particular strengths and weaknesses operating in a competitive environment. This theory is put into practice in the Marketing Management in Practice unit.

The determination of marketing budgets should also be considered when making decisions for the implementation of the marketing mix. Thus, the evaluation of such budgets using both quantitative methods such as evaluation of objectives achieved – such as sales penetration in a certain market within the time-scale, or qualitative methods such as a study of the positioning of the organization's product or brand.

Tutors and students should note that there is no specific reference to ICT as a particular driver in this part of the syllabus, but it should be remembered that ICT is also covered by the Key Skill 'Information technology'. For example, the consideration of electronic processes in the extended services mix is important, as too is the consideration of electronic communications.

### Element 4: Marketing in different contexts (15 per cent)

This part of the syllabus relates to the application of marketing in differing contexts and accounts for 15 per cent. Reference to different contexts such as international, business-to-business, large and capital projects, small medium enterprises, fast moving consumer goods, service sectors and non-profit sectors such as governments and charities is important. Each of these contexts has specific issues to consider such as budgets available, manpower, changing market places, culture, different characteristics (as with services), etc. Therefore, the marketing plan and implementation in these contexts must take account of the specific issues relating to the appropriate sector. This is practised further in the Marketing Management in Practice unit.

One of the new but important areas on the syllabus is the consideration of the virtual marketplace and direct or on-line marketing. This has a real impact on the marketing mix and planning for this is very important as there are more issues such as building trust and security, service levels, privacy, two-way communications, etc. which will need to be considered. Similarly, areas such as ethics and brand reputation are important developing areas for students.

## Delivery approach

It is important that this unit is taught using a practical approach. Therefore, tutors and students need to ensure that they are able to gain access to data either from employer's organizations or from case studies. There are many texts now that offer comprehensive case studies (which are included in the unit reading lists and on-line websites).

It is anticipated that this unit is taught usually as the second unit after Marketing Research and Information. This should ensure that the Marketing Communications unit is able to add to the learning in this unit. The Marketing Management in Practice unit provides an opportunity to apply theory developed in this unit. It also provides the summative assessment, which encompasses the theory from this unit. Tutors are encouraged to provide activities and case studies in which students learn to develop simple plans.

It is suggested that the theory may be covered via self-study, but the practical application of the theory should be developed on a continual process. This may form the basis of a student's portfolio, which is built throughout the unit. The student could choose an organization or work from their own organization's data, and each area of the syllabus should be applied and written up in relation to the gradual development of a marketing plan for the organization of choice. Student presentations of each area in class and critical reflective critiques from other class colleagues should be encouraged. It is likely that this approach would be a deviation from the 'normal' mode of delivery for most study centres. However, it would ensure that there is more development of deeper learning for this level.

This approach requires students to participate more in class and the tutor becomes more of a facilitator, therefore, busy, part-time students must understand this commitment to the course. Therefore, if this approach is undertaken, tutors should ensure that students are prepared for this at the beginning of the course. Therefore, at the recruitment stage and during the course induction this learning approach must be highlighted and the expectations of the tutors and students should be identified.

## Additional resources (Syllabus – Professional Diploma in Marketing)

### Introduction

Texts to support the individual units are listed in the syllabus for each unit. This Appendix shows a list of marketing journals, press and websites that tutors and students may find useful in supporting their studies at Professional Diploma.

## Marketing journals

Students can keep abreast of developments in the academic field of marketing by reference to the main marketing journals.

- *Corporate Reputation Review* – Henry Stewart
- *European Journal of Marketing* – Emerald
- *Harvard Business Review* – Harvard
- *International Journal of Advertising* – WARC
- *International Journal of Corporate Communications* – Emerald
- *International Journal of Market Research* – WARC
- *Journal of Consumer Behaviour An International Review* – Henry Stewart
- *Journal of the Academy of Marketing Science* – Sage Publications
- *Journal of Marketing* – American Marketing Assoc. Pubs Group
- *Journal of Marketing Communications* – Routledge
- *Journal of Marketing Management* – Westburn Pubs Ltd
- *International Journal of Market Research* – NTC Pubs
- *Journal of Product and Brand Management* – Emerald
- *Journal of Services Marketing* –Emerald
- *Marketing Review* – Westburn Pubs Ltd.

## Press

Students will be expected to have access to current examples of marketing campaigns and so should be sure to keep up to date with the appropriate marketing and quality daily press, including:

- *Campaign* – Haymarket
- *Internet Business* – Haymarket
- *Marketing* – Haymarket
- *The Marketer* – Chartered Institute of Marketing
- *Marketing Week* – Centaur
- *Revolution* – Haymarket.

## Websites

*The Chartered Institute of Marketing*

| | |
|---|---|
| www.cim.co.uk | CIM website containing case studies, reports and reviews |
| www.cim.co.uk/learningzone | Website for CIM students and tutors containing study information past exam papers and case study examples. Also access to 'the marketer' articles online |
| www.cimeducator.com | The CIM site for tutors only |

*Publications on-line*

| | |
|---|---|
| www.revolution.haynet.com | Revolution magazine |
| www.boardpublic.com | Marketing magazine |
| www.FT.com | A wealth of information for cases (now charging) |
| www.IPA.co.uk | Need to register – communication resources |
| www.booksites.net | Financial Times/Prentice Hall Text websites |

*Sources of useful information*

| | |
|---|---|
| www.acnielsen.co.uk | AC Nielsen – excellent for research |
| http://advertising.utexas.edu/world/ | Resources for advertising and marketing professionals, students, and tutors |
| www.bized.com | Case studies |
| www.corporateinformation.com | Worldwide sources listed by country |
| www.esomar.nl | European Body representing Research Organisations – useful for guidelines on research ethics and approaches |
| www.dma.org.uk | The Direct Marketing Association |
| www.eiu.com | The Economist Intelligence Unit |
| www.euromonitor.com | Euromonitor consumer markets |
| www.europa.eu.int | The European Commission's extensive range of statistics and reports relating to EU and member countries |
| www.managementhelp.org/research/research.htm | Part of the 'Free Management Library' – explaining research methods |
| www.marketresearch.org.uk | The MRS site with information and access to learning support for students – useful links on ethics and code of conduct |
| www.mmc.gov.uk | Summaries of Competition Commission reports |
| www.oecd.org | OECD statistics and other information relating to member nations including main economic indicators |
| www.quirks.com | An American source of information on marketing research issues and projects |
| www.statistics.gov.uk | UK Government statistics |
| www.un.org | United Nations publish statistics on member nations |
| www.worldbank.org | World bank economic, social and natural resource indicators for over 200 countries. Includes over 600 indicators covering GNP per capita, growth, economic statistics, etc. |

*Case sites*

| | |
|---|---|
| www.bluelagoon.co.uk | Case – SME website address |
| www.ebay.com | On-line auction – buyer behaviour |
| www.glenfiddich.com | Interesting site for case and branding |
| www.interflora.co.uk | e-commerce direct ordering |
| www.moorcroft.co.uk | Good for relationship marketing |
| www.ribena.co.uk | Excellent targeting and history of comms |

© CIM 2004

# Index

7Cs model, 102

Advertising:
   definition, 114
   and its influence on price, 117
   objectives, 115
   repositioning through, 116
   and the marketing mix, 116

Balanced scorecard, 57
   customer perspective, 59
   financial performance, 58
   innovation and learning perspective, 60
   internal perspective, 59
Brand values, 107
   brand loyalty, 108
   brand planning, 109
   brand strategies, 109
   brand threats, 111
   core and peripheral values, 108
   corporate brands, 110
   managing the brand, 111
Branding, 106
Break-even analysis, 173
Business-to-business marketing:
   buying and decision-making process in organizational markets, 245
   characteristics of business/industrial buying behaviour, 241
   decision-making process, 246
   decision-making unit, 247
   market segmentation for organizational marketing, 244
   marketing mix for organizational marketing, 248
   nature of business-to-business buyers, 243
   organizational buying, 242
   relationship marketing in organizational markets, 247

Channel effectiveness, 200
Channel members, 184
   agents/brokers/facilitators, 185
   distributors/dealers, 184
   franchisee, 185
   licensee, 185
   merchandiser, 185
   retailers, 184
   wholesalers, 184
Charities, 269
   marketing planning and control, 272
   marketing planning for, 271
   marketing segmentation and targeting, 272
Consumerism:
   ethical issues for consumers and marketers, 20
   rise in, 19
   social response to, 19
Control process, 94
   budgetary control, 96
   competitor performance, 97
   corrective action, 98
   effectiveness of marketing mix, 97
   variance analysis, 96
Corporate planning, 8
Customer retention management, 210
   customer retention in consumer markets, 211
   customer retention in not-for-profit markets, 212
   customer retention in organizational markets, 212
   marketing mix for:
      product extras, 213
      reinforcing promotions, 214
      relationship pricing, 213
      specialized distribution, 213

Database marketing, 128
Direct and interactive marketing, 126
Direct marketing, 127
   objectives, 127
   techniques, 129
      direct mail, 129
      direct response advertising, 130
Distribution, 182
   influences on, 182
   marketing issues for, 183
Distribution channels, 183
   balance of power within, 189
   channel strategy, 190
   selecting, 188
   and the customer, 187

Economic environment:
    currency/interest rate risks, 224
    three categories, 224
External marketplace, 226

FMCGs:
    marketing mix for, 254
    marketing strategy for, 251

Gap analysis, 61
Globalization, 235
    benefits of, 238
    standardization versus adaptation, 236

Horizontal channel integration, 192

Intermediaries, 185
    selection criteria, 188
Internal relationship marketing:
    internal stakeholders, 215
    techniques, 215
International marketing:
    developing an, information system, 228
        acquiring secondary data, 229
    levels of, 220
International marketing environment:
    economic environment, 224
    legal environment, 223
    political, 224
    social/cultural factors, 222
    technological environment, 225
International research, 227
Internet on channel decisions,
    impact of, 195

Legislation, 18

Macro-environment, analysis of:
    economic, 32
    environmental, 35
    legal, 35
    political, 30
    social, 33
    technological, 34
Market segmentation and competitive
        positioning, 71
    achieving segmentation effectiveness, 76
    basis for segmenting markets, 72
    business-to-business and organizational
        segmentation, 75
    continuous monitoring of segmentation, 76
    positioning, 78
    positioning alternatives, 80
    segmentation of consumer markets, 72
    targeting, 77

Marketing audit, 26
    assessing marketing environment, 29
Marketing environment:
    analysis of macro environment, 30
    analysis of the micro environment, 35
    setting of objectives, 55
        business non-financial objectives, 56
        corporate objectives, 56
        marketing objectives, 56
        programme/subsidiary objectives, 57
Marketing information system:
    areas for research and information, 49
Marketing mix:
    ethical implications:
        place, 22
        price, 21
        product, 21
        promotion, 21
Marketing of services, 255
    implementing a quality culture, 264
    importance of service quality, 263
    key components of designing a
        services mix, 262
    marketing mix in the context of services, 261
    meeting customer expectations, 259
    monitoring and evaluating service, 265
    service characteristics, 256
    service mix, 259
    services defined, 255
    structure of the services sector, 255
    uncertainties of service, 257
Marketing opportunity, 46
    role of marketing information in the planning
        process, 47
Marketing plan, 82
    implementation of, 83
        internal marketing, 85
        marketing-oriented and customer-focused
            culture, 85
        strong and committed leadership, 84
    place, 234
    pricing, 234
    product, 234
    promotional mix, 235
Marketing relationships, 206
Marketing strategy, 10
    formulation, 63
        competitive marketing strategy, 64
        growth strategies, 66
        market positioning strategies, 69
Marketing structure, 87
    financial and human resources, 91
    functional organization, 88
    product-based organization, 89
    territory-based organization, 88

*Index*

Micro-environment, analysis of the:
   business/marketing function, 36
   competitive analysis, 39
   competitors, 38
   customers, 43
   stakeholders, 43
   suppliers, 42
   SWOT analysis, 44
   threat of competitive rivalry, 40

New product development, 153
   business analysis, 156
   concept testing, 155
   idea generation, 154
   launch, 156
   product development, 155
   screening new ideas, 155
   test marketing, 156
Non-profit-making organization, 273
   managing the marketing mix, 276
   marketing planning for, 275
   motivational factors influencing not-for-profit marketing and profitable organizations, 274
   versus profit marketing, 274

Personal selling, 135
   sales force objectives, 136
Physical distribution management, 192
Planning, 12
   barriers to, 13
Planning horizons, 54
Positioning, 78
   role of a marketer in, 81
Price, 178
   correlating price with value, 168
   influences on, 166
   setting higher, 178
   stages to establish, 178
Price perception:
   and the customer, 165
   and the organization, 165
Price sensitive markets, 170
   break-even analysis, 173
   competitors, 171
   debtors and creditors, 173
   demand, 169
   marginal costing and pricing, 174
Pricing:
   objectives and strategies, 174, 176
     cost-plus pricing, 177
     differential pricing, 177
     marginal pricing, 176
     quantity discounting, 176
   in relation to demand, 166

Primary research, 230
Product, 140
   management, 143
   operations, 139
Product adoption process, 157
   consumer decision-making unit, 157
   early adopters, 160
   early majority, 161
   innovators, 160
   laggards, 161
   late majority, 161
Product life cycle, 144
   decline, 145
   development, 144
   growth, 144
   managing:
     marketing strategy for declining products, 147
     marketing strategy for growth, 146
     marketing strategy for maturity, 147
   maturity/saturation, 145
Product portfolio planning tools, 148
   BCG matrix, 149
   GE matrix, 151
   Shell Directional Policy matrix, 151
Profiling, 103
Promotional communications process, 105
Promotional mix:
   co-ordinated marketing communications, 113
   tools, 112
Promotional operations and the planning framework, 104
Public relations:
   aims and objectives, 123
   and attitude change, 124
   marketing versus corporate, 124
   techniques, 125
     internal, 125
Push and pull strategies, 103, 104, 194

Relationship management, planning for, 207
   customer loyalty, 208
   dimensions of relationship marketing, 209
   relationship based upon trust, 209
Relationship marketing, 15, 204
   definition, 204
   from transactional to, 204
   plan, 217

Sales promotions:
   definition, 118
   manufacturer to consumer, 120
     customer loyalty schemes, 121
   retailer to consumer, 120
   techniques, 118
     trade promotions, 119

SMEs, 279
   marketing mix for, 280
   marketing strategy and planning for, 279
   outline marketing plan for, 280
Social responsibility, 16
Sponsorship:
   objectives, 132
   role of, 133
   types of, 133
Strategic pricing, 175
   determinants, 169
Strategy and planning hierarchy, 7

Telemarketing, 130
   scope, 131

Vertical channel integration, 191
Virtual marketing environment, 282
   advantages of internet marketing, 285
   benefits of, 285
   disadvantages of internet marketing, 286
   dynamic marketing, 288
   price, 287
   product, 287
   promotion, 287
   virtual trends, 283